# Jammu and Kashmir
## Paradise on Earth Turned into Hell

**Sheshrao Chavan**

*Foreword by*
**Justice C.S. Dharmadhikari**

**ATLANTIC**
**PUBLISHERS & DISTRIBUTORS (P) LTD**

Published by

**ATLANTIC**

**PUBLISHERS & DISTRIBUTORS (P) LTD**

7/22, Ansari Road, Darya Ganj, New Delhi-110002
Phones : +91-11-40775252, 40775214, 23273880, 23275880
Fax : +91-11-23285873
Web : www.atlanticbooks.com
E-mail : orders@atlanticbooks.com

**Branch Office: Chennai**
Phones : +91-44-48531784, 28291383
E-mail : chennai@atlanticbooks.com



Printed & bound in India by Atlantic Print Services

# Foreword

I have a great pleasure in writing a 'Foreword' to this informative and analytical book written by Shri Sheshrao Chavan, a prolific writer.

As well said that analysing and understanding a problem is the beginning of the solution. It is by now well settled that Kashmir is an integral part of the Union of India. However, the problem before us is that we are not able to understand the difference between State or Country and the Nation or the Republic. We have not yet lifted ourselves from the parochial regional littleness to Nationwide dimensions. We forget that the Nation or the Republic is an attitude of living together. According to Victor Hugo, "The existence of a Nation is a daily plebiscite of its people to live together, just as existence of an individual is a continued affirmation of the will to live." This is the first and the foremost necessity for Nationhood. We are forgetting that Kashmirians and Indians are the members of each other. Unless we establish face to face society and the concept of neighbourhood with relationship is developed, it is quite clear and it will not be possible to achieve the goal of Nationhood. Unfortunately, today Kashmir is being treated as a tourist spot only. There is a vast difference between the concept of tourism and pilgrimage.

It is not necessary for me to analyse the problem of Kashmir, because it has been very well analyzed and put forth by the author. In ultimate analysis, he came to the conclusion that the dialogue or man to man diplomacy is the only solution, with which I agree in all humility.

Though there was partition of India, because it was thought that it was inevitable. Mahatma Gandhi in his own way had declared that he would not accept the concept of two Nations theory, meaning thereby that the people belonging to the different regions could not live together. Even the tunnel between the State of Kashmir and India should have light on both sides.

Shri Sheshrao Chavan has done yeoman service by analyzing the whole problem with an open mind to enable the readers to form their own opinion. For solving such a problem, which has become chronic, there cannot be any readymade formula. Each one of us will have to participate for searching out a solution.

I have, however, faith in our masses in general, and youths in particular. They understand the men and matters well. They can arrive at the right decision, if they are provided with facts. Kashmiris are only exploited by politicians and other vested interest to serve their own purposes. And exactly, this has kept the Kashmir problem burning for all these years. Nowadays, any dispute or problem assumes a global dimension.

Lok Nayak Jayaprakash Narayan had rightly said, "Post independence history of India and Pakistan has conclusively proved that partition has been a complete failure. It has solved no problem, but has created many more than existed before."

Kashmir has been one of the greatest and complicated problems. It cannot be, as I have repeatedly said, solved by force. It can be solved only by love, understanding and cooperation of Kashmiris, be they Muslims, Hindus and Buddhists.

I am reminded of a statement made by President Ayub Khan in the National Assembly of Pakistan. In his statement, he emphasized the need for a change of heart on both sides. If such a change of heart takes place, the dispute of Kashmir, which has assumed such a gigantic proportion would be brought to a point of solution. If India and Pakistan decide that it is in their own interest to find a way out to live together in friendship and cooperation, their economic, historical, geographical, political, social and cultural conditions would begin to operate in favour of those objectives. Of all the outstanding issues between the two countries, the dispute of Kashmir is the most intricate. But, with change of heart, I am sure that it can be solved.

Jayaprakash Narayan also said, "The disease is the deep rooted mutual distrust between India and Pakistan, each suspects the other of harbouring the blackest designs against the other. The dispute of Kashmir cannot be solved unless the distrusts are removed."

It is for both sides to get together to find out how a change of heart, in other words, replacement of the distrusts could be brought about. In my humble opinion, this could be done not by harping on disputes and differences, but by sitting down together to discover the areas of common interests on which the two countries could agree to work together for their mutual benefits. I believe that there are large areas of such kind and if they are jointly explored, discovered and worked out, the present cloud of distrust could be evaporated and a change of heart brought about. When this happens, the Kashmir dispute will not appear as forbidding as it does today.

The author has rightly said in chapter 12 that if we now look upon Kashmir as a Muslim majority area and hence entitled to secede thinking that it is not proper for it to remain in India, we would be repeating the mistake after over six decades. There is more at stake in Kashmir than merely a piece of territory. Kashmir is the symbol and touch stone of our secular structure. The dismemberment of Kashmir would begin the dismemberment of India as a whole and produce migrations and conflicts of a character and magnitude much worse and larger than the aftermath of partition. Therefore, solution has to be found which will enable India and Pakistan to live together on friendly terms. This is the real problem in India, and Kashmir is only a symptom.

Justice M.C. Chagla, in his plea before the Security Council of the United Nations said, "Kashmir is merely a symptom. It is not the disease. The disease is that Pakistan believes in a religious State; it believes in religion as the nexus between citizens."

Military operations will not be effective. Military operations may lead to war and today, a country cannot afford to wage war against other as the war will not be restricted to these two countries. The other countries may lend their direct or indirect support to either. The war is, therefore, out of question. The only alternative is man to man diplomacy as suggested by author in chapter 12. The man to man diplomacy includes exchange of cultural events, literature, games and other things of mutual interest, which will bring common men together and create an atmosphere of harmony.

All those individuals and organizations who are genuinely interested in keeping Jammu and Kashmir in India have to raise themselves above their own politics and vested interests. They should join hands in finding out the solution, which will be in the larger welfare of the people of all the three regions, namely Valley, Jammu and Laddakh.

The youths of Jammu and Kashmir are fed up and frustrated for everyday happenings, stone pelting and terrorist attacks and counter attacks by military. In the process, there are killings on both the sides. The youths of Jammu and Kashmir are looking forward for their settlement in life so that their parents can live in peace and tranquility.

I congratulate Shri Sheshrao Chavan for writing this valuable book at this crucial time.

Let me conclude with the words of Shelley who said that poets are the acknowledged legislators of the world and sang:

*Are we not formed, as notes of music are,*
*For one another, though dissimilar?*

The poet has been waiting for an emphatic 'yes' from all of us.

I welcome this book and wish it all the success.

**Justice C.S. Dharmadhikari**

# Preface

Sardar Vallabhbhai Patel in a letter written to G.D. Birla in May 1949 writes: "Here we are having a grudging time both with the weather and the problems which are arising; Kashmir, in particular, is giving us a severe headache." And it has continued to be there to a lesser or fewer degree. Today after more than 70 years, headache continues to exist between India and Pakistan in varying degrees.

The Indian Independence Act, which was based on the Mountbatten Plan of 3rd June, was passed by the British Parliament on 5th July 1947 and received royal assent or approval on 18th July 1947. A question was deliberately and not with bonafide intentions kept vague and unresolved. What about the princely states comprising 1/3rd of India? All princely states big and small became independent on that day, each of them were left to make their own decision. They can either merge with India or Pakistan or remain independent. While preparing to leave India this was deliberately kept unresolved. It was Churchill's intention to create not two states out of India but several princely states all over the country. Especially they foresaw the possibility of some large states such as Hyderabad and Travancore becoming independent. Of course, the overwhelming majority of the states all over the country cannot survive without arrangement or support from the government at the centre. British had thought that Kashmir, Baluchistan and Punjab may remain in the British sphere of influence. There were problems galore but the country had at the helm of the affairs. Sardar Patel who was in charge of states ministry, immediately realized that Lord Mountbatten could be helpful. Mountbatten and Patel adopted a pincer attack.

On the one hand they described princess as their personal friends and offered them ambassadorship, governorship and fringe privileges. On the other hand Sardar threatened them with dire consequences. Sardar Patel declared, "I hope that Indian states will bear in mind that the alternative to co-operation in general interest is anarchy and chaos." With this the problems were amicably settled for almost all the states. By 15th August 1947 only three problematic states remained, namely Junagadh, Hyderabad and Kashmir. All others merged within India. Sardar settled the problem of Junagadh and Hyderabad in his characteristic style and with clarity of purpose. Jawaharlal Nehru took charge of Kashmir for which he had emotional attachment.

British had all the way believed that it would be natural for Kashmir to merge within Pakistan but it did not happen. Before the Maharaja of Kashmir could decide on the merger of his state with either India or Pakistan, Pakistan invaded Kashmir. It was known that Maharaja wanted Independent Kashmir, a scheme unpalatable to Gandhi, Nehru and Patel.

Nehru did consider in early 60's reconciliation with Sheikh Abdullah. Bharatiya Jana Sangh (now BJP) and the left both were suspicious of Abdullah and his associates. Communist Party thought that he was in danger of falling into an imperialist trap, designed to detach Kashmir from India. Nehru was open and he received unexpected support of two stalwarts of our freedom struggle who had worked with Gandhiji, J.P. and Rajgopalachari. J.P., in a signed article in Hindustan Times, deplored the insinuation against Abdullah by politicians of inside and outside Congress. He also deplored the threats to put Sheikh back in jail and forced him into silence. Bakshi Ghulam Mohammad, the then chief Minister of Kashmir was also interested in keeping Sheikh Abdullah out.

There was confused thinking in Congress. Sheikh Abdullah after his release had expressed his desire to pay his respect to Rajaji and had the benefit of his mature advice. He went to Madras (Chennai) via Wardha where he was to meet Vinoba Bhave and he jokingly told a journalist, "He would discuss spirituality with Vinoba and practical politics with Rajaji." Good progress was being made. He also at the invitation of the President of Pakistan General Ayub Khan went to Pakistan and met him. There was possibility of settlement, but there was an attempt both from cabinet and parliament to prevent Prime Minister to come into terms with Abdullah. Pakistan's response was also positive while he was flying from Pakistan, Nehru passed away at Delhi and with that the hope of settlement of Kashmir remained as it is. There was also a feeling that if we let Kashmir go, we shall be encouraging secessions elsewhere, though baseless.

Many British Officers, Military and Civilians, who opted to serve Pakistan did their utmost to help that country against India on the problems left unresolved at Independence, the most important of them being the question of accession of princely state of Jammu and Kashmir. The British believed it would be natural for Kashmir to eventually accede to Pakistan on agreed terms. This was the pith of British Policy on Jammu and Kashmir that state had to go to Pakistan but with India's agreement. When Pakistan made invasion on Jammu and Kashmir, Jawaharlal Nehru complained to British Prime Minister Clement Attlee. Attlee's reply was evasive. The future relations of this state with Pakistan and India have obviously presented a problem and difficulty, the merits of which I do not think it incumbent of me to discuss. The main issue was who would control the main artery leading into Central Asia. The Indian proposals would leave it in their hands. The state consists of roughly three parts: Kashmir Valley, Jammu and Ladakh. Northern frontiers run in common with three countries Afghanistan, Russia and China. Lord Mountbatten was anxious to settle the Kashmir dispute before he relinquished the governor-generalship in June 1948. If the problem is not resolved by reason the sword will find the solution.

India accepted in 1948 a ceasefire promoted by UNCIP but unfortunately dropped its insistence on Pakistan's withdrawing from Gilgit. At that time situation in Kashmir was not favorable to Pakistan.

Both Maharaja of Kashmir and Sheikh Abdullah were against joining Pakistan. Sheikh Abdullah was definitely against Pakistan but the question remains whether he was definitely for India. In the letter dated 9th November Mountbatten wrote to Nehru, "I have on several occasions repeated my views on the question of sending Indian troops into western area...during my absence in London this object changed. It thus evidently became the purpose of Government of India to impose their military will on Poonch and Mirpur areas." Mountbatten wanted to neutralize Indian Military initiatives. Nehru and Sardar had no such intension. The support for Pakistan that developed in Security Council in January 1948 was mainly the result of British lobbying based on the argument that Jammu and Kashmir had 77 percent of Muslim population.

Britain's Pro-Pakistan policy on Kashmir was based on its desire to keep that part of its old Indian empire which jutted into central Asia and lay along with Afghanistan, Soviet and China. Kashmir was and remains a territorial issue, not a communal one.

Since then on and off alternatively unrest and peace have prevailed in Kashmir. United Nations while advising plebiscite in Kashmir in the presence of independent observers had also prescribed withdrawal of Pakistan's army from Pak-occupied Kashmir, which they have never done. People desire to remain with India has been unquestionably expressed by successive elections to Kashmir Assembly. There can be no need of a plebiscite. Britain and USA believe that unrest in Kashmir is for right to self-determination by the people of Kashmir. The western power had not then reconciled to India's stand. It is pure and simple insurgency in Kashmir, probably that has now been realized. After Pakistan lost out in East Bengal, where Bangladesh came into existence and it lost the war with India, it realized that it cannot win a war against India and created terrorism to hit India. In a meeting in Simla between the then Prime Minister of Pakistan Mr. Bhutto and Prime Minister Indira Gandhi, it was agreed that all disputes between India and Pakistan would be sorted out among themselves. There is no more any role for United Nations or anyone else.

**Dhiru S. Mehta**
Chairman
Navjivan Trust & Kasturba Gandhi
National Medical College, Wardha

# Acknowledgements

My first and foremost thanks go to Padmabhushan Justice Chandrashekhar Dharmadhikari for his inspiration and guidance to write a book on Kashmir with different angle for solution of the Kashmir dispute once and for all, which he has indicated in his 'Foreword' and I have suggested in Chapter 12.

I am beholden to Shri Dhiru. S. Mehta for his support in writing and completing the book. He has also written 'Preface' to the book throwing light on Kashmir dispute, which has been hanging for seven decades, for which I am thankful to him.

In one of my meetings with Padmavibhushan Shri Sharad Pawar, while writing his biography, I requested him to write 'Foreword' to the book based on his experience as Defence Minister of India and solution to settle the dispute once and for all. He was gracious enough to agree, but in view of his busy schedule he took time. By this time the MSS was sent to the Atlantic Publishers. Nonetheless, Shri Pawar snatched time to write on Kashmir dispute, which has been included in the book as 'Afterwords.' I am extremely grateful to him.

I cannot forget to extend my thanks to Shri Ankushrao Kadam, Secretary, Mahatma Gandhi Mission who has been as usual supportive in writing this hook.

My grand son Anurag has been constantly after me to complete the book at the earliest. It is he who has done the laborious task of typing the MSS along with his studies for M.Sc. in Environment Science, which he completed with distinction. I have nothing but all blessings for him.

In the last but not the least I thank Shri Harjeet Singh of Atlantic Publishers for publishing the book within the timeline.

**Sheshrao Chavan**

# Contents

# Afterword

Kashmir Valley, nestled in snow capped mountains with green meadows, gurgling brooks, blossoming gardens and sprawling lake is one of the most beautiful places on the planet. Mughals had rightly said to see its bewitching beauty that knows no bounds—"If there is a heaven on earth, it's here, it's here...."

Kashmir is the pride of India, a jewel in the crown. But, this heaven has become haven for terrorists and insurgents as if somebody has cast an evil eye on this naturally endowed place. There is a famous saying, 'Forehead is the fortune teller.' It tells us what is written in our destiny. The furrows on forehead determine the fortune. But, sadly to say that nation's forehead 'Kashmir' is deeply furrowed with festering wound, bleeding with no hopes for a healing touch and future is obscured in smouldering sentiments of Kashmiris.

If we look at the history of Kashmir, like its terrain, Kashmir has seen many upheavals since ages. From Kalhana's *Rajatarangini* to today's *Curfewed Nights* of Basharat Peer, many authors and scholars deeply explored into the core of Kashmir's history, polity and socio-economics and tried to unveil or demystify the unexplored areas of Valley. If we go through these anecdotes, we realise that the peace loving innocuous Kashmiris were often subjected to exploitations, brutalities and subjugation.

Before the advent of Islam, Hinduism, Buddhism and Shaivism attained prominence in the Valley with the Royal support. Later Islam became the predominant religion of the region. Sikhism also influenced Kashmiri culture in its own way.

Thus, Kashmiriyat has all the ingredients and elements drawn from different religions keeping its own deeply rooted cultural ethos intact. A Kashmiri always believes in peaceful coexistence; he has never been a hard-liner.

Generally, majority does not like to be ruled by minority but during British Raj, Kashmir, a Muslim majority state, was being ruled by Hindu Kings. In 1947, Maharaja Hari Singh was ruling Kashmir but would often spend much of his time in Bombay or in hunting in valley or surrounded by courtiers and favourites. Naturally, Muslims who were reeling under poverty, illiteracy and unemployment would often feel themselves oppressed and marginalised.

This led to the rise of Sheikh Abdullah who in 1930s began to lead the cause of Muslims in Valley. Although a Muslim, he was very close to Jawaharlal Nehru. Jawaharlal Nehru even had tried to enter Valley in protest of Sheikh Abdullah's arrest.

Kashmiris were neither inclined to Muslim League nor had aspirations for merging with Pakistan. So, when tribesmen invaded Kashmir, Kashmiris were shaken with that dastardly act of their co-religionists. Historian Amar Devi Gupta has depicted the horrors of invasion as "At Baramula, the tribesmen invaded the houses of peace loving Kashmiri Muslims and plundered them and raped their young girls. Shrieks of terror and agony of those girls resounded across the town of Baramula." Had Indian Army been delayed by a day, Srinagar would have met the same fate. I strongly believe, the generation of my age must be feeling sense of gratitude towards Indian Army that reached at the nick of the hour. The old Kashmiris know who were the saviours of life and dignity and who tried to savour their blood.

After the accession Sheikh Abdullah fought for self-determination, but never yielded to instigations from Pakistan. He kept Pakistan at bay and safeguarded people from its sinister activities. He later realised that pursuit for self-determination was like running behind shadows. It was his pragmatic decision to give away demand for plebiscite and settle the issue with maximum autonomy and special status to Kashmir. It was his experience and not the age that coaxed him to compromise. Only after his death, Pakistan could vigorously sponsor insurgent activities and infiltration of terrorists.

Till 1989, the situation had almost gone out of control. With the rise of JKLF, the youth raised arms with a fervent desire for independence. The incidents like Gaukadal incident and Lal Bazar incident in 1990 triggered the movement of Azadi. In March 1990, Mirwaiz's funeral procession was gun fired that claimed 50 lives and added fuel to the separatist movement. The high handedness of few civil and army officers further worsened the crisis. Islamic militants selectively targeted Kashmiri Pandits who had to take refuge in Jammu. Such type of ethnic cleansing had never happened in Valley. Once tourist destination became terrorists haven, completely crippling the tourism based economy.

Since 1989, the Kashmir conundrum is unresolved; security forces have no respite. After every 10 years, something major has happened. In 1997-98 Kashmiri Pandits were killed in Sangrampora and Wandhama massacres. Then in 1999, Kargil War brought both India and Pakistan on the brink of full-fledged war. But, during this war the Valley was exceptionally silent; it re-asserted Kashmiris' aversion towards Pakistan. But in 2009, Shopian murder case rocked the entire Valley; men, women, children took to the streets shouting for Azadi. Since then Kashmir is relentlessly boiling. Last year, Kashmir witnessed massive protests after killing of Hizb commander Burhan Wani. This time even school children, even girls took part in hurling stones on security forces. Burhan Wani is a martyred hero for them.

The Central Government has to take immediate step to stem the tide of dissent. I am sure nothing is out of control yet. There are more than 20 different separatist groups in Jammu and Kashmir raising cause of self-determination. They differ in their ideology, some are hardliners; some are moderates; some prefer Pakistan's tutelage; some are wary of Pakistan. In 1993, All Party Hurriyat Conference, a grand alliance of all these separatist groups was formed but weakened by the internal fissures. Even they know the potential danger from Pakistan if Kashmir is separated from India. This has left Kashmiri people in a state of confusion and commotion. Kashmiri people should understand that Sheikh Abdullah's decision to reconcile and endorse Indira-Abdullah accord of 1974 was the right decision, because Pakistan will never let Kashmir independent. People of Kashmir must not forget bitter memories of invasion. Voice of PoK people is completely smothered with no hope for independence or even autonomy. They are living in abject poverty with no sign of development. I believe that even recognising LoC as international border won't bring peace to Kashmir. It would neither stop Pakistan's meddling nor calm down resentment amongst the people of valley.

What India needs to do is to resume dialogue with Kashmiri people as said by the author in Chapter 12, especially youths, artisans and even with separatist groups without compromising its territorial integrity. Since Burhan Wani's killing, tourism has come to a complete halt. Shikaras and hotels are empty. Shawls, rugs and handicrafts are unsold rendering labourers and artisans jobless. I have also learnt that machine made fake handicrafts, shawls and other garments are being massively sold in the name of 'Kashmiri' in other parts of India. This would completely destroy small and cottage industries of Kashmir. The government must take urgent action against the fake manufacturers. The government should provide assured market to Kashmiri handicraft, furniture, artefacts and garments in India and abroad. This would not only help them to earn but it will enable them to interact with other people. Life in isolation is not an independent life unless it is self-reliant. Revival of tourism and handicraft industries will certainly encourage inter-dependence and interaction and make people self-reliant. Exchange of arts and culture will create positive environment for communication and conciliation and pave the way for peaceful co-existence.

Sense of insecurity, trust deficit, instinct of aloofness create voids and keep Kashmiris away from mainstream. Any untoward act or incident against the minorities, like beef ban or attack on cow, anywhere in India reflects adversely on the psyche of Kashmiris and evokes strong reactions across the valley. Heavy presence of Army though indispensable creates unrest in the valley. There should be a gradual shift of burden of responsibilities from Army to State Police for maintaining Law and Order. Army men are always outsider and local police are their own people. Being administered by own people is less disturbing. But modernisation of state police force is necessary to bring them at par with Army. Task is not easy but not impossible either.

The immediate issue in Kashmir is to locate the right type of leaders with grassroots hold on people, and to encourage them to take an active leadership role in sorting out the problems. The State has been starved of local leadership in the last two decades, with too much blatant interference from New Delhi.

Wrong policies in the past marred the chances of settlement of issues in Kashmir. For example, the Muslim United Front in Kashmir was formed out of political existence in 1986 for its extremist views by "leaders," who today cannot even step into the State. The authorities are, today, prepared to discuss the Kashmir problems with the groups that are far more extremists and militants than MUF.

Since the new government has taken over at the centre, vigilance in Kashmir has been intensified, with the defence forces playing a crucial role. The Law and Order situation in the State is not manageable. The fact, however, remains that the minds of vast section of people have to be won over.

An effective dialogue should be opened with the sensible and moderate elements in Jammu and Kashmir. Simultaneously, the interference from Delhi that has been a marked feature should also cease, leaving room for greater participation of local leadership in rebuilding the economy of the State. Visible, effective and equitable economic development of the State is one area where the Union Government can easily establish its credentials with the people of Kashmir.

It is commendable that Shri Sheshrao Chavan in his 80s has penned down the book on Kashmir. I have read his books on Gandhi and Ambedkar and Sardar Vallabhbhai Patel. He is a prolific writer with progressive thoughts. His insights in Kashmir issue will definitely help readers to understand the hearts of Kashmiris. The book will also help the administrators of valley to enter in people's shoes and address their woes. I wish all the best for this book.

**Sharad Pawar**
Former Defence Minister
Government of India

# Introduction

Jammu and Kashmir has been a perennial headache to India. His Highness Rajrajeshwar Maharajadhiraj Shri Hari Singh is primarily to blame for the territory becoming a dispute. Had he decided on the accession of Jammu and Kashmir to either India or Pakistan before the middle of August 1947, when the Crown representative Lord Mountbatten, had the authority to see through, there would have been no trouble. But the Maharaja dilly dallied.

Though India wanted the apple of Kashmir in its basket, there is no doubt that if Maharaja Hari Singh had decided to accede to Pakistan, New Delhi would have accepted it. Lord Mountbatten told Kuldeep Nair who was High Commissioner of India to UK on 1st October 1971, at his sprawling mansion, Broadlands, near London, that Sardar Patel, then Deputy Prime Minister, agreed to let Kashmir go to Pakistan if the State so wished. By sending its irregular troops into the State, Pakistan spoiled the whole thing.

The dispute of Jammu and Kashmir revolves round aggression, accession, cease-fire, plebiscite as well as resolutions of the Security Council of the United Nations.

## Aggression

Considerable parts of Jammu and Kashmir had been overrun by raiders from outside, well-armed and well-equipped, and they had sacked and looted the towns and villages and put many of the inhabitants to the sword.

Ninety-five villages in the Jammu Province were destroyed by the raiders from Pakistan. Bhimber town had also been sacked and destroyed. Other towns were besieged and considerable part of Poonch and Mirpur areas was in possession of the raiders. There had been continuous organized aggression from West Punjab into Kashmir State. The raiders possessed the latest type of modern arms. It was reported that they used flame-throwers and a disabled tank had been discovered with them.

Jawaharlal Nehru, in his speech in the Constituent Assembly on 2nd November 1947 said:

> On the night of 24 October, I learnt of another raid, this time from the Abbottabad-Mansara Road which enters Kashmir near Muzaffarabad. We were told that armed and well-equipped persons in over one hundred lorries had broken in, had sacked Muzaffarabad and killed many persons there, including the District Magistrate, and were proceeding along the Jhelum Valley road towards Srinagar. The State forces were spread out in small numbers all over the State and they could not stop this armed and well-organised raid. The civil population, Hindu and Muslim, fled before the raiders.
>
> The raiders had sacked several towns and had destroyed the great Power House at Mohoora which supplies electricity to the whole of the Kashmir. They were on the point of entering the valley. The fate of Srinagar and the whole of Kashmir hung in the balance.
>
> The month of December showed an intensification of military pressure on the State. Nearly 19,000 raiders had been reinforced in the Uri area and 15,000 raiders were operating against the western and south-western borders of the State. Incursions by the raiders into the State territory, involving murder, arson, loot and the abduction of women, were continuing. The booty was being collected and carried to tribal areas to serve as an inducement to the tribesmen to swell the ranks of the

> raiders. In addition to those actively participating in the raids, a large number of tribesmen and others, estimated at 100,000, had been collected in different places in the districts of West Punjab bordering upon the Jammu and Kashmir State, and many of them were receiving military training under Pakistan nationals, including officers of the Pakistan Army. They were being looked after in Pakistan territory, fed, clothed, armed and otherwise equipped and transported to the territory of the Jammu and Kashmir State with the help, direct and indirect, of Pakistan officials, both military and civil. The equipment of the invaders included modern weapons, such as mortars and medium machine-guns; the men wore the battle dress of regular soldiers, fought in regular battle formation and used the tactics of modern warfare. Man-packed wireless sets were in regular use and even mark 'V' mines were being employed.
>
> More than once, the Government of India had asked the Pakistan Government to deny invaders, facilities which constituted an act of aggression and hostility against India, but without any satisfactory response. On the 22nd December, I handed personally to the Prime Minister of Pakistan in New Delhi a letter in which the various forms of aid were briefly recited, and his Government were asked to put an end to such aid, promptly and without reservation.

## Accession

Maharaja Hari Singh asked for protection and signed the Instrument of Accession. India accepted the Instrument of Accession on the condition that the fate of Jammu and Kashmir will be ultimately decided by the people of the State.

On the accession, the representative of Pakistan in the Security Council said:

> India obtained the accession of the State of Jammu and Kashmir by fraud and violence and that large-scale massacre, looting and atrocities on the Muslims of Jammu and Kashmir State have been perpetrated by the

> armed forces of the Maharajah of Jammu and Kashmir and the Indian Union and by the non-Muslim subjects of the Maharajah and of the Indian Union.

In reply, V.K. Krishna Menon in his speech in the Security Council said:

### *The Accession is complete*

> It has been suggested time and again that there is something like provisional accession, that you can go in and come out.
>
> We are a federation; we are not a confederation, and the units that accede to federation stay in once they have acceded. There is no provision in our Constitution, there is no contemplation in our Constitution for the secession, and that is not peculiar to us. Once that accession has taken place there is no provision in this to go out. When Kashmir acceded, that matter was finished. Therefore, there is no such thing as going out.

## No Power can Transfer Kashmir to Pakistan

Jayaprakash Narayan in his convocation address at Mysore University on 29 November 1965 said:

> He could not conceive of any power on earth being able to transfer Kashmir from India to Pakistan, nor can I see how Pakistan can ever take the valley by force from India.

## Cease-fire Line

India and Pakistan accepted cease-fire on 1st January 1949. Each side remained in possession of areas it was occupying. But cease-fire was followed more in breach.

## Plebiscite

With regard to Plebiscite, Shri V.K. Krishna Menon and Justice M.C. Chagla in their speeches in the Security Council said:

### *V.K. Krishna Menon*

If an offer is made and it is not accepted at the time it is made, it cannot be held for generations over the heads of those who made it. *It is quite true that at one time we told Pakistan, "Let us go to the United Nations together and ask for a plebiscite". They did not agree. When they did not agree, that offer lapsed. They cannot come here nine years later and say, "You mentioned the word 'plebiscite". That is the position.* We have made many offers to Pakistan at various times. Some of these offers may be reconsidered, if necessary, when the time comes. *But, if an offer made to an opposing party is not accepted within a reasonable time, it cannot be maintained that it is still an open offer. The offer terminates when it is not accepted.*

### *Justice M.C. Changla*

"The promise given that we would ascertain the wishes of the people through a plebiscite no longer held good for two reasons: first, the promise was conditional upon Pakistan vacating her aggression, which she never did. Even today the part of Kashmir remains in the occupation of Pakistan. Secondly, a resolution passed in 1948 cannot be permitted in international law to hold the field indefinitely when conditions under which the resolution was passed had materially changed. Kashmir had already expressed its clear intention through three general elections. A plebiscite had no greater sanctity than a general election held through a secret ballot where the whole adult population went to the polls. Further, a plebiscite on a narrow communal issue was bound to rouse communal frenzy and passion, and disturb the life of the State which had remained peaceful and undisturbed."

On Pakistan's perpetual harping on plebiscite, Chagla said: "Pakistan's perpetual harping on a plebiscite in Jammu and Kashmir is not an outcome of its faith in democratic principles. I should have thought of democracy, like charity, begins at home, and before Pakistan preaches to us how we should ascertain the wishes of the people of a part of our country she should first make at least a beginning in establishing democratic institutions at home."

Shri V.K. Krishna Menon and Justice M.C. Chagla forcefully presented India's case in the Security Council, but their pleas went on deaf ears. This is what M.V. Kamath said about marathon speech made by Menon in the Security Council:

Shri M.V. Kamath, who was then P.T.I. Reporter in New York in his book *A Reporter at Large* at pages 364-66 writes:

Truth to say, he (Menon) did a first class job. If the Security Council were an impartial Court of Justice, and he was a lawyer for the defendant, he would have won hands down. His eight-hour speech was a remarkable *tour de force.* Half a dozen bright Indians had worked for him day and night to get all sorts of political, diplomatic and legal precedents and the speech, for all its rambling nature, was a work of art. Escott Reid has done him an injustice by saying that "Menon's speech in New York had not served to convert one of India's friends to India's side" and by adding that "the case which India had put had not impressed the West". The point is that the West was not *willing* to be impressed. As an Indian saying goes, you can wake a man who is asleep but cannot wake someone who is wide awake but pretends to snore.

I listened to Menon's speech, morning and afternoon, with my earphones, sitting in my office and arranged to get the UN staff 'takes' even as I was taking down my notes. One thing I was sure of: no matter how well any Western agency covered the speech, they would never be able to feel the passion and the anger behind it and reflect it in their copy. Only an Indian could do so. And I did. For once I forgot my personal dislike for Menon. He was my country's spokesman and he was standing up to the West. I would not desert him; I couldn't have done that, anyway. I was a *PTI* reporter and I had a job to do. But this was one speech I put my heart and soul in to report. I had a beautiful lead. The story went. Wagle, at the Bombay end, did not change a word or put in an extra comma. It was the front page lead, full seven columns in almost all papers. It is a coverage I am immensely proud of.

*The New York Times* which had printed the full text of Ferozekhan Noon's speech dismissed Menon's eight-hour marathon address in less than that many inches. The great newspaper displayed its meanness and pusillanimity by deliberately ignoring Menon's speech what made the news was the length of the speech, not its content. And the fact that

Menon had swooned. There was a joke current among Western correspondents that when a woman swooned she could be revived by waving smelling salts in front of her nose but when Menon swooned, one had only to wave a microphone in front of his lips. I don't flatter myself that my well-displayed report impressed Nehru. In the circumstances prevailing, he would have got the full text of Menon's speech verbatim within 24 hours of his making it. But the Prime Minister did say in an interview to the press that in speaking with passion, Menon had "represented the passion of India." He had indeed. In his book *Envoy to Nehru,* by way of comment on Nehru's remark, Escott Reid writes "Menon may have faithfully represented the passion of India but he did not present on behalf of India, arguments which were convincing to most friends of India in the West". That could not be true.

Jayaprakash Narayan in his article published in *Hindustan Times* on 1st February 1972 wrote:

> The plebiscite issue is dead for ever. Even the Sheikh cannot put back the clock of history. No question can be raised now about the accession of Jammu & Kashmir to India. Anyone who thinks otherwise is living in a fool's paradise and has failed to grow with the time and grasp the historic significance of the tremendous changes that have taken place in the Indian subcontinent.

## Monumental Mistake

Jawaharlal Nehru, who was too starry-eyed in his view of United Nations made a Himalayan blunder in taking the matter to the Security Council of the United Nations.

For over six decades India has looked up to the Security Council in vain for justice and fairplay on its straight and simple plaint of Pakistan's aggression against Indian territory.

If the weak and aggrieved among the nations of the world could not get justice at the UN, that international body would have failed in its sole function and purpose. It would be fatal for the UN, and the world as a whole, if people's faith in international institutions withered away.

By taking Kashmir to UN, we only confounded an already complex matter by the intervention of international players with their wheels within wheels.

It may be relevant to mention a question Lord Home, the then British Foreign Secretary asked Mr. T.N. Kaul in 1961, when he was Acting High Commissioner for India in UK. Lord Home asked Kaul: "Why did you take the Kashmir question to the UN when you had a very strong case legally, constitutionally, historically as well as on economic, strategic and other considerations." Kaul's reply was: "We did so on the advice of your Representative, Lord Mountbatten". It silenced Lord Home.

Gandhiji did not favour the Kashmir issue being taken to the United Nations where he was certain that India would get only what he called "monkey justice." The Sardar endorsed this view and held that if Pakistan had a grievance, it was open to that country to go anywhere it chose. He felt that India's precipitate action in rushing to the world body was a great mistake.

Sardar Patel had also said: "The forum of the United Nations has become a forum for the exchange of abuses and bitter and hostile criticism between the two blocks in which the world is being sought to be divided some what reminiscent of the old Papal Bull which divided the colonies of the world between Spain and Portugal in the Middle Ages."

Sardar Patel was more realistic about the Anglo-American domination of the World Organization when he opposed the reference of the Kashmir issue to the United Nations.

Sardar Patel feared that the UN deliberations would get bogged down in the game of power politics, and that the comparatively simple issue referred to it would be lost sight of. And this is what exactly happened. He also thought that if the matter was at all to go to the United Nations, it was better that India figured as a defendant rather than a complainant.

At the time when Kashmir issue was still a live one at the UN, Nehru overriding idealism and sense of fair play made the whole matter embarrassingly complicated.

Repeated failures of the Security Council during over six decades have made the people pessimistic and very doubtful about the potency of the UN to solve the Kashmir issue. There also appears to be no immediate prospect of India and Pakistan ending the deadlock by mutual negotiations as suggested by the Security Council of the United Nations representative. Both the governments are too much committed to their respective viewpoints and are therefore afraid to lose face if they in any way amend or alter their respective attitudes even a little. This is most deplorable as not only the fate and future of forty lakhs of Kashmiris hang in the balance but the well-being of the entire sub-continent depends on the peaceful settlement of the Kashmir issue. If the dispute drags on as at present it will never allow good relations to be established on a permanent footing between the two countries and will remain like an open sore to poison the entire Indo-Pakistan relationship.

## Stand from Jawaharlal Nehru to Manmohan Singh

The stand taken by every Prime Minister from Jawaharlal Nehru to Manmohan Singh has been given in Chapter 4. Unfortunately, all of them have failed to settle the Jammu and Kashmir dispute in spite of Tashkent Declaration; Simla Agreement; Agra Summit; Lahore Declaration; and Delhi and Kashmir Agreement.

### *Stand of Individuals and Organizations*

The Jammu and Kashmir has been in the grip of Muslim leaders and organizations. Their true colours have been revealed in Chapter 6.

There have been elements in the National Conference who exhibited a marked Islamic orientation. Some times these elements acted as fanatically as any fundamentalist group would act.

Muslim Organizations hardly with any exception in Jammu and Kashmir has been working against India with a view either to join Pakistan or remain independent.

## *Article 370*

Shri Jagmohan, who was Governor of Jammu and Kashmir, in his diary in August 1986 wrote: "Article 370 is nothing but a feeding ground for the parasites at the heart of paradise. It skins the poor. It deceives them with its mirage. It lines the pockets of the 'power elites'. It fans the ego of the new 'sultans'. In essence, it creates a land without justice, a land full of crudités and contradictions. It props up politics of deception, duplicity and demagogy. It breeds the microbes of subversion. It keeps alive the unwholesome legacy of the two-nation theory. It suffocates the very idea of India and fogs the very vision of a great social and cultural crucible from Kashmir to Kanyakumari."

On October 2, 1988, the birthday of Mahatma Gandhi, his statue was to be installed in the new High Court complex at Srinagar by the Chief Justice of India, Justice R.S. Pathak. But a few Muslim lawyers objected. They threatened to cause disturbance at the time of the function. The Chief Minister gave in to the bullying tactics. The function was cancelled.

What were the implications of what happened? A secular Kashmir, part of a secular India, could not have, even in its highest seat of justice, the statue of the Father of the Nation, of a sage who laid down his life for communal harmony and about whom Albert Einstein had said that "generations to come would scarcely believe that such a man ever trod on the earth". Who was the person spearheading the move against the installation? It was none other than Mohammad Shafi Butt, an advocate of the J&K High Court and an active member of the National Conference. He went to the extent of saying, "We shall not hesitate to secede from India if we are not assured a place of honour and dignity in terms of the safeguards provided for the people of the State under Article 370 of the Constitution."

What is the mental make-up of those who held key positions in the State, drew high salaries, and are still enjoying pension and other benefits from the Indian Exchequer? Here is Mufti Baha-ud-Din Farooqi, former Chief Justice of the J&K High Court, speaking through the writ petition filed by him:

> India annexed the Jammu & Kashmir State by manipulation, fraud and force against the declared wishes of the people of the State.

In the same writ petition, Mufti Baha-ud-Din goes on to affirm:

> The people of the State scented mischief and continued the freedom struggle with added determination.... That soon after the Indian Army landed in Kashmir, it mounted a powerful offensive on freedom fighters imposed a reign of terror in the State.

The ex-judge and ex-member of the National Conference considers that the raiders from Pakistan were freedom fighters and that the Indian Army did not go there to defend Kashmir but to establish a reign of terror. Note, further, his averment:

> The Indian Government worked on the plan to weaken and dismember Pakistan and to maintain hegemony on Kashmir through sheer might.

In Kashmir, the demand for retaining Article 370 emanates from a clever strategy to remain away from the mainstream, to set up a separate fiefdom, to fly a separate flag and to secure greater power and patronage, not for the good of the masses, not for serving the cause of peace and progress or for attaining cultural unity amidst diversity, but for serving the interests of the 'new elites', the 'new sheikhs'.

### *Sardar Patel and Article 370*

Looking to the detailed discussion of V. Shankar with Sardar Patel as given in Chapter 9, I am constrained to say that had Sardar Patel allowed the Congress Parliamentary Party to go its way, the Article 370 would not have gone through the Constituent Assembly and the country would have been saved from its consequences.

The Vajpayee Government tried to abrogate Article 370, but could not succeed. In the last Jammu and Kashmir State Assembly elections, BJP in its manifesto promised to do away with Article 370, but as the elections drew nearer, it had to sleep over it. And in the PDP-BJP alliance for forming the government,

BJP had to yield for maintaining status quo on Article 370. This provides enough reading in between the lines.

I am reminded of what J.P. Mathur, a founder member of Bhartiya Jan Sangh said and I quote: "Even if the BJP ever got the majority, it might not be able to repeal Article 370."

In fact, Justice M.C. Chagla observed, "Through Article 370, the whole of the Indian Constitution could be applied to Jammu and Kashmir." Chagla wanted the separate Constitution of Jammu and Kashmir to be scrapped.

## Solution Once and for All

Under the circumstances obtaining, a fresh approach needs to be adopted and that approach according to me could be Man to Man Diplomacy as explained in Chapter 12.

I make myself bold to say that most of the leaders in India are too timid and weak to speak out the truth, to advocate unpopular policies, and, if the need arose to face the wrath of people.

May I say without appearing to flatter Narendra Modi that some of his bold decisions are indications that he is attempting to give courageous leadership to solve the problems of India including Jammu and Kashmir.

Speaking on the unrest in J&K in his monthly radio programme 'Mann Ki Baat', he said: "From the interactions I had with all parties on Kashmir, one thing emerged, which can be put in simple words as 'ekta' and 'mamata'. These two are the basic mantra," he said.

The Prime Minister seems to have made up his mind to follow Atal Bihari Vajpayee's threefold formula *Insaniyat, Jambhooriyat and Kashmiriyat.*

Kashmir has cost a great deal and it is time that the major political parties in Kashmir, namely PDP, National Conference and All Parties Hurriyat Conference must introspect and change their political stands for the sake of peace and prosperity of Jammu and Kashmir instead of keeping the youth of Kashmir hostage to their political designs. Unfortunately, the working of the political system here is as said by Sajad Padder (Centre for International Relations, Islamic University of Science and Technology, Awantipora, Jammu and Kashmir): "Koi Azadi Ke Naam Par, Koi Autonomy Ke Naam Par, Aur Koi Bharat Mata Ke Naam Par, Sab Mile Hue Hai" (They are all together whether in the name of freedom, autonomy or Bharat Mata).

The youth in particular and people of Jammu and Kashmir in general should understand the designs of politicians and come together to solve the Kashmir embrilgo once and for all.

All eyes are set on Prime Minister Narendra Modi. Mehbooba Mufti has already said that if Narendra Modi cannot solve the dispute, no one else can solve it. I am inclined to agree with Mehbooba.

The choice before Narendra Modi is either to go down in history as saviour of Jammu and Kashmir or fall in line with his predecessors.

Jammu and Kashmir has become a gangrin in the body of India. It does not appear to be curable. It has to be amputed, if the body is to be saved. All methods adopted so far including dialogue and military operations have not brought desired results. The deteriorating situation does not make me optimistic.

Military operations may lead to war, which will not be confined only to India and Pakistan. Superpowers for obvious reasons will jump into it. It needs no pundit to say that USA, UK and China will lend hidden support to Pakistan.

I am conscious that all these factors will have to be taken into consideration before going for amputation. I am reminded of what Sardar Patel said about partition and I quote: "Deceased limb has been amputed." Sardar Patel could say it because he was Sardar Patel.

Narendra Modi is carving his image as Sardar Patel of India today. But he will have to take into account global scenario in the context of Jammu and Kashmir vis-à-vis India and Pakistan.

Jammu and Kashmir more or less has become a sentimental issue for both India and Pakistan, which is unfortunately being exploited for political existence. Setting aside the sentiments and politics inherent in it, I feel Jammu and Kashmir may be divided in three States on the basis of linguistic states. Kashmir valley, Jammu and Laddakh have Muslim, Hindu and Buddhist population respectively in majority it may evoke hostile reaction, but what else could be thought of to solve the Kashmir problem once and for all, when the plebiscite has been consistently ruled out and the dialogues do not yield results.

# 1

# Jammu and Kashmir from Dawn of History

The history of Kashmir, with a few illuminating exceptions, is a long and lamentable tale of conspiracies and collusions; of incessant upheavals, intrigues and counter-intrigues; of repulsive pettiness and nauseating profligacy; and of monstrous vices and abominable crimes. It has often been said that history repeats itself. But in the case of Kashmir, history appears to have repeated itself many times over, both as tragedy and as farce. Vincent A. Smith correctly remarked, "Few regions in the world could have had worse luck than Kashmir in the matter of Government."

The history of Kashmir would reveal what a beautiful cradle it has been of ancient culture. "The ancient India has nothing more worthy as its early civilization that the grand ruins of Kashmir." The remnants of hundreds of temples, stupas and viharas and numerous schools of thought would show how in ancient times it has been a nursery of two great religions of India—Hinduism and Buddhism—and how these religions met and mingled in the mind-scape of the people. Kashmir's own creative contribution to the Hindu thought, particularly to the evolution of the monistic philosophy of Saivism, known as 'Trika Sastra', has been truly historic. And when Islam made its appearance in the middle of the fourteenth century, it acquired its own distinct hue in the Valley.

## Antiquity

There are good geological and mythological reasons to believe that the Kashmir Valley was once a vast span of water, similar to a huge dam, walled by high mountains. There were some habitations of the higher ranges which were not under water. Over the years, as a result of violent geological upheavals such as earthquakes, the mountain walls were breached at a few points and the water gushed out, forming the Valley in its present shape.

## Sources

Fortunately enough, the State boasts of having a long and chequered history extending to thousands of years past. All this we owe to a great extent to Kalhana, a Kashmir Pandit who wrote *Rajatarangini* (the River of Kings) in round about 1149 A.D. composed in eight canons of Sanskrit verse it is the history of the various dynasties which ruled Kashmir from the earliest period to the time of the author. Undoubtedly, it is a monumental work in the field of Sanskrit literature and no other writer has approached Kalhana's attainments even remotely. His lucid and superb style can easily be judged from the following lines:

> Such is Kashmir, the country which may be conquered by the force of spiritual merit but not by armed force... where there are hot baths in winter, comfortably landing places on the river banks, where the rivers being free from aquatic animals are without peril, where realising that the land created by his father is unable to bear heat the hot-rayed sun honours it by bearing himself with softness even in summer. Learning, high dwelling—houses, saffron, iced water, grapes and the like—what is a common place there is difficult to secure in Paradise.

The main source of Kashmir's history is Kalhana's epic historical poem, *Rajatarangini* (River of Kings). The observations made in the poem on the various aspects of life shows the depth of Kalhana's mind and also the range of his perception. The book is of such great merit that it has itself become an invaluable part of Kashmir's history and also of ancient Indian literature. The book was written in A.D. 1148-50. While it provides insight into the entire period of ancient Kashmir, it gives a fairly accurate and exhaustive account of the events and social and economic conditions from the eight century onwards. This book has long attracted the attention of historians, Europeans and Indians.

Kashmir's scenic beauty, salubrious climate and sacred shrines have given it the apt title of "Tourist Paradise". Kashmir, as G.T. Vigne prophesied in 1835, has become the *sine quo non* of the travelers to the East. Thomas Moore has also described the Kashmir Valley in his immortal *Lalla Rookh* in the following lines:

> Who has not heard of the Vale of Cashmere
> With its roses the brightest that earth ever gave
> Its temples, and grottos, and fountains as clear
> As the love-lighted eyes that hang over their wave!

## Period of Hindus and Buddhist Kings

Gonanda, the first known King of Kashmir, was a relation and friend of Jarasandha, King of Magadha. The latter was father-in-law of Krishna, King of Mathura. Gonanda went to the help of Jarasandha, but he was defeated and killed by Krishna. Jarasandha's son, Damodara, then became the King of Kashmir. To avenge his father's death, he proceeded to fight Krishna. But he, too, was killed. Yasovati, Damodar's widow, who was pregnant at the time of her husband's death, ascended the throne with the support of Krishna. When a son was born to her, he was formally crowned as the king under the name of Gonanda II.

After Gonanda II, Kashmir was ruled by at least 43 kings. They were all weak and insignificant. Therefore, Asoka (273-232 B.C.) extended his control over Kashmir. He encouraged Buddhism in the Valley. During his time, viharas and stupas were built at Vita Staktra and Sus Kaletra. Asoka founded the ancient capital, Srinagar, about five kilometers away from the present city. According to Kalhana, it was "resplendent with wealth".

After Asoka's death, the Mauryan Empire began to disintegrate. Jalauk, Asoka's son, became an independent monarch of Kashmir. Meanwhile, there was revivalism of Hinduism in North India, and the wave of revivalism also reached Kashmir. Under its influence, Jalauka destroyed a few Buddhist viharas and built two new temples at Srinagari and Nandi-Kshetra.

Three centuries later, Kashmir passed under the control of the Kushans. Amongst the known Kushan rulers were Kaniska, Huska and Juska. Kaniska was the most powerful monarch whose rule extended to north-western India and Central Asia. Kashmir was the fulcrum of his activities for the spread of Buddhism which he earlier adopted. Buddhism became the State religion and Kashmiri missionaries carried its message to China and far-off places in South-Central Asia. The fourth Buddhist Council was held by Kaniska at a place called Kundalvara.

The Kushans were followed by a number of local rulers including Abhimanyu, Vibhisana I, Indrajit, Ravana and Vibhisna II. Their names, which are familiar to the readers of the *Ramayana* suggest close affinity between Kashmir and North India. During the reign of these kings, Saivism made headway. Buddhism suffered. One of the kings, Nana, burnt thousands of viharas and granted Buddhist villages to the Brahmins.

In the first half of the sixth century A.D., Mihira-Kula, a Hun general, came to occupy Kashmir's throne. He rose to power in North India after the decline of the Gupta Empire. But he lost the war against a confederacy of Indian chiefs. He escaped to the Valley and seized power. He ruled from A.D. 515 to 550. He was a cruel king. Kalhana mentions that the people could forecast his arrival by seeing the vultures that flew ahead of him. His sadistic disposition became a part of the Kashmir's sayings. While crossing the pass near Hastivanj, an elephant fell down the hill. Mihira-Kula so enjoyed the terrified cry of the dying elephant that he caused the fall of another 100 elephants to feel the repeated thrill of the scene.

After Mihira-Kula, the Huns ruled Kashmir for some time. But the local rulers soon regained power, and the second Gonanda dynasty came into being. During the role of this dynasty, King Vikramaditya of Ujjain exercised a loose suzerainty over Kashmir.

Hiuen Tsang, the celebrated Chinese traveller, came to Kashmir in A.D. 631. At that time, the Karkota dynasty was ruling over Kashmir, and its founder, Durlabhavandhana, was the king. Hiuen Tsang was well received. He stayed in the Valley for two years, and visited almost all the important places associated with Buddhism.

According to Hieun Tsang, the king of Kashmir held sway over as distant places as Taxila, Hazara, Poonch and Rajouri. He was a powerful monarch, and had a vast kingdom to rule. He controlled the route from Kabul to Kashmir. But he was not totally independent. Emperor Harshavardhana, whose capital was Kannauj, exercised a weak form of suzerainty over Kashmir. The economy of Kashmir was in good shape. The Valley was full of fruits and flowers. Buddhism was fairly widespread. There were about 5,000 Buddhist monks and over one hundred Buddhist monasteries. There were also four Asokan 'Chaityas', each containing a very small relic of Buddha's body. The sacred of Kashmir. But Harshavardhana took it away.

Hieun Tsang thought poorly of the Kashmiris of the time. He recorded: "They are volatile and timid; they are good-looking but deceitful. They are fond of learning and follow both Buddhism and Hinduism."

The most outstanding king of the Karkota dynasty was Lalitaditya who ruled for 37 years from A.D. 724 to 761. He was motivated by an ambition similar to that of Alexander the Great. This would be evident from what he is believed to have stated to his ministers: "For rivers, the ocean is the limit but nowhere is there a limit for those aspiring to be conquerors." He is believed to have gone as far as the banks of Cauvery in South India and also to Konkan and Kathiawar in the west. In the east, he extended his hold up to Bengal. In the north-west of the Valley, he established his sway over Ladakh and a portion of western Tibet. He had in his employment a brilliant Chinese general, Cankunya. Lalitaditya also had some contacts with the Chinese Emperor. Most probably he and the Chinese ruler cooperated with each other to check the power of Tibet.

Lalitaditya's most memorable act was the construction of the glorious temple of Martanda, in honour of the sun-god, at a site now called Matan. About his famous construction, Stein said, "The ruins of this splendid temple are still the most striking objects of ancient Hindu architecture in the Valley." In the same strain, Young husband observed, "The temple is built on the most sublime site of Parthenon, or of the Taj, or of St. Peters. It is second only to the Egyptians in massiveness and strength and to the Greeks in elegance and grave. No one without an eye for natural beauty would have chosen that special site for the construction of a temple and no one with an inclination to the empirical and transient would have built in on so massive and enduring a scale."

Lalitaditya was a staunch follower of Hinduism. He worshipped Lord Vishnu intensely. But he was equally liberal towards Buddhism. In fact, his rule is considered as "the golden period of Kashmir Buddhism". On a single vihara—Raja Vihara—he is believed to have spent about 84,000 tolas of gold. He patronized learned men without any distinction of creed and territorial loyalty. He brought to his court two great poets from Kannauj—Bhavbhuti and Vakpatiraja.

Due to the misrule of Lalitaditya's successors, the dynasty collapsed by the middle of the ninth century.

For the next century and a half, the course of Kashmir's history was influenced by the looks and dispositions of two women. One, Jayadevi, gave a new dynasty, Uptala, which produced one of the finest kings of Kashmir—Avantivarman; and the other, Didda, dominated this scene for about 50 years and set in motion forces which ultimately led to the decay and decline of Hindu rule in Kashmir. Both were women of captivating beauty and charming features.

From all points of view, Avantivarman's time was a glorious in Kashmir's history. There was peace; there was development; there was justice; there was understanding between the king and his ministers; there was piety and even awareness of conversation;

and there was attachment to higher ideals of religion, art and culture. The king's pious disposition can be seen from the fact that he used to listen to the recital of *Bhagwadgita* from his sickbed, and he passed away while listening to the 'slokas' from this holy book.

Avantivarman's successor, Samkarvaraman, disturbed the peace and prosperity of the kingdom by restoring to unnecessary military expeditions. He imposed heavy taxes and levies and resorted to forced labour, 'begar'. It used to be said that the king had 'spared nothing from his exactions except breathing'.

The successors of Samkaravarman were kings of poor caliber. The Uptala dynasty ended in A.D. 939, when Yasaskaradeva, a Brahmin, was crowned king. But the rule of the Brahmin dynasty lasted only ten years. In A.D. 949, Parva Gupta, chief minister of the Brahmin king, enacted a coup, killed the king, and ascended the throne.

It was during the reign of the Gupta dynasty that Didda, the daughter of the king of Lohrin, came to the forefront. Lohrin is presently located in Poonch district. Didda was married to the second Gupta King, Ksema Gupta (A.D. 950-58). She dominated the Kashmir scene for about 50 years, first as queen, then as regent for her son and grandsons, and finally a direct ruler.

She became a regent for the minor king Abhimanyu II, and vanquished her adversaries one by one. As Kalhana observes, "The lame queen whom no one thought capable of stepping over a cow's footprint got over the ocean-like host of her enemies, just as god Hanuman got over the ocean." She died in A.D. 1003.

Before death, Queen Didda was able to manipulate the crown for Samgramaraja, a member of her family from Lahora—the principality to which she herself belonged before her marriage. Thus, a new dynasty, the first Lohara dynasty (A.D. 1003-1101), came into being. With this, the Kshatriyas came to rule Kashmir.

During the time of Samgramaraja (A.D. 1004-28), Sultan Mahmud of Ghazni skirted Kashmir after defeating Trilochanapala of the Sahi Kingdom. Samgramaraja's successor,

Ananta (A.D. 1028-63), a weak king, came under the influence of the Sahi princes of Punjab, who took refuge in Kashmir after Mahmud Ghazni.

Ananta was followed by Kalsa (A.D. 1063-89) and Harsa (A.D. 1089-1101). The latter made himself infamous by plundering the wealth of temples and dishonouring divine images. In this regard, Kalhana observes, "To defile the statues of gods, Harsa had excrement and urine poured over their faces by naked mendicants."

Harsa's conduct show to what low depth the kingdom of Kashmir had descended. To use the expression of Kalhana: "In the form of Harsa, some demon had descended to the earth to destroy this land hallowed by gods, tirthas and risis."

Among the kings of the second Lohara dynasty, there were only two who deserve notice. They were Uccale (A.D. 1101-11) and Jaya Simha (A.D. 1128-55).

After the death of Jaya Simha in 1155, the process of decline and decay which had started during the time of Didda and Harsa, and which was temporarily halted by Uccale and Jaya Simha, hastened. The next two hundred years saw only weak and selfish kings who showed no will to set the house in order. An effete and insignificant dynasty of Bopadeva (A.D. 1171-1286) was followed by an equally indolent and impotent dynasty of Damra (A.D. 1286-1320).

It was in the atmosphere of the moral decay, economic decline, and social and political disruption that foreign adventurers started arriving in the Valley. Two such foreigners were Shah Mir and Rinchana. The former settled in a village near Baramulla and the latter in the Lar. Both were helped by the Damra King. Suhadeva, by grant of 'jagirs', and both were destined to play crucial roles in shaping the course of the future history of Kashmir.

A fatal blow was struck to the Hindu kingdom of Kashmir by the invasion, in 1320, of Dulacha, a Mongal warrior and adventurer who hailed from Turkistan. As no vigil was kept at the passes, Dulacha swept everything before him. King Suhadeva exhibited woeful cowardice. He tried to buy off the invaders but failed. Dulacha entered the Valley as "a lion enters the cave of a deer". The people of Kashmir died as "insects in a fire". Men were put to sword and women and children taken away as slaves. The invaders looted and burnt the villages and cities that came in their way. In the words of Jonaraja, "Kashmir became almost like a region before creation."

Rinchana who hailed from Ladakh and had migrated to Kashmir after his father, local chief, had been killed in the power-struggle with the Baltis—took advantage of the disorderly condition and—unmindful of the good deed done to him by King Suhadeva, plundered the area around the Lar Valley.

Jonaraja colorfully described the situation: "Dulacha was like a billow in the water; and on the hill, Rinchana was like a tempest, while the chief men in the town (Srinagar), the prosperous and the rich, were struck with the fear. As the kite swoops on the young ones of the bird thrown out of their nest, so the swift army of Rinchana seized the people of Kashmir". The only obstacle in the way of Rinchana was the Chief Minister Rama Chandra who had proclaimed himself as king after the flight of Suhadeva in the wake of Dulacha's invasion. Rinchana got Rama Chandra murdered by deceitful means and seized the throne. Thus, the kingdom of Kashmir came to be ruled by a Ladakhi Buddhist.

## Muslim Sultans

To conciliate the people, Rinchana married the daughter of Rama Chandra, Kota Rani. He restored order and set up an efficient and just administration under the charge of Shah Mir.

He then embraced Islam, a religion which a section of his subject had already adopted. He assumed the title of Sultan Sadar-ud-Din. Kashmir, thus, got its first Muslim ruler. The first Muslim Rule was, however, short-lived. Rinchana died in 1323, leaving behind a minor son, Haider. The courtiers invited Upyandeva, brother of the late King Suhadeva, to accept the throne. He did so.

King Upyandeva was a weak and lazy ruler. At that time, another invader, Achala, a Turko-Mongol adventurer, appeared in the Valley. Upyandeva fled to Ladakh, but Kota Rani and Shah Mir joined hands and defended the Valley. Achala retreated.

Upyandeva died in A.D. 1338. To forestall Shah Mir, Kota Rani kept the death of her husband secret for four days, and, after moving to the safe fort of Indrakot, proclaimed herself as the next ruler. In the struggle that followed, Shah Mir came out victorious and assumed kingship under the title of Sultan Shams-ud-Din.

Muslim rule in Kashmir commenced on a favorable note. Shah Mir's regime (A.D. 1339-42), though brief, acted like a soothing balm on an aching body. The Sultan adopted a humane, enlightened and just approach. He reduced the taxes and treated Hindus and Muslims alike.

The next important Sultan was Shihab-ud-Din (A.D. 1352-73) grandson of Shah Mir. In fact, his rule has been called, "from the political and military point of view, as the most glorious epoch in the history of Muslim Sultanate in Kashmir". He not only curbed the growing power of feudal chiefs and consolidated his position but also undertook extensive military expeditions to the north, north-west and south of Kashmir. As Jonaraja puts it, "Deer-eyed women attracted not his mind, nor the pleasure of drinking, nor the light of the moon; only the march with his army was dear to him."

He also built a new town on higher ground near Hari Parbat and named it Laxminagar after his queen Laxmi. He was a just ruler and generally tolerant of Hindus.

Hindal, the younger brother of Sultan Shihab-ud-Din, succeeded him. He assumed the title of Qutub-ud-Din (A.D. 1373-89). It was during his time that Sayyid Ali Hamdani came to Kashmir and Islamic practices began to be adopted rather strictly.

The Islamic zeal attained fanatical proportions under the next ruler—Sultan Sikandar (A.D. 1389-1413) who came to be known as 'But-Shikan', destroyer of idols. "There was no city, no town, no village, no wood, where the temples of gods remained unbroken." The Hindus were subjected to '*jizia*', and forbidden to apply '*tilak*' on their forehead. Sikandar also introduced an institution of Sheikh-ul-Islam to ensure that the injunctions of Islam were fully observed.

A relentless campaign for conversion of Islam was launched, under the charge of the Sultan's chief minister, Malik Saif-ud-Din. The chief minister's original name was Suha Bhatta. He renounced his Hindu faith to accept Islam. The zeal of this newly converted minister knew no bounds. He unleashed a reign of terror against those who resisted conversion. It is believed that the Sultan and his chief minister threw into the Dal Lake all the sacred books of the Hindus that they could lay their hands on, and seven maunds of sacred threads of murdered Brahmins were burnt. It is from this period that the predominance of Muslims in the population of the Valley begins.

During Sultan Sikandar's regime, a large number of Sufi saints and Islamic scholars came to Kashmir from Persia and Central Asia. About 700 Sayyids accompanied Mohammad Hamdani, son of Ali Hamdani. Through them, the influence of Islam spread further in Kashmir. A large number of mosques were also built at that time, including the famous Bijbehara Mosque and the Jama Masjid in Srinagar.

Sikandar's policy was continued by his son, Sultan Ali Shah. He too remained under the influence of the chief minister Saif-ud-Din.

The next Sultan, Zain-ul-Abidin (A.D. 1420-70), turned out to be the most tolerant and benevolent ruler that Kashmir has known. It has been correctly remarked that "history can give few examples where the policy of the father was so completely reversed by the son. Where Sikandar destroyed, Zain-ul-Abidin restored; where the former banished, the latter recalled." Zain-ul-Abidin's reign, following that of Sikandar and Ali Shah, was, in the words of historian Srivara, "like the cooling sandal paste after the heat of summer in a desert had departed."

All restrictions against the Hindus were removed. Cow slaughter was banned. Killing of fishes in the springs considered sacred by Hindus were prohibited. He also allowed rebuilding of demolished temples. He himself got a few of them reconstructed. He recalled pundits who had fled the Valley due to persecution, and assigned them responsible positions on merit. He got Hindu Shastras as well as the Mahabharata translated into Persian.

Sultan Zain-ul-Abidin was a many splendoured genius. In the sphere of religion, he was precursor of Akbar; in the field of construction, he proved to be the Shah Jahan of Kashmir. He distinguished himself equally in the realm of learning, art and culture. He had an innovative mind and introduced a number of canals which not only helped in draining out water from marshy and low-lying areas, thereby making them fit for cultivation, but also in providing irrigation facilities to parched areas.

Zain-ul-Abidin not only revived old art and crafts but also introduced a number of new ones. "Kashmir became a smiling garden of industry" and made significant progress in wood carving, paper-making, silk, shawl and carpet weaving. This is what Mirza Haider wrote in Tarikh-i-Rashidi in 1543: "In Kashmir one meets with all those arts and crafts which are, in most cities, uncommon, such as stone polishing, stone-cutting, bottle-making, gold-beating. This is all due to Sultan Zain-ul-Abidin."

Zain-ul-Abidin has justly earned the reputation of being the greatest Sultan of Kashmir who reigned for half a century. Srivara was right in saying that "the King's virtuous mode of government in the 'Kali Yuga' became glorious like the very middle of 'Satya Yuga'. At the time of his death, it was felt that the "crown became lusterless, the earth and sky became gloomy, justice and generosity, learning and power, glory and pomp, peace and tolerance departed".

Sultan Zain-ul-Abidin's sons proved unworthy of their illustrious father. In the intrigues and the counter-intrigues that followed his death, the caucus of the Sayyids gained ascendency at the court, making the Sultan a mere puppet in its hands. In the early stages of their arrival in the Valley, the Sayyids were respected. But they soon acquired power and position which caused much heart-burning amongst other courtiers. Their arrogance also alienated the people whom, to use the expression of Srivara, they "treated as grass". The administration became callous. "Accepting bribes were considered by the officers as virtue, oppressing the subjects was regarded as wisdom and the addiction to wine and women was reasoned as happiness."

The fortunes of the Sultanate in Kashmir began to decline rapidly. The next 120 years saw only intrigues and conspiracies. One weak Sultan followed another, while factions of the courtiers—the Sayyids, the Magreys, the Chaks and the Dars—indulged in their power games in the most unscrupulous manner. Religious differences added to the fury of the conflicts. The Chaks were fanatically attached to the Shia faith, and the Sayyids and the Magreys were equally strong in their adherence to the Sunni faith, and, as a result, the people suffered. Their miseries were compounded by the epidemic that swept the Valley in 1515-16. As the chronicler Shuka puts it: "The number of the dead could not be counted either in the villages or in the capital. Men could hardly get a piece of cloth at their last moment. Friends did not weep for friends, what to speak for sorrowing for others."

It was in this unsettled conditions that Mirza Haider Dughlat, a Mughal general, entered the Valley. He was in the service of Humayun. When the latter was defeated by Sher Shah at Kannauj in 1540 and his army was in retreat, Mirza Haider moved into the Valley in November 1540 with only 400 soldiers. He met with practically no resistance. He was aided and abetted by the Magreys and the Sayyids. He soon established his full control and ruled the Valley for the next eleven years (1541-51) in the name of Humayun.

After Mirza Haider's death, the local factions returned to the scene. In the ensuing scramble for power, the Chaks emerged victorious. Things came to such a pass that in 1561, in the open court, Ali Chak snatched the crown from the Sultan and put it on the head of his brother Ghazi Chak. Thus was founded the Chak dynasty. But it did not change the conditions materially. Conflicts and conspiracies continued. A section of the Kashmiri nobility approached Akbar with the request that he should annex Kashmir.

From the near anarchic conditions, Kashmir was rescued by the Mughals who established their full control over it in 1589, when Emperor Akbar himself came there.

## The Mughals

In *Ain-i-Akbari*, Abul Fazl recorded: "On all the sides, mountains, which raise their heads to heaven, act as sentinels. Though there are six or seven roads, yet in all of them there are places where if some old women rolled down stones, the bravest of the men could not pass. On this account, former princes did not think of conquering it and prudence turned them away from such a wish." But this natural fortress fell to Akbar easily not only because of the superior might of the Mughal Empire but also because the people of Kashmir had become sick of the mismanagement of their Sultans. The defense of the passes had been badly neglected. More often than not, the defenders themselves joined the invaders.

Even before Akbar, the Mughals had been treating Kashmir as a part of their empire. First, Kamran held it for a few months in 1531, and then Mirza Haider Dughlat ruled Kashmir on behalf of Humayun from 1541 to 1551.

In 1589, Kashmir became a province of the Mughal Empire. It was ruled through a Governor, known as Subedar. Kashmir became a hub of Central Asian trade. Akbar himself visited the Valley thrice—first in 1589, then in 1598, and again in 1601.

Some notable reforms were also carried out by the Mughals. For example, Jahangir put an end to an evil practice of sati and infanticide. In some areas of the kingdom, even Muslims came under the influence of the prevailing Hindu customs and buried their women alive along with their dead husbands. Unwanted female children were also killed.

Akbar's successor, Jahangir, fell in love with Kashmir. He visited the Valley six times. In his memoirs, he has paid glowing tributes to its beauty. He wrote, "Kashmir is the garden of eternal spring, a delightful flowerbed, and heart-expanding heritage for 'dervishes'. Its pleasant meads and enchanting cascades are beyond all description. There are running streams and fountains beyond count." About a site near the present-day Gulmarg, the Emperor observed, "It is a page that the painter of destiny has drawn with the pencil of creation."

Sukh Jiwan Mal established unquestioned sway over Kashmir. He declared his allegiance to the Mughal Emperor who granted him the title of Raja.

When force did not yield results, Abdali resorted to stratagem. Through his agent he wrecked the cordial relations between Raja Sikh Jiwan Mal and his chief minister, Abdul Hassan Bandey. Taking advantage of the situation, Abdali sent his third expeditionary force in 1762 under the leadership of Nur-ud-Din Khan Bamzi. A major portion of Raja Sukh Jiwan Mal's army deserted him. He was captured, blinded and sent to Ahmad Shah Abdali at Lahore, where he was mercilessly killed by throwing him under the feet of an elephant.

With the re-establishment of Afghan rule, the miseries of the people redoubled.

The Afghan misrule in Kashmir touched its lowest ebb. In 1783, George Forster, an officer of the East India Company, visited Kashmir. While recounting the cruelties perpetrated by Karim Dad Khan, Forster described how for minor offences the alleged culprits were tied together in pairs and thrown into the river, and how women are sexually abused. About Asad Khan, Forster recounted the story that was current at that time. "A film on one of his eyes has baffled the attempts of many operators, and being impatient at the want of success, he told the last surgeon who had been called in, that if the disorder was not remedied within a limited time, allowing but a few days, his belly should be cut open; the man failed in the cure and Asad Khan verified his threat."

Asad Khan, intoxicated by power, declared himself independent in 1784 and assumed the title of Nadir Shah II.

Jabbar Khan, the last Afghan Governor, persecuted the Hindus relentlessly. A Pandit nobleman, Birbal Dhar, unable to see any longer the Kashmiris being tormented and tortured, approached Maharajah Ranjit Singh for help and provided him with valuable information about the strength and deployment of Jabbar Khan's forces. Ranjit Singh has earlier made two unsuccessful attempts to capture Kashmir, once in 1812 and again in 1814. This time success greeted Ranjit Singh. The

Sikh forces, under the able command of Misser Dewan Chand, defeated Jabbar Khan at Shopiyan on July 15, 1819, and triumphantly marched into the capital the next day.

Thus ended 67 years of Kashmir's nightmare.

## The Sikhs

Maharaja Ranjit Singh was so happy over the annexation of Kashmir that he ordered special illumination of Lahore and Amritsar for three nights. He nursed a deep desire to visit Kashmir. In a letter, he wrote, "Would that only once in my life I could enjoy the delight of wandering through the gardens of Kashmir fragment with almond blossoms, and sitting on the fresh green turf!" But he was not destined to have his wish fulfilled. Although he ruled for 17 years after his forces conquered Kashmir, Ranjit Singh could not visit it even once.

Sikh rule in Kashmir lasted only 27 years (1819-46). But it saw ten Governors.

The last Governor, Imam-ud-Din, was made to surrender possession of Kashmir to Raja Gulab Singh in 1846 in pursuance of the Treaty of Amritsar.

## Rise of the Dogras

Gulab Singh, founder of the Dogra dynasty, was a gifted person. He was born in 1792 in a family which traced its ancestry to Raja Ranjit Deo, the famous ruler of the Jammu region from 1742 to 1780.

In the various military campaigns undertaken by Ranjit Singh, Gulab Singh exhibited his unmatched skills, courage, loyalty, and organizational ability, particularly in regard to the sieges of Multan and Jalandhar and subjugation of the tribes of Yusafzai in 1819 which enabled the Maharaja to capture Peshawar. In recognition of Gulab Singh's services and as part of his overall strategy to create a subordinate military power between the Sikh and the Afghan domains, Ranjit Singh granted a number of estates, including Jammu, to Gulab Singh. The title of Raja was conferred upon him, and he was given permission to raise his own force.

Jacquemont, who travelled through Gulab Singh's territory in 1831, observed, "Gulab Singh is more the master of his own house than is Ranjit Singh in distant possession."

The most significant military achievement of Raja Gulab Singh was the inclusion of Ladakh in his province. In 1834, with the implied consent of Ranjit Singh and the East India Company, Gulab Singh deputed his most brilliant general, Zorawar Singh, to conquer Ladakh, the most strategic area having borders with China and Tibet, and also a nerve centre of wool trade with Central Asia. At that time, Ladakh was an independent kingdom under the suzerainty of the Grand Lamas of Tibet.

K.M. Pannikar in his book, *Gulab Singh: Founder of Kashmir* (Martin Hopkins, 1930) writes: "In a country barren of historical achievements in India, Gulab Singh stands out as a solitary figure of political eminence. He is the only ruler in India's long history, who could be said to have extended the geographical boundaries of India. No previous Indian ruler, not even Samudra Gupta, Akbar, has ever dreamt of invading Tibet and although Zorawar, who ventured too far paid the penalty for his adventure, the Maharaja's forces ruled the Tibetan army and extended the border of India to the other side of Himalayas."

Buddhism travelled to Ladakh from India via Kashmir. The description given by Hui Ch'ao, a Chinese pilgrim, who travelled in the territory in A.D. 727, argues that Buddhism which came from India had established its hold on the people of Ladakh at a time when even Tibet had not become Buddhist. Ladakh became a part of "the spiritual and cultural empire of Tibet."

When the Anglo-Sikh conflict came to a boiling point, Gulab Singh cleverly turned the situation to his advantage. While the Sikhs wanted his help because he was their most important feudatory chieftain, the British interests lay in not permitting the combination of the Sikh and the Dogra powers. Gulab Singh deftly interposed himself between the two warring parties. On the one hand, he professed loyalty and friendliness to the Lahore Durbar, and, on the other, he remained in secret touch with the British. He wanted to use his trump card only when the power of the Sikh army had been broken.

Gulab Singh realistically accepted the position of 'subordinate alliance' to the British and in the process secured a vast princely State free from the vagaries of the Lahore Durbar. The Sikhs lost all their power and position which they had built over the last fifty years.

Gulab Singh died in 1857. Eleven years of Dogra rule witnessed the gradual establishment of order in the State. But in the reign of his successor Maharaja Ranbir Singh the northern frontier tribes again became troublesome and expeditions had to be sent against them. Thus came about the subjugation of Gilgit and adjacent territories.

Ranbir Singh was succeeded in 1885 by his eldest son Pratap Singh. After the new Maharaja's accession, a British Resident was appointed in place of an officer on special duty. The Resident and his assistants were empowered to try civil suits in which both parties were British subjects or the defendant was a Briton or an Indian subject of Britain. A council was constituted for the administration of the State with Raja Sir Amar Singh, the Maharaja's younger brother, and two officers of the Government of India as members. Amar Singh played a major part in the administration till his death in 1907.

## Treaty of Lahore and Amritsar

After the defeat of the Sikhs, two separate treaties were executed. The Treaty of Lahore, which incorporated the terms of settlement between the Sikhs and the British Government, was signed on March 9, 1846. A week later, on March 16, 1846, a separate treaty, known as the Treaty of Amritsar, was signed between Raja Gulab Singh and the British Government. It may be noted that by virtue of the first treaty the Sikhs ceded certain areas to the British Indian Government on account of their inability to pay the indemnity of rupees one and a half crore that was demanded by the British; and by virtue of second treaty, the British Government transferred 'for ever in independent possession' some of the ceded areas, including Kashmir, because of Gulab Singh's willingness to pay ₹ 75 lakh out of the total amount of the terms of the treaties, and not in consequence of a 'sale deed'.

The Dogra dynasty lasted for a little over hundred years. This period saw four Maharajas—Gulab Singh (1846-57); Ranbir Singh (1857-85); Pratap Singh (1885-1925); and Hari Singh (1925-52). But the dynasty was always at the mercy of the British Government. Maharaja Gulab Singh himself had no illusion about it. He wrote to the Governor General: "I am ready to sacrifice my life and property as a proof of my obedience to Your Highness. Anyone who is faithful to the Honourable Company has to remain faithful with his heart and soul."

In view of the British Government's pervasive and decisive intervention in the affairs of Jammu and Kashmir, it would be more appropriate to call the period of 1846 to 1947 as the period of Dogra-British rule rather than of Dogra rule alone.

# 2

# Political Awakening

On account of the pressure of the British Government and also on his own initiative, the Maharaja undertook constitutional reform on moderate scale. This was done through the Constitution Acts of 1924 and 1927.

In 1924, a deputation presented a memorial to the Viceroy, Lord Reading, on his visit to Srinagar. The memorial demanded that land ownership rights be given to peasants, that more Muslims be employed in the State services, that they be given better facilities for education, that beggar be abolished and all the mosques in the possession of the government handed over to the Muslims. A new era in the history of the State began with the accession of Maharaja Hari Singh in September 1925.

In his book, *Kashmir in Crucible* (Pamposh Publications), Premnath Bazaz observes that in the late twenties, Kashmiri Pandits stole a march over the Muslims; they launched a movement which is known as 'Kashmir for Kashmiris'. Under the leadership of Shankarlal Koul, the Kashmiris started a publicity campaign demanding recruitment of educated sons of the soil in government services, ban on the sale of land to outsiders, freedom of the press, freedom of association and assembly, and creation of an elected legislature to voice the views of the people on all affairs of State. It was a result of this campaign that the Maharaja was induced to enact the State Subject Law imposing restrictions on the entry of non-Kashmiris in government services and on sale of agricultural land on them. But this measure of reform failed to adequately meet the people's demand.

Things were now moving very fast on the Indian subcontinent. In December 1929, the Indian National Congress adopted on the banks of the Ravi at Lahore a resolution setting complete independence as its goal. A mass civil disobedience movement followed which electrified the subcontinent from Gilgit to Cape Comorin. Kashmir too felt its repercussions. Its people were deeply excited with what was taking place in the rest of the country.

In 1930, a new organization called the Reading Room Party was formed in Srinagar by a few Muslim graduates to discuss the problems of the community. Among them was Sheikh Mohammed Abdullah. The party organized meetings, at which speeches were made emphasizing the hardships of the people of the State. The State Government responded by offering them government jobs. Abdullah was appointed as a teacher in a government school but he left his post after a few months. He then founded the Muslim Conference, of which he became president.

Thus began the struggle for demonstration of the administration of Jammu and Kashmir. It had its origin in the widespread discontent among the Muslim masses who, like the Hindus of Hyderabad State, were inadequately represented in the State services and in its economic and industrial life in general, though they constituted 78 per cent of the total population of Jammu and Kashmir and were about 94 per cent of the population in the Kashmir Valley.

Sheikh Abdullah's fight for democratic rights for Muslims made him a popular figure. As the popularity of the Muslim Conference grew, it led to tension between Hindus and Muslims and to communal riots in Srinagar in June 1931. Hindus suffered heavily. The State Government arrested 300 people, including Abdullah. But the Muslim Conference continued its agitation, and in July 1931 there was a massive demonstration against the State Government and the Maharaja. Muslim demonstrators had gathered outside the jail in Srinagar where another Muslim was on trial. The crowd forced its entry into the jail, causing the police to open fire. As a result, 21 people were killed.

Communal disturbances caused the Maharaja on the insistent of British Resident to appoint a Commission, with B.J. (later Sir Bertrand) Glancy of the Political Department of the Government of India as chairman and with four non-official representatives of the Hindus and Muslims of Jammu and Kashmir provinces as members, to inquire into the religious grievances of the people.

After the inquiry, a reforms conference with Glancy as president was held to give effect to the Maharaja's desire to associate his people with the administration of the State. The result was the establishment in 1934 of the Jammu and Kashmir Praja Sabha. The right to vote was given to about 6 per cent of the population, including women.

Having convinced that the party which challenged autocracy and worked for the establishment of responsible government should be non-communal so that all progressive forces in the State could rally round it, Sheikh Abdullah moved the following resolution in the Working Committee of the Muslim Conference in June 1938:

> Whereas in the opinion of the Working Committee the time has now come when all progressive forces in the country should be rallied under one banner to fight for the achievement of responsible government, the Working Committee recommends to the General Council that in the forthcoming session of the Conference the name and constitution of the organization be so altered and amended that all such people who desire to participate in this political struggle may easily become members of the Conference irrespective of their caste, creed or religion.

Sheikh Abdullah further said: "In order to secure responsible government, it is essential that we invite Hindus, Sikhs, Buddhist and Harijans to join us. They too are steeped in ignorance.

They too pay taxes. They too face hunger. The institution of the responsible government is as necessary for them as for us."

Certain members of the Muslim Conference, notably Bakshi Ghulam Mohammad and Mirza Afzal Beg, opposed this resolution. Ghulam Abbas (who later became leader of the Muslim Conference in Pakistan-occupied Kashmir) supported it, but the Sheikh's advocacy carried the day and the resolution changing the organization's name to National Conference was adopted.

One effect of the agitation of the National Conference was that further constitutional advance was announced by proclamation. Its main features were: the number of elected members in a house of 75 was raised to 40; the Sabha was given the right to elect a Deputy President from its non-official members; provision was made for appointing non-official members as Under Secretaries to work with the Maharaja's Ministers; the Praja Sabha was given the right to vote on most of the demands made by government for budget appropriations; the Sabha was given the right to legislate on taxes.

In 1944, the National Conference adopted, as its manifesto, a program called Naya Kashmir. It envisaged a pattern of parliamentary democracy in the State, with independent judiciary, and also a program of social, economic and educational reforms.

The Naya Kashmir plan envisaged a scheme of constitutional reform for the State, a bill of rights and a frame of representative political institutions besides a national economic plan and a plan for cultural and educational development. The plan pledged to secure the people of the State, right to equality, right to self-determination, emancipation from operation, poverty and ignorance and superstition and ensure them participation in the historic resurgence of the peoples of the East and the working masses of the world. The preamble of the plan read:

> We the people of Jammu, Kashmir, Ladakh and the frontier regions, including Poonch and Chinani Illaqas—commonly known as Jammu and Kashmir State—in order to perfect our Union in the fullest equality and self-determination, to raise ourselves and

> our children forever from the Abyss of operation and poverty, degradation and superstition from medieval darkness and ignorance, into the sunlit valleys of plenty ruled by freedom, science and honest toil, in worthy participation of the historic resurgence of the people of the East and the working masses of the world, and in determination to make our country a dazzling gem upon the snowy bosom of Asia, do propose and propound the Constitution of our State.

In the summer of 1944, in an attempt to establish his hold in Jammu and Kashmir, Jinnah visited the State. He came on the plea of rest but accepted receptions in his honour. In the reception given by the National Conference, both Sheikh Abdullah and Jinnah indulged in what may be called exercises in ambivalence. At the reception held by the Muslim Conference, Jinnah came out openly in its favour. He said: "The Muslims have one platform, on Kalma, and one God. I would request the Muslims to come under the banner of the Muslim Conference and fight for their rights."

Jinnah also presided over the annual session of the Muslim Conference. In his address, he described the National Conference as a band of gangsters.

Jinnah and the Muslim League did not give much quarter to Sheikh Abdullah, and Chowdhry Ghulam Abbas and the Muslim Conference were preferred. This seems to have convinced Sheikh Abdullah that his political future would be bleak if his State joined Pakistan. In his autobiography, *Atish-e-Chinar*, Sheikh Abdullah acknowledges the hostility which Jinnah displayed towards him. He writes: "At that time, Jinnah was intoxicated by power. He thought it beneath his dignity to talk to a poor and resourceless nation. When this equation of power went against him, he woke up in panic in his dream. But by this time, the snake had passed; only its line remained."

During Jinnah's visit, Moulvi Yusuf Shah also came in for some sharp tongue-lashing from Jinnah. He described the Moulvi as a "rotten egg." He also told the Moulvi, "I advice you to remain aloof from politics. In Kashmir, we want a leader, and not a Mullah."

Throughout the rest of India, the Congress and the Muslim League were emerging as the two political parties. The question most Kashmir leaders posed to themselves was whether the National Conference should align itself with the Congress or the Muslim League. One section of opinion thought that it should remain neutral, but as Abdullah and his associates drew closer to the All-India States Peoples' Conference and came in contact with Indian leaders, particularly Mahatma Gandhi, Jawaharlal Nehru and Khan Abdul Ghaffar Khan, they were greatly influenced by them. Thus, the National Conference began to work in close liaison with not only the States Peoples' Conference but also the Indian National Conference.

Nehru accompanied by Khan Abdul Ghaffar Khan, visited Kashmir. The tour evoked a tremendous demonstration of popular support and increased the prestige of the National Conference. The visit proved a turning-point in the political career of Abdullah as well as of the freedom movement in the State.

The arrival of the Cripps Mission in India at that time also raised new hopes. In a telegram to the Mission, the National Conference said:

> As Mission is at the moment reviewing relationship of Princes with the Paramount Power with reference to treaty rights, we wish to submit that for us in Kashmir re-examination of this relationship is vital matter because hundred years ago in 1846 land and people of Kashmir were sold away to servitude of Dogra House by British for seventy-five lakhs of Sikh rupees equivalent to fifty lakhs of British Indian rupees. As such the case of Kashmir stands on unique footing and people of Kashmir press on Mission their unchallengeable claims to freedom on withdrawal of British power from India.

In August 1942, when the Congress launched the Quit India movement, the Working Committee of the National Conference adopted an official resolution supporting it. To enforce this decision, the 23rd of August was celebrated throughout Kashmir as National Day.

Nehru, Abdul Gaffar Khan and Maulana Abul Kalam Azad were present by special invitation at the Sopore session of the National Conference in August 1945 when Abdullah proposed his programme for building a new Kashmir. He declared that "the future and independence of Jammu and Kashmir State are inextricably linked with the future and independence of India."

## Quit Kashmir Movement

On 10 May 1946, the National Conference under the leadership of Sheikh Abdullah, launched the "Quit Kashmir" movement. In his speech on 17 May 1946, he said: "The tyranny of the Dogras has lacerated our souls. It is time for action, you must fight slavery and enter the field of '*Jihad*' as soldiers. Every man, woman and child will shout "Quit Kashmir." The Kashmiri people expressed its will. I ask for plebiscite on this question." On 20 May, he was arrested. The other prominent leaders of the National Conference were also detained.

Mr. Jinnah, reacting to the slogan, "Quit Kashmir" issued a statement in which he described the movement as "an agitation carried on by a few malcontents who were out to create disorderly conditions in the State."

Nehru was enraged at the behaviour of Maharaja Hari Singh's Government, and the reign of terror he had let loose. He called Srinagar a city of the dead and said conditions were reminiscent of Punjab under General Dyer. And he had fulsome praise for Sheikh Abdullah. He said: "Everyone who knows Kashmir also knows the position of Sheikh Abdullah there. He is the Sher-e-Kashmir (the lion of Kashmir) loved by the people. In the remotest valleys, he has been and is one of my most valued colleagues in the States Peoples movement whose advice has been sought in all important matters. Does anybody think that we are going to desert him?"

He further said: "The Blimps have ceased to rule in most of countries. It is the unfortunate fate of Kashmir today to be in charge of Blimps." He declared that he would personally lead a team of lawyers to defend Sheikh Abdullah at his trial. There could be no peace in Kashmir, he said, until Sheikh Abdullah was released. Such were the relations between the two.

Lord Wavell tried to persuade Nehru not to go to Kashmir, but he was adamant. Congress leaders pointed out that he was needed for the Cabinet Mission discussions, but Nehru did not relent. On 15 June, he sent a telegram to Hari Singh's Government informing that he was coming. Srinagar sent a reply: he would not be allowed to enter the province. At one O'clock on the afternoon of 19 June, Nehru along with Asaf Ali, Dewan Chaman Lal, Tilak Raj Chadha and others, reached the Kohala bridge by car, about 140 miles from Srinagar on the Srinagar-Rawalpindi road. After lunch, they began walking across the bridge. The District Magistrate served an order prohibiting Nehru from entering; he and his party continued walking. Nehru told the District magistrate that he had not obeyed any order of the British Government for two decades, and he was hardly likely to obey the orders of Hari Singh and his disliked Prime Minister, Rai Bahadur Pandit Ram Chandra Kak. A military cordon was placed in Nehru's way. "Perhaps," Nehru told his companions, "the Kashmir State authorities do not know that they are dealing with the president-elect of the Indian National Congress."

Nehru, fearless as ever, walked across and pushed the bayonets aside. By a stroke of good fortune Bhagwan Singh was a tactful and intelligent man. He ordered his troops aside, politely asked Nehru to come across the bridge and informed him that he was under arrest. He was taken to a dakbunglow at Uri, 96 miles from Srinagar.

Dr. Karan Singh, in his book *Heir Apparent* at page 40 writes:

> The news reached us in Gulab Bhavan, and Pandit Kak, the then Prime Minister, reported to my father with subdued pride and excitement that Jawaharlal had been arrested. I was stunned. Here was the most charismatic leader of the national movement for freedom, the author of the *Autobiography* and *Discovery of India,* the declared Prime Minister of the Indian Republic, and, instead of welcoming him and seeking his cooperation, we had arrested him. I have no doubt that his arrest was the turning point in the history of the State.... The die

had been cast, and it was only a matter of time before disaster struck.

Hari Singh Government allowed the counsel arranged for Sheikh Abdullah by Nehru, Baldev Sahay, and Avdesh Narayan to come to Srinagar, but would not allow Nehru to move freely. And Nehru would not leave without meeting Sheikh Abdullah. In Delhi, the Congress Working Committee was getting frantic. Vital matters relating to the Cabinet Mission were awaiting a final decision and Nehru expected to lead interim government was sitting in a jail in Kashmir. Finally, the Congress President Abul Kalam Azad ordered Nehru to return to Delhi. Gandhi sent a word that Nehru's presence in Delhi was most essential. Nehru at first refused, requesting the Working Committee to proceed without him. Azad replied: "Remember that you are under an organization which you have adored for so long. Its needs must be paramount to you and me..." Nehru relented. He informed Azad: "I am prepared to return immediately in obedience to the Working Committee on the understanding that I will come back to Kashmir later." Nehru left Kashmir.

The Congress Working Committee and Sardar Patel do not seem to have been in favour of Nehru breaking the law and getting arrested in Kashmir. Sardar Patel has referred in disparaging terms to his action in a letter, he wrote on 11 July 1946, to D.P. Mishra: "He (Nehru) has done many things recently which have caused us great embarrassment. His action in Kashmir, his interference in Sikh election to the Constituent Assembly, his press conference immediately after the AICC are all acts of emotional insanity and it puts tremendous strain on us to set matters right. But in spite of all his innocent indiscretions, he has unparalleled enthusiasm and burning passion for freedom."

Nehru wrote to Sardar Patel on 20 July 1946 as under:

> It is not my intention to raise any major issues in Kashmir at this stage. I shall see Sheikh Abdullah and join in consultation about his defence. I shall also visit parts of the city and meet some people. I do not propose to hold public meetings and the like, though it may happen, of course the crowds gather occasionally where I go.

The trial of Sheikh Abdullah began on 22 July 1946. Nehru went to watch the proceedings on 25 July, stayed for four days and met his friend four times. Sheikh Abdullah himself, perhaps settled the issue when, in a 3000 word statement pleading not guilty, he said: "I stand by whatever I said or written in regard to the fundamental rights of the people of Jammu and Kashmir. My trial for sedition is something more than a personal charge against me. It is, in effect, the trial of the entire population of Jammu and Kashmir." The Session Judge of Badambagh cantonment sentenced Sheikh Abdullah to three years simple imprisonment and a fine of ` 1500 on the charge of sedition.

Nehru kept complaining to Gandhiji that while India was on the way to freedom, Sheikh Abdullah was still in jail, and the Congress had done nothing to get him out. He wanted to visit Kashmir, Gandhiji advised against this, and said that he himself will go. Before leaving for Kashmir on 29 July, Gandhiji said:

> I am not going to suggest to the Maharaja to accede to India and not to Pakistan. This is not my intention...the people of Kashmir should be asked whether they want to join Pakistan or India. Let them do as they want.
>
> The trip enabled stops in the Punjab, in Lahore and Rawalpindi and in Wah, where Hindu and Sikh refugees were camping, as well as a visit to the Punja Sahib Gurudwara. In Kashmir, huge crowds came to his prayer meetings. Gandhiji met Hari Singh and his wife, Hari Singh's premier, Ramchandra Kak, and Begum Abdullah, the detained leader's wife. From the Maharaja, Gandhi elicited the admission that the wishes of the people would prevail.
>
> On his way back, Gandhiji said in Wah (where Sushila Nayyar was asked to stay on to assist the refugees) that Kashmir "had the greatest strategic value, perhaps, in all India". And in a note (6 August) to Nehru and Patel, he quoted the assessment of Abdullah's colleague, Bakshi Gulham Mohammad, that if Abdullah and his co-prisoners were released, all bans removed, and premier Kak replaced, 'the result of the free vote of the

> people...would be in favour of Kashmir joining India". (*Collected Works of Mahatma Gandhi,* Vol. 96, pp. 192-94)

Sheikh Abdullah was eventually removed to a comfortable place in Srinagar in September 1947. Under pressure from the government of independent India led by his friend, Jawaharlal Nehru, and released by the end of the month on what has been described in certain quarters as his qualified apology to the Maharaja. In his letter of 26 September 1947, Sheikh Abdullah wrote: "I assure Your Highness that myself and my party have never harboured any sentiment of disloyalty towards Your Highness' person, throne or dynasty. I assure Your Highness the fullest and loyal support of myself and my organization. Not only this, but I assure Your Highness that any party within or without the State, which may attempt to create any impediments in our efforts to gain our goal, will be treated as our enemy...."

However, after the assumption of power, Sheikh Abdullah cast to the winds the faithfulness he had pledged, and demanded of the Maharaja: "To quit the valley bag and baggage and leave the Kashmiris alone to decide their future by themselves."

Some prominent leaders of the National Conference, including Ghulam Abbas, joined the Muslim Conference. In October 1946, the Muslim Conference launched Direct Action campaign under the leadership of Mirwaiz Moulvi Yusuf Shah. Chowdhry Ghulam Abbas and a few other leaders of the Muslim Conference were arrested.

Mirwaiz Moulvi Yusuf Shah displayed extreme hostility to the Indian National Congress and the National Conference. Deploring what he called interference of the Congress, he said in a statement on 25 September 1946:

> The Hindu capitalists want to get the State into their grip, but I warn that if the Government of Jammu and Kashmir gets terrified at the might of the Congress and strikes an unholy alliance with the National Conference fascists, it will have to face the terrific opposition of the Muslims. And this sinister alliance will be smashed to pieces. The Muslims of Kashmir have warded off

> Pandit Nehru's invasion in 1940, 1945 and 1946. Now he is again out to make a fresh attempt and it is the duty of the Kashmiri Muslims particularly and all the well-wishers of the country to smash up this onslaught.

In his statement, on 10 May 1947, Chowdhry Hamidullah Khan, President, Muslim Conference said:

> If Kashmir has to keep itself aloof from carnage and bloodshed, it should lose no time in adopting a strong and bold policy. His Highness the Maharaja Bahadur should declare Kashmir independent immediately. A separate Constituent Assembly to frame the Constitution for the State, according to the wishes of people, should be established at once. His Highness the Maharaja Bahadur will receive the cooperation of Muslims in carrying out this policy. The Muslims form 80% of the population. They are represented by the Muslim Conference. The Muslims will welcome the Maharaja Bahadur as the first constitutional ruler of independent and democratic Kashmir.

## Indian Independence Act

On 17 June 1947, the Indian Independence Act was passed by the British Parliament providing for transfer of power to two newly created Dominions—India and Pakistan. A part of India having a preponderating Muslim majority was constituted into Pakistan which assumed power of a Dominion on 14 August 1947. The major part of India achieved independence on the midnight of 14/15 August.

The future of the Princely States was defined in a memorandum (dated 12 May 1946) on States Treaties and Paramountcy presented by the Cabinet Mission to the Chancellor of the Chamber of Princes in India. Since paramountcy lapsed on 15 August the Princes were free to accede to one or the other Dominion or become independent. All but three States, namely Junagad, Hyderabad and Kashmir acceded to either Dominion before 15 August 1947.

# 3
# Before and After Accession

Maharaja Hari Singh was under the advice of his Rajguru Swami Sant Dev. Rajguru had predicted to the Maharaja that a still bright future awaited him, implying thereby that he would, with the lapse of paramountcy become independent. The poor Maharaja lost even what he had before August 1947. Interestingly, when the Maharaja left Srinagar for Jammu at 2 a.m. on October 27 in a hurry, he found that the Swami Sant Dev who had been advising him to stay at Srinagar, was going ahead of the caravan.

## Lord Mountbatten's Visit to Kashmir

Lord Mountbatten visited Kashmir in the third week of June 1946 at the request of Maharaja of Kashmir. He spent four days discussing the situation and arguing with the Maharaja. He told the Maharaja that independence was not in his opinion, a feasible proposition and that the State would not be recognized as a Dominion by the British Government. He assured the Maharaja that, so long as he made up his mind to accede to one Dominion or the other before 15th August no trouble would ensue, for whichever Dominion he acceded to would take the State firmly under its protection as part of its territory. He went so far as to tell the Maharaja that, if acceded to Pakistan, India would not take it amiss and he had a firm assurance on this from Sardar Patel himself. Lord Mountbatten went further to say that, in view of the composition of the population, it was particularly important to ascertain the wishes of the people. The Maharaja appeared quite incapable of making up his mind and so Lord Mountbatten asked for a meeting with him and his Prime Minister on the last morning of his visit. At the last moment, the Maharaja sent a message to say that he was confined to bed and begged to be excused.

Dr. Karan Singh, in his book, *Heir Apparent*, has said:

> I suspect that in his heart of heart my father still did not believe that the British would actually leave... Independence could perhaps have been an attractive proposition but to carry that off would have required careful preparation and prolonged negotiations and diplomatic ability.... Instead of taking advantage of Mountbatten's visit to discuss the whole situation meaningfully and trying to arrive at a rational decision, he first sent the Viceroy out on a prolonged fishing trip to Thricker (where Mountbatten shocked our staff by sun-bathing in the nude) and then—having fixed a meeting just before his departure—got out of it on the plea that he had suddenly developed a severe attack of colic. Mountbatten, as has been recorded by his aide Campbell-Johnson, saw through the deception without any difficulty and returned to Delhi. Thus the last real chance of working out a viable political settlement was lost.

Lord Ismay visited Srinagar on a 'holiday' during the Independence Day celebrations in India and met Maharaja at the instance of Lord Mountbatten. According to Philip Ziegler, he applied pressure on the Maharaja. When Ismay referred to the Muslim population of Kashmir, the Maharaja replied that the Kashmir Valley's Muslims (where two-thirds of the Muslims of Kashmir lived) were very different from the Punjabi Muslims. "All he would talk about was Polo in Cheltenham in 1935 (Ismay was then military secretary to the viceroy, Lord Willingdon] and the prospect of his colt in the Indian derby" (*The Untold Story of India's Partition,* Narendra Singh Sarila, p. 345).

The Maharaja was in a Micawberish frame of mind, hoping for the best while continuing to doing nothing. Dr. Karan Singh, in his book, *Heir Apparent* says:

> The situation was so complex that even a person far more aware of contemporary realities than my father would have found it virtually impossible to come to a neat, peaceful solution. If he had acceded to Pakistan, the Hindu areas of the State would have been virtually liquidated in the wake of the communal frenzy sweeping across north India at the time. If, on the other hand, he had earlier acceded to India he would have run the risk of alienating a large section of his Muslim subjects who constituted seventy-five percent of the State. In retrospect the only rational solution would appear to have been to take the initiative in promoting and presiding over a peaceful partition of his State between the two new nations. But that would have needed clear political vision and careful planning over many years. As it turned out, the State, was in fact, partitioned, but in a manner that caused untold suffering and bloodshed, poisoning relations between India and Pakistan right down to the present day.

Dr. Karan Singh further says: "My father's only positive reaction to the rapidly approaching partition was to offer to sign a Standstill Agreement with both the 'Dominions' as they were then called. Pakistan signed the agreement, but soon thereafter, began exerting pressure on the State by interfering with essential supplies. At that time all the major communication system into the State lay through Pakistan, the road from Kohala and the two railheads at Rawalpindi and Sialkot. Thus Pakistan launched a virtual economic blockade to force my father to accede to it, while India asked for further clarification before signing the agreement."

The Government of Jammu and Kashmir complained that, in an effort to coerce that State into acceding, the Pakistan authorities had cut off the supply of food, petrol and other essential commodities, and hindered the free transit of travelers between Kashmir and Pakistan. At this time the Government of Jammu and Kashmir requested the Government of India for 5,000 gallons of petrol which Pakistan had been unable to provide. India sent only 500 gallons to meet the immediate necessity of preventing a complete breakdown of transport in Srinagar.

Military pressure was also applied by Pakistan in the form of hit-and-run border raids. This was along a 450-mile frontier, resulting in the State troops being dispersed and deployed along a wide distance with no adequate reserve, and rendering the defenses too thin to resist an all-out attack.

Early in October, Major-General Janak Singh was replaced by Mehr Chand Mahajan as Prime Minister of Jammu and Kashmir. On 15 October, the latter complained to the British Prime Minister that the Government of Pakistan had broken the Standstill Agreement by discontinuing supplies of essential articles, and that the railway service from Sialkot to Jammu had been stopped without any reason. He represented that the whole of the State border from Gurdaspur to Gilgit was threatened with invasion and that it had already begun in Poonchh. He asked that the Dominion of Pakistan should be advised to deal fairly with Jammu and Kashmir and to adopt a course of conduct consistent with the good name and prestige of the Commonwealth of which it claimed to be a member. On 18 October, the Jammu and Kashmir State sent a protest to the Governor-General and the Prime Minister of Pakistan against the breaches of the Standstill Agreement and the continuous raid. To this Jinnah replied on 20 October protesting against the tone and language of the communication and ascribing the delay in the dispatch of essential supplies to the 'widespread disturbances' in East Punjab and the disruption of communications caused thereby particularly by the shortage of coal.

On the evening of 24 October, the Government of India received a desperate appeal of help from the Maharaja. They also received from the Supreme Commander information regarding the raiders' advance and probable intentions. On the morning of 25 October, a meeting of the Defense Committee was held, presided over by Lord Mountbatten. This committee considered the request of the Maharaja for arms and ammunitions as also for reinforcement of troops. Lord Mountbatten emphasized that no precipitate action should be taken until the Government of India had fuller information. It was agreed that Menon should fly to Srinagar immediately in order to study the situation on the spot and make report to the Government of India.

Accompanied by Army and Air Force officers and by D.N. Kachru, Menon flew by a BOAC plane to Srinagar.

From the aerodrome, they went straight to the residence of the Prime Minister of the State. Mehr Chand Mahajan apprised them of the perilious situation and pleaded for the Government of India to come to the rescue of State. From his residence, they proceeded to the Maharaja's palace. The Maharaja was completely unnerved by the turn of events and by his sense of lone helplessness. There were practically no State Forces left and the raiders had almost reached the outskirts of Baramula. At this rate they would be in Srinagar, in another day or two.

They left Srinagar in the first flight of the morning of 26 October and immediately on his arrival in Delhi Menon went straight to a meeting of the Defense Committee. He reported his impressions of the situation and pointed out the supreme necessity of saving Kashmir from the raiders. Lord Mountbatten said that it would be improper to move Indian troops into what was at the moment an independent country, as Kashmir had not yet decided to accede to either India or Pakistan. If it were true that the Maharaja was now anxious to accede to India, then Jammu and Kashmir would become part of Indian territory. This was the only basis on which the Indian troops could be sent to the rescue of the State from further pillaging by the aggressors. He further expressed the strong opinion that, in view of the composition of the population, accession should be conditional on the will of the people being ascertained by a plebiscite after the raiders had been driven out of the State and law and order had been restored. This was readily agreed to by Nehru and other ministers.

Soon after a meeting of the Defense Committee, Menon flew to Jammu accompanied by Mahajan. On arrival at the palace, he found it in a state of utter turmoil with valuable articles strewn all over the place. The Maharaja was asleep; he had left Srinagar the previous evening and had been driving all night. Menon woke him up and told him of what had taken place at the Defense Committee meeting. He was ready to accede at once. He then composed a letter to Governor-General describing the pitiable plight of the State and reiterating his request for military help. He further informed the Governor-General that it was his intention to set up an interim government at once and to ask Sheikh Abdullah to carry the responsibilities in this emergency with Mehr Chand Mahajan, his Prime Minister. He concluded by saying that if the State was to be saved, immediate assistance must be available at Srinagar. He also signed the Instrument of Accession.

With the Instrument of Accession and the Maharaja's letter Menon flew back at once to Delhi. Sardar was waiting at the aerodrome and they both went straight to a meeting of the Defense Committee which was arranged for that evening. There was a long discussion, at the end of which it was decided that the accession of Jammu and Kashmir should be accepted, subject to the proviso that a plebiscite would be held in the State when the law and order situation allowed. It was further decided that an infantry battalion should be flown to Srinagar the next day. This decision had the fullest support of Sheikh Abdullah, who was in Delhi at that time and who had been pressing the Government of India on behalf of the All-Jammu and Kashmir National Conference for immediate help to be sent to the State to resist the tribal invasion. Even after the decision had been reached Lord Mountbatten and the three British Chiefs of Staff of the Indian Army, Navy and Air Force pointed out the risks involved in the operation. But Nehru asserted that the only alternative to sending troops would be to allow a massacre in Srinagar, which would be followed by a communal holocaust in India. Moreover, the British residents in Srinagar would certainly be murdered by the raiders, since neither the Pakistan Commander-in-Chief nor the Supreme Commander was in a position to safeguard their lives.

Never in the history of warfare has there been an operation like the airlift of Indian troops to Srinagar. On 27 October and on subsequent days, an operation put through with no previous thought, let alone organized planning, and at such remarkably short notice. The Defense Headquarters consisting of British and Indian officers worked almost nonstop from 26 October. In the early hours of the morning of 27 October, over a hundred civilian aircraft and RIAF planes were mobilized to fly troops, equipment and supplies to Srinagar. The RIAF and civilian pilots and ground crews rose to the occasion and work heroically to make the airlift a success.

Lord Mountbatten, who had been Chief of Combined Operations and Supreme Allied Commander, South East Asia, said that in all his war experience he had never heard of an airlift of this nature being put into operation at such short notice and he complimented all concerned on the astonishing performance. It has been suggested in certain quarters that the facts that so many Indian troops could be flown into Srinagar at such short notice was proof of its having been a pre-planned affair. A note signed by the three British Commanders-in-Chief of the Army, Air Force and Navy is given below to prove a clear refutation of this allegation:

> It has been alleged that plans were made for sending Indian forces to Kashmir at some date before 22nd October, on which day the raid on that State from the direction of Abbotabad began.

The following is a true time-table of events, as regards decisions taken, plans made, orders given, and movements started, in this matter:

1. On 24th October, the C-in-C, Indian Army, received information that tribesmen had seized Muzzafarabad. This was the first indication of the raid.
2. Prior to this date, no plans of any sort for sending Indian forces into Kashmir had been formulated or even considered.
3. On the morning of 25th October, we were directed to examine and prepare plans for sending troops to Kashmir by air and road, in the case this should be necessary to stop the tribal incursions. This was the

first direction which we received on this subject. No steps had been taken, prior to the meeting, to examine or prepare such plans.

4. On the afternoon of 25th October, we sent one staff officer of each, the Indian Army and the RIAF, by air to Srinagar. There they saw officers of the Kashmir State Forces. This was the first contact with the officers of our Headquarters and officers of the Kashmir State Forces on the subject of sending Indian troops to Kashmir.
5. On the afternoon of 25th October, we also issued orders to an infantry battalion to prepare itself to be flown, at short notice, to Srinagar, in the event of the Government of India deciding to accept the accession of Kashmir and send help.
6. On the morning of 26th October, the staff officers, mentioned in sub-paragraph (4) above, returned from Srinagar and reported of their meetings with officers of the Kashmir State Forces.
7. On the afternoon of 26th October, we finished our plans for the dispatch by air of troops to Kashmir.
8. At first light on the morning of 27th October, with Kashmir's Instrument of Accession signed, the movement by air of Indian Forces to Kashmir began.

No plans were made for sending these forces, nor were such plans even considered, before 25th October, three days after the tribal incursion began.

The storm finally broke on 25th October. It was Dussehra and, the annual Darbar was held in Srinagar as usual. By then serious trouble had broken out on the borders, and Maharaja sent Brigadier Rajender Singh Jamwal, who had taken over from General Scott as Chief of the Army Staff of the Jammu and Kashmir State Forces, to go to Uri and fight to the last man and the last bullet.

Rajender Singh left for the border of Uri-Domel on the night of 22nd October and, in a series of brave last-ditch manoeuvres, succeeded in holding the advancing hoarders back to three vital days before they could reach Baramulla, thus gaining the critical time that was required for the Instrument of Accession to be signed and Indian Army to begin arriving by air at Srinagar. Hopelessly outnumbered, his Muslim officers and troops turning hostile, the critically wounded Brigadier insisted that he be left on the roadside with only a revolver in his hand, as he had promised Maharaja that the enemy would advance only over his dead body. He was the first gallantry award winner of independent India, being awarded the Maha Vir Chakra posthumously for his outstanding act of bravery and sacrifice.

A simple but moving memorial now stands at the spot on the road to Uri where he took his last stand and fell to enemy bullets after his own were expended, as commanded by his ruler (*Heir Apparent*, Dr. Karan Singh, Oxford University Press, pp. 56-57).

On 1 November, Lord Mountbatten, accompanied by Lord Ismay, flew to Lahore and had a long conference with Jinnah. Jinnah contended that the accession of Kashmir to India had been brought about by violence. Lord Mountbatten retorted that the violence had come from the tribal invaders. He went on to say that, as the Indian troops in Srinagar were being built up, it was now remote that the tribesmen would ever be able to enter Srinagar. Jinnah then proposed that both sides withdraw at once and simultaneously. When Lord Mountbatten asked to explain how the tribesmen could be induced to remove themselves, Jinnah's reply was: "If you do this I would call the whole thing off." Lord Mountbatten then suggested a plebiscite should be held in the State. Jinnah objected and said that, with the presence of Indian troops in the State and with Sheikh Abdullah in power, the people of the State would be far too frightened to vote for Pakistan. Lord Mountbatten then suggested a plebiscite under the auspicious of United Nations Organization. But Jinnah pressed for a plebiscite to be held under the joint control and supervision of the Governors-General of India and Pakistan. Both Lord Mountbatten and Lord Ismay were at pains to explain to Jinnah that the fact that he was also President of the Muslim League gave him a special position in Pakistan which Lord Mountbatten did not enjoy in India.

Jinnah might therefore be able to offer joint control, but Lord Mountbatten, being a strictly constitutional Governor-General, was in no position to accept the offer. The conversations were inconclusive. Lord Mountbatten returned to Delhi.

This was followed on 4 November by a broadcast from Lahore by Liaqat Ali Khan. He laid stress on the 'immoral and illegal ownership' of Kashmir resulting from the 'infamous' Amritsar Treaty of 1946. He contended that it was a dishonest rewriting of history to present the rebellion of the enslaved people of Kashmir to the world as an invasion from outside just because some outsiders had shown active sympathy with it. He contended that it was not Kashmir but a tottering despot that the Indian Government and their camp followers were trying to save and that accession of Kashmir to India was a fraud perpetrated on its people by its cowardly ruler with the aggressive help of the Government of India.

Sardar Patel and Baldev Singh, the Defense Minister, visited Srinagar on 3 November. They discussed the political situation with Kashmir ministers and the military position with Brigadier L.P. Sen, who was in command of our troops. They returned to Delhi on 4 November and gave a detailed report of the military situation to the Defense Committee. Brigadier Sen had certainly done all that could be expected with the resources available to him, but they had no doubt whatever that the army needed to be strengthened. This view was accepted. It was decided to establish a new divisional headquarters (Jammu and Kashmir Division) in Kashmir: Major-General Kalwant Singh was selected to take over command of the new division. He was instructed to concentrate all his efforts on the taking of Baramula, for that place commands the entrance to the Valley of Kashmir and it was felt that its recapture would reduce the chances of further tribal incursions.

Major-General Kalwant Singh left from Srinagar the next day. On 8 November, his forces occupied Baramula. When the Indian troops entered the city they found that it had been stripped by the tribesmen of its wealth and its women. Out of a normal population of 14,000, only one thousand were left.

The devastation by the raiders was indeed ghastly, reminiscent of Nadir Shah's sacking of Delhi. A number of foreign correspondents bore testimony to the arson and pillage, loot and rape which had been indulged in by the tribesmen in Baramula.

On 21 November, Nehru made a statement in Parliament. After a rapid review of the events of the previous four weeks, he reiterated his promise that the people of Kashmir would be given the chance to decide their future under the supervision of an impartial tribunal such as the United Nations Organization.

In the first week of December, Liaqat Ali Khan came to Delhi to attend another meeting of the Joint Defense Council. Lord Mountbatten was anxious that Nehru should take the opportunity of discussing the Kashmir issue with him. But Nehru had just received from Liaqat Ali Khan a telegram which was most objectionable and contained very offensive references to Sheikh Abdullah. He was not therefore disposed, at first, to meet the Pakistan Prime Minister. Subsequently, however, he agreed. Lord Ismay later had a meeting with Mohammad Ali and Menon and they produced a draft as a basis for discussion between two Prime Ministers. The terms of the draft were that the Government of Pakistan would use all their influence to persuade the Azad Kashmir forces to cease fighting and the tribesmen to withdraw from Kashmir territory as quickly as possible; that the Government of India would withdraw the bulk of their forces from Kashmir territory as soon as the fighting had ceased and the tribesmen began to withdraw, leaving only small contingents at certain points at the frontier; that simultaneously with the cessation of hostilities, an approach would be made to the UNO jointly by both the governments requesting them to hold a plebiscite in Kashmir under their auspices and to send to Kashmir a commission which would make recommendations to the Government of India, Pakistan and Kashmir as to the steps which should be taken to ensure a fair and unfettered plebiscite; that in order to create proper conditions, all citizens of the State who left it on account of the tribal invasion would be welcome to return and to exercise their franchise; outsiders who had recently entered the State would not be entitled to participate in the plebiscite; there would be no victimization;

all political prisoners would be released as soon as possible; and no restrictions would be imposed on legitimate political activity. All felt at the time that there was every possibility of an amicable settlement.

Liaqat Ali Khan returned to Karachi and a day or two later Mohammad Ali followed.

Meanwhile Sardar Patel and Baldev Singh, who had visited Kashmir again, reported to the Defense Committee that there were large concentrations of tribesmen in certain places in West Pakistan; that no sooner had Liaqat Ali Khan returned to Karachi from Delhi that he encouraged more raiders to enter Kashmir and made speeches to the effect that Pakistan would never give up Kashmir; and the raiders had indulged in the most ghastly atrocities including wholesale murder of non-Muslims and abduction and auctioning to Kashmir girls. Their reports corroborated certain independent reports which Nehru had already received. This naturally hardened the attitude of Government of India. Lord Mountbatten, however, used his influence with both Prime Ministers to keep alive the spirit of negotiations. When Liaqat Ali Khan telegrammed to Nehru urging the continuance of talks, Nehru at once responded and accompanied Lord Mountbatten to the meeting of the Joint Defense Council which was held at Lahore on 8 December.

The two Prime Ministers and Lord Mountbatten discussed the Kashmir problem from three in the afternoon until almost midnight. Nehru said that the first step should be a declaration by the Government of Pakistan that they would use all their influence to persuade the raiders who had entered Kashmir from outside to withdraw and to take steps to see that no further invaders would go in. He pointed out that Pakistan had made no effort to prevent the raids taking place through from Pakistan territory. In fact, Pakistan had become the base of operations against the State which had acceded to India and became part of Indian territory. This amounted to little less than an act of war and indeed it was being treated as such by the Pakistan newspapers which were openly talking of the Indian troops as 'the enemy'. Before there could be a plebiscite, the fighting must cease and the obvious was to stop fighting was to withdraw the raiders.

Liaqat Ali Khan said that nothing would be easier for him than to sign an appeal calling on the raiders to withdraw. But they would certainly take no notice of such an appeal. The results would be that the relations between the two Dominions would deteriorate still further. India would accuse Pakistan of not having made the appeal. Another result of such an appeal would be that the position of Liaqat Ali Khan's Government would be seriously compromised. It was too young and to moderate a government to be strong. It was being continuously attacked in the vernacular press for its failure to support the Azad Kashmir Government and if it fell it was probable that an extremist government would take its place. He wanted a neutral administrator to be appointed in place of Sheikh Abdullah.

Nehru replied that the Government of India could not withdraw all their troops from Kashmir for, if they did so, the State would be at the mercy of the armed men from Poonchh and other areas, and chaos would undoubtedly ensue. Nor could they promise a neutral administration. The administration was entirely a matter for the people of Kashmir to decide. Sheikh Abdullah had been fighting for responsible government for over fifteen years and he and his followers had made considerable sacrifices to attain their objective. The National Conference was the premier political organization in the State, analogous to the Congress organization in India or the Muslim League in Pakistan. His was the first responsible ministry the State ever had. It had succeeded the autocratic rule of the Maharaja and had knit the people together on non-communal lines. Nothing came to these discussions. And thus yet another attempt at a negotiated settlement proved fruitless. It was at this meeting that Lord Mountbatten suggested that the United Nations Organization might be called upon to fill the third-party role to mediate between India and Pakistan, but no decision was reached on his suggestion.

After the Lahore meeting of the two Prime Ministers, Lord Mountbatten was convinced that a negotiated settlement between the two Dominions on the question of Kashmir was practically impossible. He was also apprehensive that, if a solution was not found, the fighting in Kashmir might degenerate into open war between the two Dominions, a contingency which he was anxious to avoid at all costs. He therefore pressed both Gandhiji and Nehru to adopt his original suggestion to invoke the good offices of the United Nations Organization. Nehru ultimately accepted the suggestion, though some of his colleagues had misgivings about the wisdom of the State.

That very same day, but after the application of the Security Council had been dispatched, Liaqat Ali Khan's reply was received. It was a lengthy catalogue to counter-charges. It alleged that the Government of India were out to destroy Pakistan. He wanted the intervention of the UNO to extend from the question of Junagadh to that of genocide.

# 4

# Complaint with United Nations

It is too well known that at the instance of Lord Mountbatten, Jawaharlal Nehru agreed to invoke the good offices of the United Nations Organization and lodged a formal complaint with the Security Council of United Nations on 1 January 1948.

The representative of India to UNO submitted the representation to the President of the Security Council under Article 35 of the Charter of the U.N., which provides that any member may bring any situation whose continuance is likely to endanger the maintenance of international peace and security to the attention of the Security Council. The text of the representation and the resolutions of the Security Council thereon along with correspondence are reproduced below.

## Indian Complaint to the Security Council

**Letter dated 1 January 1948 from the Representative of India to the President of the Security Council**

The Government of India have instructed me to transmit to you the following telegraphic communication:

1. Under Article 35 of the Charter of the United Nations, any member may bring any situation whose continuance is likely to endanger the maintenance of international peace and security to the attention of the Security Council. Such a situation now exists between India and Pakistan owing to the aid which invaders, consisting of nationals of Pakistan and of tribesmen

from the territory immediately adjoining Pakistan on the north-west, are drawing from Pakistan for operations against Jammu and Kashmir, a State which has acceded to the Dominion of India and is part of India. The circumstances of accession, the activities of the invaders which led the Government of India to take military action against them, and the assistance which the attackers have received and are still receiving from Pakistan are explained later in this memorandum. The Government of India request the Security Council to call upon Pakistan to put an end immediately to the giving of such assistance, which is an act of aggression against India. If Pakistan does not do so, the Government of India may be compelled, in self-defence, to enter Pakistan territory, in order to take military action against the invaders. The matter is, therefore, one of extreme urgency and calls for immediate action by the Security Council for avoiding a breach of international peace.

2. From the middle of September 1947, the Government of India had received reports of the infiltration of armed raiders into the western parts of Jammu province of Jammu and Kashmir State; Jammu adjoins West Punjab, which is a part of the Dominion of Pakistan. These raiders had done a great deal of damage in that area and taken possession of part of the territory of the State. On 24 October, the Government of India heard of a major raid from the Frontier Province of the Dominion of Pakistan into the Valley of Kashmir. Some two thousand or more fully armed and equipped men came in motor transport, crossed over to the territory of the State of Jammu and Kashmir, sacked the town of Muzaffarabad, killing many people and proceeded along the Jhelum Valley road towards Srinagar, the summer capital of Jammu and Kashmir State. Intermediate towns and villages were sacked and burnt, and many people killed. These raiders were stopped by Kashmir State troops near Uri, a town some fifty miles from Srinagar, for some time, but the invaders got around them and burnt the power house of Mahora, which supplied electricity to the whole of Kashmir.

3. The position, on the morning of 26 October, was that these raiders had been held by Kashmir State troops and part

of the civil population, who had been armed, at town called Baramulla. Beyond Baramulla there was no major obstruction upto Srinagar. There was immediate danger of these raiders reaching Srinagar, destroying and massacring large number of people, both Hindus and Muslims. The State troops were spread out all over the State and most of them were deployed along the western border of Jammu province. They had been split up into small isolated groups and were incapable of offering effective resistance to the raiders. Most of the State officials had left the threatened areas and the civil administration had ceased to function. All that stood between Srinagar and the fate which had overtaken the places en route followed by the raiders was the determination of the inhabitants of Srinagar, of all communities, and practically without arms, to defend themselves. At this time Srinagar had also a large population of Hindu and Sikh refugees who had fled there from West Punjab owing to communal disturbances in that area. There was little doubt that these refugees would be massacred if the raiders reached Srinagar.

4. Immediately after the raids into Jammu and Kashmir State commenced, approaches were informally made to the Government of India for the acceptance of the accession of the State to the Indian Dominion. It might be explained in parenthesis that Jammu and Kashmir form a State whose ruler, prior to the transfer of power by the United Kingdom to the Dominions of India and Pakistan, had been in treaty relations with the British Crown, which controlled its foreign relations and was responsible for its defence. The treaty relations ceased with the transfer of power on 15 August last, and Jammu and Kashmir like other States acquired the right to accede to either Dominion.

5. Events moved with great rapidity, and the threat to the Valley of Kashmir became grave. On 26 October, the ruler of the State, His Highness Maharaja Sir Hari Singh, appealed urgently to the Government of India for military help. He also requested that the Jammu and Kashmir State should be allowed to accede to the Indian Dominion. An appeal for help was also simultaneously received by the Government of India

from the largest popular organization in Kashmir, the National Conference, headed by Sheikh Mohammad Abdullah. The Conference further strongly supported the request for the State's accession to the Indian Dominion. The Government of India were thus approached not only officially by the State authorities, but also on behalf of the people of Kashmir, both for military aid and for the accession of the State to India.

6. The grave threat to the life and property of innocent people in the Kashmir Valley and to the security of the State of Jammu and Kashmir that had developed as a result of the invasion of the Valley demanded immediate decision by the Government of India on both the requests. It was imperative on account of the emergency that the responsibility for the defence of Jammu and Kashmir State should be taken over by a Government capable of discharging it, but, in order to avoid any possible suggestion that India had utilized the State's immediate peril for her own political advantage, the Government of India made it clear that once the soil of the State had been cleared of the invader and normal conditions resorted, its people would be free to decide their future by the recognized democratic method of a plebiscite or referendum which, in order to ensure complete impartiality, might be held under international auspices.

7. The Government of India felt it their duty to respond to the appeal for armed assistance because:

(a) They could not allow a neighboring and friendly State to be compelled by force to determine either its internal affairs or its external relations;

(b) The accession of Jammu and Kashmir State to the Dominion of India made India really responsible for the defence of the State.

8. The intervention of the Government of India resulted in saving Srinagar. The raiders were driven back from Baramulla to Uri and are held there by Indian troops. Nearly 19,000 raiders face the Dominion forces in this area. Since operations in the Valley of Kashmir started, pressure by the raiders against the western and south-western border of Jammu and Kashmir State has been intensified. Exact figures are not available. It is

understood, however, that nearly 15,000 raiders are operating against this part of the State. State troops are besieged in certain areas. Incursions by the raiders into the State territory, involving murder, arson, loot, and the abduction of women continue. The booty is collected and carried over to the tribal areas to serve as an inducement to the further recruitment of tribesmen to the ranks of the raiders. In addition to those actively participating in the raid, tribesman and others, estimated at 100,000 have been collected in different places in the districts of West Punjab bordering Jammu and Kashmir State, and many of them are receiving military training under Pakistani nationals, including officers of the Pakistan Army. They are looked after in Pakistan territory, fed, clothed, armed and otherwise equipped, and transported to the territory of Jammu and Kashmir State with the help, direct and indirect, of Pakistani officials, both military and civil.

9. As already stated, the raiders who entered the Kashmir Valley in October came mainly from the tribal areas to the north-west of Pakistan and, in order to reach Kashmir, passed through Pakistan territory. The raids along the south-west border of the State, which had preceded the invasion of the valley proper, had actually been conducted from Pakistan territory, and Pakistan nationals had taken part in them. This process of transmission across Pakistan territory and utilization of that territory as a base of operations against Jammu and Kashmir State continues. Recently, military operations against the western and south-western borders of the State have been intensified, and the attackers consist of nationals of Pakistan as well as tribesmen. These invaders are armed with modern weapons, including mortars and medium machine-guns, wear the battle dress of regular soldiers and, in recent engagements, have fought in regular battle formation and are using the tactics of modern warfare. Man-pack wireless sets are in regular use and even mark V mines have been employed. For their transport the invaders have all along used motor vehicles. They are undoubtedly being trained and to some extent led by regular officers of the Pakistan Army. Their rations and other supplies are obtained from Pakistan territory.

10. These facts point indisputably to the conclusion

(a) that the invaders are allowed transit across Pakistan territory;

(b) that they are allowed to use Pakistan territory as a base of operations;

(c) that they include Pakistan nationals;

(d) that they draw much of their military equipments, transportation, and supplies (including petrol) from Pakistan; and

(e) that Pakistan officers are training, guiding, and otherwise actively helping them.

There is no source other than Pakistan from which they could obtain such quantities of modern military equipment, training or guidance. More than once, the Government of India had asked the Pakistan Government to deny to the invaders facilities which constitute an act of aggression and hostility against India, but without any response. The last occasion on which this request was made was on 22 December, when the Prime Minister of India handed over personally to the Prime Minister of Pakistan a letter in which the various forms of aid given by Pakistan to the invaders were briefly recounted and the Government of Pakistan were asked to put an end to such aid promptly; no reply to this letter has yet been received in spite of a telegraphic reminder sent on 26 December.

11. It should be clear from the foregoing recital that the Government of Pakistan are unwilling to stop the assistance in material and men which the invaders are receiving from Pakistan territory and from Pakistan nationals, including Pakistan Government personnel, both military and civil. This attitude is not only unnatural, but constitutes active aggression against India, of which the State of Jammu and Kashmir forms a part.

12. The Government of India have exerted persuasion and exercised patience to bring about a change in the attitude of Pakistan. But they have failed, and are in consequence confronted with a situation in which their defence of Jammu

and Kashmir State is hampered and their measures to drive the invaders from the territory of the State are greatly impeded by the support which the raiders derive from Pakistan. The invaders are still on the soil of Jammu and Kashmir and the inhabitants of the State are exposed to all the atrocities of which a barbarous foe is capable. The presence, in large numbers, of invaders in those portions of Pakistan territory which adjoins parts of Indian territory other than Jammu and Kashmir State is a menace to the rest of India. Indefinite continuance of the present operations prolongs the agony of the people of Jammu and Kashmir, is a drain on India's resources and a constant threat to the maintenance of peace between India and Pakistan. The Government of India have no option, therefore, but to take more effective military action in order to rid Jammu and Kashmir State of the invaders.

13. In order that the objective of expelling the invaders from Indian territory and preventing him from launching fresh attacks should be quickly achieved, Indian troops would have to enter Pakistan territory; only thus could the invader be denied the use of bases and cut off from his sources of supplies and reinforcements in Pakistan. Since the aid which invaders are receiving from Pakistan is an act of aggression against India, the Government of India are entitled, under international law, to send their armed forces across Pakistan territory for dealing effectively with the invaders. However, as such action might involve armed conflict with Pakistan, the Government of India, ever anxious to proceed according to the principles and aims of the Charter of the United Nations, desire to report the situation to the Security Council under Article 35 of the Charter. They feel justified in requesting the Security Council to ask the Government of Pakistan:

(1) to prevent Pakistan Government personnel, military and civil, from participating or assisting in the invasion of Jammu and Kashmir State;

(2) to call upon other Pakistani nationals to desist from taking any part in the fighting in Jammu and Kashmir State;

(3) to deny to the invaders: (a) access to any use of its territory for operations against Kashmir, (b) military and other supplies, (c) all other kinds of aid that might tend to prolong the present struggle.

14. The Government of India would stress the social urgency of the Security Council taking immediate action on their request. They desire to add that military operations in the invaded areas have, in the past few days, been developing so rapidly that they must, in self-defence, reserve to themselves the freedom to take, at any time when it may become necessary, such military action as they may consider the situation requires.

15. The Government of India deeply regret that a serious crisis should have been reached in their relations with Pakistan. Not only is Pakistan a neighboring but, in spite of the recent separation, India and Pakistan have many ties and many common interests. India desire nothing more earnestly than to live with her neighbor-State on terms of close and lasting friendship. Peace is to interest of both States; indeed to the interests of the world. The Government of India's approach to the Security Council is inspired by the sincere hope that, through the prompt action of the Council, peace may be preserved.

16. The text of this reference to the Security Council is being telegraphed to the Government of Pakistan."

**Resolution Adopted at the 29th Meeting of the Security Council, 17 January 1948**

The Security Council having heard statements on the situation in Kashmir from representatives of the Governments of India and Pakistan;

Recognizing the urgency of the situation; taking note of the telegram addressed on 6 January by its President to each of the parties and of their replies thereto; and in which they affirmed their intention to conform to the Charter;

Calls upon both the Government of India and the Government of Pakistan to take immediately all measures within their power (including public appeals to their people) calculated to improve the situation and to refrain from making any statements and from doing or causing to be done or permitting any acts which might aggravate the situation;

And further requests each of those governments to inform the Council immediately to any material change in the situation which occurs or appears to either of them to be about to occur while the matter is under consideration by the Council, and consult with the Council thereon.

**Resolution of the Security Council of 20 January 1948**

**(Setting forth terms of reference of the Commission)**

The Security Council

Considering that it may investigate any dispute or any situation which might, by its continuance, endanger the maintenance of international peace and security; that, in the existing state of affairs between India and Pakistan, such an investigation is a matter of urgency;

Adopts the following resolutions:

(A) A commission of the Security Council is hereby established, composed of representatives of three members of the United Nations, one to be selected by India, one to be selected by Pakistan, and the third to be designated by the two so selected.

Each representative on the Commission shall be entitled to select his alternates and assistants.

(B) The Commission shall proceed to the spot as quickly as possible. It shall under the authority of the Security Council and in accordance with the directions it may receive from it, it shall keep the Security Council currently informed of its activities and of the development of the situation. It shall report to the Security Council regularly, submitting its conclusions and proposals.

(C) The Commission is invested with a dual function:

(1) to investigate the facts pursuant to Article 34 of the Charter;

(2) to exercise, without interrupting the work of the Security Council, and mediatory influence

likely to smooth away difficulties; to carry out the directions given to it by the Security Council; and to report how far the advice and directions, if any, of the Security Council have been carried out.

(D) The Commission shall perform the functions described in Clause C:

(1) in regard to the situation in Jammu and Kashmir State set out in the letter of the Representative of India addressed to the President of the Security Council, dated 1 January 1948, and in the letter from the Minister of Foreign Affairs in Pakistan addressed to the Secretary-General, dated 15 January 1948; and

(2) in regard to other situations set out in the letter from the Minister of Foreign Affairs of Pakistan addressed to the Secretary-General, dated 15 January 1948; when the Security Council so directs.

(E) The Commission shall take its decision by majority vote. It shall determine its own procedure. It may allocate among its members, alternate members, their assistants, and its personnel, such duties as may have to be fulfilled for the realization of its mission and the reaching of its conclusions.

(F) The Commission, its members, alternate members, their assistants and its personnel, shall be entitled to journey, separately or together, wherever the necessities of their tasks may require, and in particular, within those territories which are the theatre of the events of which the Security Council is seized.

(G) The Secretary-General of the United Nations shall furnish the Commission with such personnel and assistance as it may consider necessary.

**Resolution of the Council of 21 April 1948**

**(Additional terms of reference of Commission and terms of plebiscite)**

The Security Council

Having considered the complaint of the Government of India concerning the dispute over the State of Jammu and Kashmir, having heard the Representative of India in support of their complaint and the reply and counter-complaints of the Representative of Pakistan;

Being strongly of the opinion that the early restoration of peace and order in Jammu and Kashmir is essential and that India and Pakistan should do their utmost to bring about a cessation of all fighting;

Noting with satisfaction that both India and Pakistan desire that the question of the accession of Jammu and Kashmir to India or Pakistan should be decided through the democratic method of a free and impartial plebiscite;

Considering that the continuation of the dispute is likely to endanger international peace and security;

Reaffirms the Council resolution of 17 January;

Resolves that the membership of the Commission established by the resolution of the Council of 20 January 1948 shall be increased to five and shall include, in addition to the membership mentioned in that resolution, representative of...and..., and that if the membership of the Commission has not been completed within ten days from the date of the adoption of this resolution the President of the Council may designate such other Member or Members of the United Nations as are required to complete the membership of five;

Instructs the Commission to proceed at once to the Indian subcontinent and there place its good offices and mediation at the disposal of the Governments of India and Pakistan with a view to facilitating the taking of the necessary measures, both with respect to the restoration of peace and order and to the holding of a plebiscite by the two Governments, acting in co-operation with one another and with the Commission, and further instructs the Commission to keep the Council informed of the action taken under the resolution, and to this end;

Recommends to the Governments of India and Pakistan the following measures as those which in the opinion of the Council are appropriate to bring about a cessation of the fighting and to create proper conditions for a free and impartial plebiscite to decide whether the State of Jammu and Kashmir if to accede to India or Pakistan.

**A. Restoration of Peace and Order**

1. The Government of Pakistan should undertake to use its best endeavours:

(a) to secure the withdrawal from the State of Jammu and Kashmir of tribesmen and Pakistani nationals not normally resident therein who have entered the State for the purposes of fighting and to prevent an intrusion into the State of such elements and any furnishing of material aid to those fighting in the State.

(b) to make known to all concerned that the measures indicated in this and the following paragraphs provide full freedom to all subjects of the State, regardless of creed, caste, or party, to express their views and to vote on the question of the accession of the State, and that therefore they should co-operate in the maintenance of peace and order.

2. The Government of India should:

(a) when it is established to the satisfaction of the Commission set up in accordance with the Council's resolution of 20 January that the tribesmen are withdrawing and that arrangements for the cessation of the fighting have become effective, put into operation in consultation with the Commission a plan for withdrawing their own forces from Jammu and Kashmir and reducing them progressively to the minimum strength required for the support of the civil power in the maintenance of law and order;

(b) make known that the withdrawal is taking place in stages and announce the completion of each stage;

(c) when the Indian forces shall have been reduced to the minimum strength mentioned in (a) above, arrange in consultation with the Commission for the stationing of the remaining forces to be carried out in accordance with the following principles;

(i) that the presence of troops should not afford any intimidation or appearance of intimidation to the inhabitants of the State,

(ii) that as small a number as possible should be retained in forward areas,

(iii) that any reserve of troops which may be included in the total strength should be located within their present base area.

3. The Government of India should agree that, until such time as the Plebiscite Administration referred to below finds it necessary to exercise the powers of direction and supervision over the State forces and police provided for in paragraph 8, they will be held in areas to be agreed upon with the Plebiscite Administrator.

4. After the plan referred to in paragraph 2(a) above has been put into operation, personnel recruited locally in each district should so far as possible be utilized for the re-establishment and maintenance of law and order with due regard to protection of minorities, subject to such additional requirements as may be specified by the Plebiscite Administration referred to in paragraph 7.

5. If these local forces should be found to be inadequate, the Commission, subject to the agreement of both the Government of India and the Government of Pakistan, should arrange for the use of such forces of either Dominion as it deems effective for the purpose of pacification.

**B. Plebiscite**

6. The Government of India should undertake to ensure that the Government of the State invite the major political groups to designate responsible representatives to share equitably and fully in the conduct of the administration at the Ministerial level, while the plebiscite is being prepared and carried out.

7. The Government of India should undertake that there will be established in Jammu and Kashmir a Plebiscite Administration to hold a plebiscite as soon as possible on the question of the accession of the State to India or Pakistan.

8. The Government of India should undertake that there will be delegated by the State to the Plebiscite Administration such powers as the latter considers necessary for holding a fair and impartial plebiscite, including, for that purpose only, the direction and supervision of the State forces and police.

9. The Government of India should at the request of the Plebiscite Administration make available from the Indian forces such assistance as the Plebiscite Administration may require for the performance of its functions.

(a) The Government of India should agree that a nominee of the Secretary-General of the United Nations will be appointed to be the Plebiscite Administrator.

(b) The Plebiscite Administrator, acting as an officer of the State of Jammu and Kashmir, should have authority to nominate his assistants and other subordinates and to draft regulations governing the plebiscite. Such nominees should be formally appointed and such draft regulations should be formally promulgated by the State of Jammu and Kashmir.

(c) The Government of India should undertake that the Government of Jammu and Kashmir will appoint fully qualified persons nominated by the Plebiscite Administrator to act as special magistrates within the State judicial system to hear cases which in the opinion of the Plebiscite Administrator have a serious bearing on the preparation for the conduct of a free and impartial plebiscite.

(d) The terms of service of the Administrator should form the subject of a separate negotiation between the Secretary-General of the United Nations and the Government of India. The Administrator should fix the terms of service for his assistants and subordinates.

(e) The Administrator should have the right to communicate direct with the Government of the State and with the Commission of the Security Council, and, through the Commission, with the Security Council, with the Governments of India and Pakistan and with their representatives with the Commission. It would be his duty to bring to the notice of any of all of the foregoing (as he in discretion may decide) any circumstances arising which may tend, in his opinion, to interfere with the freedom of the plebiscite.

10. The Government of India should undertake to prevent and to give full support to the Administrator and his staff in preventing any threat, coercion or intimidation, bribery or other undue influence on the voters in the plebiscite, and the Government of India should publicly announce and should cause the government of the State to announce this undertaking as an international obligation binding on all public authorities and officials in Jammu and Kashmir.

11. The Government of India should themselves and through the government of the State declare and make known that all subjects of the State of Jammu and Kashmir, regardless of creed, caste or party, will be safe and free in expressing their views and in voting on the question of the accession of the State and that there will be freedom of the Press, speech and assembly and freedom to travel in the State, including freedom of lawful entry and exit.

12. The Government of India should use and should ensure that the government of the State also use their best endeavours to effect the withdrawal from the State of all Indian nationals other than those who are normally residents therein or who on or since 15 August 1947 have entered it for a lawful purpose.

13. The Government of India should ensure that the government of the State release all political prisoners and take all possible steps so that:

(a) all citizens of the State who have left it on account of disturbances are invited, and are free, to return to their homes and to exercise their rights as such citizens;

(b) there is no victimization;

(c) minorities in all parts of the State are accorded adequate protection.

14. The Commission of the Security Council should, at the end of the plebiscite, certify to the Council whether the plebiscite has or has not been really free and impartial.

**C. General Provisions**

15. The Governments of India and Pakistan should each be invited to nominate a representative to be attached to the Commission for such assistance as it may require in the performance of its task.

16. The Commission should establish in Jammu and Kashmir such observers as it may require for any of the proceedings in pursuance of the measures indicated in the foregoing paragraphs.

17. The Security Council Commission should carry out the tasks assigned to it herein.

## UNCIP Resolution of 13 August 1948

The United Nations Commission for India and Pakistan having given careful consideration to the points of view expressed by the Representatives of India and Pakistan regarding the situation in the State of Jammu and Kashmir, and

Being of the opinion that the prompt cessation of hostilities and the correction of conditions the continuance of which is likely to endanger international peace and security are essential to implementation of its endeavours to assist the Governments of India and Pakistan in effecting a final settlement of the situation,

Resolves to submit simultaneously to the Governments of India and Pakistan the following proposal:

### Part I: CEASE-FIRE ORDER

A. The Governments of India and Pakistan agree that their respective High Commands will issue separately and simultaneously a cease-fire order to apply to all forces under their control in the State of Jammu and Kashmir as of the earnest practicable date or dates to be naturally agreed upon within four days after these proposals have been accepted by both governments.

B. The High Commands of the India and Pakistan forces agree to refrain from taking any measures that might augment the military potential of the forces under their control in the State of Jammu and Kashmir.

C. For the purpose of these proposals "forces under their control" shall be considered to include all forces, organized and unorganized, fighting or participating in hostilities on their respective sides.

D. The Commanders-in-Chief of the forces of India and Pakistan shall promptly confer regarding any necessary local changes in present dispositions which may facilitate the cease-fire.

E. In its discretion and as the Commission may find practicable, the Commission will appoint military observers who, under the authority of the Commission and with the co-operation of both Commands, will supervise the observance of the cease-fire order.

F. The Government of India and the Government of Pakistan agree to appeal to their respective peoples to assist in creating and maintaining an atmosphere favourable to the promotion of further negotiations.

## Part II: TRUCE AGREEMENT

Simultaneously with the acceptance of the proposal for the immediate cessation of hostilities as outlined in Part I, both governments accept the following principles as a basis for the formulation of a truce agreement, the details of which shall be worked out in discussion between their Representatives and the Commission.

### A

18. As the presence of troops of Pakistan in the territory of the State of Jammu and Kashmir constitutes a material change in the situation since it was represented by the Government of Pakistan before the Security Council, the Government of Pakistan agrees to withdraw its troops from the State.

19. The Government of Pakistan will use its best endevours to secure the withdrawal from the State of Jammu and Kashmir of tribesmen and Pakistan nationals not normally resident therein who have entered the State for the purpose of fighting.

20. Pending a final solution, the territory evacuated by the Pakistani troops will be administered by the local authorities under the surveillance of the Commission.

## B

1. When the Commission shall be notified the Government of India that the tribesmen and Pakistan nationals referred to in Part IIA-2 hereof have withdrawn, thereby terminating the situation which was represented by the Government of India to the Security Council as having occasioned the presence of Indian forces in the State of Jammu and Kashmir, and further, that the Pakistani forces are being withdrawn from the State of Jammu and Kashmir, the Government of India agrees to begin to withdraw the bulk of their forces from that State in stages to be agreed upon with the Commission.

2. Pending the acceptance of the conditions for a final settlement of the situation in the State of Jammu and Kashmir, the Indian Government will maintain within the lines existing at the moment of cease-fire the minimum strength of its forces which in agreement with the Commission are considered necessary to assist local authorities in the observance of law and order. The Commission will have observers stationed where it deems necessary.

3. The Government of India will undertake to ensure that the Government of the State of Jammu and Kashmir will take all measures within its power to make it publicly known that peace, law and order will be safeguarded and that all human and political rights will be guaranteed.

## C

1. Upon signature, the full text of the truce agreement or a communiqué containing the principles thereof agreed upon between the two governments and the Commission will be made public.

## Part III

The Government of India and the Government of Pakistan reaffirm their wish that the future status of the State of Jammu and Kashmir shall be determined in accordance with the will of the people and to that end, upon acceptance of the truce agreement, both governments agree to enter into consultations with the Commission to determine fair and equitable conditions whereby such free expression will be assured.

**Letter from the Prime Minster of India to the Chairman in Reply to the Commission's Resolution of 13 August 1948**

Excellency,

On 17 August, my colleague, the Minister without Portfolio, and I discussed with you and your colleagues of the Commission now in Delhi the resolution which you had presented to us on the 14th instant. On the 18th, I had another discussion with you, in the course of which I tried to explain to you the doubts and difficulties which members of my government, and representative of the Government of Kashmir whom we consulted, had felt as the result of a preliminary but careful examination of the Commission's proposals.

1. During the several conferences that we had with the Commission when it first came to Delhi, we placed before it what we considered the basic fact of the situation which had led to the conflict in Kashmir. This fact was the unwarranted aggression, at first indirect and subsequently direct, of the Pakistan Government on Indian Dominion territory in Kashmir. The Pakistan Government denied this, although it was common knowledge. In recent months, very large forces of the Pakistan regular army have further entered Indian Union territory in Kashmir and opposed the Indian Army which was sent there for the defence of the State. This, we understand now, is admitted by the Pakistan Government, and yet there has been at no time any intimation to the Government of India by the Pakistan Government of this invasion; there has been a continual denial and the Pakistan Government have evaded answering repeated inquiries from the Government of India.

In accordance with the resolution of the Security Council of the United Nations adopted on January 17, 1948, the Pakistan Government should have informed the Council immediately of any material change in the situation while the matter continues to be under the consideration of the Council. The invasion of the State by large forces of the regular Pakistan Army was a very material change in the situation, and yet no information of this was given, so far as we know, to the Security Council.

The Commission will appreciate that this conduct of the Pakistan Government is not only opposed to all moral codes as well as international law and usage, but has also created a very grave situation. It is only the earnest desire of my government to avoid any extension of the field of conflict and to restore peace that had led us to refrain from taking any action to meet the new situation that was created by this further intrusion of the Pakistan Army into Jammu and Kashmir State. The presence of the Commission in India has naturally led us to hope that any arrangements sponsored by it would deal effectively with the present situation and prevent any recurrence of aggression.

2. Since our meeting of 18 August, we have given the Commission's resolution our most earnest thought. There are many parts of it which we should have preferred to be otherwise and more in keeping with the fundamental facts of the situation, especially the flagrant aggression of the Pakistan Government on Indian Union territory. We recognize, however, that if a successful effort is to be made to create satisfactory conditions for a solution of the Kashmir problem without further bloodshed, we should concentrate on certain essentials only at present and seek safeguards in regard to them. It was in this spirit that I placed the following considerations before Your Excellency:

1. That paragraph A3 of Part II of the resolution should not be interpreted, or applied in practice, so as:

(a) to bring into question the sovereignty of the Jammu and Kashmir Government over the portion of their territory evacuated by Pakistan troops;

(b) to afford any recognition of the so-called "Azad Kashmir Government"; or

(c) to enable this territory to be consolidated in any way during the period of truce to the disadvantage of the State.

1. That from our point of view the effective insurance of the security of the State against external aggression, from which Kashmir has suffered so much during the last ten months, was of the most vital significance and no less important than the observance of internal law and order and that, therefore, the withdrawal of Indian troops and the strength of Indian forces maintained in Kashmir should be conditioned by this overriding factor. Thus at any time the strength of the Indian forces maintained in Kashmir should be sufficient to ensure security against any form of external aggression as well as internal disorder.

2. That as regards Part III, should it be decided to seek a solution of the future of the State by means of a plebiscite, Pakistan should have no part in the organization and conduct of the plebiscite or in any other matter of internal administration in the State.

3. If I understood you correctly, A3 of Part II of the resolution does not envisage the creation of any of the conditions to which we have objected in paragraph 3(1) of this letter. In fact, you made it clear that the Commission was not competent to recognize the sovereignty of any authority over the evacuated areas other than that of the Jammu and Kashmir Government.

As regards paragraph 3(2), the paramount need for security is recognized by the Commission, and the time when the withdrawal of Indian forces from the State is to begin, the stages in which it is to be carried out and the strength of Indian forces to be retained in the State, are matters for settlement between the Commission and the Government of India.

Finally, you have agreed that Part III, as formulated, does not in any way recognize the right of Pakistan to have any part in a plebiscite.

3. In view of this clarification, my government, animated by a sincere desire to promote the cause of peace, and thus to upload the principles and prestige of the United Nations, have decided to accept the resolution.

**Letter dated 25 August from the Chairman of the Commission to the Prime Minister of India**

I have the honour to acknowledge the receipt of your communication dated 20 August 1948, regarding the terms of the resolution of the United Nations Commission for India and Pakistan which the Commission presented to you on 14 August 1948.

The Commission requests me to convey to Your Excellency its view that the interpretation of the resolution as expressed in paragraph 4 of your letter coincides with its own interpretation, it being understood that as regards point (1) (c) the local people of the evacuated territory will have freedom of legitimate political activity. In this connection, the term "evacuated territory" refers to those territories in the State of Jammu and Kashmir which are at present under the effective control of the Pakistan High Command.

The Commission wishes me to express to Your Excellency its sincere satisfaction that the Government of India has accepted the resolution and appreciates the spirit in which this decision has been taken.

I wish to avail myself of this opportunity to renew to Your Excellency the assurances of my highest consideration.

**Letter dated 20 August 1948, from the Prime Minister of India to the Chairman of The UNCIP Concerning Northern Territories (S/1100 Para 80)**

Excellency,

You will recall that in our interview with the Commission on 17 August, I dealt at some length with the position of the sparsely populated and mountainous region of Jammu and Kashmir State in the north. The authority of the Government of Jammu and Kashmir over this region as a whole has not been challenged or disrupted, except by roving bands of hostiles, or in some places like Skardu which have been occupied by irregulars of Pakistan troops. The Commission's resolution, as you agreed in the course of our interview on the 18th, does not deal with the problem of administration or defence in this large area. We desire that, after Pakistan troops and irregulars have withdrawn from the territory, the responsibility for the administration of the evacuated areas should revert to the Government of Jammu and Kashmir and that for defence to us. (The only exception that we should be prepared to accept would be Gilgit.) We must be free to maintain garrisons at selected points in this area for the dual purpose of preventing the incursion of tribesmen, who obey no authority, and to guard the main trade routes from the State into Central Asia.

**Letter dated 25 August 1948, From the Chairman of the UNCIP to the Prime Minister of India, Concerning Northern Territories**

I have the honor to acknowledge receipt of your letter of 20 August 1948, relating to the sparsely populated and mountainous region of the State of Jammu and Kashmir in the north.

The Commission wishes me to confirm that, due to the peculiar conditions of this area, it did not specifically deal with the military aspect of the problem in its resolution of 13 August 1948. It believes, however, that the question raised in your letter could be considered in the implementation of the Resolution.

**Aide Memoire No. 1 (21 December 1948)**

His Excellency, Dr. Lozano, accompanied by his Alternate, Mr. Samper, and His Excellency Mr. Colban, Personal Representative of the Secretary-General of the United Nations, met the Prime Minister yesterday. The Hon'ble Shri Gopalaswami Ayyangar and Sri G.S. Bajpai were also present. The discussions of the Commission's plebiscite proposal fell into two parts: (1) General, (2) Particular in reference to individual clauses.

2. The Prime Minister drew attention to Pakistan's repeated acts of aggression against India. In spite of the presence of Pakistan troops in Jammu and Kashmir, which is Indian territory now, and the offensive action of Pakistan troops, the

Government of India had accepted the Commission's Resolution of 13 August; Pakistan had not accepted the Resolution. In paragraph 143 of its Repòrt, the Commission had referred to its conference with the Prime Minister on the conditions attached by the Government of Pakistan to its acceptance of the Resolution of 13 August. As stated in paragraph 144 of the Report, the Prime Minister had informed the Commission that he stood on his original premises that the Pakistan forces must be withdrawn from the State before the Government of India could consider any further steps. This had specific reference to an amplification of Part III of the Resolution of 13 August. Nevertheless, the Government of India have agreed to informal conversations in Paris which had resulted in the formulations of the proposals now put forward by the Commission. The Government of India naturally wondered how far this process of rejection of proposals put forward by the Commission of Pakistan and the adoption of a responsive attitude on the part of the Government of India towards the Commission's proposals could continue. The Commission must realize that there were limits to the forbearance and spirit of conciliation of the Government of India. The Prime Minister emphasized (1) that, if the Government of India were to accept the Commission's plebiscite proposals, no action could be taken in regard to them until Parts I and II of the Commission's Resolution of 13 August had been fully implemented; (2) that in the event of Pakistan not accepting these proposals, or having accepted them, not implementing Parts I and II of the Resolution of 13 August, the Government of India's acceptance of them should not be regarded as in any way binding upon them; (3) Part III of the Commission's Resolution of 13 August provided "that the future status of the State of Jammu and Kashmir shall be determined in accordance with the will of the people and to that end, upon acceptance of truce agreement, both governments agree to enter into consultations with the Commission to determine fair and equitable conditions whereby such free expression will be assured." To present proposals appeared to limit the method of ascertaining the will of the people regarding the future status of the State of Jammu and Kashmir through a plebiscite. While the Government of India adhered to their position in regard to a plebiscite, they had pointed out that, in the view of the difficulties of holding a plebiscite in present conditions in Kashmir, other methods of ascertaining the wish of the people should also be explored. The Commission had itself recognized the difficulties of carrying out a plebiscite in Kashmir. The Government of India feel that the exploration of other methods should not be ruled out.

3. As regards (1), Dr. Lozano enquired whether there should be objection to the appointment of a Plebiscite Administrator until Parts I and II of the Resolution of 13 August had been implemented. Both he and Mr. Colban thought that the Plebiscite Administrator could do useful exploratory work even before arrangements for holding a plebiscite could be taken in hand. The Prime Minister pointed out that it was always open to the Commission to employ advisers or experts for work within its terms of reference. The Government of India, however, would regard the appointment of a Plebiscite Administrator, as such, premature until Parts I and II of the Resolution of 13 August had been implemented. Dr. Lozano accepted (2). As regards (3), he said that the Commission wished the possibility of a plebiscite to be explored first. Should the Plebiscite Administrator, however, find a plebiscite to be impracticable, the way would be open to consider other methods for ensuring a free expression by the people of Jammu and Kashmir of their wish regarding the future status of the State.

4.B.1. Preamble. The phrase "The Governments of India and Pakistan simultaneously accept" is incorrect in that either government may not accept the principles supplementary to the Resolution of 13 August. Even if both governments accept them, the acceptance cannot be simultaneous. The wording should be changed accordingly.

B.3(b). The question was raised whether the form of words employed was intended to give to the Plebiscite Administrator powers of interference in the administration of the State, e.g. by "direction and supervision of the State Forces and Police," mentioned in paragraph B.8 of the Security Council's Resolution of 21 April 1948. Dr. Lozano said that this was not the intention of the Commission and that the words quoted above had been deliberately omitted. The Prime Minister pointed out that all that the Plebiscite Administrator could in reason expect was that, for the purpose of organising and conducting the plebiscite and ensuring its freedom and impartiality, the Government of Jammu and Kashmir should give him such assistance as he might require. Dr. Lazano said that a Plebiscite Administrator of international standing and commanding general confidence, who would be appointed after consultation with the Government of India, could be expected to act reasonably and that the Commission did not intend that he should usurp the functions of the State Government in the field of normal administration and law and order. His functions and powers would be limited to ensuring that the plebiscite was free and impartial.

B.4(b). The Prime Minister drew attention to the fact that the Azad Kashmir forces which had been armed and equipped by Pakistan and were under the operational command of the Pakistan Army ran into tens of thousands. Their presence in the territories referred to in A.3 of Part II of the Resolution of 13 August, even after demobilization, would be a constant threat to the territory under the control of Indian and State forces, a deterrent to the return of many refugees, and an obstacle to the free expression of opinion regarding the future status of the State by those who might be opposed to the accession of the State to Pakistan. Dr. Lozano pointed out that it was the Commission's intention that there should be large-scale disarming of these forces, though it would not be possible to require withdrawal from these territories of genuine inhabitants of these areas.

B.6(a). Dr. Lozano agreed that it was not the Commission's intention that the Pakistan Commission should operate outside Pakistan. Thus, the Pakistan Commission would not operate in the territory referred to in A.3 of Part II of the Resolution of 13 August. The Prime Minister then raised the question of the "free return" to the State of all citizens who had left it on account of the disturbances. He said that the tendency of Pakistan would be to push as many people as possible into Jammu and Kashmir. If the plebiscite was to be limited, as it should be, to genuine citizens of the State, the entry of persons claiming to be citizens into the State will have to be most carefully checked. How was this to be achieved? Dr. Lozano said that the Commission fully realized the necessity of an accurate and effective check but had not gone into details. Possibly those returning to the State could be stopped and examined at the frontier. The Prime Minister pointed out that, considering the length of the frontier and the ease with which people could slip across the border over mountain tracks, a check on the frontier would be neither easy nor effective, except by the employment of large forces.

Apart from the problem of entry, there is the even more important problem of the rehabilitation and protection of those who have left the State on account of recent disturbances. Homes have been destroyed; property has been lost; there has been wholesale dispossession of persons from the land that they used to cultivate. It is not enough to "invite" these persons to return to the State. They have to be given full security and to be housed, fed and put in a position to maintain themselves. It may be necessary to lodge these returning citizens of the State temporarily in campus for distribution to their homes. They could not, however, be expected to remain in relief camps for long or to take part in a plebiscite from such camps. The administrative and economic implications of this task were at once significant and onerous. They must receive full attention.

B.6(b). It is assumed that the Government of Jammu and Kashmir will decide whether or not a person entered the State for a lawful purpose.

B.7(b). India is a secular State; the United Nations also are a secular organization. Pakistan aims at being a theocratic State. An appeal to religious fanaticism could not be regarded as legitimate political activity. Dr. Lozano agreed that any political activity which might tend to disturb law and order could not be regarded as legitimate. The same test would apply to freedom of the Press and of speech.

As regards the freedom of lawful entry and exit, this must obviously be governed by B.6 of the proposals. It is assumed that in the territory under their control, entry and exit will be regulated by rules framed for the purpose by the Government of Jammu and Kashmir, with due regard to the security of the State and the maintenance of law and order. Dr. Lozano said that a system of permits would probably be necessary.

B.7(c) Persons guilty of ordinary offences against law and order will not be regarded as political prisoners.

In all their negotiations the Government of India have emphasized the paramount need of ensuring the security of the State. The Commission recognized this in their Resolution of 13 August; they have also provided in 4(a) of the plebiscite proposals that measures with regard to the final disposal of Indian and State Forces will be taken with due regard to the security of the State. The Government of India wish to emphasise the supreme importance which they attach to adequate provision for the security of the State in all contingencies.

**UNCIP Resolution of 5 January 1949 (s/1430, PARA 143)**

The United Nations Commissions for India and Pakistan, having received from the Governments of India and Pakistan, in communications dated 23 December and 25 December 1948, respectively, their acceptance of the following principles which are supplementary to the Commission's resolution of 13 August 1948:

1. The question of the accession of the State of Jammu and Kashmir to India or Pakistan will be decided through the democratic method of a free and impartial plebiscite.

2. A plebiscite will be held when it shall be found by the Commission that the cease-fire and truce arrangements set forth in Parts I and II of the Commission's resolution of 13 August 1948, have been carried out and arrangements for the plebiscite have been completed.

(a) The Secretary-General of the United Nations will, in agreement with the Commission, nominate a Plebiscite Administrator who shall be a personality of high international standing and commanding general confidence. He will be formally appointed to office by the Government of Jammu and Kashmir.

(b) The Plebiscite Administrator shall derive from the State of Jammu and Kashmir the powers he considers necessary for organizing and, conducting the plebiscite and for ensuring the freedom and impartiality of the plebiscite.

(c) The Plebiscite Administrator shall have authority to appoint such staff of assistants and observers as he may require.

4. (a) After implementation of Parts I and II of the Commission's resolution of 13 August 1948, and when the Commission is satisfied that peaceful conditions have been restored in the State, the Commission and the Plebiscite Administrator will determine, in consultation with the Government of India, the final disposal of Indian and State armed forces, such disposal to be with due regard to the security of the State and the freedom of the plebiscite.

(b) As regards the territory referred to in A-2 of Part II of the resolution of 13 August, final disposal of the armed forces in that territory will be determined by the Commission and the Plebiscite Administrator in consultation with the local authorities.

5. All civil and military authorities with the State and the principal political elements of the State will be required to co-operate with the Plebiscite Administrator in the preparation for and the holding of the plebiscite.

6. (a) All citizens of the State who have left it on account of the disturbances will be invited and be free to return and to exercise all their rights as such citizens. For the purpose of facilitating repatriation there shall be appointed two commissions, one composed of nominees of India and the other of nominees of Pakistan. The Commission shall operate under the direction of the Plebiscite Administrator. The Governments of India and Pakistan and all authorities within the State of Jammu and Kashmir will collaborate with the Plebiscite Administrator in putting this provision into effect.

(b) All persons (other than citizens of the State) who on or since 15 August 1947, have entered it for other than lawful purpose, shall be required to leave the State.

7. All authorities within the State of Jammu and Kashmir will undertake to ensure, in collaboration with the Plebiscite Administrator, that:

(a) there is no threat, coercion or intimidation, bribery or other undue influence on the voters in the plebiscite;

(b) no restrictions are placed on legitimate political activity throughout the State. All subjects of the State, regardless to creed, caste or party, shall be safe and free in expressing their views and in voting on the question of the accession of the State to India or Pakistan. There shall be freedom of the Press, speech and assembly and freedom to travel in the State, including freedom of lawful entry and exit;

(c) all political prisoners are released;

(d) minorities in all parts of the State are accorded adequate protection; and

(e) there is no victimization.

8. The Plebiscite Administrator may refer to the United Nations Commission for India and Pakistan problems on which he may require assistance, and the Commission may in its direction call upon the Plebiscite Administrator to carry out on its behalf any of the responsibilities with which it has been entrusted.

9. At the conclusion of the plebiscite. The Plebiscite Administrator shall report the result thereof to the Commission and to the Government of Jammu and Kashmir. The Commission shall then certify to the Security Council whether the plebiscite has or has not been free and impartial.

10. Upon the signature of the truce agreement the details of the foregoing proposals will be elaborated in the consultations envisaged in Part III of the Commission's resolution of 13 August 1948. The Plebiscite Administrator will be fully associated in these consultations.

Commends the Governments of India and Pakistan for their prompt action in ordering a cease-fire to take effect from one minute before midnight of January 1, 1949, pursuant to the agreement arrived at as provided for by the Commission's resolution of 13 August 1948; and

Resolves to return in the immediate future to the subcontinent to discharge the responsibilities imposed upon it by the resolution of 13 August 1948, and by the foregoing principles.

## Agreement between Military Representatives of India and Pakistan Regarding the Establishment of a Cease-Fire Line in the State of Jammu and Kashmir

29 July 1949

### I. Introduction

(A) The military representatives of India and Pakistan met together in Karachi from 18 July to 27 July 1949 under the auspices of the Truce Sub-Committee of the United Nations Commission for India and Pakistan.

(B) The members of the Indian delegations were: Lieutenant-General S.M. Shrinagesh, Major-General K.S. Thimayya, Brigadier S.H.F.J. Manekshaw. As observers: Mr. H.M. Patel, Mr. V. Sahay.

(C) The members of the Pakistan delegation were: Major-General W. J. Cawthorn, Major-General Nasir Ahmed, Brigadier M. Sher Khan. As observers: Mr. M. Ayub, Mr. A.A. Khan.

(D) The members of the Truce Sub-Committee of the United Nations Commission for India and Pakistan were: Mr. Hernando Samper (Colombia), Chairman; Mr. William L.S. Williams (United States); Lieutenant-General Maurice Delvoie, Military Adviser; Mr. Miguel A. Marin, Legal Adviser.

### II. Agreement

A. *Considering*

1. That the United Nations Commission for India and Pakistan, in its letter dated 2 July 1949, invited the Governments of India and Pakistan to send fully authorized military representatives to meet jointly in Karachi under the auspices of the Commission's Truce Sub-Committee to establish a cease-fire

line in the State of Jammu and Kashmir, mutually agreed upon by the Governments of India and Pakistan;

2. That the United Nations Commissions for India and Pakistan in its letter stated that "The meetings will be for military purposes; political issues will not be considered," and that "They will be conducted without prejudice to negotiations concerning the truce agreement";

3. That in the same letter the United Nations Commission for India and Pakistan further stated that "The cease-fire line is a complement of the suspension of hostilities, which falls within the provisions of Part I of the resolution of 13 August 1948, and can be considered separately from the questions relating to Part II of the same resolution";

4. That the Governments of India and Pakistan, in their letters dated 7 July 1949, to the Chairman of the Commission, accepted the Commission's invitation to the military conference in Karachi.

B. ***The delegation of India and Pakistan, duly authorized, have reached the following agreement:***

1. Under the provisions of Part I of the resolution of 13 August 1948, and as a complement of the suspension of hostilities in the State of Jammu and Kashmir on 1 January 1949, a cease-fire line is established.

2. The cease-fire lines run from Manawar in the south, north to Keran and from Keran east to the glacier area, as follows:

(a) The line from Manawar to the south bank of Jhelum River at Urusa (inclusive of India) is the line now defined by the factual positions about which there is agreement between the parties. Where there has hither—to not been agreement, the line shall be as follows:

(i) in the Patrana area: Kohel (inclusive to Pakistan) north along the Khuwala Kas Nullah up to Point 2276 (inclusive to India), thence to Kirni (inclusive to India).

(ii) Khambha, Pir Satwan, Point 3150 and Point 3606 are inclusive to India, thence the line runs to the factual position at Bagla Gala, thence to the factual position at Point 3300.

(iii) in the area south of Uri the positions of Pir Kanthi and Ledi Gali are inclusive to Pakistan.

(b) From the north bank of the Jhelum River the line runs from a point opposite the village of Urusa (NL 972109), thence north following the Ballaseth Da Nar Nullah (inclusive to Pakistan), up to NL 973140, thence north-east to Chhota Qazinag (Point 10657 inclusive to India), thence to NM 010180, thence to NM 037210, thence to Point 11825 (NM 025354, inclusive to Pakistan), thence to Tutmari Gali (to be shared by both sides, posts to be established 500 yards on either side of the Gali), thence to the north-west through the first "R" of Burji Nar to north of Gadori, thence straight west to just north of point 9870, thence along the black line north of Bijidhar to north of Batarasi, thence to just south of Sudhpura, thence due north to the Kathaqazinag Nullah, thence along the Nullah to its junction with the Grangnar Nullah, thence along the letter Nullah to Kajnawala Pathra (inclusive to India), thence across the Danna ridge (following the factual positions) to Richmar Gali (inclusive to India), thence to Thanda Katha Nullah, thence north to the Kishanganga River. The line then follows the Kishanganga River up to a point situated between Fagri and Tarban, thence (all inclusive to Pakistan) to Bankoran, thence north-east to Khori, thence to the hill feature 8930 (in Square), thence straight north to Point 10164 (in square 9057), thence to Point 10323 (in square 9161), thence north-east straight to Guthur, then to Bhutpatra, thence to NL 98070, thence following the Bugina Nullah to the junction with the Kishansagar River at Point 4739. Thereafter the line follows the Kishansagar River to Kerwan and onwards to Point 4996 (NL 975818).

(c) From Point 4996 the line follows (all inclusive to Pakistan the Famgar Nullah eastward to Point 12124, to Katware, to Point 6678, then to the north-east to Sarian (Point 11279), to Point 11837, to Point 13090 to Point 12641, thence east again to Point 11142, thence to Dhakki, thence to Point 11415, thence to Point 10301, thence to Point 7507, thence to Point 10685, thence to Point 8388, thence south-east to Point 11812. Thence the line runs (all inclusive to India) to Point 13220, thence across the river to the east to Point 13449 (Durmat), thence to Point 13220, thence to Point 14586 (Anzbari), thence the Point 13554, thence to Milestone 45 on the Burzil Nullah, thence to the east to Ziankal (Point 12090), thence to the south-east to Point 11114, thence to Point 12216, thence to Point 12867, thence to the east to Point 11264, thence to Karo (Point 14985), thence to Point 14014, thence to Point 12089, thence following the track to Point 12879. From there the line runs to Point 13647 (Karobal Gali, to be shared by both sides). The cease-fire line runs thence through Point 17392, thence through Point 16458, thence to Marpo La (to be shared by both sides), thence through Point 17561, thence through Point 17352, thence through Point 18400, thence through Point 16760, thence to (inclusive to India) Dalunang.

(d) From Dalunang eastwards the cease-fire line will follow the general line Point 15495, Ishmam, Manus, Gangam, Gunderman, Point 13620, Funkar (Point 17628), Marmark, Natsara, Shangruti (Point 17531), Chorbat La (Point 16700), Chalunka (on the Shyok River), Khor, thence north to the glaciers. This portion of the cease-fire shall be determined in detail on the basis of the factual position as of 27 July, 1949, by the local commanders assisted by United Nations military observers.

(C) The cease-fire line described above shall be drawn on a one-inch map (where available) and then be verified mutually on the ground by local commanders on each side with the assistance of the United Nations military observers, so as to eliminate any no-man's land. In the event that the local commanders are unable to reach agreement, the matter shall be referred to the Commission's Military Adviser, whose decision shall be final. After this verification, the Military Adviser will issue to each High Command a map on which will be marked the definitive cease-fire line.

(D) No troops shall be stationed or operate in the area of the Burzil Nullah from south of Minimarg to the cease-fire line. This area is bounded on the west by the ridge leading north-east from Dudgaikal to Point 13071, to Point 9447, to Point 13466, to Point 13463, and on the east of the ridge running from Point 12470 to Point 11608, to Point 13004, to Point 13976, to Point 13450. Pakistan may, however, post troops on the west of the above ridges to cover the approaches to Kamri Bal Pass.

(E) In any dispositions that may be adopted in consequence of the present agreement troops will remain at least 500 yards from the cease-fire line except where the Kishansagar River continues the line. Points which have been shown as inclusive to one party may be occupied by that party, but the troops of the other party shall remain at a distance of 500 yards.

(F) Both sides shall be free to adjust their defensive positions behind the cease-fire line as determined in paragraphs A through E, inclusive, subject to no wire or mines being used when new bunkers and defenses are constructed. There shall be increase of forces or strengthening of defenses in areas where no major adjustments are involved by the determination of the cease-fire line.

(G) The action permitted by paragraph F above shall not be accompanied or accomplished by the introduction of additional military potential by either side into the State of Jammu and Kashmir.

(H) Except as modified by paragraph A to G, inclusive, above, the military agreements between the two High Commands relating to the cease-fire of 1 January, 1949, shall continue to remain operative.

(I) The United Nations Commission for India and Pakistan will station observers where it deems necessary.

(J) The delegations shall refer this agreement to their respective Governments for ratification. The documents of ratification shall be deposited with the United Nations Commission for India and Pakistan not later than 31 July 1949.

(K) A period of thirty days from the date of ratification shall be allowed to each side to vacate the areas at present occupied by them beyond the cease-fire line as now determined. Before the expiration of this thirty-day period there shall be no forward movement into areas to be taken over by either side pursuant to this agreement, except the mutual agreement between local commanders.

In faith whereof the undersigned sign this document in three original copies.

Done in Karachi on 27 July 1949.

For the Government of India:

S.M. Shrinagesh

For the Government of Pakistan:

J. Cawthorn Major-General

For the United Nations Commission for India and Pakistan:

Hernando Samper

M. Delvoie

The UN Commission achieved little except to bring about a cease-fire on 1 January 1949 followed by a cease-fire line for the observance of which a group of UN observers was posted on each side. Its resolution required the withdrawal of Pathan tribesmen and Pakistani nationals and its armed forces from the State. India's responsibility for internal security as well as the legality of the Jammu and Kashmir Government was recognized by the Commission. After Pakistan had carried out its obligations and in consultation with India, arrangements were to be considered for the holding of a plebiscite. As Pakistan never honoured its obligations, the resolution about plebiscite became infructuous.

Maharaja Hari Singh intensely felt that Kashmir issue may be kept on dragging in UN. Therefore, he wrote to Sardar Patel a letter on 31 January 1948 in which he said:

In his letter of 31 January 1948 to Sardar Patel, Maharaja Hari Singh said:

In the situation described above a feeling comes to my mind as to the possible steps that may be taken no make so far as I am concerned a clean breast of the situation. Sometimes I feel that I should withdraw the Accession that I have made to the Indian Union. The Union only provisionally accepted the Accession and if the Union cannot recover back our territory and is going eventually to agree to the decision of the Security Council which may result in handing us over to Pakistan then there is no point in sticking to the Accession of the State to the Indian Union. For the time being it may be possible to have better terms from Pakistan but that is immaterial because eventually it would mean an end of the Dynasty and end of the Hindus and Sikhs in the State. There is an alternative possible for me and that is to withdraw the Accession and that my kill the reference to the UNO because Indian Union will have no right to continue the proceedings before the Council if the Accession is withdrawn. The result may be a return to the position the State held before the Accession. The difficulty in the situation however will be that the Indian Troops cannot be maintained in the State except as volunteers to help the State. I am prepared to take over command of my own Forces along with the Forces of the Indian Army as volunteers to help the State. I am prepared to lead my Army personally and the command, if the Indian Union agrees, also their troops. It would certainly hearten my people and the Troops. I know my country much better than any of your General will know it even during the next several months or years keep on sitting here doing nothing. It is for to consider whether the Indian Union will accept this in both the situations whether after the withdrawal of the Accession or even if the Accession continues. I am tried of my present life and it is much better to die fighting than watch helplessly the heart-breaking misery of my people.

The Sardar's reply came on 9 February. The operative paragraph was short but categorical. He wrote:

> I fully realize what an anxious time you must be having. I can assure you that I am no less anxious about the Kashmir situation and what is happening in the U.N.O., but whatever the present situation may be, a counsel of despair is entirely out of place. (*Hair Apparent*: Dr. Karan Singh, pp. 88, 89)

# 5

# Stand of India: Jawaharlal Nehru to Narendra Modi

After India and Pakistan could not resolve the dispute through bilateral talks on Kashmir, Nehru on the insistence of Lord Mountbatten lodged complaint with the United Nations Security Council.

Commonwealth Relations secretary Philip Noel-Baker, U.N. representative Sir Alexander Cadogan and Lord Hasting Ismay former Chief of Staff of Mountbatten met acting Secretary of State Lovett in Washington in January 1948 before the beginning of Security Council deliberations on Kashmir.

Lovett said that U.S. involvement might attract Soviet interest, making it harder to solve the Kashmir dispute.

When the Security Council met on Kashmir in early 1948, American diplomats followed the British line in trying to reach a satisfactory solution. By March 1948, the Security Council settled on a draft resolution proposed by China. Pakistan did not favour the proposal because it left Sheikh Abdullah in office during the plebiscite.

Jinnah said that a fair plebiscite was impossible, if Sheikh Abdullah, a Congress quisling remained in power. He went on to beg the United States not to be misled by British claims that they knew the situation better than we did.

Ultimately, the United States joined Britain, Canada and China in supporting a modified proposal. The Security Council unanimously adopted a resolution on 21 April 1948 on which neither India nor Pakistan was happy.

Prime Minister of Pakistan Liaquat Ali Khan declared that the Kashmir resolution showed complete lack of understanding of oriental psychology and that as long as Sheikh Abdullah remained head of the Kashmir Government, the voters would not take risk in voting against him.

Paul Alling took over as first US Ambassador to Pakistan. He expressed American hope for friendly India-Pakistan relations to which Jinnah replied that nothing was dear to his heart. Jinnah said that he had told Nehru, Gandhi and others that Pakistan desired a defensive understanding with India on military level with no time limit. He alleged that India and Mountbatten had been less than fair and that he was firmly convinced that Pakistan was a victim of conspiracy.

### Ceasefire but No Settlement

During 1948 UN worked hard for ceasefire and lay ground work for plebiscite in Kashmir. After the United States reluctantly agreed to become a member of the UN Commission for India and Pakistan (UNCIP), the UN representative on the Commission, Ambassador to Burma Klahr Huddle found little to choose between the Indians and the Pakistanis. Prime Minister Nehru in Huddle's view adopted a self-righteous intransigent stand, while Foreign Minister of Pakistan Zafrullah Khan's attitude towards the Commission was patronizing. Although India eventually accepted the UNCIP proposals, Pakistan added so many riders that the UN team regarded Pakistan's response as rejection.

Charles Lewis who had become Charge D'Affairs again after Ambassador Alling strongly defended Pakistan's action. His dispatches of 10 and 24 September 1948 expressed little faith in UNCIP's ability to suppress or control Indian perfidy.

In October 1948, Liaquat Ali Khan met Secretary of State Marshall during UN General Assembly Session held that year in Paris. Khan described India's attitude toward Pakistan as hostile. He asserted that Pakistan wanted peace but would fight if India persisted in being aggressive. He said that the Kashmir problem could be solved by plebiscite, however, there must be no coercive forces present.

Following the meeting with Liaquat and Nehru, Marshall expressed little optimism about the prospects for a Kashmir settlement. While discussing the issue with Sir Alexander Cadogon, the British UN representative, Marshall commented that although both Nehru and Liaquat stressed the need for stability, they did not seem to be willing to suit action to their words.

On 11 December 1948, after reaching a consensus on ceasefire arrangements and on the appointment of a high level plebiscite administrator, UNCIP forwarded its proposal to Karachi and New Delhi on a take-it-or-leave-it basis. Both countries accepted the UN plan. A ceasefire took place in Kashmir on 1 January 1949. Each side remained in physical possession of the areas it was occupying. The Security Council endorsed the UNCIP proposals and reaffirmed a call for plebiscite.

In March 1949, UN Secretary Trygve Lie appointed Admiral Chester Nimitz, who had commanded American Navel Forces in the Pacific during World War I, as administrator of Kashmir plebiscite.

Nimitz waited in New York for the accord to be finalized before shifting to South Asia to conduct the voting. But it shortly became apparent that reaching an agreement would not be easy. India started raising a variety of problems, including its desire to disarm and disband all Azad Kashmir forces and to challenge Pakistan's control over Gilgit and Hunza, two small isolated, but strategic territories in Northern Kashmir that had joined Pakistan in August 1947.

After struggling without success for six months, UNCIP proposed that India and Pakistan should submit their differences to arbitration. American President Truman endorsed the idea in personal appeals to Liaquat and Nehru and urged parallel approach by British Prime Minister Clement Attlee. Truman's message to Liaquat was:

> I am sure that you will agree that peace and cooperation between your country and India are essential to the

> continuance of social and political progress on the subcontinent. The Kashmir dispute is the greatest threat to such peace and cooperation. My Government, is therefore, deeply interested in an early settlement of this dispute. In the interest of your own nation and in the interest of the world community, I urge you accept the recommendation for arbitration of true terms.

Liaquat agreed for arbitration. He replied to Truman on 8 September 1949: "Had the proposal not hinged around the eminent personality of Fleet Admiral Chester W. Nimitz and had it not been so emphatically sponsored by the president of the United States, my Government would have felt considerable hesitation in accepting it."

Nehru, however, turned Truman down. He claimed that the basic problem was the anti-Indian attitude of the Pakistan leadership. Resorting to what Americans regarded as legalistic quibbling, Nehru said that he was not opposed to arbitration, but found the proposal insufficiently precise and defined.

A week later, Dean Acheson, who had succeeded Marshall as Secretary of State conferred with Foreign Minister Zafrullah Khan. Zafrullah Khan expressed fears that India's resistance to plebiscite would lead to an interminable delay, increasing pressure on the Pakistan Government to take action. "This Government," Marshall replied, "shared Pakistan's concern in this matter. We were very pleased with Pakistan's acceptance of the arbitration proposal and greatly disappointed by reply we had received from India."

The perception also grew that Prime Minister Nehru, given his family roots as a member of a Kashmiri Brahmin community, was the principal barrier to a settlement. McGhee commented: "Nehru was the stumbling block. If he had cooperated, the Kashmir problem could have easily been solved."

A major outbreak of Hindu-Muslim violence in east Bengal triggered a potentially explosive crisis in India-Pakistan relations. As tensions rose, Truman, vacationing in Key West, Florida, telephoned Acheson to send a message to Liaquat and Nehru to find a way to resolve the problem. With American and British diplomats playing a helpful behind-the-scenes role, the Indian and Pakistani leaders were able to ease tension by reaching an agreement to improve treatment of minorities.

While Liaquat was visiting the United States in May 1950, Sir Owen Dixon, a distinguished Australian Jurist, was making UN effort to solve the Kashmir dispute. Even though Dixon came closer to success than anyone else before or after, in the end he too failed. After shuttling back and forth between Karachi and New Delhi in the piercing May heat, Dixon concluded that a statewide plebiscite was no longer feasible. Instead, he fixed on the idea initially put forward by Sir Girja Shankar Bajpai, Secretary-General of India's Ministry of External Affairs. The proposal was for India and Pakistan to keep the portions of Kashmir that they controlled, except for the Vale where a plebiscite of some other arrangement, would settle matters. After considerable difficulty, Dixon gained the agreement of Liaquat and his cabinet colleagues in Karachi. However, Liaquat insisted that Dixon obtain Nehru's assurance that he would not oppose the idea out of hand. Dixon traveled to New Delhi to meet Nehru. But Nehru rejected the proposal, claiming that it was not suitable for Kashmir. Dixon's mission came to an end.

Ambassador Loy Henderson, who had succeeded Henry Grady, thought he should continue the effort to seek a settlement and leave Sheikh Abdullah in place as long as the plebiscite administrator believed that he was supporting a fair vote. From Karachi, Warren, echoed official Pakistani views in vehemently opposing giving "Abdullah's stooge government the slightest possibility of bringing pressure on the local population either before or during the balloting."

Dr. Frank Graham made little progress after he took up the assignment. After a long talk with Nehru, Graham, almost came to the conclusion that it is useless for his mission to remain longer in south Asia. He eventually reported on his lack of progress to the Security Council on October 16, 1951.

However, Graham went ahead. His strategy was to seek points of agreement and to narrow the differences to three areas: the ratio of troops to remain in Kashmir, the period of time for the demilitarization process, and the date for the plebiscite administrator to start his work. Although Graham doubted that the Indians could block the plebiscite once Nimitz was on the scene in Kashmir. He told Ernest Gross of the US mission to the UN in December 1951 that he found little tendency on the part of India to agree to any reasonable proposition.

Until the beginning of 1952, the Kashmir dispute remained largely outside the scope of the Cold War. In keeping with its cool and distant relations with both India and Pakistan, the Soviet Union had steered clear of the issue in UN deliberation. Indicating, a significant policy shift in January 1952, however, Jacob Malik, the Soviet representative to the United Nations, tore into Graham's report to the Security Council. He blasted the envoy as a US-UK secret agent and charged that the West intended to transform Kashmir and Pakistan into a military springboard against the USSR and New China.

With Graham's efforts proving exercise in futility, the Pakistanis were becoming more downcast. Foreign Minister Zafrullah Khan told Ambassador Warren in April 1952 that his colleagues believed that Graham was an old man of the sea with his legs locked around the neck of Kashmir and would never let go. A month later, Karachi was even more unhappy when Nimitz decided to resign as plebiscite administrator after having sat idle for three years in New York. In a call on Acting Secretary of State David Bruce, Nimitz commented, "no mediation effort in Kashmir is going to succeed as long as Mr. Nehru maintains his present un-statesman-like attitude."

In June 1952, when it looked as if the Kashmir discussions had reached a dead end, Pakistan Prime Minister Nazimuddin informed Warren that Pakistan was ready to break the deadlock by offering a major concession on the question of troop withdrawal ratios. Chester Bowles, who had succeeded Henderson as Ambassador to India happened to be passing through Karachi and Warren arranged his meeting with Nazimuddin to discuss the issue. Bowles cabled Washington after the session: "it is difficult to see how Nehru can turn down this proposal." A State Department responded that it was "gratified at the Pakistani government's willingness to offer concessions in the hope of achieving demilitarization and the entrance into office of the plebiscite administrator and regards the Pakistani proposal as a statesmanlike act." But Nehru turned Bowles down. He refused asserting that "ratios were not the way to approach the problem since this implied that the Pakistanis had definite rights in Kashmir which the Indians had consistently denied."

Despite this setback, Graham held India-Pakistan ministerial talks in Geneva, Switzerland, in the fall of 1952. After these failed to advance matters, Washington and London prepared a new draft UN resolution that drew sharp fire from Bowles, by then on his way out after the defeat of the Democrats in the November 1952 UN presidential elections. Assistant Secretary of State for UN Affairs John Hickerson, and Henry Byroade, who had replaced McGhee as Assistant Secretary of State for Near Eastern South Asian and African Affairs in late 1951, rebuffed Bowles in a November 20, 1952 cable that reaffirmed our basic policy of attempting to help both parties without siding with either. Summing up the US Government's view after five frustrating years of wrestling with the Kashmir problem, Hickerson and Byroade cabled, "the Department of State considers Nehru the key figure in the settlement of the Kashmir issue. Until he is willing to indicate a sincere desire to make a settlement it probably will follow."

Truman, Acheson, and McGhee considered Jawaharlal Nehru difficult and regarded his chief foreign affairs aide Krishna Menon, as obnoxious and procommunist. Nonetheless, recognizing the geopolitical realities of the subcontinent the Truman administration held back from establishing a security relationship with Pakistan lest this antagonize India.

## First Republican President

In January 1953, Dwight Eisenhower became the first Republican President of the United States in 20 years.

Eisenhower's selection of John Foster Dulles as Secretary of State was also heartening news in Karachi.

By the time he became Secretary of State, Dulles had already formed an unfavourable impression of India and a favourable one of Pakistan. He found Nehru's neutralist foreign policy naive if not unprincipled, and much preferred Pakistan's anti-communist orientation.

In May 1953, Dulles visited India and Pakistan as part of the first trip to the Middle East and South Asia by Secretary of State.

Dulles told Nehru that the United States had no present plans that would bring it into a military relationship with Pakistan which could reasonably be looked at as un-neutral regarding India. Dulles next stop was Karachi.

Ghulam Mohammed, Bogra, Zafrullah Khan and Ayub Khan, in their meetings with Dulles, stressed their allegiance to the anti-communist case and emphasized Pakistani's desire to join the free world's defence team.

Speaking of the "potential both in manpower and bases that is available in Pakistan," Ayub declared, "Pakistan under the present Government is extremely anxious to cooperate with the United States." To allay US concerns about the impact on India, Ayub asserted, "If Pakistan were strengthened by United States economic and military aid, it would result in India dropping its present intransigent attitude on Kashmir."

Dulles cabled from Turkey, "Genuine feeling of friendship encountered in Pakistan exceeded to a marked degree that encountered in any country previously visited on this trip. Was impressed with the spirit and appearance of what we saw of the armed forces and their leaders. Have a feeling Pakistan is one country that has the moral courage to do its part in resisting communists. Believe Pakistan would be a cooperative member of any Defence scheme that may emerge in the Middle East and that we need not await formal defence arrangements as a condition to some military assistance to Pakistan."

On 1 June 1953, Dulles told the National Security Council [NSC] that "Pakistan was a potential strong point for us" and he was "tremendously impressed by the martial and religious qualities of the Pakistanis." In contrast, he described India's Prime Minister Nehru as an "utterly impractical statesman."

In India, media speculation generated by the *New York Times*, article and Ghulam Mohammed's trip triggered an uproar. Prime Minister Nehru warned Washington and Karachi that "it would be a matter of grave consequence to us, if vast armies are built up in Pakistan with the aid of American money." He told the Chief Ministers of India's States that US arms for Pakistan would bring the Cold War to the region and have very far reaching consequences on the whole structure of things in south Asia, and especially in India and Pakistan.

Speaking in Bangalore, Nehru described the arms proposals in extreme terms as "a step not only towards war, even world war, but a step which will bring war right to our doors."

Taking note of Nehru's disagreeable statements, Eisenhower sent Dulles a note about the problems of dealing with India and Pakistan on November 16, 1953 in which he wrote: "This is one area of the world where, emotion rather than reason seems to dictate policy. I know you will be watchful to see that we do not create antagonism unnecessarily." In his reply, Dulles commented that: "this is another of those situations like Trieste and Israel where emotion rules and where it is difficult to help one without making an enemy of the other."

A few days later, however, President Eisenhower told in private to *New York Times* columnist C.L. Sulzberger: "Pakistan wants to help the cause of the United States and the Western powers, but India and Afghanistan were objecting. Although the Afghans were concerned that the Russians might use US military aid to Pakistan as an excuse to move against them, Nehru and his tribe were just being a nuisance."

After Foreign Secretary Anthony Eden voiced London's doubts when he and Dulles met in Bermuda on December 7, 1953, the Secretary confirmed that the United States definitely wished to help Pakistan but said that Washington had not yet decided what arms it would give. Expressing annoyance at Nehru's reactions, Dulles commented that India did not have "the right not only to remain neutral herself but to prevent other countries from lining up with the West."

## Dim Prospect of Settlement

Dulles agreed with the recommendation from Byroade and John Hickerson to seek Eisenhower's approval for a fresh effort toward a settlement outside the UN framework. The plan was to send a high-level emissary, Paul Hoffman, the President of the Ford Foundation and the former administrator of the Marshall Plan quietly to south Asia to urge the two countries to start bilateral talks. Moreover, Dulles agreed that solving the dispute through a division or partition of Kashmir seemed a more promising approach than continuing to urge a plebiscite. Dividing the State "is the only solution that seems to have practical possibilities the Secretary's March 24, 1953, memorandum to the President stated. In approving the Hoffman mission Eisenhower expressed his personal concern about Kashmir. He wrote to Dulles: "Our world simply cannot afford an outbreak of hostilities between these two countries.... I would risk a great deal to prevent such an eventuality."

When Hoffman traveled to South Asia in April 1953, he had positive meetings with Nehru and Bogra, who both accepted the idea of India-Pakistan bilateral talks on Kashmir.

After returning to the United States Hoffman wrote to Dulles that the two Prime Ministers were going to persist in bilateral negotiations until they reached a settlement.

A month later, Dulles raised the Kashmir issue in New Delhi during his May 1953 trip to the region. Nehru readily agreed with Dulles that partition might be a better way to solve the problem than a plebiscite. Nehru suggested that the ceasefire line, with minor modifications, would provide a reasonable basis for dividing the State.

In Karachi, when Dulles took up the Kashmir question, he encountered strong opposition to the idea of dropping the plebiscite and partitioning the State as a way to settle the dispute. "We have no right to make a settlement not acceptable to the Kashmiri people. Bogra asserted recalling the troubled plebiscites in Europe after World War I. Dulles countered, "Reliance on the will of the people is a noble principle but...it is sometimes difficult to carry out in an atmosphere of mistrust with opportunities to whip up violent emotions on both sides. Foreign Minister Zafrullah Khan, who also opposed abandoning the plebiscite offered no alternative ideas, but predicted that until Kashmir was settled, there would be no peace in this part of the world.

Bogra proceeded to Delhi for a second round of talks. Surprisingly, he and Nehru agreed to name a new Kashmir plebiscite administrator by April 1954—a step the Indians had previously resisted.

Progress was short-lived, however, India refused to have an American succeed Adm. Chester Nimitz as plebiscite administrator, something the Pakistan wanted. Nehru was also angered when Pakistan was the only member of the British Commonwealth to oppose Indian participation in the UN political conference on Korea. New Delhi was further upset when the Pakistan press, contrary to the agreement reached during the Bogra-Nehru talks resumed strident attacks on India. The final derailment came with the US decision to provide arms to Pakistan after Nehru warned that this step would affect the Kashmir issue. Bogra countered that Pakistan's enhanced military strength would improve not set back the prospects for a settlement. But the Indian Prime Minister was as good as his word. Following the announcement of the arms accord the Indian position on Kashmir hardened. The bilateral talks collapsed. New Delhi soon ruled out a plebiscite asserting that the election of a constituent assembly in Kashmir in 1953 had served this purpose and further balloting was unnecessary.

## Eisenhower Visits Pakistan

Despite increasing frictions both Washington and Karachi maintained the public posture that the two countries were warm friends and sturdy allies. This was underscored in December 1959 when Dwight Eisenhower became the first US President to visit Pakistan.

The first visit to Pakistan by a serving US President, especially one as popular as Eisenhower was a major event.

In wide-ranging talks, General Ayub painted a gloomy picture of the region's security. He expressed that the change in Soviet strategy was in the offing and urged America not to lower its guard. The Soviets were trying to penetrate Afghanistan and the Chinese were building air bases near the region. In time, Ayub feared Afghanistan would pose a grave threat to us all and India might collapse. To meet this danger the Pakistani leader stressed the view that India and his country needed to cooperate. It would be fatal, he declared if India and Pakistan should remain enemies. They have a common interest in the defence of the subcontinent. Above all, Ayub emphasized this required settlement of the Kashmir dispute. A plebiscite was fine, according to him but if that is not possible he was willing to consider any alternative that ensured Pakistan, India and the people of Kashmir "a stake in the area."

The Pakistani President urged the United States to use its influence on India to find a Kashmir solution. Massive US economic aid to India, Ayub argued would be "disastrous for Pakistan in the absence of a settlement. Economic aid simply permitted India to divert other funds for arms." "Nehru still wants Pakistan to remain weak while India builds its strength." Ayub claimed. Eisenhower responded that he would talk about these matters in New Delhi but did not intend to negotiate on Kashmir. Although he could urge Nehru to get together with Pakistan to try to work out the Problem. Eisenhower said that he "saw great value in finding some way of a solution."

The high point of the South Asia Trip came during Eisenhower's stay in India, where he received a tumultuous welcome and had extensive talks with Prime Minister Nehru. During these, Nehru suggested that if Ayub agreed to a "no-war" declaration he would be less concerned about US arms aid to Pakistan. Eisenhower promptly instructed Rountree to put the proposal to Ayub stressing the great opportunity this could give [Ayub] for the modernization of his Army. As Rountree anticipated—since Nehru had proposed the no-war pledge in the past—Ayub rejected the suggestion. The Pakistani leader, according to Rountree's cabled report, stated "the effect... would be for the Pakistan public to assume that Pakistan had handed Kashmir to India on a silver platter unless the no-war pact included a mechanism to address the dispute."

Eisenhower's trip to South Asia proved a great public relations success. Even if the President was unable to get India and Pakistan together on the no-war pact the visit simultaneously strengthened US relations with the two antagonists, no mean achievement.

In early December 1953, Vice-President Richard Nixon visited New Delhi and Karachi during a 17-nation Asia trip. The Vice-President left from the Indian capital with an even more negative view of Nehru than had Dulles. In his memoirs, Nixon described Nehru as "the least friendly leader that he had met in Asia." Like Dulles, the Vice-President gained a highly favourable impression of Pakistan. In Nixon's talks in Karachi, which focused on the arms issue, Ghulam Mohammed told him, "were the US not to grant aid now, especially in view of all the publicity, it would be like taking a poor girl for a walk and then walking out on her, leaving her only with a bad name." Ghulam Mohammed said: "if Washington gave arms to Pakistan the difficulties would blow over in three or four months."

After returning to Washington, Nixon spoke out forcefully on December 24, 1953, in briefing the NSC about his Asia trip: "Pakistan, is a country I would like to do everything for. The people have less complexes than the Indians.... It will be disastrous if the Pakistan aid does not go through. This may force out the Prime Minister of Pakistan but it isn't going to force the people toward Communism." Eisenhower thus gave his blessing to a policy decision that would shape US relations with India and Pakistan for the next three and a half decades.

Dana Adams Schmidt wrote in the February 14, 1954 article in *New York Times* that "the importance of bringing in Pakistan on the defence of the Middle East is greater than the importance of preserving pleasant relations with Mr. Nehru."

In late January 1953, Dulles informed Eden when they met in Berlin that India's attitude had made it impossible for the United States to back down. If the Indians had used the diplomatic channel for their representations and made less noise, the reconsideration would have been possible. Now that they had held public meetings, etc. the United States could not give way on military aid to Pakistan.

On February 22, 1954, Karachi made formal request for US military help without specifying the nature or amount of assistance. Two days later, Eisenhower responded positively and George Allen, the US Ambassador to India, delivered a letter of explanation to Nehru. On February 25, 1954, the administration released the text of this letter and an accompanying policy statement. In this Eisenhower pledged that if our aid to any country, including Pakistan is misused and directed against another in aggression, I will undertake immediately, in accordance with my constitutional authority, appropriate action both within and without the United Nations to thwart such aggression. Neither the letter nor the policy statement, however, calmed India's furious response to the US decision to arm Pakistan.

In Karachi, Prime Minister Bogra welcomed the decision, declaring "Pakistan today enters what promises to be a glorious chapter in its history...United States military aid will enable Pakistan to achieve adequate defensive strength without the country having to assume an otherwise increasing burden on its economy." The Prime Minister went on to pledge that the aid would not be used in "any act of aggression against any nation" and to deny that Pakistan had either offered or the United States requested any bases or other military facilities.

Ayub and others in the ruling group regarded the US action as a tremendous boost for Pakistan's security.

At the March 1956 SEATO meeting, East Pakistani politician Hamidul Haq Choudhury, who had become Foreign Minister after Zafrullah Khan was elected a Judge on the International Court of Justice, pressed hard for greater US support on Kashmir. Dulles tread warily offering only continued backing for the implementation of the 1948 Security Council resolution.

In July 1957, Suhrawardy embarked on an extensive foreign trip, including a three-week official visit to the United States. During a stopover in London before going on to America, he met privately with Nehru and British Prime Minister Harold Macmillan. Suhrawardy and Nehru agreed, when Macmillan pressed them for a practical way to deal with the Kashmir problem that the only feasible answer lay in direct negotiations and some form of partition. But both Nehru and Suhrawardy said that they could not state this publicly for domestic political reasons.

In May 1961, Vice-President Lyndon Johnson stopped in Karachi during a goodwill trip through Asia.

In Johnson's talks with Ayub and even in the public welcome, bilateral policy differences were evident. Pakistan's President argued forcefully that the large US economic aid programme and India's troubles with China gave the Americans leverage to force Nehru to the bargaining table on Kashmir. Johnson responded that Pakistan's President attributed to us a capacity to influence Nehru. At a public reception Karachi Municipal Corporation Chairman H.M Habibullah, who spoke in Urdu gave vent to mounting Pakistani unhappiness by caustically criticizing US policy on Kashmir and India. More in keeping with the diplomatic pablum the Vice-President ignored these barbs to voice pride that the commitments of our alliances will be fully honoured on both sides.

In July 1961, Ayub paid his first official visit to the United States as President of Pakistan.

In extensive private discussions, Ayub hammered away at the threat his country faced from India. Although Kennedy agreed to support Pakistan on Kashmir at the United Nations if upcoming talks with Nehru failed to advance prospects of a settlement, he refused to use economic assistance to India as a lever on Kashmir. America did not give aid, Kennedy said in the expectation of getting "Nehru's support on the times that were vital to the United States but because it was in everyone's interest that India did not collapse."

## Major Changes in Pakistan

The year 1962 saw major institutional changes in Pakistan. On March 1, Ayub lifted martial law and promulgated a new constitution, which he described as "a blending of democracy with discipline." The basic law gave the President strong executive powers and established a weak national legislature.

Ayub Khan declared that the differences between India and Pakistan over Kashmir should be resolved so that India can be free from anxiety from us and vice versa. When Averell Harriman and Duncan Sandys visited New Delhi and talked with Nehru and Defence Minister Yeshwantrao Chavan to assess India's defence requirement, they were able to persuade Nehru to agree to hold talks with Pakistan for settling the Kashmir dispute.

A week after the arrival of Harriman and Sandys, it was announced that Nehru and Ayub Khan would meet to resolve their differences. There was, however, no enthusiasm for negotiations either in India or Pakistan. *Dawn*, the Pakistani newspaper, said "Negotiations are merely a trap which has been laid for Pakistan by Mr. Sandys and Harriman." And yet between 27 December 1962 and 16 May 1963 the two countries held six meetings.

## Kennedy-MacMillan Meeting

On 20 December 1962, Kennedy and British Prime Minister Harold Macmillan discussed South-Asia during their meeting in Bermuda. Macmillan told Kennedy: "We support the people who are troublesome, such as Nehru and Krishna Menon, and abandon the people who support us. It will be dangerous, if we let Ayub feel we are abandoning him."

Kennedy intervened and said: "What would be so disastrous, if the Pakistan left CENTO? What do we get from Pakistan? In return for the protection of our alliance and our assistance, what do they do for us?"

After the US-UK talks, Kennedy once again wrote to Ayub describing the Indian military aid package as reasonable but frugal. He further wrote: "Although the aid was not made contingent on Kashmir, it would be a factor in determining the extent and pace on future assistance."

On 26 December 1962, a day before the talks were slated to begin, Pakistan announced that it had reached a border agreement with China.

Despite the uproar caused by Pakistan-China agreement, the Kashmir talks began on schedule, which were attended by Pakistan's Foreign Minister Zulfikar Ali Bhutto and India's Railway Minister Sardar Swaran Singh. During the initial round in Rawalpindi, both sides reiterated their traditional position.

During the second round of talks in New Delhi on 16-19 January 1963, the two delegates seriously discussed the basis for drawing an international boundary through Kashmir. As guiding principle, Pakistan recommended the character of the population, security considerations, and the control of river waterheads. Indians objected to the first point, which they feared would lead to a resurgence of Hindu-Muslim communal trouble. In the end, two sides were able to agree on a confidential joint statement of principles calling for an international boundary line through the State of Jammu and Kashmir. They could not, however, agree how the line should be drawn.

To keep the pressure on, Washington sent Assistant Secretary of State Talbot, who met Ayub on 1 February 1963. When they talked, Talbot found that Pakistan's position had stiffened against partition of Kashmir. Ayub told Talbot: "Division of Valley would be crime against the inhabitants." Talbot also met with Bhutto, who said that the partition of the valley was suicidal and declared that it would be preferable to wait for the future rather than accept a settlement with dishonour.

Despite the rebuff, American and British diplomats advised the Indians and Pakistanis that dividing the Valley seemed to be the best way to resolve the dispute. Nehru reacted sourly: "It would surely be bad to divide such a small and economically and culturally homogeneous area." Bhutto remained equally negative, but indicated that Pakistan could accept the division of Kashmir to the north and south but not the partition of the Valley.

When the two sides met for the third round in Karachi on 8-10 February 1963, Indians put modest territorial concessions to adjust the ceasefire line. Pakistan's counter proposal was to allot India only a sliver of territory in Jammu, which had Hindu population in majority and to claim entire Valley and also ladakh and the northern-eastern part of Kashmir. Although Bhutto later indicated that the offer was only an opening gambit, it took US and UK intervention to get the embittered Indians to agree to a fourth round of talks at Calcutta in March 1963.

The announcement that Bhutto would be flying to Beijing to sign border agreement further angered the Indians and upset the Americans.

The secretary Dean Rusk warned: "If the negotiations were to fail because of Pakistan, the sympathy that Pakistan has enjoyed from other governments on Kashmir in the United Nations and elsewhere would be dissipated."

On the eve of fourth round McConaughy delivered yet another presidential letter to Ayub. In this letter, Kennedy urged that Pakistan put forward a far more forthcoming and realistic proposal. The President also said: "If the opportunity to solve Kashmir dispute were lost, it would seem almost inevitable that the issue would be, for all practical purposes, be settled on the basis of the status quo."

In talking with McConaughy, Ayub agreed that Pakistan's proposal was unrealistic. He even termed it 'Damn nonsense.' But the Calcutta round of talks on 12-14 March 1963 made no progress.

When President Kennedy reviewed the talks on 1 April 1963, he expressed pessimism that they could be salvaged. He nonetheless approved the release of a US-UK paper outlining elements of settlement as below.

Ensuring access through the Vale for defence to the north and east (i.e. India's defence of Ladakh).

Ensuring Pakistan's interest in the headwaters of the Chenab River.

Ensuring some local self-rule in the Vale and free movement of people to India and Pakistan.

Enhancing economic development efforts.

Events soon showed that Kennedy's pessimism was warranted. Ambassador Galbraith had conversation with Nehru on 15 April 1963 on the future of Valley about which he says:

"Once or twice Nehru got very angry, shouted and pounded the table, but in the end calmed down." Galbraith raised Kashmir issue again with Nehru on 20 April 1963. Galbraith notes: "Nehru took a hard line against partitioning the Valley and stressed the desire to keep the talk going, but did not suggest any improvement in the Indian brief."

In a sharp letter to Kennedy, Nehru wrote on 21 April 1963: "I am convinced that these ill-considered not ill-conceived initiatives, however, well-intentioned they may be have at least for the present made it impossible to reach any settlement on this rather involved and complicated questions."

Galbraith cabled that India's Prime Minister would have found some other escape route, if the elements paper had not surfaced. "Nehru," the Ambassador commented, "is unquestionably agree, in part at my pressure, much more at the fact that I have translated his vague talk of wanting a settlement into firm concessions, he does not want to make."

The talks remained deadlocked during the fifth round in Karachi. The only thing on which the two sides could agree was to oppose the US-UK idea of partitioning the Valley.

Having concluded that the chances for a Kashmir settlement were almost nil, Kennedy instructed Dean Rusk to tell Ayub that the US was going ahead with arms aid to India and would not tie this to progress in the Kashmir talk.

The sixth and final round of talks took place in New Delhi on 15-16 May 1963. The Indians rejected a Pakistani proposal to internationalize the Valley for six months followed by a plebiscite and, in turn, suggested that the two countries agree not to use force to change the status quo in Kashmir. The Pakistan rejected this proposal while stressing that they too believed in a peaceful settlement.

The talks failed principally over differences on alignment of the Kashmir valley. India and Pakistan drifted farther and in mid-1963, they mutually expelled diplomats.

In December 1963, the tension between the two countries was heightened when riots broke out in Srinagar over reports that the Hair of the prophet kept in Hazratbal mosque in

Srinagar was stolen. The relic was found a week later. India believed that Pakistani agents instigated the theft and subsequent riots in Kashmir.

In the Hazratbal Mosque in the Valley of Kashmir lay a sacred relic of Islam, a hair of the Prophet Mohammad, greatly cherished and worshipped by the followers of the Faith. One morning, on December 26 to be exact, the Maulvis and the Mullahs in-charge of the mosque discovered to their chagrin that the sacred relic was missing from its casket. That nearly flung a lighted match into the powder-keg. The Valley was agog with wild rumours about a conspiracy hatched to commit the theft of the sacred relic, which whipped up the Muslim masses to frenzy and passion.

The many disgruntled factions in the politics of the Valley lost no time in exploiting the crisis to their own ends. These included the pro-Abdullah elements and the pro-Pakistani Plebiscite Front and Mirwaiz Farouq groups as well as the anti-Bakshi section. This motley crowd had joined together to form an Action Committee whose triple mission appeared to be (1) to embarrass and topple the Bakshi regime headed by his nominee Shamsuddin; (2) to mount an agitation for the release of Sheikh Abdullah from detention; and (3) to press for a plebiscite in the State on the issue of accession, as demanded by Pakistan.

Right from the outset, the Union Home Ministry took direct charge of the crisis developing in the Valley. CBI officials were sent to Srinagar, and the Home Secretary, Mr. V. Vishwanathan, personally directed the investigations on the spot.

Prompt action by the Centre had produced results. Within eight days of its loss, on January 4, the sacred relic had been restored and identified as genuine by the Maulvis. The Home Secretary declared that almost all the witnesses in a position to testify to its genuineness had identified the sacred hair. Further, Mr. Vishwanathan told a press conference that the relic had been surreptitiously placed back in the mosque by the culprits following hot pursuit by CBI men, and he promised a trial of the culprits as soon as the investigations were completed.

Even though the Prophet's hair had been identified by the Maulvis and Pirs, the Action Committee insisted that the relic be identified by persons nominated by the Action Committee at a public identification ceremony. Mr. Vishwanathan turned down the demand. The State Government was equally against conceding the demand lest it led to further complications.

The authorities' reluctance to accept the demand, however, gave a handle to agitators questioning the genuineness of the relic who now charged the authorities with deceiving the people.

Such was the situation that Lal Bahadur, who was then Minister without portfolio was called upon to tackle. Before leaving New Delhi, the Minister without portfolio had studied the problem confronting him in Kashmir in every aspect of it. He had had a long discussion with Nehru and secured a carte blanche from the Prime Minister for any drastic measures he might choose to take in order to clean up the Augean Stables in the Valley. Thus, Lal Bahadur landed in Srinagar on January 30 with a clear mind as to what he wanted to do there.

Lal Bahadur held a series of parleys with individual leaders as well as groups. He also held direct talks with representatives of the Action Committee. His approach was that if the authorities were honest and sincere in their efforts and took decisions genuinely in the interests of the people, they would be supported by the people.

The opposition elements were, however, still bent on mischief. The agitation that was launched over the missing sacred hair was sought to be converted into an incendiary, subversive movement.

But Lal Bahadur's tactics verily non-plussed them. Lal Bahadur readily suggested a compromise that met the opposition's demand half-way, thereby over-ruling the Home Secretary's earlier decision. He agreed to a public exposition of the sacred relic and fixed February 3 as the date for it. He further announced that representatives of the Action Committee would be included in the identification committee comprising prominent Mullahs and Maulvis.

Seventeen esteemed men, Maulvis and Pirs, including representatives of the Action Committee, met ceremonially on the appointed day and held an hour-long official identification session, at the end of which they unanimously reaffirmed the genuineness of the relic. This verdict fully satisfied all sections of the people and nailed the controversy once and for all. And Lal Bahadur's political instinct proved right and the civilian Vishwanathan's fears entirely misplaced. Indeed, this act of trust on the part of Lal Bahadur changed the opposition's heart.

His tactful handling of a most ticklish situation won him fresh kudos. The opposition leaders in Kashmir were among the first to congratulate him and to appreciate his gesture in reposing confidence in them over the controversial issue.

In New Delhi, the executive of the Congress Parliamentary Party passed a resolution recording its appreciation of the highly competent manner in which Lal Bahadur had handled the delicate situation in Kashmir (*Lal Bahadur Shastri*: D.R. Mankekar, Publication Division Government of India, pp. 144-46).

### Pakistani Incursions

Pakistan was quietly going ahead with its secret plan to seize Kashmir. The Pakistani incursion into the Rann of Katch provoked the emotions of the Indian people.

C.P. Srivastava, Lal Bahadur Shastri's, Personal Secretary writes in his book, *Lal Bahadur Shastri: A Life of Truth in Politics* that by 5 August 1965, things had taken interesting turn when a shephered boy informed the Indian authorities in Kashmir that some inflitrators from Pakistan had come in. On 8 August, Shastri had a fulfledged discussion in his cabinet and began to monitor the situation on a personal basis and was in constant touch with Army Chief General Choudhury. Within three days Shastri became confident of handling the situation.

### Indo-Pak War

It became evident that Ayub Khan was planning a full-scale war against India. The operation commenced on 5 August 1965. By 13 August Shastri made up his mind to meet force with force. On 30 August 1965, Indian forces threw out Pakistan army unit in the Uri-Poonch sector and consolidated its position in this sector.

In the early hours of 1 September, Pakistani invaded Bhimber-Chhamb area in Kashmir with the objective of capturing Akhnoor. On 3 September, Shastri gave orders to the Indian military forces for a counter attack.

By 6 September, a full-scale war between India and Pakistan had begun, although UN Secretary General U Thant urged both countries to halt hostilities.

Ambassador Bowels had a meeting with Shastri and tried to persuade him against war. Bowels reported to the White House: "At least it is clear that we are not dealing with a mad man, who is about to fly off on an emotional tangent, although it does not mean that Shastri will necessarily come up with a wise decision, it does mean that he is unlikely to act in blind anger."

Shastri made three important conditions to Bowels, the same as he did to U Thant.

1. The report by General Robert Nimmo of the UN of his on the spot assessment must be made public.
2. Following publication of the report, Pakistan must agree to withdraw remaining infiltrators who had crossed the borders from 5 August.
3. In order to prevent a repeat performance, the UN observers team should be greatly expanded to give them effective coverage of the whole area.

Shastri also made it clear to Bowels that the US and other powers should not think that this was the time to resolve Kashmir problem (*India and the US*: Kalyani Shankar, Macmillan India Ltd., pp. 41-42).

U Thant visited India and Pakistan in September 1965. He sent messages to both Shastri and Ayub Khan asking them to order ceasefire without condition before 14 September 1965. Shastri sent a reply reiterating most of India's position and agreeing to ceasefire. However, Ayub Khan rejected ceasefire unless certain conditions were accepted. Later on 22 September, Ayub Khan reluctantly agreed for ceasefire.

After the end of Indo-Pak war on 20 October 1965, a Department of Intelligence Agency (DIA) report said that Shastri was emerging slowly from Nehru's shadow and becoming an effective leader in his own right. That beset by constant internal crisis and undeclared war with Pakistan over the Rann of Katch and Kashmir, he now appeared to be in a much stronger position than when he took over. His personality and style of leadership, nevertheless, identify him as an agile and resourceful compromiser rather than a dynamic leader in the Nehru mould.

## Tashkent Declaration

Indo-Pak war and Shastri's handling of it boosted his image within Congress Party and within country, while it proved to be disaster for Ayub Khan. The Soviets came to the rescue to tie-up the loose ends and broken peace between India and Pakistan. Soviet Premier Kosygin offered to mediate.

Ayub Khan rejected the idea initially when it was put to him, but by November he changed his mind and accepted it. The US sat back and allowed the Soviets to handle a patch up between India and Pakistan.

Giving reasons about why the Americans let the Soviets take a lead on Tashkent summit, Dean Rusk clarifies in his *Oral History*:

"We encouraged the Russians to go ahead with the Tashkent idea because we had nothing to loose. If they had succeeded in bringing about any détente at Tashkent, then there would be more peace on the subcontinent between India and Pakistan. If the Russians failed at Tashkent, at least the Russians would have the experience of some of the frustration we had had for many years in trying to sort out things between India and Pakistan. As a matter of fact I once in a semi-joking way told the Russian Ambassador that if he wanted them we would be glad to give him all our old memoranda on efforts that we have made over the past 20 years to try to solve things between India and Pakistan as a part of their preparation for Tashkent, but that did not become necessary.

Kosygin wrote a letter to Shastri on 4 September 1965 in which he said:

"We should not be frank if we did not say that the military conflict in Kashmir arouses the concern of the Soviet Government also because it has occurred in an area directly adjacent to the borders of the Soviet Union.

"I think you will agree that in the present serious situation it is hardly appropriate to place the question of the causes of the origin of the conflict in the forefront or to seek to determine who is right and who is to blame. The principal efforts should be concentrated upon the immediate cessation of military operations, the halting of the tanks and the silencing of the guns.

"In our opinion, the first step after the immediate cessation of hostilities could be the withdrawal of troops to positions behind the Ceasefire Line established by agreement between India and Pakistan in July 1949."

Shastri, in his statement in Parliament on 23 September 1965 said:

> I should like to inform the House that on 18th September 1965, I received a message from Mr. Kosygin, Chairman of the Council of Ministers of the USSR, offering his good offices for bringing about improved relations between India and Pakistan. No one can ever contest the view that ultimately India and Pakistan will have to live together as peaceful neighbours. We cannot, therefore, say no to any efforts which may help to bring about such a situation, made by those who are sincere and genuine in their feelings of good will and friendship. I have, therefore, informed Mr. Kosygin today that we would welcome his efforts and good offices.

During the two weeks prior to his departure for Tashkent, Shastri made a number of public speeches in which he spelt out his likely approach. He emphasized again and again that peace was of crucial importance for the economic development of India. Speaking at Allahabad on 18 December, Shastri said that if the Tashkent talks between him and Ayub failed, the whole country would have to remain prepared to meet any eventuality. If the talks succeeded, he said, he would be the happiest man in the world.

Significantly, the All-India Jamiat-Ulema whose general council met in New Delhi on 19 December, declared that Kashmir was an integral part of India and said:

> If any external power attacks Kashmir or interferes in its internal affairs, the all-India Jamiat-Ulema would regard it as a national duty to defend it. The general council, presided over by Maulana Fakhruddin Ahmad, congratulated Lal Bahadur Shashtri and his colleagues for the foresight, courage and determination displayed by them in the war against Pakistan.

Soviet leader Kosygin invited Shastri and Ayub Khan to Tashkent in January 1966 for summit.

Shastri and Ayub Khan reached Tashkent on 3 January 1966. Kosygin had arrived three days in advance to personally supervise the arrangements.

The USSR attached the greatest importance to securing peace between India and Pakistan by the implementation of Security Council resolution 211 of 20 September 1965 and resolution 214 of 27 September 1965.

India wanted to ensure that peace should be agreed to on terms which would provide firm assurance that there would be no repetition of aggression, open or disguised, against India. To this end India wanted a 'no-war' pact with Pakistan.

Pakistan wanted a substantive discussion on the question of Kashmir in order to secure India's agreement to the establishment of a 'self-executing machinery' for any further progress on this matter. Ayub reiterated this in a broadcast on 1 January 1966. He wanted Kosygin to 'influence and persuade Mr. Shastri to see that light of reason' and to cut the 'Gordian Knot of the problem of Jammu and Kashmir.'

Kosygin decided wisely to be an active but cautious participant in the deliberations from the very beginning. To prevent the development of an impasse, he took up the role of an intermediary. To prepare the ground for the later 'summit meeting', he met Shastri and Ayub separately in the evening of 3 January, a few hours after they reached Tashkent (*Lal*

*Bahadur Shastri—A Life of Truth in Politics:* C.P. Srivastav, Oxford University Press, pp. 330-33, 350-51).

Kosygin held separate talks with Shastri and Ayub Khan several times to find a meeting point. With talks going no where there was not much to expect. However, there was a break through with the efforts of Kosygin and the two leaders signed Tashkent declaration on 10 January 1966. The text of Tashkent Declaration is given below:

***Tashkent Declaration***

The Prime Minister of India and the President of Pakistan, having met at Tashkent and having discussed the existing relations between India and Pakistan hereby declare their firm resolve to restore normal and peaceful relations between their countries and to promote understanding and friendly relations between their peoples. They consider the attainment of these objectives of vital importance for the welfare of the 600 million people of India and Pakistan.

(i) The Prime Minister of India and the President of Pakistan agree that both sides will exert all efforts to create good neighbourly relations between India and Pakistan in accordance with the United Nations Charter. They reaffirm their obligation under Charter not to have recourse to force and to settle their disputes through peaceful means. They considered that the interests of peace in their region and particularly in the Indo-Pakistan subcontinent and indeed, the interests of the peoples of India and Pakistan were not served by the continuance of tension between the two countries. It was against this background that Jammu & Kashmir was discussed, and each of the sides set forth its respective position.

(ii) The Prime Minister of India and the President of Pakistan have agreed that all armed personnel of the two countries shall be withdrawn not later than 25 February 1966 to the positions they held prior to 5 August 1965, and both sides shall observe the cease-fire terms on the cease-fire line.

(iii) The Prime Minister of India and the President of Pakistan have agreed that relations between India and Pakistan shall be based on the principle of non-interference in the internal affairs of each other.

(iv) The Prime Minister of India and the President of Pakistan have agreed that both sides will discourage any propaganda directed against the other country and will encourage propaganda which promotes the development of friendly relations between the two countries.

(v) The Prime Minister of India and the President of Pakistan have agreed that the High Commissioner of India to Pakistan and the High Commissioner of Pakistan to India will return to their posts and that the normal functioning of diplomatic missions of both countries will be restored. Both governments shall observe the Vienna Convention of 1961 on Diplomatic Intercourse.

(vi) The Prime Minister of India and the President of Pakistan have agreed to consider measures towards the restoration of economic and trade relations, communications as well as cultural exchanges between India and Pakistan, and to take measures to implement the existing agreements between India and Pakistan.

(vii) The Prime Minister of India and the President of Pakistan have agreed that they will give instructions to their respective authorities to carry out the repatriation of the prisoners of war.

(viii) The Prime Minister of India and the President of Pakistan have agreed that the two sides will continue the discussions of questions relating to the problems of refugees and evictions—illegal immigrations. They also agreed that both sides will create conditions which will prevent the exodus of people. They further agree to discuss the return of the property and assets taken over by either side in connection with the conflict.

(ix) The Prime Minister of India and the President of Pakistan have agreed that the two sides will continue meetings both at highest and at other levels of matters of direct concern to both countries. Both sides have recognized the need to set up joint Indian-Pakistani bodies which will report to their governments in order to decide what further steps should be taken.

The Prime Minister of India and the President of Pakistan record their feelings, deep appreciation and gratitude to the leaders of the Soviet Union, the Soviet Government and personally to the Chairman of the Council of Ministers of the USSR for their constructive, friendly and noble part in bringing about the present meeting which has resulted in mutually satisfactory results. They also express to the government and friendly people of Uzbekistan their sincere thankfulness for their overwhelming reception and generous hospitality.

They invite the Chairman of the Council of Ministers of the USSR to witness this declaration.

It may be recollected that the Jana Sangh had opposed the Tashkent talks. A delegation of Jan Sangh led by Atal Bihari Vajpayee, called on Shastri and urged him not to go for the summit meeting. They were apprehensive that international pressure might force the Indian side to return Haji Pir and Tithwa, the two important posts captured by the Indian Army in Pakistan-occupied Kashmir (POK).

A few weeks before Shastri was scheduled to leave for Tashkent, Lal Krishna Advani met Shastri in his office to interview him for *Organizer*. Advani expressed the widespread fear that India might be pressured into relinquishing Haji Pir and Tithwa posts to Pakistan. The Prime Minister's response was categorical. "Rest assured," he said, "that will not happen."

Sadly, this is exactly what happened when Shastri signed the Tashkent Declaration on 10 January 1966 along with General Ayub Khan. Indians expected him to talk to Pakistan from a position of strength because India's military had already demonstrated its superiority on the battlefield. He had resisted, till the very end, any compromise deal. At one point, when

Kosygin said to him, "You will have to give up Haji Pir and Tithwa," Shastri had even retorted, "In that case, you will have to talk to some other Prime Minister."

Mysteriously, at the end of the prolonged negotiations, Shastri agreed to withdraw Indian forces from these two posts in return for a vague Pakistani assurance not to resort to arms to settle bilateral issues. The outcome of the summit was not to his liking, and he probably carried a heavy burden of guilt on his conscience. He died of a massive heart attack in Tashkent on 11 January 1966 and his body was brought back from Tashkent for the Indian public to pay homage.

As the poet Kabir has said:
*Das Kabir jatan se odhi,*
*Jyon ki tyon dhar deeni chadariya.*

In essence this means: "I have laid down my life as pure as I found it at my birth."

One of the foreigners to witness this poignant and historic finale to Shastri's life was Warren Unna of *The Washington Post.* In his dispatch from New Delhi which was published in *The Washington Post* on 13 January 1966, Unna said: "Mankind historically has reserved its greatest occasions for the final journeys of its leaders—and India today made such an occasion."

Of all great men it is Shastri who springs Confucius's definition of the perfect gentleman. "There are nine things," said Confucius, "the gentleman turns his thought to: to seeing clearly when he uses his eyes, to hearing acutely when he uses his ears, to looking cordial when it comes to his countenance, to appearing respectful when it comes to his demeanour, to being conscientious when he speaks, to being reverent when he performs his duties, to seeking advice when he is in doubt, to the consequences when he is enraged, and to what is right at the sight of gain."

When Shastri died, his life-sheet was spotlessly clean. He left no money, no house and no land. He did leave behind an example which will continue to inspire, fortify and encourage all those of every community and creed who believe that the only foundation for national life must be a dedication to truth and honesty. He never sought for himself any superlatives or fulsome praise.

Following is the joint statement on Tashkent Declaration issued by Shri Jayaprakash Narayan, Chairman A.B. Shanti Sena Mandal and Shri Manmohan Chaudhuri, President, Sarva Seva Sangh, on 28 January 1966, from Varanasi.

## Tashkent Day

The two nations of India and Pakistan were born eighteen years ago in the midst of intense mutual bitterness and it was only the martyrdom of Mahatma Gandhi that was able to restore normalcy in their relationship. Subsequently, differences, misunderstandings and disputes went on gathering momentum and the climax was reached in the Indo-Pak clash a few months ago. This was a great misfortune not only for these two countries but also for the world at large. While these two countries had to plan for greater expenditures on war preparation diverting resources from developmental programmes essential for their millions of improverished masses, their mutual hostility was also a threat to world peace. But fortunately the leaders of the two countries had not lost mental equilibrium and there were neighbours deeply interested in bridging the gulf between them and willing to persevere for the cause. The result was the Tashkent declaration, which heralded the beginning of a new and hopeful chapter in the history of Indo-Pak relations.

Our great leader, the Late Lal Bahadur Shastri sealed the compact with his life and the general acclaim with which declaration was hailed by the peoples of the two countries shows that the latter were sick of hatred and strife and were longing for the fresh air of goodwill and peace. The peoples and public men of the world have also by and large welcomed it heartily. The future of the 600 million people of this subcontinent is the magnificent and inspiring thought that moved the leaders of the two countries to end their hostility and bitterness. Now it is the duty of all of us to give concrete shape to the aspirations enshrined in the declaration.

Both countries have common roots in the historical past and a common cultural heritage. The great rivers, the Himalayas and the ocean serve them both. Their economies were also interdependent.

If we continue to think and act in terms of "the 600 million", we will be able to discover a hundred ways of cooperation and joint effort in the interest of these millions. Thus, the two countries can jointly achieve the welfare of their masses and be a force for peace and progress in the world as well.

So, it is time we pledged ourselves to make a success of the new era presaged by the Tashkent declaration and to never allow hatred and strife to darken our lives again. For this we appeal to the people of India to observe February 11 next as Tashkent day. On that day let us assemble in public meetings and affirm our support for the Tashkent Declaration. Let us also express our firm determination to seek peaceful solutions to all disputes with our neighbour and to renounce the use of force for the same. On that day let us appreciate the role of the UNO in the present-day world as a forum of world public opinion and resolve to do all we can to strengthen it as an instrument of world peace.

We can also on that day solemnly resolve to give our support to whatever steps the governments take to improve relations between the two countries, to make serious effort to understand and appreciate the hopes and aspirations the problems and difficulties and the cultural and spiritual values of our neighbours, and express our readiness to extend our helping hand during natural calamities, etc.

The last message of the Late Shastriji was "we fought resolutely to save our country, now we will have to fight still more resolutely for the sake of peace." We must pledge ourselves on the 11th February to carry out this behest with all our strength.

Alas! we forgot to celebrate Tashkent Day.

Justice M.C. Chagla, who was then Foreign Minister of India, in his book *Roses in December* at pages 413 and 414 writes: "Pakistan had never implemented the Tashkent agreement. We, on the other hand, loyally abided by the decisions. We made it a point to celebrate what we called Tashkent day and we had unilaterally removed the trade barriers. But even before the ink on the agreement was dry, Pakistan had in effect, repudiated the pact. She had obtained all the advantages she could out of the agreement, but had refused to carry out her share of the responsibilities and duties.

"The moral of Tashkent is that it is difficult to arrive at any stable agreement with Pakistan in the hope that it would be observed fully and in good faith.

"We cannot afford to rely merely on promises given by Pakistan, which have the same effect as though written on sand. And unless the assurances are backed by proper guarantees, any future summit meeting would share the same fate."

Chagla in the same book at page 447 says: "Shastri signed the Tashkent Declaration with considerable misgivings; but he signed it because he felt that war between the two countries was an evil thing. He realized what human suffering it entailed, and he wanted to put an end to it even it meant some sacrifice on the part of India. He knew that when he went back home he would have to face an angry Parliament and resentful nation. When he responded to the call of peace, he did so without thinking of his own future."

On what India did in Tashkent, President Johnson remarked: "Shastri did the right way in the cause of peace not at the end of a gun barrel."

## Simla Agreement

In July 1972, Smt. Indira Gandhi and Zulfikar Ali Bhutto, who had by then become Pakistan's Prime Minister after the exit of General Yahya Khan met in Simla for a summit meeting. Jan Sangh again reminded the government not to yield ground at Simla. A resolution passed by the party's working committee in March 1972 said:

> Ever since the end of the 14 day war with Pakistan, pressure is being mounted to force India to repatriate Pak prisoners of War (POW) and to withdraw Indian

troops from Pakistan territory, irrespective of whether or not there is an overall peace settlement between India and Pakistan. The Communist Party of India's resolution calling for withdrawal of Indian troops to the 1948 cease-fire line can well be regarded as reflecting Moscow's mind.... Any piece-meal settlement of issues that suits Pakistan would be wrong, impolite and against the best interest of India. There should be no question of withdrawing Indian troops unless all pressing issues are thrashed out and a package deal has been arrived at in the interest of durable peace between India and Pakistan.

As party president Atal Bihari Vajpayee met Prime Minister Indira Gandhi at Simla and urged her not to agree to the release of POWs and withdrawal of Indian troops without securing permanent settlement with Pakistan on the Kashmir issue. And yet, Indira Gandhi and Bhutto met and signed an agreement which came to be known as Simla Agreement. The text of the Simla Agreement is reproduced below:

*Simla Agreement on Bilateral Relations between India and Pakistan signed by Prime Minister of India, Mrs. Indira Gandhi, and President of Pakistan, Mr. Z.A Bhutto, in Simla on July 3, 1972.*

The Government of India and the Government of Pakistan are resolved that the two countries put an end to the conflict confrontation that have hitherto marred their relations and work for the promotion of a friendly and harmonious relationship and the establishment of durable peace in the subcontinent, so that both countries may henceforth devote their resources and energies to the pressing task of advancing the welfare of their people.

In order to achieve this objective, the Government of India and the Government of Pakistan have agreed as follows:

(i) That the principles and purposes of the Charter of the United Nations shall govern the relations between the two countries.

(ii) That the two countries are resolved to settle their differences by peaceful means through bilateral negotiations or by any other peaceful means mutually agreed upon between them. Pending the final settlement of any of the problems between the two countries, neither side shall unilaterally alter the situation and both shall prevent the organization, assistance or encouragement of any acts detrimental to the maintenance of peaceful and harmonious relations.

(iii) That the prerequisite for reconciliation, good neighbourliness and durable peace between them is a commitment by both the countries to peaceful co-existence, respect for each other's territorial integrity and sovereignty and non-interference in each other's internal affairs, on the basis of equality and mutual benefit.

(iv) That the basic issues and causes of conflict which have bedeviled the relations between the two countries for the last 25 years shall be resolved by peaceful means.

(v) That they shall always respect each other's national unity, territorial integrity, political independence and sovereign equality.

(vi) That in accordance with the Charter of the United Nations, they will refrain from the threat or use of force against the territorial integrity or political independence of each other.

Both governments will take all steps within their power to prevent hostile propaganda directed against each other. Both countries will encourage the dissemination of such informations as would promote the development of friendly relations between them.

In order progressively to restore and normalize relations between the two countries step by step, it was agreed that:

(i) Steps shall be taken to resume communications, postal, telegraphic, sea, land including border posts and air links including over-flights.

(ii) Appropriate steps shall be taken to promote travel facilities for the nationals of the other country.

(iii) Trade and cooperation in economic and other agreed fields will be resumed as far as possible.

(iv) Exchange in the fields of science and culture will be promoted.

In this connection delegations from the two countries will meet from time to time to work out the necessary details.

In order to initiate the process of the establishment of durable peace, both the governments agree that:

(i) Indian and Pakistani forces shall be withdrawn to their side of the international border.

(ii) In Jammu and Kashmir, the line of control resulting from the case-fire of December 17, 1971 shall be respected by both sides without prejudice to the recognized position of either side. Neither side shall seek to alter it unilaterally, irrespective of mutual differences and legal interpretations. Both sides further undertake to refrain from the threat or the use of force in violation of this line.

(iii) The withdrawals shall commence upon entry into force of this agreement and shall be completed within a period of 30 days thereof.

This agreement will be subject to ratification by both countries in accordance with their respective constitutional procedures, and will come into force with effect from the date on which the instruments of ratification are exchanged.

Both governments agree that their respective heads will meet again at a mutually convenient time in the future and that in the meanwhile the representatives of the two sides will meet to discuss further the modalities and arrangements for the establishment of durable peace and normalization of relations, including the questions of repatriation of prisoners of war and civilian internees, a final settlement of Jammu and Kashmir and the resumption of diplomatic relations.

It would be noted that the Agreement, inter alia, contained the following:

> That the two countries are resolved to settle their differences by peaceful means through bilateral negotiations or by any other peaceful means mutually agreed upon between them.

In order to initiate the process of the establishment of durable peace, both the Governments agree that:

(i) Indian and Pakistani forces shall be withdrawn to their side of the international border.

(ii) In Jammu and Kashmir, the line of control resulting from the cease-fire of December 17, 1971, shall be respected by both sides without prejudice to the recognized position of either side."

Sadly, the Simla Agreement turned out to be another betrayal. Indira Gandhi agreed to send back all POWs, return the entire 9000 square kilometers territory under the possession of the Indian Army, and pardon all war criminals, whose trial was demanded by Bangladesh. In return, Pakistan's commitments under the agreement were minor and intangible, and it could violate them, as it indeed did, without incurring a heavy cost.

In his book; *Surrender at Dacca: Birth of a Nation*, General Jacob praises Indira Gandhi's role during the war, but bemoans that she was badly advised on the Simla Pact. He says: "We had won a decisive victory in the marshes and rice paddies of Bangladesh. The advantages gained on the battlefield were frittered away at the Simla Conference." Jacob mentions that Bhutto had agreed verbally to convert the line of control into permanent border between India and Pakistan. But the Indian side failed to get an official commitment from him on this important point.

L.K. Advani had said at a public meeting in New Delhi at the time: "Indira Gandhi wasted a golden opportunity for a mass berbiage" (*My Country, My Life*, Rupa & Co. pp. 171-72).

With Indira Gandhi at the peak of her power, Bhutto played a diplomatic hand with skill when the two met at Simla. After several days of tough bargaining, Pakistan agreed as India had long sought to settle all disputes peacefully and bilaterally, including Kashmir. According to what Indira Gandhi told the Indian delegation, Bhutto also expressed willingness to settle the Kashmir dispute on the basis of the status quo with the line of control becoming the border but added that he needed time to gain political acceptance for this. Bhutto said nothing about this to the Pakistani delegation.

The United States welcomed the Simla Agreement as an important step toward the establishment of a durable peace in South Asia. Following the agreement, the US stance on the Kashmir dispute shifted. Although previously the US had supported the 1948 and 1949 UN resolutions calling for a plebiscite, after Simla agreement, Washington indicated that any settlement that India and Pakistan worked out would be acceptable.

Simla Agreement was interpreted by India as having delinked the Kashmir dispute from the UN and transferred it into a bilateral matter between India and Pakistan. Pakistan never publicly accepted that assertion (*Pakistan in the Shadow of Jihad and Afghanistan:* Mary Ann Weaver, Farran, Strauss and Giron, New York, p. 252).

## Kashmir Accord

After the Bangladesh War and Pakistan's humiliating defeat with its about 90,000 troops surrendering to the Indian Army, and the execution of the Simla Agreement which made the Kashmir issue really a bilateral one, the attitude of the recalcitrant leaders of Kashmir like Sheikh Abdullah and Mirza Afzal Beg underwent a change. Their ardour for Pakistan or independent Kashmir diminished. They started making conciliatory speeches. Mrs. Indira Gandhi also thought it expedient to arrive at some settlement with Sheikh Abdullah. Negotiations started between G. Parthasarathi and Mirza Afzal Beg, an agreement, known as the Kashmir Accord, was signed on February 24, 1975. The text of the Kashmir Agreement is reproduced below:

*Agreed conclusions which led to Sheikh Mohammad Abdullah accord with Mrs. Indira Gandhi, Prime Minister, and his subsequent assumption of office as Chief Minister in February 1975.*

1. The State of Jammu and Kashmir which is a constituent unit of the Union of India, shall, in its relation with the Union, continue to be governed by Article 370 of the Constitution of India.
2. The residuary powers of legislation shall remain with the State; however, Parliament will continue to have powers to make laws relating to the prevention of activities directed towards disclaiming, questioning or disrupting the sovereignty and territory of India or secession of a part of the territory of India from the Union or causing insult to the Indian National flag, the Indian National Anthem and the Constitution.
3. Where any provision of the Constitution of India had been applied to the State of Jammu and Kashmir with adaptations and modifications, such adaptations and modifications can be altered or repealed by an order of the President under Article 370. Each individual proposal in this behalf being considered on its merits; but provisions of the Constitution of India already applied to the State of Jammu and Kashmir without adaptation or modification are unalterable.
4. With a view to assuring freedom to the State of Jammu and Kashmir to have its own legislation on matters like welfare measures, cultural matters, social security, personal law and procedural laws, in a manner suited to the special conditions in the State, it is agreed that the State Government can review the laws made by Parliament or extended to the State after 1953 on any matter relatable to the Concurrent List and may decide which of them, in its opinion, needs amendment or repeal. Thereafter, appropriate steps may be taken under Article 254 of the Constitution of India. The grant of President's assent to such legislation would be sympathetically considered. The same approach would be adopted in regard to laws to be made by Parliament in future under the proviso to clause 2 of the Article. The State Government shall be consulted regarding the application of any such law to the State

and the views of the State Government shall receive the fullest consideration.

5. As an arrangement reciprocal to what has been provided under Article 368, a suitable modification of that Article as applied to the State should be made by Presidential order to the effect that no law made by the Legislature of the State of Jammu and Kashmir, seeking to make any change in or in the effect of any provision of Constitution of the State of Jammu and Kashmir relating to any of the undermentioned matters, shall take effect unless the Bill, having been reserved for the consideration of the President, receives his assent; the matters are:
   (a) the appointment, powers, functions, duties, privileges, and immunities of the Governor, and
   (b) the following matters relating to elections namely, the superintendence, direction and control of elections by the Election Commission of India, eligibility for inclusion in the electoral rolls without discrimination, adult suffrage and composition of the Legislative Council, being matters specified in Sections 138, 139, 140, and 50 of the Constitution of the State of Jammu and Kashmir.
6. No agreement was possible on the question of nomenclature of the Governor and the Chief Minister and the matter is therefore remitted to the Principals.

In the spirit of the Kashmir Accord, Chief Minister Syed Mir Qasim, who had taken over after the death of G.M. Sadiq on 13 December 1971 and had played a significant role in bringing about the Accord, resigned. The Congress Legislative Party elected Sheikh Abdullah as its leader. He was sworn in as Chief Minister on February 25, 1975. Three other non-Congress ministers joined his Cabinet.

The understanding between the Congress and Sheikh Abdullah did not last long. It turned out to be a love-hate relationship. While on the one hand Sheikh Abdullah lauded

"Jawaharlal's vision and statesmanship, combined with Indiraji's courage and decisiveness", on the other, he turned down the suggestion that he should join the Congress Party. Instead, he revived the National Conference and became its president on April 13, 1975, thereby creating a piquant situation in which he held the office of the Chief Minister on the sole legislative support of one political party and at the same time functioned as president of another political party.

On July 5, 1975, Sheikh Abdullah dissolved the Plebiscite Front and merged it with the National Conference. On August 15, he openly welcomed ten Congress members, including Abdul Ghani Lone, who defected to the National Conference. This created a rumpus in the Congress Party. The differences were, however, resolved, and a coordination committee comprising two representatives of each party was set up on October 13. On October 21, Sheikh Abdullah announced expansion of his cabinet in which he inducted four Congressmen who were picked by him without consulting Mrs. Indira Gandhi. She retaliated by instructing the four Congressmen not to join the ministry. The swearing-in ceremony had to be cancelled.

Thus, within a period of less than eight months, wide cracks appeared in the edifice built on the foundation of the Indira-Abdullah Accord of February 1975.

The main provisions of the Kashmir Accord were that Article 370 would remain and the residuary powers would continue to vest in the State Government. It also stipulated that "where any provision of the Constitution of India had been applied to the State of Jammu and Kashmir with adaptations and modifications, such adaptations and modifications can be altered or repealed by the Order of the President under Article 370, each individual proposal in this behalf being considered on its merits; but provisions of the Constitution of India already applied to the State of J&K without adaptation or modification are unalterable."

In essence, the Kashmir Accord did not change the constitutional relationship between the Union and the State. It was primarily a device to bring Sheikh Abdullah back to power and also give an impression that certain aspects relating to autonomy could be reviewed. Mrs. Indira Gandhi brought out the essence of the Accord when she said in her statement to Parliament on February 24, 1975, "Nobody had denied Sheikh Abdullah the previous role. In between, he seemed to have changed his mind and there was disagreement and estrangement. Now that he is again expressing his willingness to work for unity, for secularism, we welcome him."

The Kashmir Accord was, undoubtedly, beneficial in some respects. As stated by Swaran Singh in Parliament in justification of the Accord. "The need for change was that there was an influential section of public opinion in J&K which still was not in the mainstream of Indian nationalism." In the international arena also, India's case could perhaps be better understood. This was evident from the unhappiness of Pakistan over the signing of the Accord. Z.A. Bhutto gave a call for *hartal* to protest against the Accord.

But the Accord did not tackle the fundamental problems. The emotional ingredients of Article 370 remained intact. The forces which had, in the first instance, created a situation that led to the events of August 1953, were not really vanquished. Nothing was done to ensure that the communal card and the card of Kashmir's identity were not played to strengthen the personal power and position of Sheikh Abdullah and his family. Nor was any remedial measure taken to stop the unhealthy fall-outs from the politics of deception and duplicity. Avenues that could set the clock back were not effectively plugged. And Sheikh Abdullah did put a number of items in the reverse gear. He soon became a 'mini Sultan' again. There was nothing wrong in burying the unsavory past. But putting the unpleasant dirt underneath the carpet did not help. It began to ooze out and soon a suffocating atmosphere was created.

Swaran Singh hailed the Kashmir Accord as "an accession of heart and mind and an act of faith" Sheikh Abdullah described it as re-establishment of trust and confidence. He said, "We have established a solid foundation for mutual cooperation." But it was soon discovered that the solid foundation was made of spurious and substandard material. Cracks started appearing.

By 1977, the superstructure collapsed. Another illusion stood shattered.

Mir Qasim in his book, *Dastan-e-Hayat,* primarily blamed Mrs. Gandhi for the failure of the Kashmir Accord. He thought that Mrs. Gandhi was always suspicious of Sheikh Abdullah and Mir Qasim, and the decision of the Congress(I) Legislature Party on March 26, 1977, to elect a new leader and withdraw support of Sheikh Abdullah was the last nail in the coffin of the Kashmir Accord. But Mir Qasim is only partly right. He does not adequately explain as to why it was necessary for Sheikh Abdullah to convert the Plebiscite Front into National Conference, why Mrs. Gandhi was not consulted in clear terms about the nominee of her party in the State Cabinet, why Sheikh Abdullah was keen to induct A.G. Lone in his ministry, the person who had earlier deserted the Congress Party, and why the Sheikh acted in an arbitrary manner and rewarded the Plebiscite Front workers and leaders with bonanzas, such as pensions for freedom fighters. The Accord was a failure not only because a section of the Congress(I) Party of J&K was hostile to it from the very beginning but also because the basic contradictions and incompatibilities were not resolved and the concept of autonomy was allowed, as in the past, to degenerate into licence under the umbrella of the 'democratic dictatorship' of Sheikh Abdullah.

## Reverse Gear

*The Resettlement Act.* After the Kashmir Accord of 1975, and particularly after the State Assembly elections of 1977, the process of integration of the State with the Union was put in the reverse gear. Further extensions of the provisions of the Indian Constitution and Central laws to the State virtually stopped, even when these were in public interest and highly beneficial to the common folk. The bogey of autonomy was raised from time to time. The pattern of All-India Services was subverted. And the protective wall of Article 370 was raised higher. But the most glaring manifestation of the reverse gear was the Jammu and Kashmir Grant of Permit for Resettlement Act, 1982 (*Frozen*

*Turbulence*: Jagmohan, Allied Publishers Ltd., pp. 105-06, 142-44).

## Bus Yatra to Lahore

In one of his meetings with the National Security Team, Vajpayee said: "Is Guthi Ko Suljhana Hai." He was determined to cut the Gordian knot that was the country's lingering problem since independence—namely, India-Pakistan-Kashmir.

He evolved a grand plan with an enlightened strategy. The strategy was "Dialogue."

The idea of the Delhi-Lahore Bus Yatra, according to Jaswant Singh, who was then Foreign Minister came up when Prime Minister of India and Prime Minister of Pakistan—Vajpayee and Nawaz Sharif met for lunch on the side line of the U.N. General Assembly in New York on 23 September 1998 (*Kashmir: The Vajpayee Years* by A.S. Dulat and Aditya Sinah, HarperCollins Publishers India, p. 15).

Pokharn II raised both the stature of Prime Minister Vajpayee, as also the popularity of his government, immensely. After demonstrating that he was a worshipper of Shakti (power), he now set out to prove that he was, equally, a votary of shanti (peace). Establishment of enduring peace and amiable relations between India and Pakistan was a goal dear to Atalji. Now, with both India and Pakistan having become nuclear weapon states, it was all the more necessary to find lasting solutions to the contentious issues that consistently generated tension and strife.

Out of this deep commitment to peace came the novel idea of Atalji's historic bus *yatra* to Lahore on 20 February 1999. The purpose of the journey was to inaugurate a cross-border bus service between Delhi and Lahore. The Prime Minister captured the imagination of the common people both in India and Pakistan.

The then Prime Minister of Pakistan, Nawaz Sharif, welcomed Vajpayee at the Wagaha border. Speaking in a banquet in Atalji's honour, he said:

> The bus service between Lahore and Delhi is not a means only to ease travel from one country to another.

> The running of the bus between the two countries symbolizes the desire of the people to improve relations and come together. Indeed, if this was only a bus made by metal, it would not have caused such excitement and expectations, not only in our two nations but all over the world. There can be no greater legacy that we can leave behind than to do away with mistrust, to abjure and eliminate conflict, to erect an edifice of durable peace amity, harmony and co-operation.

### Lahore Declaration

On the following day, the two Prime Ministers signed the 'Lahore Declaration', containing three salient features.

(i) It reiterated the determination of both countries to 'implementing the Simla Agreement in letter and spirit'.

(ii) It recognized that 'the nuclear dimension of the security environment of the two countries add to their responsibility for avoidance of conflict'.

(iii) Pakistan agreed to join India in condemning 'terrorism in all its forms and manifestations' and affirming its 'determination to combat this menace.'

Vajpayee was in Lahore for just 26 hours. He visited the Minar-e-Pakistan, which was a monument to Muslim League Resolution of 23 March 1940 calling for the Pakistan.

Vajpayee in the visitor's book kept at the monument wrote: "A stable, secure and prosperous Pakistan is in India's interest. Let no one in Pakistan be in doubt. India sincerely wishes Pakistan well."

Vajpayee was accorded civic reception by Khwaja Ahmad Hassan, Mayor of Lahore. Replying to the reception, Vajpayee said: "His original plan was to merely cross the border, greet Nawaz Sharif and then return home. Nawaz Sharif convinced me to visit Lahore by saying 'Dar Tak Aaye Ho, Ghar Nahi Aaoge?' (You have come to the door, won't you come inside).

When Prime Minister Vajpayee courageously took the peace initiative by travelling to Lahore, in bus on 20 February 1999, little did he or any one in the NDA Government realize that a sinister conspiracy to wreck the peace process was already underway. Even as Pakistan's Prime Minister Nawaz Sharif was welcoming his guest with a hug at the Wagaha border, his own army, under the guidance of its newly appointed chief, General Parvez Musharraf, was planning an audacious cross-border incursion into the Indian territory. And barely had the ink dried on the Lahore Declaration, signed with much optimism by the two Prime Ministers, Pakistan violated it flagrantly, precipitating, in the process, a fourth war with India since 1947.

## Operation Vijay

The Indian army had informed Prime Minister Vajpayee about some strange movement of infiltrators crossing the Line of Control in Kargil district in the Ladakh region of Jammu and Kashmir.

The infiltrators were heavily armed and had entrenched themselves at heights of 16000-18000 feet along a 150-kilometer stretch on the Indian side of the Line of Control, and threatened the strategic Srinagar-Leh highway. The Cabinet Committee of Security (CCS) concluded that adequate troops, along with artillery and other equipments, should be moved to attack locations along the Line of Control. Finally, on 26 May, the Indian Army launched a counter-attack, which was code named "Operation Vijay".

All in the government were shocked by the turn of events that proved Pakistan, once again, to be unreliable and devious. For Vajpayee, the feeling of hurt and outrage was especially deep. He felt that he had been personally betrayed by his Pakistani counterpart. As he would say later, Pakistan had violated not only the Line of Control but also the line of trust. He phoned Nawaz Sharif saying "*Nawaz Saab, Yeh kya ho raha hai?* Your army is attacking our army." Surprisingly, Sharif claimed to have no knowledge of it.

Pakistan's objectives for the Kargil incursion, code-named 'Operation Badr,' were five-fold:

1. To choke the Srinagar-Leh highway, since it was the main supply line for Indian troops in Ladakh;

2. To force Indian troops to withdraw from the Siachen Glacier;
3. To use the crises to strengthen its own bargaining position so that India could be compelled to negotiate a settlement of the Kashmir dispute on favorable terms;
4. To use the Kargil war to further incite militancy in Jammu & Kashmir; and
5. To internationalise the Kashmir issue, projecting Kargil as a potential trigger for nuclear showdown.

Victory in Kargil War was one of the finest hours in the annals of India's armed forces. Defending India on what was arguably the highest battlefield in the world, with temperatures dipping on even below −15°C, which was accentuated further by the wind chill factor and forbidding terrain, was extremely challenging. Initially, Pakistani attackers had a relative locational advantage since they had occupied the heights, from where they could observe Indian soldiers in their line of sight. As such, our Army had to mount many frontal assaults, which often resulted in a hand-to-hand combat with the enemy. In spite of all these odds, our armed forces, displaying indomitable fight spirit, grit and determination, evicted every single enemy soldier from our territory and regained every inch of land from Pakistani occupation. Finally, after seventy-four days, 'Operation Vijay' became vijayi (triumphant) on 26 July 1999, which is celebrated each year as Kargil Victory Day.

Vajpayee's leadership during the Kargil war was outstanding. Never once did he seem ruffled by the unexpected turn of events. His calm and confident words inspired the nation. On 7 June, in an address to the nation, he said, "I do want to make it plain: if the stratagem now is that the intrusion should be used to alter the Line of Control through talks, the proposed talks will end before they have begun." He also urged the people, "Have confidence in the ability of our armed forces. The armed forces shall accomplish this task and ensure that no one dares to indulge in this kind of misadventure in future." However, his greatest triumph was that in the Kargil war, in contrast to the four precious wars fought under the leadership of Congress prime ministers—1948, 1962, 1965 and 1972—not one inch of Indian territory was either lost in the battlefield or 'negotiated away' in the diplomatic field.

L.K. Advani, in his book *My Life, My Country* at page 569 says: "The Vajpayee government had a larger agenda in imposing upon itself the no-crossing-the-LOC restraint. It was designed to win international support for the Indian position and to show Pakistan as the aggressor that violated the Simla Agreement and the Lahore Declaration. It helped allay fears of the international community, especially its influential constituents in the West that the conflict could spiral out of control and result in nuclear confrontation."

Advani further says: "India's missions abroad did a splendid job of presenting before foreign governments a convincing case of Pakistan's aggression in Kargil and, in the process, also its baseless claim on Jammu & Kashmir, which it had been pursuing by resorting to cross-border terrorism. The climax on the diplomatic front arrived when, faced with imminent defeat on the battlefield and total isolation from the world community, Pakistan's Prime Minister desperately sought an appointment with the US President Bill Clinton to negotiate a settlement of the conflict. Clinton agreed to the request, but only after cautioning Sharif that he ought to fly to Washington DC, for a meeting on 4th July, only if he recognized "what great mistakes Pakistan had made and moved in for immediate rectification".

Pakistani establishment's 'rectification' or rather capitulation was complete, as evidenced by the joint statement issued after Sharif's meeting with President Clinton. Pakistan swallowed the bitter pill of agreeing to 'respect the Line of Control in Kashmir, in accordance with the 1972 Simla Accord' and to take 'concrete steps' for the restoration of the 'sanctity of the LOC'. It also agreed that the 'bilateral dialogue begun in Lahore in February provides the best forum for resolving all issues dividing India and Pakistan, including Kashmir.' It is important to mention here that, soon after he received Sharif's request for a meeting with him, President Clinton phoned Prime Minister Vajpayee and invited him to join the talks. Atalji politely but firmly rejected the invitation. The contrast between the conduct of the two Prime Ministers could not have been starker. One beseeched for a meeting, in order to seek a face-saving formula from a superpower while the other turned down superpower's invitation for the same meeting, saying there was nothing to discuss since what was expected from the aggressor was crystal-clear.

## Kargil Review Committee

On 29 July 1999, that is, within three days of the conclusion of the war, the NDA Government constituted what came to be known as the Kargil Review Committee to 'Review the events leading up to the Pakistani aggression'; and 'Recommend such measures as are considered necessary to safeguard national security against such armed intrusions.'

Defense Minister George Fernandis tabled the committee's report in Parliament on 20 February 2000. The conclusion of the report was:

> The outcome of the Kargil operation was both a military and diplomatic triumph for India. The Pakistani intruders were evicted with heavier casualties than those suffered by India. The sanctity of the LOC received international recognition and Pakistan was isolated in the comity of nations. While attending to such shortcomings as have been brought to light, the nation can be proud of the manner in which the Armed Forces and the people as a whole acquitted themselves.
>
> On the eve of Bill Clinton's visit to New Delhi in March 2000, thirty-six Sikhs in Chattisinghpora village in Kashmir were gunned down by terrorists belonging to Pakistan-based Lashker-e-Taiba (LeT). Prime Minister Vajpayee described it as an 'act of ethnic cleansing'. Echoing his views, Advani said: 'Till now the militants had targeted the Hindu community in the Kashmir Valley. Now the objective is to see to it Sikhs also begin a process of migration.'

In his much-applauded address to the Indian Parliament, Clinton said, "Americans understood the pain and agony you went through during the Indian Airlines hijacking. And I saw that pain first hand when I met with the parents and the widow of the young man who was killed on that airplane. We grieve with you for the Sikhs who were killed in Kashmir-and our heart goes out to their families." Clinton visit, during which he was accompanied by his wife Hillary and daughter Chelsea, was a huge diplomatic success. It heralded what he himself called a new 'dynamic and lasting partnership' with India. The Clintons endeared themselves to Indians, and vice-versa, with a naturalness and spontaneity that marks the bilateral relationship of those countries that cherish freedom, democracy, pluralism and openness. True, India and the United States could not agree on certain issues, most notably on our nuclear weapons programme, but it was obvious to any perspective observer that America's new-found respect for India had itself much to do with our nuclear programme."

During his mere six-hour stop in Islamabad Clinton spoke about the twin evils plaguing Pakistan: 'violence and extremism.' He was also candid in reminding his hosts, in a clear allusion to Pakistan's terrorist campaign to capture Kashmir, that the new era did not support those who sought to 'redraw borders in blood'.

## Agra Summit

As a part of the overall strategy, Prime Minister Vajpayee launched another bold initiative in November 2000. On the eve of Ramzan, he announced a six-month 'ceasefire' in the counter-insurgency operations in Jammu & Kashmir.

This announcement was received well by the people of the State and helped in weaning away misguided local youth from the path of militancy.

## Terrorism or Freedom Struggle

Both Indian and Pakistani delegation arrived in Agra on the night of 14 July, after attending a banquet hosted by K.R. Narayanan at Rashtrapati Bhavan for his Pakistani counterpart. Musharraf and his team stayed at Hotel Amarvilas, where every room has a view of the Taj Mahal. Atalji and the rest of his collegues stayed at Jaypee Palace Hotel, which was also the venue of the talks.

Although it was a summit between the Indian Prime Minister and Pakistani President, Atalji had taken the well-considered decision to have all his ministerial colleagues in the CCS Agra. It included Defense Minister Jaswant Singh, Finance Minister Yashwant Sinah and Commerce Minister Murasoli Maran apart from Advani. National Security Advisor Brajesh Mishra, India's High Commissioner in Islamabad Vijay Nambiar, and other officials were also present. Sushma Swaraj, Minister for Information and Broadcasting, had come specially to oversee media arrangements. After all, the Agra Summit was the biggest media event in India's diplomatic history, with journalists from around the world having arrived there to capture an event that combined elements of conflict and peace, betrayal, hope and enigma.

At the delegation-level meeting on the morning of 15 July, Atalji presented India's approach to the summit in precise terms.

"We look forward to a detailed exchange of views on all issues, including that of Jammu & Kashmir. We cannot deny that there are vast differences between us on this. We are willing to address these differences and to move forward. But for this, it is important to create a conducive atmosphere. The terrorist violence being promoted in the State from across its borders does not help to create such an atmosphere. We will counter them resolutely. Let no one think that India does not have the resolve, strength or stamina to continue resisting terrorism and violence. We firmly believe that a framework to address the differences between us on Jammu & Kashmir would have to include the issue of cross-border terrorism in its ambit."

Prime Minister also referred to certain other specific matters, such as the release of fifty-four Indian PoWs in Pakistan, and two more Advani had discussed with Atalji in advance.

"We know that some terrorists and criminals, guilty of crimes like the bomb blasts in Mumbai in 1993 and the hijacking of the Indian Airlines flight, are living in Pakistan.

We have requested Pakistan that they should be arrested and handed over to us. They have to be brought to justice."

"Pilgrims to religious shrines in both countries have to be facilitated and their sentiments respected. The presence of known terrorists who have been allowed to stay in Sikh Gurudwaras in Pakistan is a matter of grave concern to our Sikhs. We have formally requested Pakistani authorities that these terrorists be handed over to us to face due process of law in connection with crimes for which they are wanted in India. While on the subject of religious shrines, the upkeep of Hindu temples and the treatment of Hindu pilgrims is also a matter of concern to us."

The Prime Minister and President had extensive one-to-one talks, on that day as well as on 16 July, lasting five hours. After their first round of talks, they decided to issue a mutually acceptable joint statement. The task of drafting it was entrusted to the foreign secretaries of the two countries, under the guidance of their respective ministers.

From India's point of view, two unwelcomed things happened at Agra. Firstly, the exercise of drafting a joint statement proved highly unsatisfactory. The inconclusive draft which Jasawant Singh brought from his meeting with Pakistan's Foreign Minister, Abdul Sattar, was discussed at the informal meeting of the CCS that the Prime Minister convened in his suite on the evening of the 15th. Advani noticed that there was no reference to cross-border terrorism in the draft. 'This cannot be accepted,' he said. His view was unanimously endorsed by all present in the room.

They also noticed the absence of any reference to the Simla Accord (1972) and the Lahore Declaration (1999) in the text. Musharraf seemed allergic to these pacts, as they were associated with his political rivals. He probably wanted to send a signal to his people back home that he wanted to start Indo-Pak engagement on a clean slate, all on his own terms and bearing his exclusive footprints. On India's part, they conveyed that the Simla and Lahore agreements should continue to remain the cornerstones of Indo-Pak dialogue. The rejection of the draft was communicated to the Pakistani side, after which efforts continued at the official level to rework it until 4.30 am on 16 July.

Advani says: "Sensing, perhaps, that he would not be able to take home an 'Agra Declaration', Musharraf precipitated the second unhelpful development in the form of his audacious attempt to conduct the remaining part of his summit talks with India through the media. On the morning of 16 July, he turned, what was meant to be an informal breakfast meeting at his hotel with about thirty-five prominent journalists, into a virtual hour-long press conference. Apart from arranging his telecast on Pakistan's government-run PTV, he also allowed a leading Indian TV channel to telecast it fully. Thus, we in the Indian delegation had the extraordinary spectacle of watching the Pakistani President articulate his rather combative views on Kashmir and cross-border terrorism, even as he was, that very time, holding closed door talks with the Indian Prime Minister."

In his media interaction, Musharraf insisted that India should accept the centrality of the Kashmir issue in Indo-Pak relations and said, "We can address all issues, after having addressed the main issue. No leader in Pakistan can allow the sidelining of Kashmir for the sake of economy, confidence building, nuclear, everything." He sought to justify Pakistan's support to the secessionist movement in Kashmir by drawing a parallel with India's support to Bangladesh in its war of liberation. "See history", he said. "There is tendency to stop at Kargil. I am supposed to be the Kargil man. I can understand how you feel about Kargil. You must understand how Pakistanis feel about 1971 and Saichen. How much hurt was caused when in 1967 the Mukti Bahini (Bangladesh Freedom Army) was being treated, supported by India? How much hurt did it cause to Pakistan when in violation of the Simla Accord, the Indian army intruded into Saichen?"

But what shocked Indians watching the televised press interaction the most was Musharraf's assertion about cross-border terrorism. "We are not encouraging any violence in Kashmir," he said. "This is an indigenous freedom struggle going on there. We in Pakistan keep calling it a freedom struggle....

Can someone expect that this violence (in Kashmir) can stop when the dispute itself is not resolved?"

Shri Lal Krishna Advani again in his book referred to above says:

> To be honest, the manner in which the Agra Summit concluded left all of us in the Indian delegation disappointed, none more than the Prime Minister himself. After the unfortunate denouncement of his Lahore peace initiative, he was fervently looking forward to a positive outcome in Agra. However, being a seasoned leader with his feet firmly on the ground, he knew why it was unsatisfactory. As he stated in Parliament on 24 July 2001, "In his presentations, President Musharraf focused almost exclusively on Jammu & Kashmir. Despite the obvious differences in our perspectives, we made progress towards bridging the two approaches in a draft joint document. We sought to incorporate all the issues, including Jammu & Kashmir, in composite dialogue. Eventually, however, we had to abandon the guest for a joint document mainly because of Pakistan's insistence on the settlement of Jammu & Kashmir issue, as a precondition for the normalization of relations. Pakistan was also reluctant to acknowledge and address cross-border terrorism. My cabinet colleagues and I were unanimously of the view that our basic principles cannot be sacrificed for the sake of a joint document."

Replying later to a debate in the Rajya Sabha, Atalji said: *'Atithi bhi apne karmon ke hisab se milta hai, hamare karma he aise the to hum kya karein?'* (One gets guests depending on one's karma; our karma is such that we got Musharraf)." He further said:

> I, on my part, did a lot of plain speaking ('*Kaafi khari khari baatein huin.*') I conveyed to Musharraf whatever were my pent-up feelings on Kashmir for the last forty years.... I told him we had already fought three wars and did not want another one.... I also told him that terrorism in the name of jihad would one day spell trouble for his country too.

## Musharraf's Accusation

Advani in his book referred to above writes:

> Who was responsible for the failure of the Agra Summit? Curiously, this question continues to be debated in political, intellectual and media circles in both India and Pakistan. However, even before the Pakistani delegation had departed from Agra, senior members in it, whose proximity to General Musharraf was widely known, had started pointing fingers at Advani. He was supposed to have been the 'hidden hand' that scuttled the chances of the summit's success. About a month later, Musharraf himself blamed me for the breakdown of talks.

Five years later, in August 2006, Musharraf made this accusation in an even more shocking manner when he published his memoir *In the Line of Fire*. Advani wasn't named directly, but the inference was obvious enough for everybody including the media. The following experts shed much light on the personality of Pakistan's military ruler:

> We were approaching the climax of our visit. Instead, it was an anti-climax, when…my Foreign Minister and Foreign Secretary informed me that the Indians had backed out. I could not believe my ears. "How could that be? Why?" I asked.
>
> "The Cabinet has rejected it, sir," was the answer.
>
> "Which Cabinet?" I asked. "There is no Cabinet in Agra." I became very angry, and my impulse was to leave for Islamabad immediately. The two diplomats cooled me down, asking for some time to try a redraft. I allowed it, and reluctantly cancelled my evening visit to Ajmer Sharif.
>
> The redrafting took another two or three hours of intense haggling over words and sentences. But ultimately my team returned, signaling success. They showed me the new draft, which I approved. I thought it still carried the essence of what we wanted, except that now the language was different. They returned to the other hotel to make fair copies of the draft. I assured my

> wife, saying that the 'Agra Declaration' would hit the headlines the next day.
>
> Yet, this was not to be. Just as I was about to leave for the signing ceremony, I received the message that the Indians had backed out again. This was preposterous. I decided to leave immediately, but my Foreign Minister persuaded me to call on Prime Minister Vajpayee before leaving. I consented to fulfill this diplomatic protocol, though much against my wishes....
>
> I met Prime Minster Vajpayee at about eleven o'clock that night in an extremely somber mood. I told him bluntly that there seemed to be someone above the two of us who had the power to overrule us. I also said that both of us had been humiliated. He just sat there, speechless. I left abruptly, after thanking him in a brisk manner.

Musharraf blamed Vajpayee for the failure of Summit. In his words: "There is man and there is the moment. When man and moment meet history is made. Vajpayee failed to grasp the moment and lost his moment in history" (*In the Line of Fire:* Pervez Musharraf, pp. 298-99).

Musharraf's outrageous claim that 'there seems to be someone above the two of us who had the power to overrule us' and 'both of us had been humiliated' was strongly and unequivocally refuted by Atalji himself. In a press statement, Atalji issued on 26 September, he said:

> General Musharraf's reported comments on the failure of our talks at Agra have surprised me. No one insulted the General and certainly no one insulted me. Everyone in our government was acutely alive to the fact that there could be no normalcy in Indo-Pak relations until cross-border terrorism, which had cost thousands of innocent lives, was ended.... But during our talks General Musharraf took a stand that the violence that was taking place in Jammu & Kashmir could not be described as 'terrorism'. He continued to claim that the bloodshed in the State was nothing but the people's battle

for freedom. It was this stand of General Musharraf that India just could not accept. And this was responsible for the failure of the Agra summit.

## Failure in Agra became Success in Islamabad

According to L.K. Advani, Prime Minister Vajpayee achieved the greatest diplomatic triumph of his career in January 2004. He had gone to Islamabad to attend the 12th SAARC Summit meeting. The visit provided an opportunity for him to have intensive discussions with President Musharraf. The outcome of these talks, a joint statement they issued on 6 January, was proof of the fact that India's failure in Agra had became its success in Islamabad. For it said:

> Both leaders welcomed the recent steps towards normalization of relations between the two countries and expressed the hope that the positive trends set by the Confidence Building Measures (CBMs) would be consolidated. Prime Minister Vajpayee said that in order to take forward and sustain the dialogue process, violence, hostility and terrorism must be prevented. President Musharraf reassured Prime Minister Vajpayee that he will not permit any territory under Pakistan's control to be used to support terrorism in any manner.

For the first time since it had launched the proxy war against India in the early 1980s, Pakistan acknowledged through this joint statement the existence of cross-border terrorism from the territory under its control and committed itself to disallowing it. This is precisely what we had asked Musharraf to do in Agra, which he had refused. Which is why, in his press statement on 26 September 2006, refusing the baseless accusation that Musharraf had been willing to accept our position in 2001, the Agra summit would have been successful, and the three subsequent years may have proved very valuable to take our initiative forward.

It is, of course, noteworthy that the commitment made by Pakistan in the January 2004 joint statement has not fully translated into concrete and sustained action on the ground. The terrorist infrastructure on Pak-controlled territory is still intact. Infiltration of terrorists into Jammu & Kashmir has not yet fully stopped. The ISI continues to train, arm and network with religious extremists in their murderous and subversive activities in India. It seems that the rulers in Pakistan have not yet completely abjured the temptation of using terrorism as a tool, as a covert policy of their government, to bleed India. Can our country-our people as much as our government—afford to lower its guard in these circumstances? Certainly not.

Advani in his book *My Country, My Life* writes:

> Partition (1947), three wars (1947-48; 1965; 1971), Simla Pact (1972), Lahore Declaration (1999), Kargil War (1999), failed summit at Agra (2001), Islamabad Joint Statement (2004), continuing cross-border terrorism.... Can there be no durable peace, no end to enmity and no cooperation between India and Pakistan? Is the future of our bilateral relations going to be more of the seemingly unchanging past? Can we not—indeed, should we not—give our future generations a better future? I believe that we must.

Advani further wrotes:

"The onus for changing this state of affairs rests with Pakistan since India has not cast its identity, nor does it think of its own destiny, in anti-Pakistan terms. Unfortunately, many in Pakistan continue to view their own country's identity, and its destiny, as inimical to India. This anti-India attitude is deeply ingrained in its military set-up as well as its religious establishment. On this prejudice rests a wholly mistaken notion about India's perceived weaknesses, making some in Pakistan believe that they can wrest Kashmir by bleeding India through a thousand cuts. This will never happen.

"On the contrary, as all right-minded people in Pakistan realize, Pakistan itself will have to pay a heavier price if it persists in this misadventure. For too long, many of its leaders have deluded themselves by claiming that Jammu & Kashmir is the 'unfinished business of Partition' and thereby justifying Pakistan's continued meddling in the affairs of the state. This delusion, which Musharraf exhibited in Agra by describing

Pakistan-backed terrorism in Kashmir as indigenous 'freedom struggle', is counter-productive. In the sense, Pakistan today stands at a critical crossroads. It must make the right choice for its own good, and for the larger benefit of South Asia.

"I believe that the socio-political constituency in Pakistan for peaceful and friendly relations with India has considerably expanded in recent years. We in India have to work closely with this constituency, by shedding some of the anti-Pakistan prejudices that have got accumulated over the years as a reactive response. But, as I have said earlier, the absolute precondition for any fundamental transformation in India-Pakistan relations is a decisive decimation of terrorism, fuelled by religious extremism on the one hand and state-sponsorship on the other, in Pakistan itself. Once that happens, the two countries can consider an array of creative solutions to the long-standing problems between us, including the issue of Jammu & Kashmir."

## Musharraf Meets Manmohan Singh

Musharraf had his first meeting with Prime Minister Manmohan Singh during the UN Summit in New York on September 24, 2004. It was said to be an extremely pleasant encounter. In the words of Musharraf: "I found the prime minister to be a very positive and genuine person with a desire to resolve disputes with Pakistan and establish good relations with us. Our joint statement after the meeting reflected a common desire to take the peace process forward.

"My next meeting with Manmohan Singh occurred when the Pakistani cricket team toured India and he invited me to one of the games. I accepted invitation and went to a one-day match in Delhi on April 18, 2005. I traveled via Ajmer Sharif—the visit that I had missed after the Agra summit. This, I thought, was an auspicious beginning.

"Before the match was over, we left for our discussions. During our official one-on-one meeting I suggested to the prime minister that we go back to see the last hour of the match and also distribute the prizes.

"Still, our one-on-one dialogue was most productive. We discussed Kashmir in depth. We both agreed that we had to resolve the dispute and that we needed to find a solution 'outside the box.' The prime minister did say that he could not agree to any redrawing of borders, while I said I could not agree to accepting the Line of Control as permanent. We had to find a solution satisfactory to both sides, and to the people of Kashmir especially. This meeting ended in a very positive joint declaration, which the prime minister read out to a gathering of the media. We decided to carry forward the peace process with all sincerity.

"Prime Minister Manmohan Singh invited me to dinner at his hotel in New York on September 14, 2005, during the UN General Assembly. The occasion started on a down note, with the Indians very upset at the tenor of my speech to the General Assembly. I thought they were being unnecessarily sensitive. The dialogue heated up quite a bit, perhaps because of my military gruffness, but our respective foreign ministers soon cooled the situation down. Dinner was served after about three hours of discussion, still in a tense atmosphere. The atmosphere improved after dinner, however, and we did manage to draft a bland joint statement. The media were fast to pick up the tense mood of the opposing sides and concluded that the meeting had not gone very smoothly. Still, I invited Manmohan Singh to Pakistani and he accepted readily. As I write this in June 2006, we are still awaiting his visit. The Indian cricket team toured Pakistan in early 2006. This gave India's Prime Minister an opening but he didn't take it, apparently because Indian officialdom felt that our discussions were far too serious to be mixed with something as "frivolous" as cricket. As it turned out, India won four out of five one-day international games. Prime Minister Manmohan Singh could have attended one of the games that India won, and we would have been even!

"Such intricate diplomacy with India has produced results. Our bilateral relations are better than they ever were. I have said repeatedly that the time for conflict management has passed and the time for conflict resolution has come—and come urgently, because such moments do not occur often or last long. We are moving on two parallel tracks: one track is confidence-building measures (CBMs), and the second is conflict resolution. My preference has always been to move along them simultaneously; but the Indians, it seems, want to move quickly on CBMs while only crawling forward on conflict resolution.

"The initial signs of sincerity and flexibility that I sensed in Manmohan Singh seem to be withering away. I think the Indian establishment—the bureaucrats, diplomats, and intelligence agencies and perhaps even the military—has gotten the better of him. I feel that if a leader is to break away from hackneyed ideas and frozen positions, he has to be bold. He has to dominate the establishment, rather than letting it dictate to him. I am still waiting for Manmohan Singh's 'outside the box' solution. In the meantime, I have initiated many new ideas. We await responses or any counter ideas to solve the dispute over Kashmir, without which I strongly believe permanent peace in the region will remain elusive.

"I have myself spent hours on many a day pondering a possible 'out-side the box' solution. The idea that I have evolved—which ought to satisfy Pakistan, India and the Kashmiris involve a partial stepping back by all. The idea has four elements and can be summarized as follows:

1. First, identify the geographic regions of Kashmir that need resolution. At present the Pakistani part is divided into two regions: Northern Areas and Azad Kashmir. The Indian part is divided into three regions: Jammu, Srinagar, and Ladakh. Are all these on the table for discussion, or are there ethnic, political, and strategic considerations dictating some give and take?
2. Second, demilitarize the identified region or regions and curb all militant aspects of the struggle for freedom. This will give comfort to the Kashmirs, who are fed up with the fighting and killing on both sides.
3. Third, introduce self-governance or self-rule in the identified region or regions. Let the Kashmiris have the satisfaction of running their own affairs without having an international character and remaining short of independence.

4. Fourth, and most important, have a joint management mechanism with a membership consisting of Pakistanis, Indians, and Kashmiris overseeing self-governance and dealing with residual subjects common to all identified regions and those subjects that are beyond the scope of self-governance."

In conclusion, Musharraf says:

> This idea is purely personal and would need refinement. It would also need to be sold to the public by all involved parties for acceptance. (*In the Line of Fire*: Pervez Musharraf, pp. 300-03)

## Narendra Modi

The hopes are now pinned on Prime Minister Narendra Modi on the strength of the factors in his favour. He has already revealed his mind to solve the Kashmir problem through dialogue and interaction and following Bajpayee's tri-sutri Insaniyat, Jambooriyat and Kashmiriyat.

"We will move ahead with harmony, with brotherhood, with strong will and determination for the brighter future of the youth," Modi said, Development, he said, will be pushed further in all three parts of Jammu and Kashmir—Kashmir, Jammu and Ladakh.

Saying more than half of ` 80,000 crore package given by the Centre over a year back has already been spent. "Otherwise packages remain on paper only," he said, complimenting the Chief Minister.

J&K, Modi said, had the potential to have the highest per capita income, and to realize this, the people need to walk with the government shoulder-to-shoulder. "Development is our only mantra," he said, and emphasized the importance of "Jan Bhagidari" (people's cooperation).

The nine-km-long Chenani-Nashri Tunnel, which provides an all-weather route and reduces the distance between Jammu and Srinagar by 31 km, was the state's "fate line", the Prime Minister said; it would take tourism in Kashmir to new heights. Nine such tunnels are planned for the state as part of infrastructure development, he said.

"Yeh sirf infrastructure network nahin, yeh dilon ko jodne wala network hai." (This is a network not only infrastructure, but one that connects hearts).

The (Jammu-Srinagar) highway is closed for days due to landslides and as a result the produce of farmers perish before reaching the market. This tunnel is a boon for farmers. Now, their produce, their fruits, vegetables will reach Delhi in time, and they will no longer suffer financial losses," he said.

Prime Minister Narendra Modi said: "40 years of bloodshed" in Jammu and Kashmir had benefited no one, and urged the "misguided youth" of Kashmir to choose the path of tourism over that of terrorism to ensure the state's well-being.

He invoked former Prime Minister Atal Bihari Vajpayee's famous slogan of "Kashmiriyat, Jamhooriyat, Insaniyat", and declared that this "prime motto" would be used to take the state to new heights of development. "No obstacle can stop us," the PM declared.

Modi, who was on a brief visit here to inaugurate the country's longest road tunnel between Chenani in Udhampur district and Nashri in Ramban district, advised the stone throwing youths of the Valley that stones could be used for better purposes—that of building infrastructure.

If they ignored the "invaluable tradition of Sufi culture", they would lose the present and put the future in darkness, the PM told the youth. He hit out at the rulers of Pakistan who were eyeing Kashmir, saying "they can't even take care of themselves".

Modi promised to stand shoulder-to-shoulder in the development of Jammu and Kashmir and sought the cooperation of the people in this regard.

## Need for Development and Dialogue to Resolve Situation

Narendra Modi expressed "deep pain" over the Jammu & Kashmir situation and emphasized the need to pursue development and dialogue for a lasting solution to the state's problems at a meeting with opposition leaders from J&K.

In an interaction that lasted 75 minutes, he expressed his commitment to the development of the state and its people and appealed for restoration of normalcy. "We need to find a permanent and lasting solution to the problem within the framework of the Constitution," a release from the Prime Minister's office (PMO) quoted Modi as saying.

The opposition delegation spoke of the need for a political solution and while government is ready for dialogue, a senior government functionary said any engagement with the Hurriyat alliance is unlikely.

According to junior minister for PMO Jitendra Singh, the PM told the delegation comprising National Conference chief Omar Abdullah, Congress's Ghulam Ahmed Mir and CPM's M.Y. Tarigami, among others, that "those who lost their lives during recent disturbances were part of us, our nation...whether the lives lost are of our youth, security personnel or police, it distresses us."

# 6

# Opinion of Political Pandits and Legal Luminaries

Jawaharlal Nehru at the instance of Lord Mountbatten lodged a formal complaint to the Security Council of the UNO through his representative on 1 January 1948.

Sardar Patel was away from Delhi, when the Kashmir issue was taken to the UNO. Nehru wrote a letter to Sardar Patel in which he said: "During your absence the Kashmir situation, more specially in regard to the reference to the United Nations had developed and we had to take a number of decisions. We have missed you here, because your advice would have been valuable, but we could not afford to postpone our decisions owing to the urgency of the matter" (*Sardar Patel's Correspondence*: Durga Das, Vol. 6, p. 148).

On his return Sardar Patel's unofficial comment was: "Even a District Court pleader will not go as a complainant. Later, he did not hesitate in telling the British Under Secretary of State Aurthur Henderson: "Unfortunately it is my experience that an attitude of an average Englishman in India is instinctively against us.... We should never have gone to UNO, not only has the dispute been prolonged, but the merits of our case have been completely lost in the interaction of power politics. ...we were so terribly disappointed at the attitude of your delegation. It was, we maintain, the attitude of Noel Baker that tilted the balance against us. But for his lead, I doubt if the USA and some other powers would have gone against us."

Sardar Patel wrote to Gopalaswami Ayyangar on 4 June 1948: "I have followed the Kashmir proceedings of the UNO with considerable surprise and pain. It is difficult to follow British diplomacy in this affair. However for good or evil, we are in it and we must do our best."

In reply, Gopalaswami Ayyangar in his letter of 5 June 1948 to Sardar Patel said: "The ways of Security Council have been extraordinary and in dealing with the Kashmir question, it has behaved in a manner which has surprised even a person like me with three months day-to-day contact and experience with its members. Its last resolution giving the Commission the direction to make enquiries about Junagadh genocide and implementation of Inter-Dominion agreements is dishonest surrender to Pakistan intrigues."

Gopalaswami Ayyangar further said: "As you say, we have entangled ourselves with a set of persons who will not see things straight and we have to do our best under the circumstances in which we find ourselves today. We are today informing the Security Council that in view of our previous clear indications to it, its Commission cannot, on arrival here, proceed to take steps to implement the tasks cast upon it by a resolution by which we have declined to accept in essentials. But we have only intimated our willingness to confer with it, if it comes over in spite of our objections. We are asking further to let us know in advance the point or points on which it proposes to confer with us. The Council apparently wants to put its Commission out, to plant it in India and slowly to hustle us into agreeing to all things recommended in its resolution. I am not sure even the telegram we are sending today will have the intended effect of making it hesitate to carry out the program of the Commission coming out to this country."

This is what Sardar Patel felt about United Nations: "The affairs of the United Nations continue to give rise to apprehension. The forum of the UNO has become a platform for the exchange of abuses and bitter and hostile criticism between the two blocks in which the world is being sought to be divided (somewhat reminiscent of the old Papal Bull which divided the colonies of the world between Spain and Portugal in the Middle Ages). Whether it is the question of disarmament or the atom bomb or the Berlin issue, this cleavage manifests itself in its worst form...."

Sardar Patel feared that the United Nations deliberations would get bogged down in the game of power politics, and that the comparatively simple issue referred to it would be lost sight of. He also thought that if the matter was at all to go to the United Nations, it was better India figured as a defendant rather than a complainant.

In December 1947, Nehru took away Kashmir from Patel's charge and placed it under the charge of N. Gopalaswami Ayyangar. This hurt Patel deeply and he wrote to Nehru: "Your letter dated 23 December 1947 has been received just now at 7 p.m. and I am writing immediately to tell you that it has caused me considerable pain. ...your letter makes it clear to me that I must not and cannot continue as a member of Government and hence I am hereby tendering my resignation."

Nehru sent his reply to Patel on the same day in which he said: "I am sorry what I wrote to you gave you pain. It seems that our approaches are different, however, much we may respect each other. If I am to continue as Prime Minister, I cannot have my freedom restricted and I must have a certain liberty of direction. Otherwise it is better for me to retire. If unfortunately either you or I have to leave the Government, let this be done with dignity and goodwill. On my part I would gladly resign and hand over reins to you."

On the next day, Patel replied to Nehru: "I have no desire to restrain your liberty of direction in any manner nor have I done so in the past. The question of your resignation or your abdicating your functions does not arise at all. I am at one with you in that the decision be taken with dignity and goodwill and I will strain every nerve to help you in doing so but you will not, I am sure, want me to continue long as an ineffective colleague" (*Sardar Patel's Correspondence*, Vol. 6, pp. 10-13).

The Kashmir issue was thereafter dealt with in the Ministry of External Affairs under the personal supervision of Nehru, who was advised by Gopalaswami Ayyangar. Sardar Patel, out of deference to Nehru in this, as in other matters, did not press his views, and was content to advise when suitable occasions arose. One such occasion may be recalled. Pakistan had in the discussions in the United Nations totally denied its direct involvement in Kashmir. This involvement could no longer be concealed when the United Nations Commission on India and Pakistan actually came to the sub-continent. In its resolution of 13 August 1948, the Commission referred to the presence of Pakistan troops as constituting a "material change" in the situation as it was represented by the Government of Pakistan before the Security Council and its proposal was that the Government of Pakistan "agrees to withdraw its troops" from the State. Sardar Patel's firm advise was that Pakistan should accept the resolution and the clear fact of its military aggression before India agreed to further discussions. But the discussions went on, until India had to agree to cease-fire and a consequential line and the further resolution of 5 January 1949 which was biased in favour of Pakistan's views and placed India and Pakistan virtually on a plane of equality. These discussions diluted the UN Security Council's resolution of August 1948, blurred the fact of Pakistan aggression, left large areas of the State in Pakistan control and laid more emphasis on the plebiscite than on the basic issue of aggression.

## Monumental Mistake

K. Natwar Singh who was in Indian Foreign Service and also India's Foreign Minister, in his autobiography *One Life is not Enough* says:

> Taking the Kashmir issue to the Security Council of the United Nations was a monumental mistake. By doing so, Nehru converted a domestic matter into an international one. What was even more erroneous was his going to the Security Council under Chapter VI of the UN Charter, which addresses itself to disputes. He should have taken the Kashmir problem to the Security Council under Chapter VII, which deals with aggression. In the case of Kashmir, he allowed his personal feelings to cloud his professional judgement; a major failing

for a statesman of his stature. Members of the Security Council rightly said that, by doing so, India had accepted that a dispute exists.

"After the draft of the communication which India was to send to the UN Security Council was prepared, Mountbatten suggested that the Indian draft be shown to Liaquat Ali Khan, the Prime Minister of Pakistan. It was so outrageous a proposal that even Pandit Nehru refused to oblige him. Sardar Patel was not in favour of even a limited reference on Kashmir to the United Nations, which he called 'Dis-United Nations'. Pandit Nehru had the good sense to show the draft to Gandhiji, who made a vital correction by cutting out in pencil the words 'independent status'".

## Nehru Regretted Accepting Mountbatten's Advice

Natwar Singh says: "It is now well known that Jawaharlal Nehru deeply regretted accepting the advice that Mountbatten gave him. At a meeting called by Mountbatten on 25 February 1948, Pandit Nehru said, 'That it had been an act of faith by the Government of India, at a time when the situation was rapidly deteriorating to make their reference to the Security Council in the first place. If this faith was now proved to be misplaced, the consequences would have to be borne by those who had made the reference.' Sardar Patel, who was also present at that meeting, did not mince his words. He said that Pandit Nehru, in particular, had reposed great faith in the United Nations. But the Security Council had been meddling in power politics to such an extent that very little of that faith had been left uneroded. He pointed out that it had been the Governor General who had induced the government to refer the issue to the United Nations in the first place. Mountbatten had no choice but to accept what Sardar Patel said.

"Not only this, Pandit Nehru even agreed to a plebiscite in Kashmir for ascertaining the views of the people. He also agreed to a representative of the UN Security Council to conduct these elections. Furthermore, he mentioned that he had no objections to taking the Kashmir issue to the International Court of Justice at The Hague.

"The Indian delegation to the first meeting of the Security Council was led by Sir Gopalaswami Ayyangar. He was a PCS officer of the Madras Presidency who was appointed Dewan of Kashmir in 1937 and had served there till 1943. He was a wise and soft-spoken man of unimpeachable integrity. But he was not familiar with the manner in which the Security Council functioned. The Pakistan delegation was led by Sir Muhammad Zafarulla Khan, the Foreign Minister and a very eminent lawyer who had decided to migrate to Pakistan after Partition. Gopalaswami Ayyangar put forward his case in a mild manner. Zafarulla got the better of him. Sheikh Abdullah was also a member of the delegation. It is now well known that even in 1948, Sheikh Abdullah had an independent Kashmir at the back of his mind. An American writer has written that Indians had made Abdullah a member of the delegation in the expectation that he would be an effective spokesperson for India's cause. They could not have calculated that he would undercut their position by calling for Kashmir's independence in a private conversation with the US delegate in the Security Council Warren Austin. Nehru had put all his Kashmiri eggs in the Abdullah basket.

"At the Security Council, the Kashmir issue became entangled in the Cold War between the two superpowers, the USSR and the US. But for the Soviet Union's support, India would have been isolated in the Council. From the very beginning, the dice was loaded against us. Pakistan was being aggressive and being openly supported by the UK and the US.

"It was only after Jawaharlal Nehru's death in May 1964 that it became possible to view the Kashmir issue in a different way" (*One Life is not Enough*: K. Natwar Singh, Rupa & Co. pp. 114-17).

Narendra Singh Sarila, who was a diplomat, in his book, *The Untold Story of India's Partition*, at page 366 says: "Jawaharlal Nehru was one of the few who was intensely interested in global affairs and kept in touch with world leaders. However, he did not prove knowledgeable on how the United Nations' Security Council functioned; that its members acted in the context of power pulls and in their own national interests, rather on the basis of merit or the high ideals enshrined in the UN Charter."

Perhaps the history of Kashmir would have been different if only the State had been allowed to remain within the jurisdiction of Sardar Patel. It was however, taken away from him by Nehru at the instance of Sheikh Abdullah. "But for Jawaharlal Nehru," says K.M. Munshi, "who under the influence of Sheikh Abdullah, took away the portfolio of Kashmir from the Sardar's State Ministry, Kashmir would never have become the problem that it has been." The Sardar seriously doubted the rightness of Nehru's policy towards Kashmir and refused to share his abounding confidence in the Sheikh. He was, however, not alone in entertaining such misgivings. Some of the members of the Union Government wondered what precisely could be the ultimate aim of Sheikh Abdullah concerning that State. "Gandhiji," writes Pyarelal, "was not himself free from misgivings. He, however, said: 'If Sheikh Abdullah is erring in the discharge of his duty as the chief of his Cabinet or as a devout Muslim, he should certainly step aside and give place to a better man.' Gandhiji did not favour the Kashmir issue being taken to the United Nations where he was certain that India would get only what he called 'monkey justice.' The Sardar endorsed this view and held that if Pakistan had a grievance, it was open to that country to go anywhere it chose. He felt that India's precipitate action in rushing to the world body was a great mistake" (*The Indian Triumvirate*: V.B. Kulkarni, Bharatiya Vidya Bhavan, p. 393).

## Krishna Menon's Speech

V.K. Krishna Menon's marathon speech lasting for eight hours spread over two days before the Security Council of the United Nations has been taken from Dr. Milk Raj Anand's book, *Kashmir at the Security Council.*

I knew Dr. Mulk Raj Anand personally and have had privilege of having interaction with him on varied subjects of mutual interest including Partition of India, in which Kashmir figured. I remotedly foresee then that I would be writing on Jammu and Kashmir. Dr. Mulk Raj Anand has left for Divine Abode. I pledge my deep sense of gratitude to the memory of

> that, in the existing state of affairs between India and Pakistan, such an investigation is a matter of urgency.

*On 21 April the Council adopted another resolution.*

*On 5 May of that year, the Government of India formally informed the Security Council of its rejection of certain parts of this resolution, and that correspondence is contained in document S/734/Corr. I. India, however, expressed its willingness to confer with the Commission.* The letter stated:

> The Government of India has given the most careful consideration to the resolution of the Security Council concerning their complaint against Pakistan over the dispute between the two countries regarding the State of Jammu and Kashmir. The Government of India regret that it is not possible for them to implement those parts of the resolution against which their objections were clearly stated by their delegation, objections which, after consultation with the delegation, the Government of India fully endorse.
>
> If the Council should still decide to send out the Commission referred to in the preamble of the resolution, the Government of India would be glad to confer with it.

Thus, the Security Council resolutions adopted earlier in the year had been disregarded by Pakistan in the sense that it had introduced other forces and heavy fighting had been taking place in the northern area and despite the injunctions of and the undertakings given to the Security Council that any material change in the situation should be reported, a considerable offensive was taking place in the Northern areas;

> As a result of this heavy fighting, the Commission was naturally concerned about the immediate objective of achieving a cease-fire.
>
> Sir Mohammed Zafrullah Khan stated that three main reasons had motivated the entry of Pakistan troops into Kashmir: protection of the territory of Pakistan from possible aggression by Indian forces; prevention of a

faitaccompli in Kashmir by the Government of India; and prevention of the influx of refugees into Pakistan.

When the Commission, under its Chairman, Mr. Graffe, interviewed the Prime Minister, the following points were submitted on behalf of the Indian Government: (1) The regular Pakistani forces should be withdrawn from the State of Jammu and Kashmir, (2) Indian forces should remain along fixed lines and occupy certain advanced strategic positions and (3) the evacuated territories situated outside of the fixed line should be provisionally administered by existing local authorities, or, if necessary, by local authorities to be designated by the Commission, and should be supervised by observers of the Commission, but remain under the sovereignty of the State of Jammu and Kashmir until the final settlement of the dispute between India and Pakistan.

At its meeting on 13 August *finally formulated the resolution which forms the basis of the Kashmir question so far as the Security Council is concerned. This is the well-known resolution of 13 August 1948 which brought about a cease-fire.*

The representative of Pakistan stated:

The main provisions of this international agreement for a plebiscite are:

(i) Cease-fire and demarcation of cease-fire line.

(ii) Truce agreement providing, *inter alia,* for (a) withdrawal of tribesmen and Pakistan nationals... (b) withdrawal of Pakistan troops and the bulk of the Indian Army... (c) a plebiscite to be conducted....

Part I, paragraph E, is relevant in this connexion:

E. The Government of India and the Government of Pakistan agree to appeal to their respective peoples to assist in creating and maintaining an atmosphere favourable to the promotion of further negotiations.

Neither before 13 August nor after 13 August until the present time, as the Council will come to see when we deal with present conditions, has there been any appearance that this has been done by the Government of Pakistan as reflected in the public opinion of Pakistan.

Now that the cease-fire has been established, so far as the Government of India is concerned that is an agreement into which it has entered and which should be supervised by an international body of observers.

Part II relates to the truce agreement. The plan of this programme is that first there should be a cease-fire, then there should be third part. Part II is divided into three sections: A, B, and C. Paragraph 1 of Section A states:

> 1. As the presence of troops of Pakistan in the territory of the State of Jammu and Kashmir constitutes a material change in the situation since it was represented by the Government of Pakistan before the Security Council, the Government of Pakistan agrees to withdraw its troops from that State.

The second paragraph states:

> The Government of Pakistan will use its by endeavour to secure the withdrawal from the state of Jammu and Kashmir of tribesmen and Pakistan nationals not normally resident there who have entered the State for the purpose of fighting.

*That there has been no withdrawal of these nationals to the extent that is required in this matter. What are called other armies in Kashmir are under the control of the Pakistan command.* They are officered by Pakistan officers, and the administration is under Pakistan control. Therefore, to say that paragraph 2 of the truce agreement has been carried out is not accurate.

The third paragraph states:

> Pending a final solution, the territory evacuated by the Pakistan troops will be administered by the local authorities under the surveillance of the Commission.

What is the position today.

> *The administration in that area is directly under Pakistan administration through its own officials, and the authorities in Kashmir* are controlled from Karachi.

Section B begins with "When". It states:

> When the Commission shall have notified that Government of India that the tribesmen and Pakistan nationals referred to in Part II A hereof have withdrawn, thereby terminating the situation which was represented by the Government of India to the Security Council as having occasioned the presence of Indian forces in the State of Jammu and Kashmir, and further that the Pakistan forces were being withdrawn from the State of Jammu and Kashmir, the Government of India agrees to begin to withdraw the bulk of their forces from that State in stages to be agreed upon with the Commissions.
>
> *Pending the acceptance of the conditions for a final settlement of the situation in the State of Jammu and Kashmir, the Indian Government will maintain, within the lines existing at the moment of the cease-fire the minimum strength of its forces which, in agreement with the Commission, are considered necessary of law and order.*
>
> The Government of India will undertake to ensure that the Government of the State of Jammu and Kashmir will take all measures within their power to make it publicly known that peace, law and order will be safeguarded....

Part III states:

> The Government of India and the Government of Pakistan reaffirm their wish that the future status of the State of Jammu and Kashmir shall be determined in accordance with the will of the people and to that end, upon acceptance of the Truce Agreement both Governments agree to enter into consultations with the Commission to determine fair and equitable conditions whereby such free expression will be assured.

*No truce agreement has been signed, because Pakistan armies have not vacated and, what is more, there are continued violations.*

*So far as we are concerned, the commitment is for the acceptance of a truce agreement. It is not to hold a plebiscite but to enter into consultations.*

*First of all, there is no truce agreement. Therefore, if number two does not happen number three is out of court.*

Now *this resolution was not accepted by Pakistan.* We accepted this resolution.

*But still there was no cease-fire. The fighting was going on in the northern areas.*

So, by 25 December, we had a situation where the resolution of the Commission, as passed in its private sitting on the 11th, was accepted by both governments, and that became the resolution of 5 January, the resolution was first set up by the Commission and put to the two governments; their agreement was obtained, and it was formalized.

> that Parts I and II of the resolution are not implemented, and that therefore the Government of India cannot be regarded as being bound by those resolutions, because that is the consecutive character. It is a concertina resolution Unless (A) is accomplished, (B) cannot be undertaken; unless (b) is accomplished, (C) cannot be undertaken. Apart from what (C) means—something to which I have referred—(B) has not been implemented, and so unless there is a truce, unless there is evacuation, how does the Security Council even contemplate the idea of anything in the nature of an assessment of the will of the people in the occupied areas of Pakistan, with forty-five battalions of these forces, the entire army of Pakistan, right up on our frontier?

What the resolution of 5 January does is to elaborate the ways in which a plebiscite should be taken. Practically, the whole of this resolution deals with the methodology of this plebiscite; but it is not as though it is laid down categorically. There are so many "ifs" and "whens" in this which are integral to the commitments made by India.

What is this resolution of 5 January 1949? It reads as follows:

> The Untied Nations Commissions for India and Pakistan, having received from the Governments of India and Pakistan, in communications dated 23 December and

25 December 1948, respectively, their acceptance of the following principles which are supplementary to the Commission's resolution of 13 August 1948:

1. The question of the accession of the State of Jammu and Kashmir to India or Pakistan will be decided through the democratic method of a free and impartial plebiscite.

paragraph 2 of this resolution of 5 January governs the first one:

2. A plebiscite will be held when it shall be found by the Commission that the cease-fire and truce arrangements set forth in Parts I and II of the Commission's resolution of 13 August 1948 have been carried out.

.... And arrangements for the plebiscite have been completed.

Hence, the whole of the resolution of 5 January is concerned with the minutiae of the plebiscite, but even in that, it makes it quite clear at what time it will be taken. This is a plan of action. It is a blueprint. But you cannot operate it, you cannot pull the trigger on it until Parts I and II are in operation. Part I is in operation; therefore, there is no fighting—and, so far as we are concerned, it will remain in operation. But Part II is not in operation; and, what is more, the conditions that could have made Part II in operation have been breached before this without the knowledge of the Security Council and without conveying the information and afterwards, and is being breached continually. In fact, a division of Kashmir which is wrong both de jure and de facto, has taken place. This is sheer violation of all the commitments made by the Government of Pakistan to the United Nations.

We are not a theocracy, we are a modern secular State governed on democratic principles, where the right of citizenship is based on residence, upon domicile, and upon loyalty to the Constitution. Therefore, we totally disregard this argument with regard to Muslim majorities and Hindu minorities.

## The Accession is Complete

It has been suggested time and again that there is something like provisional accession, that you can go in and come out.

We are a federation; we are not a confederation, and the units that accede to federation stay in once they have acceded. There is no provision in our Constitution, there is no contemplation in our Constitution for the secession, and that is not peculiar to us.

Once that accession has taken place there is no provision in this to go out.

When Kashmir acceded, that matter was finished. Therefore, there is no such thing as going out.

In the telegram of 31 October 1947, from New Delhi to Karachi, the government says:

> Kashmir's accession to India was accepted by us at the request of the Maharaja's Government and the most numerous representative popular organizations in the state, which is predominantly Muslim. Even then it was accepted on the condition that, as soon as the invader had been driven from Kashmir soil and law and order restored, the people of Kashmir would be able to decide the question of accession.

I continue to read from my Prime Minister's communication to me:

> I had suggested to Pakistan to make a joint request to the United Nations to undertake a plebiscite in Kashmir, Pakistan did not accept this, and in fact continued its aggression for a year subsequently—that is, throughout 1948.

If an offer is made and it is not accepted at the time it is made, it cannot be held for generations over the heads of those who made it. It is quite true that at one time we told Pakistan, "Let us go to the United Nations together and ask for a plebiscite". They did not agree. When they did not agree, that offer lapsed. They cannot come here nine years later and say, "You mentioned the word 'plebiscite'". That is the position. We have made many offers to Pakistan at various times. Some of these offers may be reconsidered, if necessary, when the time comes. But, if an offer made to an opposing party is not accepted within a reasonable time, it cannot be maintained that it is still an open offer. The offer terminates when it is not accepted.

It has been said that we obtained ,this accession on the one hand by force and on the other hand by fraud.

So far as force is concerned, I would say this: Force did play a part in this accession. Force affected the timing so that the Maharaja had no alternative but to ask for protection.

We used no force in connection with the accession.

General Lockhart, the British Commander-in-Chief of our Army, and Air Marshal Elmhurst, the head of the Air Force at that time categorically stated that any suggestion that there was any conspiracy in connexion with the accession was entirely wrong.

Before the Maharaja had made up his mind, we asked the Governor-General to tell him to accede to Pakistan if he so wished. Lord Mountbatten told the Maharaja categorically that we would not regard such accession to Pakistan as an unfriendly act.

Thus, there was no question of our trying to inveigle the Maharaja into any kind of accession.

The plebiscite, I think, has, first of all two aspects, and one aspect has two sub-aspects.

One aspect is the commitment we may have made to the people of Kashmir, that is to say, what came out of us by our own volition in the context of the national life of India. That is represented by the communication made by Lord Mountbatten to the Maharajah on the 27th, which states that "it is wish of the Government in accordance with our policy"—he did not say anything about a plebiscite—"to have a reference to the people." That might be any kind of reference; it might be a referendum; it might be a plebiscite; it might be a general election; it might be Gallup Poll; it might be anything. That was the position at that time, but let us assume that it was a plebiscite. Even he attached conditions to it: when the soil was cleared of the invader and peace and order was restored.

Therefore, our first commitment, if it is a commitment, is to the people of Kashmir. No other party comes into it. Secondly, it is in consonance with the policy of the Government of India. Policies of governments are matters which the governments alone can decide. Thirdly, it was effective when the soil was cleared of the invader; and, fourthly, when peaceful conditions had been restored.

Therefore, that condition, even so far as we are concerned, does not exist. But we did our best. We hung this up for sometime, right from 1948 till about 1952, hoping that something would happen.

Our commitments for a plebiscite are, first of all, conditioned by the withdrawal of Pakistani forces and nationals by the large-scale disbandment and disarmament of the Azad Kashmir army, by the restoration of the unity of the country, by the return of refugees, by the restoration of law and order and by conditions of Security.

The plebiscite is not Pakistan's business but has to be taken by a Plebiscite Administrator, who has to decide its terms. And in any case none of these things can take place so long as the territory—more than 42,000 square miles out of 84,000—is under occupation.

It was Sir Owen Dixon, who said that no plebiscite would ever be adequate because, supposing the plebiscite by majority decided for Pakistan, there would be even more trouble. And, what is more, how would the adequacy of this plebiscite be justified in the present conditions?

Oppenheim says:

Kashmir was in no way historically connected with the present Pakistan, and therefore, its entry into that territory, irrespective of our claims, is an act of invasion.

> Sir Owen Dixon, now Chief Justice of Australia, went to India and to Kashmir and to Pakistan and he tried to establish, in the same way as General McNaughton did, a parity between India and Pakistan. What is more, he also brought in Azad Kashmir as though it were a de jure Government, and he also tried to establish parity between the State forces and militia on the one hand and Azad forces on the other.
>
> Sir Own Dixon's came to two or three important conclusions,

> One conclusion he came to was that a wholesale plebiscite was neither desirable nor possible. So he suggested alternative plans for what has been called a compartmental plebiscite. It was not India that rejected them. Pakistan rejected from wholesale.

The president of the Security Council took votes on the resolution S/3778 by show of hands.

Australia, China, Colambia, Cuba, France, Iraq, Philippines, Sweden, United Kingdom of Great Britain and Northern Ireland, United States of America voted in favour. U.S.S.R abstained.

The result of the voting was: 10 in favour; none against; and one abstained. The draft resolution was adopted.

"This is the message that Krishna Menon sent across to the Security Council in 1957 and it still holds good, in fact more than ever before."

Shri M.V. Kamath, who was then P.T.I. Reporter in New York in his book *A Reporter at Large* at pages 364-66 writes:

> Truth to say, he did a first class job. If the Security Council were an impartial Court of Justice, and he was a lawyer for the defendant, he would have won hands down. His 8-hour speech was a remarkable *tour de force.* Half a dozen bright Indians had worked for him day and night to get all sorts of political, diplomatic and legal precedents and the speech, for all its rambling nature, was a work of art. Escott Reid has done him an injustice by saying that "Menon's speech in New York had not served to convert one of India's friends to India's side" and by adding that "the case which India had put had not impressed the West". The point is that the West was not *willing* to be impressed. As an Indian saying goes, you can wake a man who is asleep but cannot wake someone who is wide awake but pretends to snore.
>
> I listened to Menon's speech, morning and afternoon, with my earphones, sitting in my office and arranged to get the UN staff 'takes' even as I was taking down my

notes. One thing I was sure of: no matter how well any western agency covered the speech, they would never be able to feel the passion and the anger behind it and reflect it in their copy. Only an Indian could do so. And I did. For once I forgot my personal dislike for Menon. He was my country's spokesman and he was standing up to the West. I would not desert him; I couldn't have done that, anyway. I was a *PTI* reporter and I had a job to do. But this was one speech I put my heart and soul in to report. I had a beautiful lead. The story went. Wagle, at the Bombay end, did not change a word or put in an extra comma. It was the front page lead, full seven columns in almost all papers. It is a coverage I am immensely proud of.

*The New York Times* which had printed the full text of Ferozekhan Noon's speech dismissed Menon's eight-hour marathon address in less than that many inches. The great newspaper displayed its meanness and pusillanimity by deliberately ignoring Menon's speech What made the news was the length of the speech, not its content. And the fact that Menon had swooned. There was a joke current among western correspondents that when a woman swooned she could be revived by waving smelling salts in front of her nose but when Menon swooned, one had only to wave a microphone in front of his lips. I don't flatter myself that my well-displayed report impressed Nehru. In the circumstances prevailing, he would have got the full text of Menon's speech verbatim within 24 hours of his making it. But the Prime Minister did say in an interview to the press that in speaking with passion, Menon had "represented the passion of India." He had indeed. In his book *Envoy to Nehru,* by way of comment on Nehru's remark, Escott Reid writes "Menon may have faithfully represented the passion of India but he did not present on behalf of India, arguments which were convincing to most friends of India in the West". That could not be true.

## Justice Chagla

Justice Mr. M.C. Chagla, who was Chief Justice of Bombay High Court, India's Ambassador to the United Nations and U.K. and also External Affairs and Education Minister of the Government of India was specially sent by Jawaharlal Nehru to represent India in the Security Council on Kashmir. I have given below Chagla's views on Kashmir and excerpts of the speech he made in the Security Council.

With regard to India's position of Kashmir Chagla said:

> Our position on Kashmir was clear, unambiguous and unequivocal. Broadly speaking, our stand was that constitutionally, legally and politically, Kashmir was an integral part of India. With the signing of the Instrument of Accession, constitutionally and legally Kashmir had become a part of India as much as Maharashtra or any other State was a part of India. As a transitional measure, our Constitution had enacted that there should be special relations in certain matters between India and Kashmir which differed from the Centre-State relations in regard to other States. It was an established fact, which was admitted by Pakistan herself, that Pakistan had committed aggression in Kashmir and, therefore, against India.

Dealing with the question of accession, Chagla repudiated the Pakistan Foreign Minister's charge that India had obtained the signature of the Ruler on the instrument of Accession at a time when the people of Jammu ahd Kashmir had risen in rebellion against the Ruler, and had ousted his authority from the State. Chagla argued that this was a complete distortion of facts and said: "It was the tribal raiders and Pakistan nationals, aided and abetted by the Pakistan Government, who carried the fire and sword into Kashmir and compelled the Ruler to turn to India in an hour of extreme peril, and he quoted Sheikh Abdullah:

> When for the first time the people of Srinagar saw the incoming planes from India and the tanks of the Indian Army passing through the streets here, their

disappointment and anguish was turned to joy and happiness. The people here, Muslims, Hindus and Sikhs, heaved a sigh of relief, knowing that their honour and dignity could not be safe-guarded. We must not forget that time.

Even today, several people including press in Western countries feel that there should be plebiscite in Kashmir and the people of Kashmir should decide whether they want to remain in India or Pakistan. The right of self-determination for people in any part of India may look romantic but it is totally impracticable and uncalled for. Without the so-called plebiscite, 562 Princely States have acceded to India. So as far as communal angle is concerned India is the second largest Muslim country in the world next only to Indonesia. Pakistan is not even third or fourth in the line. Even the UNO resolution which talks of plebiscite in Kashmir is with a clear rider that Pakistan must first withdraw its troops from Pak-occupied Kashmir. Pakistan failed to honour its obligations in this respect. Thus, the UNO resolution about plebiscite has rendered infructuous.

With regard to plebiscite, Chagla said: "The promise given that we would ascertain the wishes of the people through a plebiscite no longer held good for two reasons: first, the promise was conditional upon Pakistan vacating her aggression, which she never did. Even today the part of Kashmir remains in the occupation of Pakistan. Secondly, a resolution passed in 1948 cannot be permitted in international law to hold the field indefinitely when conditions under which the resolution was passed had materially changed. Kashmir had already expressed its clear intention through three general elections. A plebiscite had no greater sanctity than a general election held through a secret ballot where the whole adult population went to the polls. Further, a plebiscite on a narrow communal issue was bound to rouse communal frenzy and passion, and disturb the life of the State which had remained peaceful and undisturbed."

Chagla further said: "Politically, a new dimension to the problem had been added by the collusion between Pakistan and China against India. Kashmir was our life-line for the defence of our country against possible Chinese aggression in the north-west and it would be national suicide on our part to give up that life-line. With regard to the facts, it was a bare-faced lie to say that Kashmir was in open revolt. And with regard to the question of integration, it was for India and Kashmir to determine how they should regulate their mutual relations. The question of integration did not arise because Kashmir was integrated with India a long time ago".

On Pakistan's perpetual harping on plebiscite, Chagla said: "Pakistan's perpetual harping on a plebiscite in Jammu and Kashmir is not an outcome of its faith in democratic principles. I should have thought of democracy, like charity, begins at home, and before Pakistan preaches to us how we should ascertain the wishes of the people of a part of our country she should first make at least a beginning in establishing democratic institutions at home. I need hardly say that since the State's existence it has never sufficiently trusted its own people to permit them to participate in a general and direct election for the creation of legislative and parliamentary bodies.

"To Pakistan everything is communal. She cannot understand how Hindus and Muslims can live peacefully in Kashmir and have best of relations. Her philosophy is that in the very nature of things Muslims must hate the Hindus and the Hindus must hate the Muslims."

Chagla continued: "Pakistan does not want India to be strong; she wants to weaken India, both internationally and domestically. Her recent flirtations with China are clear evidence of this fact. In this context, Kashmir assumes great importance. Pakistan has been complaining of India's changing the *status quo* with regard to Kashmir, and yet she has given away to China, in the border agreement, over 2,000 square miles of Kashmir territory. Pakistan has no right or title to it, and yet she has been generous at another country's expense. If ever there was a blatant case of change of *status quo*, such a change was made by Pakistan, not India. But, apart from the fact that legally and constitutionally Kashmir is part of India, apart from the fact that we do not subscribe to the theory that Hindus and Muslims are two nations, and that Kashmir is the symbol and guarantee of our secularism, Kashmir has now assumed vital importance because of the continuing menace of China. A mere glance at the map of India will be sufficient to illustrate this."

On the principles of self-determination, Chagla said: "Pakistan has made great play with the idea of self-determination. She has tried to appeal to world opinion by proclaiming that her interest in Kashmir arises from the fact that the people of that State have been denied the right of self-determination. Now, in the first place, we must determine what are the connotations of the word 'self' in this expression. What is the 'self' which has the right to determine whether it would be a part of one country, or part of another country, or would be independent? It is clear that the 'self' contemplated in the enunciation of this democratic principle is not, and cannot be, a constituent part of a country. It can be operative only when one is dealing with a nation as a whole, and the context in which it can be applicable is the context of conquest or of foreign domination, or of colonial exploitation. It would lead to disastrous consequences if the expression were extended to apply to the integral part of any country or sections of the population to secede. The principle of self-determination cannot, and must not, be applied to bring about the fragmentation of a country or its people. Let us not forget that the United States fought a bloody civil war to prevent, not a small part, but the whole of the south of the United States from seceding and constituting itself into an independent country."

He added: "Many countries today have living in them people of different races, religions and cultures, and the future of the world depends upon the evolution of multi-racial States and nations in different parts of the world. Pakistan's thesis is a reactionary and obscurantist one. The thesis of self-determination which Pakistan advocates has been used in the recent past by colonialists and neo-colonialists from the disruption of newly emerging States. Pakistan would have the hands of the clock set backwards, and would go back to the days when countries permitted only one religion and persecuted those who followed another faith....

"The fact is that Kashmir, since the dawn of history, has been a part of India, a repository of Indian culture and heritage.

It has shared fully the vicissitudes of Indian history. It has been part of the empire of Asoka and Akbar. Srinagar, the capital of Kashmir, was founded by the great Emperor Asoka in the third century B.C. the people of Kashmir are blood of our blood and flesh of our flesh, and Jammu and Kashmir are one of the sixteen States of the Indian Union, and the people of Kashmir as Indian citizens, share in the total freedom which India enjoys."

"The representative of Pakistan had repeated the slander against India that Kashmir is under India's 'colonial rule.' Kashmir became part of India not as a result of conquest, nor is it a case of one race ruling over another; Kashmir has been part of India since time immemorial, and the people of Kashmir and the rest of India are racially and ethnically the same. Even religiously, although in that part of India Muslims might be in a large majority, this majority professes the same religion as the 50 million Muslims in India. It is here that the basic difference between Pakistan and ourselves arises. The bond that Pakistan finds with the people of Kashmir, and which makes the representative of Pakistan say that the people of Kashmir are their kith and kin, is not common nationality; it is not a common race; it is not common traditions or common history, but the mere bond of religion. We emphatically deny and repudiate a philosophy which equates nationality with religion. The basic philosophy on which our State is based, and our Constitution is enacted, is a multi-racial society, a society in which people of different religions can live together happily and can be treated as equals before the law and can enjoy the same rights and opportunities.

"Fifty million Muslims live with their Hindu brethren in all parts of the country, in every village, town and city. To us the very thought of exchange of Hindus and Muslims is abhorrent. We realize that India would break up and disintegrate if it cannot give all the communities which live in it protection and full rights."

In his final speech on the debate which he delivered on 18 May 1965, Chagla made a strong appeal to Pakistan: "India is an example of a society where inter-communal harmony exists. My appeal to Pakistan is, 'Do not interfere with this experiment. Let the experiment go on, because the future of the world depends on inter-communal societies succeeding.'

"As one paper described it, the Security Council started with a fanfare and ended in a fiasco. Seven members of the Council suggested a consensus statement which would require the U.N. Secretary-General to join the talks between India and Pakistan as a good offices officer. The U.S.S.R. and Czechoslovakia opposed this idea, and supported the Indian stand. The result was that the Security Council left the Kashmir question to be settled bilaterally between India and Pakistan. The Secretary-General was to extend his good offices only if both parties wanted his help."

Chagla described the Council deliberations as unrealistic and an exercise in futility. He pointed out that the Council had neither passed a resolution nor arrived at a consensus; there was only a summing-up by the President which was based on a statement containing the facts of the debate.

Chagla had again to go to the Security Council in September 1965. This was under very different circumstances. Pakistan had sent raiders into Kashmir, followed by contingents of its regular army. It was a clear case of gross and unprovoked aggression. The Security Council passed two resolutions on September 4 and 6, 1965, calling for a cease-fire. Our objection on these resolutions was that they equated India and Pakistan, refused to recognize the fact that Pakistan was the aggressor, and also refused to condemn its aggression. Chagla's task, therefore, was to persuade the Council to fix the responsibility for the aggression and to provide effective guarantees against future aggression by Pakistan.

In his speech delivered on September 17, 1965, Chagla said: "We have here a finding of the Secretary-General, based upon first-hand information from General Nimmo, that this conflict started on August 5, with armed men from the Pakistan side invading our country. I cannot understand or imagine how there could be a clearer finding of aggression than we have here.

"It is important to note that the resolution of the Security Council also mentions the date as August 5. That, to our mind, is the crucial date. What happened on that date? What happened on that date was that Pakistan invaded India. Kashmir is a part of India and the invasion of Kashmir was an invasion of India and, aggression on Kashmir was aggression on India."

On the question of condemning the aggression by Pakistan, Chagla made the following observations:

"What is the utility of this Council if it will not condemn aggression on these facts? If you are satisfied—and I ask you to say that you are satisfied—and respect the Secretary-General's report, and if you are satisfied that aggression was committed by Pakistan on August 5, I say that it is your duty to condemn this aggression. Otherwise, international law has no meaning and international society cannot exist. Not only must this aggression be condemned, but also Pakistan must be asked to vacate this aggression. An aggressor cannot get away with the fruits of his aggression. I beg you, Mr. President, and members of the Council, "Do not equate the aggressor and the victim, do not bracket them together". My one objection to the resolutions of September 4 and 6, if I may say so with due respect to the Security Council, is that you treat both India and Pakistan alike, that you call upon both of them to do something without distinguishing in any way whatsoever the role played by Pakistan and the role played by India."

Chagla brought to the Council's notice the fact that the Pakistan Government was telling its people that it was waging a *jihad* against India:

> Pakistan's other objective was to make this a religious war. We are living in the modern age. We have learned to understand that religion is something personal and intimate. It is your contact with your Creator. It is your attempt to understand the inscrutable mystery of existence. We do not wear our religion on our sleeves now. We do not ostentiously brandish it in the face of people. But I am sorry to say that Pakistan is still in the medieval age.

He then quoted from a speech by Sheikh Abdullah he once made to the Security Council to demonstrate what Pakistani's conception of a religious war was:

> These raiders abducted women, massacred children; they looted everything and everyone; they even dishonoured the Holy Koran and converted mosques into brothels, and today every Kashmiri loathes the invading tribesmen and their archinspirers who have been responsible for such horrors in a land which is peopled by an overwhelming majority of Muslims.

Chagla then described the true nature of the war between India and Pakistan: "This is a war between two ideologies. Let us face it. On the one hand, there is a religious State; and on the other a secular State. This is the conflict; it is not Kashmir. Kashmir is merely the symptom; it is not the disease. The disease is that Pakistan believes in a religious State; it believes in religion as the nexus between citizens. We believe in a secular State, in a multi-racial society. And it is also a fight between a free society and democratic institutions on the one hand, and dictatorship and regimentation on the other. These are the issues involved in this war. And I think, if I may say so, that it is in the interest of Asia and the world that our free society, our multi-communal federation, should survive.

"The attack on Kashmir is an attack for the purpose of breaking up our federation, of breaking up our way of life, of preventing us from carrying on our great experiment of men of different religions and different languages living peacefully together. You in this country are trying the same experiment. Other countries are trying it. But Pakistan does not want it; she does not believe in it and wants to break it up."

Chagla referred to the blackmail that was being practiced by Pakistan:

> But may I say this—and here I am echoing what my friend, the representative of Malaysia said—that this would be a vary serious thing for the Security Council, it would be a vary serious thing for international relations, it would be a very serious thing for international peace, if Pakistan could get a settlement of the Kashmir problem, could get a plebiscite, at the point of the gun or bayonet. I call this blackmail. You invade a country, you spread terror in the country, you bomb civilians,

> you do everything that is in your power, and then you turn around and say: "I agree to a cease-fire, provided you settle the problem of Kashmir and hold a plebiscite in Kashmir".

Ultimately, the Security Council passed a resolution, fixing the time when the cease-fire should come into force. We had unconditionally accepted the cease-fire, but up to that time Pakistan had not. I need not go into the theatricals indulged in by Bhutto, who woke up the President at dead of night, had a meeting convened in the early hours of the morning, and after vilifying India to his heart's content and putting out threats against her once more, accepted the cease-fire on behalf of his country.

The broad conclusion Chagla drew from these debates in the Security Council was that it was futile for the Security Council to try to interfere in Indo-Pakistan relations. The nature of these relations must be left to be settled bilaterally between the two countries without any intervention from any outside power. Undoubtedly, the Council has to play its legitimate role when hostilities have broken out, but the Council should not sit on the fence, ignoring admitted or patent facts and refuse to pass judgment and condemn the aggressor, when it sees one. Failure to take a stand is simply a way of stultifying oneself.

While speaking on South Africa on another occasion, Chagla said: ".... All the members of the United Nations had joined this organization on the basis of the Charter. Its provisions bind everybody. Is it suggested that any of the signatories can with impunity violate one of the binding terms of the Charter, and the U.N. Organization has no right to take any action against the offending members? If that be the true interpretation of the domestic jurisdiction clause, I do, gentlemen, in all seriousness, ask you to treat this Charter as a scrap of paper. Tear it up, and have done with it. We are sitting here wasting our time."

The observations of Chagla speak volumes on the United Nations.

## Chagla's Confirmed Views about Pakistan

Lal Bahadur Shastri, when he constituted his Cabinet, was thinking of appointing Chagla as External Affairs Minister. But he was persuaded both by a section of the press and of the public not to give him the foreign affairs portfolio because of his confirmed views about Pakistan which, they thought, would seriously hamper any negotiations for a settlement between the two countries.

Chagla had his own views about Pakistan, which I have produced below in his own words:

"I did not in any case want to adopt a hard line towards Pakistan but a firm line, and there is a vital distinction between these two attitudes. It was my conviction that we should negotiate with Pakistan from strength and not from weakness, and that we had too often taken decisions merely out of a certain concern about Pakistan's reactions. I felt that Pakistan's reaction could be easily anticipated, because whatever we did Pakistan would condemn so long as it pursued a policy of 'Hate India'. The greatest and the real obstacle in the way of a settlement between our two countries was the nature of the foundation on which Pakistan's foreign policy structure had been erected. Pakistan had come into existence by reason of the two-nation theory which we completely repudiated. But although this theory might have been all right for the creation of Pakistan itself, and for giving the Muslims a country which they could call their own, it had no relevance to the relations between two independent countries.

"But Pakistan went on harping on this theory, asserting that Hindus and Muslims could never be united, and claimed Kashmir on the basis of this very theory, inasmuch as Kashmir was a State with a large Muslim majority. I knew of no earthly way by which this ideological obstacle could be removed. Kashmir is the be-all and end-all of Pakistan's foreign policy. Whatever may be the subject matter of discussion, Pakistan will always bring up Kashmir in the end.

"The second plank is Pakistan's foreign policy was hatred of India. The Government of Pakistan kept deceiving its people quite deliberately by telling them that India had aggressive designs on their country. We had repeated, times without number, in public an in Parliament that we have no designs on even an inch of Pakistan territory, and we have even offered to President Ayub a no-war Pact—an offer also repeated on many occasions—which conclusively demonstrated our sincerity and the rejection of which by Pakistan demonstrated on her side the warlike intentions of her military rulers. Pakistan consistently refused to sign a no-war pact. Despite all this, one had to work hard to bring about cordial relations between the two countries and we did work hard. I hoped the day would come when, as in North America where there is not a single soldier guarding the long frontier dividing the United States from Canada, we too could have an open and unarmed frontier between our two countries. But this could only be brought about, not by giving in to Pakistan, but by taking a firm line and making it clear beyond doubt where we stood and intended to stand. This was particularly so with regard to Kashmir. There could be no wavering on this question. Kashmir was not negotiable—it is part of India—and the sooner Pakistan realized that, the better it would be for our two countries.

"It is true that while Pakistan was communal and theocratic, we were secular, and the two ideologies were entirely different, even antithetical. But countries with different ideologies could have peaceful relations, and leave each country to follow its own way of life and its own way of thinking. I further thought that apart from Kashmir there were many subjects on which we could arrive at a mutually beneficial settlement. Kashmir could be kept in cold storage, each country sticking to its own views about it, while we settle matters which might be peripheral, but which were bound to lead to an improvement in the general situation. It would be easier to settle the Kashmir problem in a friendly and cordial atmosphere created by a series of prior agreements on other matters rather than in an atmosphere which was still charged with hatred and distrust.

"As soon as I took office, I instructed my officials to get into touch with Aziz Ahmed, the Pakistan High Commissioner, and see whether officials of two countries could meet and settle outstanding questions like trade and commerce, air flights between the two countries, telecommunications, and so on. Aziz Ahmed's response to this was that nothing could be settled unless Kashmir was settled first. I might say that Kashmir had become like King Charle's head in all the negotiations and talks which I attempted to initiate. After a prolonged and tiresome dialogue, the only subject Pakistan was prepared to discuss was telecommunications."

Chagla can be said to be prophetic in analyzing the attitude and approach of Pakistan. The same will continue to be until India takes a hard and firm line.

The forceful pleas made by Krishna Menon and Justice Chagla, however, went on deaf ears.

# 7

# Stand of Individuals and Organizations

## Sheikh Abdullah

Of Sheikh Abdullah, it was said that he could be a communalist in Kashmir, a communist in Jammu, and a nationalist in Delhi.

Before Sheikh Abdullah lost power in 1953, he generally sang the song of secularism. But when the Congress Party was established as a separate political entity in Jammu and Kashmir, he issued a 'Fatwa' religious decree, labeling the Congress Party as an organization of infidels, 'kafirs.' He declared that it would be a sin to offer the funeral prayer 'namaz-e-janaza,' for Muslims who were members of Congress Party.

Sheikh Abdullah politicized religion; he paved the way for fundamentalism and built an emotional bedrock against India. His secularism was phony, a mere stance to suit his power game. He was a mere power seeker. His stance was determined by the strategy of his power game. Nowhere has the faith of the unlettered populace been so unashamedly exploited, and nowhere has it been so cynically blinked at, as in Kashmir.

After gaining power, consequent upon the signing of the 1975 Kashmir Accord, Sheikh Abdullah once again became the high priest of secularism. But what Sheikh Abdullah did during the State Assembly election in 1977, showed that he exploited Islam to the hilt. At first, after Indira Gandhi lost Lok Sabha elections in 1977 and Janata Government came to power, he wooed the Janata Party and asked two members of

Parliament belonging to his party—Begum Akhtar Jahan and Abdul Ahad Vakil—to support it in the Lok Sabha. But as soon as the Janata Party decided to fight State Assembly elections on its own, he berated it on communal grounds. In April 1977, he observed, "Kashmir Congress is a dirty gutter. Democracy will undoubtedly thrive under Janta Party. We yearn to be its ally. Jansanghis are our brothers." But barely after a month, in June 1977, he said, "Janta Party is anti-Muslim, Jan Sanghi in new garb. The hands of Jan Sangh leaders are still soiled with Muslim blood." He sent his workers with Quran in hand, exhorting the Kashmiri Muslims not to vote for a party of the infidels.

The same phenomenon of duplicity and deception of Sheikh Abdullah was noted with regard to accession. Basically, Sheikh Abdullah was neither for India nor for Pakistan. It was his power game that got precedence over everything else. What suited him at a particular moment was all that mattered. From 1947 to 1952, he went on proclaiming that accession of Kashmir to India was based on fundamental principles and was irrevocable. In 1948, he told Jawaharlal Nehru, "We have made our choice and linked our destiny with India, and nothing can separate us now." On March 7, 1949, he announced, "We have decided to work with and die for India."

In a letter in July 1951, Sheikh Abdullah wrote to Nehru: "I have stated again and over that we have acceded to India because of the two luminous stars of our hope there—Gandhiji and yourself. That is why, despite several affinities between us and Pakistan, we did not join it, because we thought our programs were not in conformity with their thoughts."

While he was making such solemn declarations, Sheikh Abdullah was sounding various quarters for support to the idea of having an independent Kashmir. As early as January 28, 1948, he discussed the subject of independence with the American officials. This is evident from the note sent by Warren Austin to the State Department after an interview with Sheikh Abdullah on January 28, 1948. Again in April 1948, Sheikh Abdullah gave an interview to Michael Davidson of *Scotsman* in which he said, "Independent Kashmir, guaranteed by United

Nations, may be the only solution." He suggested to Sir Owen Dixon in 1950 that one possible solution of the Kashmir issue would be independent Kashmir. At that time, he also wanted to enter into bilateral talks with the leaders of Azad Kashmir.

By now the Sheikh was clearly on the warpath. Despite repeated suggestions to visit Delhi, and an invitation from Jawaharlal to do so on 3 July, he refused to go to Delhi and discuss the whole situation. Maulana Azad came up to Srinagar for a few days, but instead of taking advantage of his visit to sort out differences, Sheikh Abdullah pointedly ignored him and he was virtually insulted by the National Conference workers. The Sheikh's speeches became more and more strident, and it became increasingly clear that he was seriously working on the idea of some sort of independent status for Kashmir which, inevitably, would imply a virtual negation of the Accession to India. At about this time Adlai Stevenson visited Srinagar and had long talks with the Sheikh. It is not known what exactly transpired, but the general impression was that in some way the Sheikh received encouragement from these conversations for his independence theory.

This was the working of the mind of a person whom Nehru, in a letter to the Maharaja of Jammu and Kashmir on November 13, 1947, described as the only person who could deliver the goods in Kashmir. Nehru said:

"As I pointed out to you, the only person who can deliver the goods in Kashmir is Sheikh Abdullah. He is obviously the leading popular personality in Kashmir. The way he has risen to grapple with the crisis has shown the nature of the man. I have high opinion of his integrity and his general balance of mind. He has striven hard and succeeded very largely in keeping communal peace. He may make any number of mistakes in minor matters, but I think he is likely to be right in regard to major decisions.

"But the real point is that no satisfactory way out can be found in Kashmir except through Sheikh Abdullah. If that is so, full confidence must be placed in him. There is no half-way house between full confidence and half and half affair which has little advantage and many disadvantages. Even if a risk has to be taken in giving this full confidence, that risk has to be taken. There is no other way as far as I can see it both from the short-term point of view and the long-term one. Sheikh Abdullah is earnestly desirous of co-operating and is amenable to any reasonable argument. I would suggest to you to keep in close personal touch with him and deal with him directly and not through intermediaries."

And now see what Sheikh Abdullah writes about Nehru in his *Atish-e-Chinar*: "Nehru used to call himself an agnostic. But he was also a great admirer of the past heritage and the Hindu spirit of India. His interpretation of the Indian history, though not always based upon accurate knowledge, approximates to the interpretation of revivalists like K.M. Munshi and Dayanand Saraswati. He considered himself as an instrument of rebuilding India with its ancient spirit."

What Sheikh Abdullah did after August 1953 was equally inconsistent. Most of his speeches and actions were wholly irreconcilable with his earlier stand. He virtually toed the Pakistani line. He remained in touch with Pakistani authorities through the workers of 'War Council' and 'Plebiscite Front.' With the help of Pakistani agents, he managed to have his letter sent to the Security Council. He even entered into a criminal conspiracy to overthrow the government with the help of men, material and money from Pakistan. When he was released on January 8, 1958, he entered the Valley with a great deal of fanfare and made anti-India speeches at various places. He continued to whip up mass hysteria by exploiting the religious faith of the poor, non-discerning populace and exhorting them to act as martyrs of Islam had acted against the oppressors.

There was validity in the criticism of his detractors who said that the place of honour about which Sheikh Abdullah talked for 22 years meant "Chief Ministership for himself and subsequently for his son, Dr. Farooq Abdullah; membership of Parliament for his wife, Akbar Jahan; ministership for his son-in-law, G.M. Shah; and lucrative posts for his other friends and relations.

What is true of Sheikh Abdullah is also true, to some extent of G.M. Shah and Dr. Farooq Abdullah. When G.M. Shah was the Chief Minister, he was all out for India; for him, accession was irrevocable and final. When he went out of power, he started saying, "Every Kashmiri Muslim is a Pakistani. I am also a Pakistani; a great mistake was made by acceding to India." Till 1975, when the National Conference was out of power, Dr. Farooq Abdullah kept company with Amanullah Khan. In 1974, he even went to the extent of saying, "For independence of Kashmir every child would give his blood." His recorded speech was believed to have been broadcast from Azad Kashmir Radio from January 22 to 26, 1990, to incite Kashmiris to rise in revolt against India.

A.G. Lone, at one stage, was a Congress Minister. At that time, India was seen by him as the heaven of secularism and democracy, and accession was considered as a sound and valid decision. But the moment he lost office, he put on different spectacles. India became communal and colonial, and accession was described as a tragic blunder. When he found that incitement of violence would pay him richer political dividend, he went to the extent of praising the Sikh assassins of General A.S. Vaidya and virtually goaded the Muslim youth to emulate them.

In 1986, a Pakistani journalist, who originally held from Baramulla came to see Jagmohan when he was Governor of Jammu and Kashmir. During the course of their talk, Jagmohan asked him as to what impression he had gathered during his visit. He said: "I can say something definitely only about the politicians as I met a large number of them. Those who are in power at the moment are with India and those who are not, are for Pakistan" (*Frozen Turbulence in Kashmir*: Jagmohan, Allied Publishers Limited, pp. 132, 134-38, 140-41).

Shri Jagmohan, in his book referred to above says: "The brand of democracy which Sheikh Abdullah and his coterie cultivated in Kashmir was largely based upon negative factors and forces. It was built around medieval instincts and sectarian emotions. It stoked the personality cult, and did not hesitate to employ intimidatory tactics. It was essentially manipulative and fascist in character. It created imprisoned and prejudiced minds and then hijacked them to the ballot boxes. Clearly, such a spurious coin could not hold ground for long.

"What I have stated above would be evident from the way Sheikh Abdullah prepared the ground for dynastic succession, and also from the manner in which the National Conference fought the elections during the period beginning from the Kashmir Accord (February 1975) to the Rajiv-Farooq Accord (November 1986)."

On August 21, 1981, Sheikh Abdullah made a speech at Iqbal Park, Srinagar in which he said:

> In 1930 Pt. Motilal Nehru had entrusted the presidentship of the Indian National Conference to the new generation led by Pandit Jawaharlal Nehru, and we have seen how that had served well. I find myself standing on the same delicate crossroads. I am handing over the presidentship of the National Conference to the new generation represented by Dr. Farooq Abdullah. This is a great honor and big test. The crown that I am putting on his head is full of thorns; I hope that Dr. Farooq Abdullah will be worthy of it. I pray to God that he may come out successful in the test.

Sheikh Abdullah further said: "I have nursed this nation, the Kashmiri people, with a lot of care, and have bathed this nation with tears. I have dedicated the best part of my years in the service of the nation. I would like that the younger generation should be worthy of the trust.

"Colleagues, my heart is full, keeping the greatness of the occasion in view. I am grateful to God that He had selected me for discharging a great trust. I am grateful that He gave me strength since 1931.

"I thank all those friends and colleagues who were my fellow-travelers and who supported me on all difficult occasions. If I did not have their trust and confidence, I could not have discharged the trust given to me. I bow my head to these colleagues who had risked their lives in the freedom struggle. I also pay my respects to the martyrs who sacrificed their lives in the service of nation, those sisters who sacrificed their own 'suhag' for the country." In the same speech, Sheikh Abdullah brought in the communal factor: "In India even after 34 years, Muslims live with a fear psychosis." At the same time he knew that, at that moment, when he was manoeuvring to have his son installed in his place, it was not expedient to rub the central leaders, such as Indira Gandhi beyond a point. He, therefore, also quoted what Abul Kalam had said at the Ramgarh Congress Session: "I am a Muslim and I am proud to be so. The culture of Islam is my health and it is my duty to protect it. But, with all this, I feel proud that I am an Indian and it is our duty to forge ahead with the Indian national cause."

The occasion of the speech was annual convention of the National conference, but the real purpose was the 'coronation of Dr. Farooq Abdullah'.

Shri Jagmohan, in his book *Frozen Turbulence in Kashmir*, at page 153 says: "The democracy which Sheikh Abdullah, Farooq Abdullah and National Conference built in Kashmir was exploitative in nature. It drew sustenance from techniques which could provide only temporary gains to the wielders of power. The hate propaganda created revulsion against India on the one hand, and, on the other hand, hid the poor and corrupt performance of the State Government."

Jagmohan further says: "...the tragic irony becomes all the more pronounced when it is remembered that this was being done by a party about whose supreme leader, Sheikh Abdullah, President Sanjiva Reddy said in October 1977 at Srinagar: "For his achievements, Sheikh Abdullah deserves to be called Sher-i-Kashmir (lion of Kashmir) as also Sher-i-Bharat (lion of India)."

About Sheikh Abdulla's idea of 'New Kashmir' Amin Chughtai, a noted Urdu poet of Jammu versified in his Urdu stanzas, the gist of which is: "It is the desire of the Sheikh that a new Kashmir should come into being, and thereafter it should become his personal fiefdom. If any one says anything to oppose him, the Bakhshi's stick should at once turn into a sword and take care of the opponent."

For quite a length of time, Sheikh Abdullah has been issuing 'Fatwas' against Congressmen, describing them as 'dirty insects of the gutter' who were even unworthy of burial in Kashmir; and yet in February 1975, he had no hesitation in becoming the leader of the Congress Legislative Party and functioning as Chief Minister with its support.

The anti-India propaganda was carried out by Sheikh Abdullah even in foreign press and outside India when he accompanied by Afzal Beg, went for Haj pilgrimage in 1965. In an article published in *Foreign Affairs Quarterly* in April 1965, he lambasted the attitude of the Government of India and justified his demand for a plebiscite. He intentionally embraced India by suggesting in a press interview at Cairo that President Nasser of Egypt should intervene to bring about unification of the two parts of Kashmir. He also demanded that the Algiers Afro-Asian Conference (1965) should discuss Kashmir as a problem of divided people. He even met Chou En-Lai to elicit support for his views on Kashmir. Chou invited him to Peking.

The Government of India took strong exception to the hostile activities of Sheikh Abdullah and Mirza Afzal Beg. Both of them were detained when they returned from Haj on May 8, 1965.

Sheikh Abdullah did not hesitate to use Islam to attain his political ends, whenever he found it expedient to do so. After his death, his son Dr. Farooq Abdullah, and the National Conference, as a party, adopted a similar line. In fact, all along, there have been elements in National Conference who exhibited a marked Islamic orientation. Sometimes these elements acted as fanatically as any fundamentalist group would act. For instance, Attaullah Suhrawardy, a senior leader of the National Conference and a former Minister and Deputy Speaker, made the following remarks in a speech in Jammu and Kashmir State Legislative Assembly:

> I am first a Muslim then an Indian. Islam does not need the support of any one for its spread. It is spreading on its own. At the time of partition there were only four and half a crore of Muslims in the country. However, in spite of bloody communal riots in Bhivandi, Moradabad, Aligarh and other areas, killing thousands of Muslims,

> the population of Muslims has increased to 14 crores. As for the question of conversion of all to Islam, it is the fundamental duty of a Muslim to strive for conversion and any Muslim who does not remember this duty, does not deserve to be called a Muslim.

From May 1983 to February 1986, the Congress (I) had been telling the nation that Dr. Farooq Abdullah was a security risk and Rajiv Gandhi himself called him anti-national and accused him of having links with subversive and pro-Pakistan elements, still, the Congress (I) entered into an "Accord" with him, fought State Assembly elections in March 1987 together, and joined the Ministry as the only coalition partner. This was befitting to the dictum that in politics there are no permanent friends or foes; it is only common interest.

Speaking in the course of a debate in the Lok Sabha on change of Government in Jammu and Kashmir, the Congress (I) MPs virtually portrayed Dr. Farooq Abdullah as a traitor. Rajendra Kumari Bajpai, for instance, said: "Dr. Farooq Abdullah has always contacts with people who thought in terms of separating Kashmir from India. He has personal relations with leaders of the Kashmir Liberation Front. After coming to power also, he continued his contacts with these people and that was why he had started giving encouragement to Jama'at-e-Islami and Jama'at-e-Tulba which were their militant wings. These people started raising slogans which had never been heard earlier." Zain-ul-Bashir commented that "there was a constant link between the extremists of Punjab and the Chief Minister of Jammu and Kashmir." B.R. Bhagat charged: "Facts had borne out clearly that Dr. Farooq Abdullah was indulging in anti-national activities."

Kamal-ud-Din Ahmed also expressed grave misgivings about the patriotism and sincerity of Dr. Farooq Abdullah. He said: "The events in Punjab and Kashmir confirmed that there was a very serious conspiracy for the balkanization and disintegration of our country. Dr. Abdullah had been in the company of organizations like, Akali Dal, Plebiscite Front, Jama'at-i-Islami, Jama'at-i-Tulba and JKLF. It was a serious matter which the entire country had to take note of. Dr. Abdullah also aligned himself with Moulvi Farooq who did not believe in the accession of Kashmir to India. The way Dr. Farooq Abdullah conducted the Kashmir Government had compelled the MLAs to part company with him."

The existence of corruption on a large scale during Sheikh Abdullah's rule was recognized by Dr. Farooq Abdullah, when he became Chief Minister after Sheikh's death in September 1982.

Dr. Farooq Abdulla's ministry was no paragon of virtue or in any way different from the previous regime.

A cabinet sub-committee was appointed under the Chairmanship of Deputy Chief Minister D.D. Thakur to go into the allegations of corruption and improprieties committed by Dr. Farooq Abdullah. This sub-committee, castigated Dr. Farooq Abdullah for his aberrations, malpractices and anti-national activities. But nothing came out of these inquiries and counter-inquiries.

Dr. Farooq Abdullah joined hands with Mirwaiz Maulvi Farooq, though the later did not abandon his pro-plebiscite and pro-Pakistan stance. Dr. Farooq Abdullah spoke different languages at different places. But in the Valley, he subtly enlisted the support of the groups which once formed the core of the 'Plebiscite Front' and which formally parted company with Sheikh Abdullah when he entered into the 1975 Kashmir Accord. Dr. Abdullah propagated in the Valley: "This election is a plebiscite to allow the people to say which political party, National Conference or Congress (I) party, they liked."

The Valley and the Muslims overwhelmingly voted for the National Conference and the non-Muslim dominated area of the Jammu region and the Hindus for the Congress (I).

The State Congress Chief, Mufti Mohammad Sayeed, bemoaned, "This is exactly like Bhutto's 1978 election in Pakistan. It has no legitimacy. It is based upon fraud."

## Politics in Sheikh Abdullah Family

Politics was in the blood of Sheikh Abdullah's family. His eldest daughter, Mrs Khalida Shah, was as politically ambitious as her brother Dr Farooq Abdullah.

G.M. Shah, Khalida's husband, always felt that he had a better claim for Chief Ministership of the State and the leadership of the National Conference. He was not reconciled to Sheikh Abdullah's decision to pass on the crown to his son. He lay low for sometime. He made an outward show of loyalty to Dr. Farooq Abdullah. During the State Assembly election of 1983, he managed through his mother-in-law to secure party tickets for eight of his supporters. He saw his opportunity when the relationship between Congress (I) and National Conference soured, and the former sent encouraging signals to him. About half a dozen erstwhile ministers who were unceremoniously dropped by Dr. Farooq Abdullah joined hands with G.M. Shah.

Dr. Farooq Abdullah criticized the Congress (I). He threatened that if the Central Government did not give liberal financial assistance, he would turn to Saudi Arabia for help. He called the Congress (I) Party in Kashmir as a group of 'burglars and goondas,' who could not remain without power.

By the end of January 1984, it was no longer secret that G.M. Shah and his supporters had decided to topple Dr. Farooq Abdullah's Ministry with the help of Congress (I).

## Separate Conventions

The rupture between G.M. Shah and Dr Farooq Abdullah was formalized when their groups decided to have separate conventions of the party. G.M. Shah decided to have his convention on May 23, 1984, and Dr Farooq Abdullah a few days later.

The convention, organized on May 23 by the dissidents headed by G.M. Shah, removed Dr Farooq Abdullah from the presidentship of the party and expelled him from the primary membership of the National Conference. In his place, the convention elected Mrs. Khalida Shah as the leader of the National Conference. They called their group the "real National Conference."

The resolution passed at this convention said that the election of Dr Farooq Abdullah as party leader was a "Himalayan blunder," that the period of his 18-month presidentship was a black spot in the history of the National Conference.... That he was entering into alliance with known communal and pro-Pak elements like the Awami Action Committee, and that during his stewardship of the State, its economy has gone down.

G.M. Shah presented to the Governor Jagmohan a letter on June 28, 1984, signed by 12 MLAs in which it was stated: "...Dr Farooq Abdullah, during the last nineteen months or so, has miserably failed in following the principles and the programmes of the party and its late leader. ...throwing to winds the directions of Sher-i-Kashmir and the party, he entered into an unholy alliance with anti-social elements and fundamentalists. G.M. Shah who had given his life and blood for the party was expelled from the party along with D.D. Thakur, a close confidant of the late leader, and a large number of other senior leaders."

Concluding the letter the signatories said: "We submit that Dr Abdullah and his Government having lost the support of the majority of the Lower House of the Legislature has no moral or constitutional right to recommend the dissolution of the House. We therefore, pray that any such recommendations as and when made may kindly be ignored and rejected.

"We would further submit that Shri G.M. Shah in whose leadership we have total faith and who has the confidence of the other sections of the House also be called upon to form a Government which shall be stable and which we are sure would carry out the policy and programmes of our leader, Sher-i-Kashmir."

### Plebiscite Front

The Plebiscite Front was founded by Mirza Afzal Beg on August 9, 1955. The basic objective of the Plebiscite Front was to press for the demand for holding a plebiscite under the auspices of the United Nations to decide the future of Jammu and Kashmir. This demand was voiced at every public meeting that the Front organized. The Front kept secret links with Pakistan wherefrom it received substantial financial and propaganda support. According to a report published in Pakistan in 1976, the Front received about ` 7.5 crores from Pakistan during the period between 1954 and 1974.

The activities of the Plebiscite Front increased following the withdrawal, in April 1964, of the Kashmir Conspiracy Case. After a brief spell of moderation, virulent propaganda against India was set in motion.

In January 1968, Sheikh Abdullah was released. The propaganda of the Plebiscite Front again started making deeper inroads.

The Plebiscite Front did not participate in the first two State Assembly elections on the ground that these were held under the Constitution of the State which it did not recognize.

After the Bangladesh War, the Plebiscite Front got a big psychological setback. Its rank and file also showed signs of exhaustion. At this time, Sheikh Abdullah started making statements that he would be holding negotiations with the Central Government. These negotiations conducted by Mirza Afzal Beg, ultimately led to the signing of the Kashmir Accord and the disbandment of the Plebiscite Front—rather its virtual conversion into National Conference.

Dr. Farooq Abdullah in his public utterances appealed to the people of Kashmir to rally round the Plebiscite Front functioning on both sides of the ceasefire line and categorically stated that he stood firmly for the inalienable right of the Kashmir people to determine their future.

## Jamaat-i-Islami—Hind

Jamaat-i-Islami Hind was founded in India in 1938 by Sayyid Abul A'la Maududi, when he circulated its draft constitution amongst a few prominent Muslims of his way of thinking. This draft was adopted with a slight modification in 1941.

Maududi migrated to Pakistan after partition and the Jamaat was split into three Jamaats, namely Jamaat-i-Islami Hind; Jamaat-i-Islami Pakistan and Jamaat-i-Islami Jammu & Kashmir.

The Jamaat-i-Islami of Jammu and Kashmir was formed in 1942 at Shopian by Maulvi Ghulam Ahmad Ahar in collaboration with Syed Shab-ud-Din and other like minded persons.

Both in theory and practice, Jamaat-i-Islami of Jammu and Kashmir is on the same wavelength as of Jamaat-i-Islami of Pakistan. It rejects secularism and socialism. It denounces what it calls 'Indian Colonialism' and 'Brahminical imperialism.' It contemptuously libels the Union Government as a Delhi Darbar. It does not recognise the accession of Kashmir to India. It works for Kashmir's merger with Pakistan. It believes in Islam-inspired political mobilization. It advocates the establishment of Nizam-e-Mustafa in accordance with Maududi's ideas. It criticizes modern norms of social and moral behaviour. It wants the Kashmiri society to be reformed and re-fashioned in accordance with the principles and ideas of 'Shariat.'

A clear idea about aims, objectives and motivation of the Jamaat-i-Islami of Jammu and Kashmir emerges from the writings and speeches of Syed Ali Shah Jeelani. In his book *Ye Bhee Ek Rukh Tha Tasveer-e-Kashmir Ka* in Urdu, he articulates his views in a poetic and colorful style which has great fascination of the Kashmiri youth who, as a class, are given to sentimentality and emotionalism.

About the role of Sheikh Abdullah, Geelani comments: "Since 1931 we have been playing with our blood but the leader in whom we reposed our trust betrayed us. For the last 40 years, the youth has been a victim of deception. Now he has steadied himself. He has started distinguishing between friends and foes. He is now moving with confidence and courage."

In respect of his political beliefs, he makes it clear: "The politics of socialism and secularism is totally unsound. I do not like any Muslim to adopt socialism and secularism as his political ideal."

In another booklet titled *Mukadama-e-Ilhaq* (Trial of Accession), Jamaat-i-Islami speaks to the people in these words: "Your enemies are bent upon destroying your identity and faith. They are pressing in full strength with their army and weapons. If you ignore this warning, be sure that the history of Muradabad will be repeated here. Like the lands of Bhiwandi, Chaibasa, Aligarh, Hyderabad, Jabbalpur and Assam, your hands would be dyed with blood. You are facing a ruthless imperialist power whose Brahminical psyche is bringing new troubles for you every day. If you do not understand even now, you will not find any place in the pages of history."

Such views, expressed in a highly emotional and religious tone, continued to be propagated with impunity for a number of years till January 1990. No counter strategy was formulated and implemented. Nothing effective or concrete was done to educate the people about the inaccuracy of the Jamaat-i-Islami propaganda and the pitfalls of fanaticism and fundamentalism and the fatal injury which the hegemony of Pakistan would cause to Kashmir's identity and culture.

Consequently, the Jamaat-i-Islami, with one or two brief intervals of low fortune, continued to gain strength. On the political plane, it went on advocating, with increasing belligerency, that accession of Kashmir to India was not final, that 'jihad' was a legitimate weapon for the Muslims, that the Iranian revolution was worthy of emulation, and that Gen. Zia-ul-Haq's programme of Islamising Pakistani society and state was inspiring and admirable. On the social plane, the Jamaat-i-Islami carried out a virulent campaign against family planning saying that the programme was un-Islamic and a clever device of the Central Government to convert the Muslim majority into a minority in the State. On the educational plane, it went on planting seeds of fundamentalism and parochialism through its 150 schools and madrassas. A typical example of what was being taught to the children was the following portion of a poem prescribed for Class III:

> Little children, be very calm
> I will tell you what is Islam.
> You may be few and without army.
> But you must fight for Islam.

Another passage from a book for primary classes reads: "We are Kashmiri and our country is Kashmir. It is surrounded by India, China and Iran."

Because of Jamaat-i-Islami's operation at social, educational and cultural levels and the growing number of its workers, it had always more strength beneath the surface than above it.

When the Kashmir Accord was signed by Sheikh Abdullah in 1975, the Jamaat-i-Islami strongly opposed it. A number of active workers of the Plebiscite Front, who were not in favour of the Accord and who were in the same wavelength as of the Jamaat-i-Islami were intending to do. The Youth Organizations got set-back in 1977 when Zulfikar Ali Bhutto was executed in Pakistan.

The set-back of the Jamaat-i-Islami was short-lived. It quickly regained its position and, in fact, strengthened it. This was due partly to the maladministration and consequent frustration amongst the youth, upon which the Jamaat-i-Islami encashed, and partly to the proclivity of the National Conference leaders to whip up and make use of those very emotions which constituted the base of the Jamaat-i-Islami. This was the electoral strategy which Sheikh Abdullah adopted in 1977, Dr. Farooq Abdullah in June 1983 and G.M. Shah in 1984. The dangers inherent in this phenomenon were forcefully pointed out by Jagmohan, when he was Governor of Jammu and Kashmir to the Union Government. In his letter of 12 February 1985 to the Prime Minister Rajiv Gandhi, he wrote:

"This is about firing and other incidents that took place in Srinagar yesterday in connection with observance of first death anniversary of Maqbool Butt.

"On surface, the trouble is connected with Maqbool Butt Day. But underlying cause is the increasing strength of the anti-national forces which received a tremendous boost by the sudden decision of the Chief Minister to release Syed Ali Shah Geelani, leader of the Jamaat-i-Islami and his followers. This decision was announced by the Chief Minister on December 6, 1984, in a dramatic fashion. Even when the issue involved the security of the State, he did not care to consult me or the Central Government. In fact, I came to know about the decision only from the newspaper reports.

"Ever since the aforesaid release, Geelani has been making highly objectionable speeches, preaching Islamic fundamentalism and accusing India of forcible occupation of Kashmir. Of late, he has been organizing training camps in which ring leaders of Jamaat-i-Islami have been exhorting the party cadres to propagate that by joining Pakistan, the Kashmiris would have not only served the cause of Islam but also secured, like Pakistanis a large number of jobs in the Muslim world.

"What is most disconcerting is that, notwithstanding the secessionist and treasonable activities which have been mentioned even in the otherwise sketchy reports of the State intelligence, no action has been taken against Geelani. This has naturally emboldened other anti-national groups like Mahaz-e-Azadi, People's League, Kashmir National Liberation Front, etc.

"I may take this opportunity to indicate that, in violation of Article 44 of the J&K Constitution and the Rules of Business, the Chief Minister is keeping me in the dark with impunity by withholding information even with regard to vital matters involving the security of the State and creating parallel police cadres, etc.

"For the consumption of the public and the Central Government, the Chief Minister has been making a few pro-national statements. In actual practice, however, he has been doing everything to encourage communal, pro-autonomy and secessionist forces. These forces are more pernicious than others, because they preach Islamic fundamentalism mixed with pro-Pak sentiments. Once these forces become part of Kashmiri ethos, permanent damage will be done. No amount of subsequent political engineering would be able to solve the basic problems that would be created. Whatever solution may be thought of, the present situation needs to be remedied."

Rajiv Gandhi, unfortunately, remained insensitive to all such pleadings and warnings (*My Frozen Turbulence in Kashmir*: Jagmohan, Allied Publishers Limited, pp. 174-80, 181-63).

The Jamaat-i-Islami of Jammu and Kashmir considers the insurgency in Jammu and Kashmir as armed struggle in the nature of *jihad*, holy war against *kufr* (false beliefs) and liberation of the faithful.

In accordance with the ideology of Jamaat-i-Isalmi of Jammu and Kashmir, the State of Kashmir should not be a secular State but a theocratic, i.e. Islamic State.

According to Geelani, the Muslims of Kashmir have no territorial nationality—they are not Indian or Kashmiri Muslims. They belong to the Universal Muslim Brotherhood—the *Ummah*, the Islamic *Millat* which transcends national boundaries. Again, according to Geelani, a true Muslim, can at best, be *watan dost* (love his country, the land of his birth) but he cannot be *watan parast* (worship his mother land or father land). Geelani has characterized nationalism as a "Poisnous philosophy" in conflict with the concept of 'community of religion'—*millat-e-iman.*

According to Geelani, Muslims and Hindus in Kashmir as well as in India belong to two-nations. They cannot co-exist for Muslims to stay among Hindus is as difficult as it is for a fish to stay in a desert. Liberation of Kashmir from India is, therefore, a must. To quote Geelani:

> To advocate that one Muslim group (*qaum*) be kept apart from the rest would be against the very definition of a people (*millat*) whose communal identity is based only on one creed (*kalmia tayyiba*) especially so when that group shares common ideological, cultural and communal relations with neighbouring Muslim group as well as common border. For such a group to maintain a separate political identity of its own is against broader interests of the entire Muslim *millat.*

Geelani further supports the cession of Kashmir from India and the ideological thesis for incorporation of Kashmir in Pakistan with allegations that the Indian State has been anti-Muslim and anti-Islam.

Geelani has charged India with extreme hostility towards the religious and moral sensibilities of Muslims and the tenets of Islam. Islamic laws have been violated and religious rights of Muslims have been trampled upon, the Muslims oppressed. He has warned the Kashmiris that Indians would destroy the mosques and desecrate the Holy Quran by using it for cleaning dust and rubbish. He has described Indians and their armies as the enemies of Kashmiris bent upon destroying their identity and faith.

To quote Geelani again:

> "The extreme oppression that the Kashmiri Muslims are having to face is an open challenge for the entire Muslim *ummah*. All Muslims must now move ahead, help the oppressed Muslims and stop the hands of the oppressors." This according to him makes Jihad a binding obligation (*farz*).

Even at his age of 87, Syed Ali Geelani continues to be adamant in his stand on Kashmir. During 2016 uprising in Kashmir he said: "We do not accept the Indian Constitution at all. So the talks within the frame work of Indian Constitution is out of question." The separatist leader while addressing a rally in south Kashmir over telephone said: "The statement of Prime Minister Narendra Modi about talks on Kashmir, under the Indian Constitution is wastage of time and it has been going on for the last seven decades."

Mehboob Baig a senior PDP official made an appeal to Geelani in which he said: "that he (Geelani) must think of Mehbooba as his daughter, who also happens to be the first Kashmiri woman to lead our State, invoking her status as the new elder of the Mufti family. She is not a conventional politician that we deal with most of the times. If she does not bring about a change, she will be the first to own up and make way." He further said: "I appeal to Geelani sahib to give her an opportunity. She understands the pain and pulse of the people as she has risen from the grassroots." But his appeal went on deaf ears of Geelani.

New Delhi considers Syed Ali Geelani, the biggest hurdle in its efforts to resolve the Kashmir issue and find a solution within the ambit of the Indian Constitution. In fact, Geelani's stance has been unwavering; the solution for Kashmir lies in plebiscite, a vote to determine whether Kashmir will go to India or Pakistan, a promise made by India's first Prime Minister Jawaharlal Nehru. While he wants Kashmir to become part of Pakistan, he had repeatedly said that he would accept the results of plebiscite, if people vote for India.

Geelani realizes that this is no ordinary protest. It is a public endorsement of Wani's call for "Kashmir's freedom from India". And this is what Geelani has exactly been saying even before Wani was born.

On its part, the centre has been trying to match Geelani's perseverance with some tough talk of its own—indicating that it was likely to harden its stance against separatists and curtail the alleged 'largesse' they get from New Delhi, a position from which the Centre has since backtracked. But as it is evident from the way he responded to the all-party delegation at his gate, Geelani is not known to keep his door open, not to any peace talk with New Delhi, unless as he says, 'Kashmir's Azadi on the table.'

Geelani supporters say that he is not against dialogue per se. During the 2010 uprising, Geelani put five demands before New Delhi to begin talks. His first demand was that New Delhi should accept Kashmir as an "international dispute;" the other four demands, including demilitarization and withdrawal of cases against youth, were linked to creating atmospherics. New Delhi did not respond.

When Geelani wrote to SAARC leaders in August 2016, he put forth a list of confidence building measures before New Delhi. But as usual, he insisted that New Delhi must accept Kashmir as a dispute first. National Conference leader and former Chief Minister Omer Abdullah says that "unlike other separatists, Geelani is willing to say No and stick to it. He did not want to meet the members of the all-party delegation and he shut his door. I do not think that the government pressure is going to work on him. You cannot force him to buckle down by refusing him or his family members their passports or by taking away their security."

Geelani was firm that the talks with New Delhi can only happen once when the government accepts that Jammu and Kashmir is a dispute. However, the group led by Mirwaiz Umar Farooq, the man seen as the 'dove' by New Delhi, wanted talks. The killing of one of Hurriyat's top leaders, Abdul Gani Lone of the People's Conference allegedly by militants in 2002, also led to the widening of the rift. In September 2003, the Hurriyat split into two camps—the Geelani faction and the Mirwaiz faction. Finally, Geelani left the Jamaat-i-Islami and formed his own party—the Tehreek-e-Hurriyat, Jammu and Kashmir in August 2004. Now with the PDP-BJP Government launching a major crackdown against Jamaat across Kashmir and booking most of its leaders under the Public Safety Act to quell the current protests, the Jamaat cadre has come around to Geelani's position.

The most important development is the unity of the separatists. After more than a decade, even as the two Hurriyats exist separately, the recent protests have brought Geelani and Mirwaiz on the same platform. Geelani's statement during this uprising are not his alone, they represent the stand of a united alliance. This has given his words a new strength. And, as he knows that this may be his last defiance, Geelani is not allowing his failing health and old age to come in his way.

A second rung Hurriyat leader says that all separatist leaders realize that New Delhi is not willing to even throw the bait of dialogue because they see Kashmir's complete integration and assimilation into the Indian Union alone as a solution to the Kashmir problem, with no tolerance even for the degree of autonomy advocated by pro-India parties such as the PDP and NC.

"Our leadership has understood this big shift, if you remember, when Modi took over as Prime Minister, Mirwaiz sahib was expecting that he would restart the dialogue process that had been initiated by Bajpayee. That was not the case," he says, adding that moderate separatist leaders "have woken up after being mistreated for decades by successive governments. Geelani sahib has been vindicated. The promise of dialogue was only a farce aimed at managing the status quo," he says.

Another Hurriyat activist says that until now, every time Kashmir erupted, successive governments in New Delhi would follow a single script to calm tempers; open channels with sections of separatist leadership and promise them dialogue. But when the calm was restored, the process too would end.

"It was not only the Indian leadership that distrusted Geelani sahib; the moderates always felt that he was an unnecessary hurdle. Thus every effort was made (among the separatists) to isolate him as an anti-dialogue hardliner who cannot see logic. That is not the case any more. All the top leaders have decided to come together on a joint platform. Their statements are on behalf of all. So now, whatever Geelani sahib says is the view of Mirwaiz sahib and Malik sahib (Yasin Malik).

This is why Mirwaiz does not see any merit in "talks for the sake of talks." He sounded extremely upset about the way the current government was responding to the uprising.

"They (government) are killing our youngsters, blinding our children day after day. They want complete surrender. That will never happen," he said. "We have always been ready for talks but not talks for the sake of talks. That is unacceptable."

"This time," Mirwaiz said, "there are other serious fears, which did not exist earlier. The Hindutava agenda of this government is seen with a lot of apprehension. They regularly talk about assimilation of Kashmir and it is the RSS that drives this government's Kashmir policy," he said. "This is not Bajpayee's BJP. We know that now. Every body knows how we put our lives and credibility at stake when we agreed to hold direct talks with New Delhi earlier."

Unlike Geelani, Mirwaiz believed that engagement itself was a good beginning. Although his family's stronghold in downtown Srinagar was staunchly pro-Pakistan, he held direct talk with the Vajpayee and Manmohan Singh Governments and openly supported then Pakistan President Pervez Musharaff's four point plan to address Kashmir. This plan announced on December 25, 2003, was based on suzerainty without international borders for Kashmir on either side of the Line of Control. This major policy shift was followed by several big changes in Pakistan's Kashmir policy. With Musharaff replacing self determination with self-governance, ruling out complete independence and encouraging a direct dialogue between Kashmiri groups and New Delhi.

Once again the separatist camp was divided, with Mirwaiz supporting this solution and Geelani opposing it. Irked, Musharaff sidelined Geelani but he did not give in. The deal could not become a reality because New Delhi developed cold feet and soon an agitation led by lawyers forced Musharaff's ouster.

Yasin Malik, meanwhile has a different appeal in Kashmir. He represents those who seek a Kashmir independent of both India and Pakistan. While he began his journey as a militant commander of Jammu Kashmir Liberation Front as teenager, he has been an ardent advocate of non-violence ever since he was released in 1994 and has been campaigning for a meaningful dialogue for a permanent solution to Kashmir ever since.

Malik was one of the pioneers of militancy in Kashmir who crossed over to Pakistan for arms training in late 1980s. He was one of four area commanders, the others being Hamid Sheikh, Ashfaq Majid and Javid Mir and they came to be known as HAJY group. The four of them were JKLF top leaders. Malik's stint as a militant was short lived. In 1991, he was arrested and jailed for three and half years. After his release on May 17, 1994, Malik emerged a changed man. He became an ardent advocate of non-violence and declared a unilateral ceasefire. Despite JKLF giving up arms, scores of Malik's collegues were killed. In 2007, Malik even launched a statewide door to door campaign, the *Safr-e-Azadi* (journey for freedom) to mobilize support for Indo-Pak peace process and create a space for Kashmiri voices in the dialogue.

Malik was one of the first separatist leaders to be arrested when the 2016 uprising erupted. One of the reasons for the government's suspicion of Malik is the appeal of his message of Kashmir's independence from both India and Pakistan.

Unlike other separatist leaders, Malik has not been part of any of the factions of the Hurriyat. In fact, he was always trying to unite the separatists.

While Geelani has an ardent support base, he has his share of critics. Apart from those who see his politics rooted in religious identity as divisive, there are many among the separatists who disagree with his politics. "His politics is reactionary. Each time a situation emerges, he responds to it. We have been asking what is next after a strike call? This question was there in 2008 and

2010 too," says a Hurriyat leader belonging to the moderate camp.

He says Geelani stays away from taking unpopular decisions. His politics is shaped by his biggest adversary, Sheikh Mohmad Abdullah, the founder of the National Conference. Referring to Sheikh's decision to side with India in 1947, he says Geelani sahib wants to die as an unwavering leader. He wants to be remembered as a leader who did not surrender. He knows age is not on his side. So he does not want to muddy his hands in murky realpolitik.

Senior PDP leader and Education Minister Naeem Akhtar says: "In a way, Geelani represents the Kashmir problem as it is, the Kashmir conundrum. He is one of those old guards, who have been part of the story, the tragic story of Kashmir. The final verdict on him will come from history. It depends on his own strength. Whether he wants to continue to be part of the problem or solution, that is his choice."

## Masarat Alam

Masarat Alam is a militant turned political leader. He could well be Geelani's successor. Alam whose political career as a separatist leader started in 1996, first came on the radar of fellow separatists in 2007. Alam was a top commander of pro-Pakistan militant outfit Hizbollah. After his arrest and release 13 months later, he joined separatist outfit Muslim League and later became its chief. In 2003, when the Hurriyat Conference split, Alam joined the Geelani led faction. He rose to prominence in 2008 during the Amarnath land row agitation that was followed by pro-freedom protests in the Valley. He also led the 2010 uprising. Since 2010, Alam has spent his days—barring a month in March 2015—in jail booked under PSA.

## Mohmad Ashraf Sherai

A long-term associate of Geelani from Kupwara, Sherai is seen by many as his natural successor. But the veteran Sherai is reluctant to take up any post. Sherai quit with the Jamaat-e-Islami and became a member of the Tehreek-e-Hurriyat. Sherai, like Alam is known to take positions that are more hardline than

Geelani. Sherai, Hurriyat insiders say was against calling off the shutdown in 2010 and expressed his displeasure from jail.

## Mirwaiz writes to

Hurriyat Conference Chairman Mirwaiz Umar Farooq issued a call for help from Pope Francis in the Vatican, the Dalai Lama, the Imam of Kaba, the Shankaracharyas and ambassadors of various countries in New Delhi, as well as the United Nations, the European Union and Organizations of Islamic Corporations regarding the urgent and grave situation in Jammu and Kashmir.

In a letter, Mirwaiz wrote: "The Hurriyat believes that a war is being waged against us by the democratic Indian State, in total violation of all democratic norms. The security machinery of India has embarked upon the strategy of ruthlessly crushing us and our resistance."

He further said: "The expectation that society remain passive or non-violent in the midst of this brutalization is unrealistic. The younger population of the State has been on the streets for the past one and half months, with fatal consequences.

"As I write to you, the present phase of the unceasing and unprecedented violence in Kashmir is over 40 days old. Now a sense of extreme urgency has built up due to inexplicable lack of response from the international community to the explosive human tragedy. Why is the international community being a mute spectator?" Mirwaiz asked.

He said the Indian security forces have admitted using 1.3 million pallets in 32 days in Kashmir.

"The indiscriminate and heartless use of the pallet gun at point-blank range on teenagers with devastating consequences, has elicited enough negative reactions in editorials in Indian mainstream media," Mirwaiz said.

"What is restraining the international community against this extraordinary breach of democratic norms and humanitarian impulses?" Mirwaiz asked.

## Kashmir on Brink of Joining IS War

The former deputy chief minister of Jammu and Kashmir and a Member of Parliament (PDP), Muzaffar Husain Baig, has cautioned that the six decade long conflict in Kashmir is on the verge of joining the global religious war. Its resolution requires a defter strategy than hitherto deployed, he added.

Saying that there have been three preceding stages of the Kashmir conflict, Baig said: "This, the fourth stage in the struggle of Kashmir is in danger of becoming religious extremism, which is not a political goal, but a religious vision; that Muslims must have their own State and they cannot live in a Hindu State."

Explaining the issue from a historical perspective, Baig who was also Law and Parliamentary Affairs Minister of Jammu and Kashmir from 2002 to 2006, said that the conflict that arose out of the direct legacy of partition of India and Jinnah's two-nation theory has changed for the worse. "Although, terrorism hit Kashmir in 1990, when thousands of Kashmiri Muslims and hundreds of Kashmiri Pundits were massacred, it was still a part of the local struggle." Baig said: "It was not a part of world vision for the revival of Khilafat or Islamic State and hegemony of religious extremism. Now, there is a danger of it becoming a part of the international struggle," he said. Violence in Kashmir, he eared, "will be magnified from now on." Until now the older and rural population voted in Kashmir. Now, that may be in danger because this new uprising, has gone into rural Kashmir. It appears religious extremism is infecting the hearts and minds of the youth. Even the women are participating in the struggle, not in a big way but since the excessive use of force and pellet guns, they have started coming to the centre stage," he said.

Mehbooba Mufti, Jammu and Kashmir Chief Minister made an impassioned and emotional appeal to protesters in the Valley on the eve of the visit of all party delegation in Sept 2016 to give her one chance to address their concerns as she had been in office for only two months when the current crisis engulfed the State.

Mehbooba reiterated her views that violence is the handiwork of a 5% as the rest of the population is keen on peace while stating that children of the poor are victims in the violence wracking the valley since July 8, 2016.

She further said: "Those who are backing the instigators, the persons who are urging the children to attack CRPF camps are not interested in peace. They are interested in bloodshed as their children are not getting hurt."

Referring to the previous protests in 2008 and 2010, she said there was a reason for anger but this time around an encounter with a militant had sparked off the violence. There were encounter before...even now and will be in the future, she said, clearly suggesting that there was a plan and brain behind the current upsurge. She said that attention will be given to the agenda of alliance, between PDP and BJP adding that the Prime Minister reiterated his commitment that the political, economic and developmental initiatives enumerated in the agenda will be implemented with sincerity of purpose.

She spoke strongly in favour of a political process initiated through an all-party delegation and team of interlocutors who the people of J&K feel can convey their views to New Delhi.

Mehbooba had some sharp words for Pakistan, which she said, squandered a 'golden opportunity' to help normalize the Kashmir solution when Home Minister Rajnath Singh had visited Islamabad. Instead of reaching out to him, Pakistan behaved inappropriately with a guest even as Modi's earlier initiatives went a begging, she said.

"Instead of helping to set things right in Kashmir, Pakistan has been trying to provoke. Mehbooba said: *"Modiji ne to initiative le liya. Woh Lahore chale gaye. Ab Pakistan ko aana hoga*" (Modi took initiative. He went to Lahore. Now Pakistan has to come forward).

She continued: "Modi's majority in Parliament offers a chance for peace. If things do not happen during his tenure, it will not happen ever. I am sure that the Prime Minister will not forget to find a lasting solution to Kashmir issue."

Mehbooba who called for a team of interlocutors appointed to interact with stakeholders in J&K advised Pakistan: "Things that they talk about like UN resolutions, the time for UN resolution is over. If Pakistan has any sympathy for the situation, it should not support instigators."

She also wrote a letter to the entire separatist leadership asking them to take a lead and engage with the MPs saying it would be a start of a credible and meaningful political dialogue and resolution process to end the stalemate. She further wrote: "Cutting across party lines and political positions, the country's political leadership has reached out and it is for us to collectively lend it credence and credibility."

Requesting the separatist leaders to indicate a time and place of their convenience for exchange of ideas with delegation, she said that to convert our conviction and commitment of a peaceful and prosperous J&K into reality. It is important that you share your thoughts and beliefs with this distinguished group who represent the people of India and not only the Government of India.

Mehbooba's meeting with Modi assumes political significance as it further cemented the impression that PDP and BJP are largely in sync in assessing the cause and likely redressal strategies for the troubled State. Mehbooba said Modi is keen that bloodshed in the valley ends as soon as possible and wants to reach out to the people for a dialogue.

Mehbooba told *Times of India* on 24 August 2016: "Everyone who is ready to reject violence and help restore peace in Kashmir should be engaged in any dialogue to resolve the conflict. People provoking youth to 'gherao and attack' security camps should stop abetting violence in order to create a conducive atmosphere for talks."

Mehbooba who met the Prime Minister in Delhi said: "What I am concerned about and told the Prime Minister is that people have lost faith in dialogue. So, first dialogue as an institution has to be restored. We need people who have very credible background and can communicate with the other side."

Asked whether talking to Hurriyat members would help, she reiterated that the dialogue should involve everybody who wants a peaceful resolution. Stressing a need for the peaceful atmosphere to hold talks she added, "People who want a solution to the Kashmir problem should understand that it is not going to come in days or months. Do we make life miserable until solution arrives? Do we want our boys to be killed? Do we want to do them something which is going to provoke retaliation? That is something for everyone to think.

"Violence and killings" Mehbooba, said: "only further complicate issue rather than help solve it. Kashmir has been witnessing violence for last 27 years, but nothing has been achieved, except for killings that have left children orphaned and women widowed, she added.

Mehbooba said Hurriyat members should use whatever influence they have on young boys who indulge in violence to ensure that some sense prevails. If we let them attack camps of security forces and make them believe that this is going to resolve the problem, we are misleading them and putting them in a very dangerous spot, she added.

Asked whether these provocative actions are being deliberately undertaken, the chief minister said, "That is something that should not happen because every attack on security forces means somebody is injured even if there is maximum restraint by security personnel."

"If we want and we should want, that our country and Pakistan should have dialogue, then that decision has to be taken here (in India) and not there in Pakistan," she said.

"Pakistan has to understand that we have to live and die together, we are similar countries. We want better relations between the two because whenever there is an atmosphere of war, its impact is in Jammu and Kashmir. See, there is a fight on whether to show a film or not, but trade continues on Waghah border," she said referring to the protest over release of the movie, *Ae Dil Hai Mushkil* for featuring a Pakistani actor.

Speaking on the support of police and security forces for restoration of peace in Jammu and Kashmir, Mehbooba said her party—PDP—joined hands with BJP to create a conducive situation for dialogue.

"If we want peace and situation to improve in Jammu and Kashmir, we need to collectively work for that. Dialogue is needed to establish peace and we cannot force anyone to hold talks on the basis of guns, batons and stones. Dialogue is possible only when the situation is good and conducive. Our agenda of alliance has a commitment that we will hold dialogue with everyone in Jammu and Kashmir," she said.

Suggesting a road map for calming tension in the Valley amidst the protests over the killing of militant Burhan Wani, Mehbooba said that police should reach out to youth in Kashmir.

"The children who have gone from the homes—they may have picked up guns or not, but are missing from their homes and want to join militancy. They are small boys, our police should try if they can return to their homes," she said.

"If it is possible, the local boys who have gone to join militancy in past two, three or four years, who are missing, instead of getting them killed in encounters, if they can be brought back to their homes and made part of our mainstream, if we can give bats, balls in their hands instead of guns and give them education. Resolving this issue is the work of elders, the chief minister said.

On the revocation of AFSPA, Mehbooba said that, "black laws" will have to go, but added that a peaceful atmosphere and end to militancy was required.

"I know that today the situation is not such but tomorrow, a year after or two or four years after we will have to repeal AFSPA. We cannot keep it in force for ever," she said.

"We have to create a situation so peaceful in Jammu and Kashmir by ending militancy, infiltrators, that we can slowly remove the AFSPA initially from a few areas and then others," she said.

Hurriyat Conference asked Mehbooba to be on the side of her people and join their just struggle, a day after the ruling PDP asked Syed Ali Shah Geelani to give her a chance to address the grievances of the people.

"We have three-pronged relations with Mehbooba—human, national and religious. But she has utterly failed to uphold any of these," a Hurriyat spokesman said.

"Humanity teaches us to respect and honour human beings irrespective of their caste, creed or culture, but she, by her barbaric armed forces and uncontrolled police, has turned this heavenly land into the hell. Here every house is mourning the demise of their loved ones," the spokesman said.

The Hurriyat was re-acting to the PDP chief spokesman Mehboob Baig's appeal to Geelani to treat Mehbooba as his daughter and help her restore peace in Kashmir which has seen its worst unrest in recent years after security forces killed a militant Burhan Wani last month sparking violence that has killed about 70 people.

## All-party Delegation

A delegation of 27 representatives of all political parties visited Kashmir on 3 and 4 September 2016, nearly two months after the valley erupted in anger over the killing of the Hizbul Mujhaideen militant Burhan Wani.

In Kashmir's context, when it comes to the bigger political questions, the elected government has never been seen as representative. This is not just in the case of the present PDP-BJP Government, but even governments before it. When Union Home Minister Rajnath Singh visited Kashmir in July 2016, associations of fruit sellers, hotel owners, tour operators and government employees were the only people, who could be persuaded to meet him. They asked Singh to hold talks with all stakeholders meaning thereby 'the separatists.'

Rajnath Singh issued no exclusive invitation to anybody including the Hurriyat for talks to end the 47-day unrest in the valley, with the death toll rising to killing of Burhan Wani and one of the youths of 18 years Amir Mir of Ratnipora village in Pulwana district of South Kashmir.

In response to Singh's overture, Hurriyat Conference Chairman Mirwaiz Umar Farooq said that the centre should open dialogue with all stakeholders including Pakistan. He said that the government has habit of blaming the separatists, Pakistan or traitors for the problem and not the establishment.

Syed Shah Ali Geelani ruled out a meeting with the All-Party delegation saying he does not want to be a part of photo-session.

Civil society and trade bodies stayed away from meeting the Home Minister. The Chairman of Kashmir Chamber of Commerce and Industry, Mushtaq Ahmad, boycotted the meeting saying that they saw no change on the ground in the last 47 days of unrest. Pellets are being used, civilian killings are continuing, so at this point of time meeting any minister or official will prove hoax, Ahmad said.

Jammu and Kashmir Congress chief G.M. Mir said: "A delegation of party functionaries called on Rajnath Singh and apprised him about the turbulent situation for the last 47 days. The delegation sought immediate ban on pellet guns and other lethal weapons for controlling the protesters."

Former chief minister and National Conference chief Omer Abdullah too met Singh and conveyed the stand of his party for opening political dialogue with all the stakeholders. PDP delegation also stressed the need for a political dialogue with the stakeholders in Jammu and Kashmir.

Rajnath Singh held two rounds of meetings on 18 and 21 September 2016 with experts including former Jammu and Kashmir interlocutor M.M. Ansari, *Milli Gazette* editor Zafrul Islam Khan, Rajya Sabha member Shahid Siddiqui, former Judge Ishrat masroor Quddusi, Supreme Court advocate Ahok Bhan and former AAP leader Mufti Shameem Karmi.

During these meetings, experts objected to the use of pellet guns in the valley and demanded that they be replaced by modern crowed control measures like water cannons, rubber bullets, and tear gas. The Home Minister regretted the pellet injuries, but said the other measures were not found to be effective.

M.M. Ansari said: "We expressed the view that the serious injuries sustained by the youth had allenated three generations in Jammu and Kashmir and could increase the base of militants."

Ansari also questioned the Modi Government's reluctance to engage with the Hurriyat, reminding that even Vajpayee Government had included them in the Jammu and Kashmir dialogue. "This rigidity against including separatists has antagonized sections in Kashmir," Ansari said.

Incidently, the government is now dusting the various studies in Jammu and Kashmir including the interlocutors report for any meaningful suggestions.

"The centre is giving push to recruitment in central forces as well as schemes like *Udaan* and *Himayat*. Over 1.40 lakh jobs are being generated, covering recruitment of 10,000 special police officers and 1300 central force personnel, besides training of 23000 youth under Udaan and one lakh jobs under Himayat," said an official.

From holding a plebiscite to decide the fate of Kashmiris to implement an autonomy resolution passed by Jammu and Kashmir Assembly, from discussions with separatists and Pakistan to fast-tracking delimitation of constituencies, from UT status for Leh to a permanent camp secretariat in Jammu.

These and other demands made by political parties and organizations in memorandums during their meetings with all-party delegation find mention in a Home Ministry's summery of issues raised for the follow up meetings of the all-party delegation which was held in Parliament House.

Delegations that met the all-party team voiced their following concerns:

1. Promises made by the State Government have not been kept.
2. Implement the PDP-BJP agenda for alliance.
3. Hold elections to local bodies, allow West Pakistani refugees to participate.
4. Form SC/ST and minority Commissions in the State.
5. Minority community leaders should be nominated as MLCs, Rajya Sabha MPs.
6. Package for Muslims since many were killed in the 1990s on the lines of one for Kashmiri pandits.
7. Review AFSPA, reduce footprint of military and paramilitary forces in civilian areas.
8. Engage the media and regularize state government advertisements.

9. Check radicalization in madrassas and mosques.
10. Investigate funding of Kashmir unrest, newly built mosques.
11. Crack down on drug smuggling.
12. End infiltration from Pakistan, cross-border terrorism.
13. Grant protection and benefits to minorities in the State.
14. ST status for Paharis, minority status for Sikhs.
15. Implement relief and rehabilitation package for Kashmiri migrant.
16. Complete registration of migrants in various camps.
17. Investment by the Shrine Board in Jammu.
18. Government jobs for ex-service men of Jammu and Kashmir.
19. Centre should resolve appointment of guides or scouts.
20. Corruption a major issue since public servants are not investigated.
21. Increase quality of education, open more Higher Secondary Schools.
22. Youth exchange programme between Jammu and Kashmir and other states.
23. Take steps for industrialization to increase private sector employment.

The all-party delegation was also told that the relief for 2014 floods had not been distributed properly since some received ` 3000, others ` 5,00,000 and still others no money at all. It was also told that recommendations of the all-party delegation that visited the State in 2010 had still not been implemented. Some of those who met the delegation urged for a review of implementation of the recommendations of the five working groups constituted by the State Government, and for an all-party delegation visit to the Laddakh region (*Times of India,* 28 September 2016).

All party delegation returned to Delhi saying that it has done its best. This has been the case with Congress/UPA as with the BJP/NDA. The UPA even sent three persons as interlocutors. They were treated with contempt and their report trashed. This is because no one really wants to solve the Kashmir problem. Politicians want to relive the same story again and again. The same clitch cast of separatists. Hurriyat, Jihadists, Pakistani intrusions, militancy and diplomatic, are staple ingredients. There will be more shootings, more funerals, more pellet guns till the next All-Party Parliamentary Delegation.

**National Conference with Separatists**

The National Conference asked its workers to be "part of this struggle", referring to the protests triggered by the killing of Hizbul Mujahideen militant Burhan Wani. The opposition party also threw its weight behind the separatists, calling their agitation a "justice struggle".

Speaking on the 11th founder anniversary of NC founder Sheikh Mohammed Abdullah, Farooq Abdullah said, "I want to tell the workers of NC that do not be out of this struggle. I warn you. We are a part of this struggle. We have fought every time for the interests of this state."

The NC president and former Union Minister also urged separatist leaders to move forward, saying his party was with them as long as they took the "nation forward in the right manner".

"I want to tell Hurriyat leaders not to go their separate ways, be united and we are also standing with you. Do not think of us as your enemies, we are not," he said.

Regarding the five-month long protests, Abdullah said the NC was with those who were agitating for the rights of the people of Kashmir.

Abdullah said people had been fighting for their rights and that many had been injured or jailed. "The fire that has started will not be extinguished until India and Pakistan do justice with us. The more they suppress it, the more it will rise," he said.

Taking dig at Prime Minister Narendra Modi, Abdullah said people of India had been fooled by Modi's comments on stopping water to Pakistan.

"What did Modi say in Jalandhar, that he would stop water to Pakistan. Which river water did he stop? The (river) that are already with them," he said.

Abdullah said there was no option other than dialogue to solve the Kashmir issue. "I hope that one day he (Modi) will talk to Pakistan.... Both the countries should show restraint," he said.

# 8

# Article 370 of Constitution—A Breading Ground for Separatist Emotions

Article 370 as adopted by the Constituent Assembly is given below:

1. Notwithstanding anything in this Constitution:
   (a) the provisions of article 238 shall not apply in relation to the State of Jammu and Kashmir;
   (b) the power of Parliament to make laws for the said State shall be limited to—
      (i) those matters in the Union List and the Constitution List which, in consultation with the Government of the State, are declared by the President to correspond to matters specified in the Instrument of Accession governing the accession of the State to which the Dominion Legislature may make laws for that State; and
      (ii) such other matters in the said Lists as, with the concurrence of the Government of the State, the President may by order specify.

**Explanation**—For the purpose of this article, the government of the State means the person for the time being organized by the President as the Maharaja of Jammu and Kashmir acting on the advice of the Council of Ministers for the time being in office under the Maharaja's Proclamation dated the fifth day of March 1948;

(c) the provisions of article 1 and of this article shall apply in relation to that State;

(d) such of the other provisions to this Constitution shall apply in relation to that State subject to such exceptions and modification as the President may by order specify: Provided that no such order which relates to the matters specified in the Instrument of Accession of the State referred to in paragraph (i) sub-clause (b) shall be issued except in consultation with the Government of the State:

Provided further that no such order which relates to matters other than those referred to in the last preceding proviso shall be issued except with the concurrence of that Government.

2. If the concurrence of the Government of the State referred to in paragraph (ii) of sub-clause (b) of clause (i) or in the second proviso to sub-clause (d) of that clause be given before the Constituent Assembly for the purpose of framing the Constitution of the State is convened, it shall be placed before such Assembly for such decision as it may take thereon.

3. Notwithstanding anything in the foregoing provisions of this article, the President may, by public notification, declare that this article shall cease to be operative or shall be operative only with such exceptions and modifications and from such date as he may specify:

Provided that the recommendations of the Constituent Assembly of the State referred to in clause (2) shall be necessary before the President issues such a notification.

## Effects of Article 370

One of the strongest roots of Kashmiri separatism and alienation lies in Article 370 of the Constitution of India, which gives special status to the State of Jammu and Kashmir. A fierce nation-wide controversy has often been raised about it.

While pondering over the need for fundamental reforms during Governor's Rule, in Kashmir, Shri Jagmohan, who was then Governor of Jammu and Kashmir in his diary in August

1986 wrote: "Article 370 is nothing but a feeding ground for the parasites at the heart of paradise. It skins the poor. It deceives them with its mirage. It lines the pockets of the 'power elites'. It fans the ego of the new 'sultans'. In essence, it creates a land without justice, a land full of crudités and contradictions. It props up politics of deception, duplicity and demagogy. It breeds the microbes of subversion. It keeps alive the unwholesome legacy of the two-nation theory. It suffocates the very idea of India and fogs the very vision of a great social and cultural crucible from Kashmir to Kanyakumari. It could be an epicenter of a violent earthquake in the Valley-an earthquake, the tremors of which would be felt all over the country with unforeseen consequences."

Over the years, Article 370 has become an instrument of exploitation in the hands of the ruling political elites and other vested interests in bureaucracy, business, the judiciary and bar. It has set in a vicious circle. It breeds separatist forces which in turn sustain and strengthen Article 370. Apart from the politicians, the richer classes have found it convenient to amass wealth and not allow healthy financial legislation to come to the State. The provisions of the Wealth tax, the Urban Land Ceiling Act, the Gift Tax, etc., and other beneficial laws of the Union have not been allowed to operate in the State under cover of Article 370. The common masses are prevented from realizing that Article 370 is actually keeping them impoverished and denying them justice and also their due share in the economic advancement.

The sum and substance of Article 370 is that with regard to Jammu and Kashmir, in addition to Defence, Foreign Affairs and Communication, the Union Parliament can make laws with regard to the items in the Union and Concurrent Lists but only with the concurrence of the State Government. This puts the Jammu and Kashmir State on a special footing. While the Union Parliament has unfettered powers to make laws for all the States in respect of items included in the Union and Concurrent Lists of the Constitution, it can do so with regard to Jammu and Kashmir only with the consent of the State Government.

## Delhi Agreement

In regard to political and constitutional issues, the fundamental question was: what would be the constitutional structure of the State and how it would fit into the overall framework—political, legal and financial—laid down by the Constitution of India. With Sheikh Abdullah's hidden ambition to carve out a virtual Sheikhdom for himself and his coterie and with his uncanny technique of exploiting India's difficulty with regard to holding of plebiscite, difference arose between him and the Central leader, particularly in regard to the issues of fundamental rights, citizenship, jurisdiction of the Supreme Court, Election Commission, Comptroller and Auditor General, emergency provisions, etc. A broad agreement, known as the Delhi Agreement, was arrived at. It was announced in the Union Parliament on July 24, 1952, by Nehru. On August 19, the Constituent Assembly of the State also approved it.

The provisions of the Delhi Agreement included abolition of the hereditary rulership; vesting of the residuary power in the State; continuance of special citizenship rights for the 'State subjects'; flying of a separate flag for the State with the national flag also finding a supremely distinct place; and, subject to certain restrictions and limitations, extension of provisions of the Indian Constitution in respect of fundamental rights, emergency powers of the President and jurisdiction of the Supreme Court.

Immediately after the announcement of the Delhi Agreement, the State Constituent Assembly proceeded to abolish the institution of the hereditary monarchy. The formal resolution was passed on August 21, 1952. The Head of the State was designated as the Sadar-i-Riyasat. He was to be elected by the State Legislative Assembly for a period of five years from amongst the persons who were "State Subjects of Class I". He was to be recognized by the President of India and hold office at his pleasure.

There was a substantial section of Indian opinion which thought that Sheikh Abdullah was being unduly appeased and national interests were being sacrificed. The Jammuites were particularly unhappy. They were incensed at the derogatory remarks which the Sheikh frequently made against the Dogra dynasty. For instance, on June 10, 1952, while speaking in the Constituent Assembly on the report of the Basic Principles Committee, Sheikh Abdullah said, "The people, under the guidance of National Conference, have sacrificed their lives, have gone to jails, and have lived in narrow cells inhabited by serpents and scorpions. Hundreds of womenfolk have been dishonoured, hundreds made to crawl on their bellies and thousands rendered martyrs by shedding their blood." Such observations showed little regard for facts or truth. These were also, in the changed circumstances, not called for. They merely added to tensions in Jammu.

The agitation in Jammu was led by the Praja Parishad. The main plank of the agitation was, "Ek desh mein do vidhan; ek desh mein do nishan; ek desh mein do pradhan nahin challenge"—"in one country, two constitutions; in one country, two flags; in one country, two prime ministers", would not be tolerated.

At the national level, it was strongly supported by Jana Sangh which was highly critical of the Delhi Agreement and reacted to it in these words; "Sheikh Abdullah has secured most unreasonable of his demands without conceding anything substantial. Every concession that Nehru has secured is limited by a proviso which almost nullifies it. This is not likely to gain Kashmir for India but will certainly endanger the security and development of Jammu and Kashmir."

Even with regard to the Delhi Agreement of which Nehru was severely criticized by the Praja Parishad, the stance of Sheikh Abdullah turned out to be insincere. In fact, to let him abolish the hereditary rulership and allow him to deal with the remaining items of the Delhi Agreement later was another mistake. If it had been insisted that all parts of this agreement should be implemented at one go, most of the subsequent troubles could have been avoided. After securing implementation of what suited him, Sheikh Abdullah referred the remaining clauses of the Agreement to the sub-committees of the Constituent Assembly, causing intentional delay. Even Nehru was dismayed by his crafty approach. He felt that he had been caught on the wrong foot. In his letters of August 6 and 7, 1952, to Abdullah, he lamented that his position in Parliament would become untenable if changes were made by the Kashmiri leaders in the Delhi Agreement. Again, on June 28, 1953, Nehru wrote to Abdullah: "To me it has been a major surprise that settlement arrived at between us should be by-passed or repudiated. That strikes at the root of all confidence. My honour is bound up with my word." But Abdullah was unmoved. He even avoided visiting Delhi for discussion, though he was invited by Nehru himself. Arrogance of power and visions of an independent Sheikhdom had wholly seized him (*Frozen Turbulence*: Jagmohan, pp. 95-97).

It would be noticed from the contents of Article 370 that it was transitional in nature. The Constituent Assembly of Jammu and Kashmir ratified the State's accession to India in February 1956. With this ratification, the issue of accession was finally settled but the issues in regard to jurisdiction of Parliament to subjects other than Defence, Foreign Affairs and Communication were kept flexible. The President could, extend provisions of the Indian Constitution to the State of Jammu and Kashmir.

The first order of the President of India, under Article 370, was issued in 1950. The order applied to the State of Jammu and Kashmir those provisions of the Indian Constitution which were related to the three subjects stipulated in the Instrument of Accession. The proposals to extend more items of the Indian Constitution to Jammu and Kashmir were further discussed by the representatives of the Union Government and the State Government. At that time Sheikh Mohammad Abdullah was the Prime Minister of Jammu and Kashmir. Consequent upon the discussions, an understanding is known as the Delhi Agreement (1952) in pursuance of which the President of India issued the Constitution (Application to Jammu and Kashmir) Order 1954. Under this Order, a number of provisions of the Indian Constitution were extended to the State. This order was amended from time to time extending more provisions of the Indian Constitution to the State. Separately, the Constitution of Jammu and Kashmir was amended in 1966 to change the denomination of Sadar-e-Riyasat to that of Governor and the Prime Minister to Chief Minister.

The position, in brief, today is that besides the subjects of Defence, Foreign Affairs and Communication, a number of provisions of the Indian Constitution stand extended to the State of Jammu and Kashmir. Important amongst these extensions are Article 356 and the jurisdiction of the Supreme Court, the Election Commission, and the Comptroller and Auditor General.

There is, however, still a vast area which remains under the exclusive jurisdiction of the State Government. It includes a substantial portion of the Concurrent List and also Residuary Powers. Article 352, which enables the President to declare a proclamation of financial emergency, is also not applicable. Neither can the President suspend the Constitution of the State, nor can he give any direction under Article 365.

The State has a Constitution of its own which is an unfortunate by-product of Article 370. No other State of the Indian Union has a separate Constitution. All other States have uniform structure; it is laid down in part IV of the Constitution of India.

The provisions of Jammu and Kashmir Constitution create a number of problems, particularly in regard to the right to hold property, right to citizenship, and right to settlement. The citizens of India do not automatically become the citizens of Jammu and Kashmir. They have no constitutional right of settlement in the State. The Constitution of India recognizes only one citizenship. But the citizens of Jammu and Kashmir enjoy double privileges—one as citizen of India and the other as citizen of the State. Those who are not citizens of Jammu and Kashmir are subjected to a number of disabilities. They cannot hold any property in the State. They have no right to vote in the election to the State Assembly or local bodies or panchayats and co-operative societies, etc. What is still more unjust is that if a woman, belonging to Jammu and Kashmir, gets married to a person who is not a citizen of Jammu and Kashmir, she loses her property; she cannot even inherit property from her parents. The unhealthy position is compounded by the fact that the

State has its own flag and its own emblem. On the government buildings, the National Flag and the State Flag are flown and the Ministers belonging to National Conference usually fly the National Flag as well as the flag of the National Conference.

On October 2, 1988, the birthday of Mahatma Gandhi, his statue was to be installed in the new High Court complex at Srinagar. The function had been announced. The Chief Justice of India, R.S. Pathak, was to do the formal installation. But a few Muslim lawyers objected. They threatened to cause disturbance at the time of the function. The Chief Minister gave in to the bullying tactics. The function was cancelled.

What were the implications of what happened? A secular Kashmir, part of a secular India, could not have, even in its highest seat of justice, the statue of the Father of the Nation, of a sage who laid down his life for communal harmony and about whom Einstein had said that "generations to come would scarcely believe that such a man ever trod on the earth". Who was the person spearheading the move against the installation? It was none other than Mohammad Shafi Butt, an advocate of the J&K High Court and an active member of the National Conference, who was later given party ticket for the Srinagar Lok Sabha seat in the elections held in November 1989.

At that time, there was a National Conference (F)-Congress (I) Ministry in office, such was its lack of adherence to principles, such was its disposition to cling to power, such was the character of Congressmen who formed part of the Ministry that not even a little finger was raised when the function was cancelled (*Frozen Turbulence*: Jagmohan, pp. 126-27).

Both for plan and non-plan finances, Jammu and Kashmir is heavily dependent upon the Union Government. Its five-year plans are wholly funded by the Centre. A substantial part of its non-plan expenditure is also met by the Union.

Abrogation of Article 370 would, in fact, help in removing poverty and backwardness, which, in turn, would help in rejuvenating Kashmiri culture and enhancing the cultural personality of the State as a whole. No culture can advance in isolation. It requires cross fertilization. It requires the 'stimulus of contact'.

Sheikh Abdullah resorted to his familiar technique of arousing parochial feelings and planting apprehensions in the minds of Kashmiris about the abrogation of Article 370. He went to the extent of saying, "We shall not hesitate to secede from India if we are not assured a place of honour and dignity in terms of the safeguards provided for the people of the State under Article 370 of the Constitution. We shall remain part of India only with dignity and honour. There had been much watering down of Article 370 since 1953. We have to strengthen it with all our might.

The Union Government enacted the Religious Institutions (Prevention of Misuse) Act, 1988. It was made applicable to all the States of the Union except J&K. Because of Article 370, the concurrence of the State Government was needed for extension of this law to the State Government. But the same was not given. Why? Because J&K is different; its personality, its identity, is different. What an argument for not having a law which aimed at prevention of misuse of religious premises for political purposes!

Nowhere was this law more needed than in the State of Jammu and Kashmir. Nowhere were religious places misused more than here. Nowhere were the seeds of fanaticism and fundamentalism sown more assiduously than from the pulpits of mosques here, every Friday. Nowhere has it been preached more regularly than here that Indian democracy was un-Islamic, Indian secularism was un-Islamic, and Indian socialism was un-Islamic. And yet, neither the State Government which was ruled by two supposedly secular parties, nor the Union Government took the matter seriously. The Union Government did not discharge its obligations to pressurize or persuade the State to fall in line with the rest of the country. What intrigued most was that the law, which was considered good for about 100 million Muslims in other parts of India, was not considered good for four million Muslims of Kashmir.

After 1977, Sheikh Abdullah acquired almost unlimited powers. And corruption acquired new fangs and depth in

Kashmir. The power-circle grew closer; the roles of politicians and civil servants virtually merged; the curtain of Article 370 acquired a thicker and more malevolent texture; and increasing reliance came to be placed upon money-power and exploitation of parochial emotions rather than on solid, sound and honest work. And one could easily see the operation of the well-known dictum of Lord Action: "Power corrupts, and absolute power corrupts absolutely."

The Ladakhi Association vehemently complained that "Being assured of Article 370, the Kashmiris have trained their guns on the minuscule Buddhist population with the ultimate objective of assimilating them in the Islamic faith. The State Government, dominated by Kashmir Muslims, have been openly encouraging conversion of Ladakhi Buddhist to Islam. The Underlying idea has been to disturb the balance of population in favour of Muslims. Conversion has assumed a menacing proportion in the recent years. The Islamic fundamentalists and zealots have been encouraged by the State Government to carry out a relentless campaign of conversion. By using monetary power and fraudulent propaganda means they have converted hundreds of Buddhist girls to Islam. Underlying the conversion campaign is the design to Islamic Ladakh and to consolidate the Valley based on separatist and secessionist politics."

Another ground of strong resentment was the appointment of certain Kashmiri officers who allegedly established a nexus with 'Argoras'—a tiny community of Kashmiri Sunni Muslim elite traders who settled in Ladakh years ago—and misappropriated the plan funds and thus deprived Ladakh of whatever little development that could have taken place.

Yet another grievance of the Ladakhis was that in Dr. Farooq Abdullah's ministry of 1989, there were 30 ministers, but not a single one from their region. They raised a number of other questions: "How does the government justify the inclusion of departments such as tourism, power and horticulture in the district plan of Leh, when in other districts these departments receive funds from the State sector? How is it that the World Bank aided Social Forestry Scheme received ` 24 crores in the last four years and Leh district was not covered at all? At the senior level, the local officers are not appointed in Ladakh on the plea that they would not be objective, but why is this criterion not employed in Kashmir where exactly the opposite tune is played?"

The people of the Jammu region nurse a long-standing grievance that, under cover of Article 370 and the State Constitution, the decisions over the years have been so manipulated by the Valley-leaders that the power structure in the State has permanently tilted in favour of the Kashmir region.

The Ladakhis, too, highly resentful that the leverage of Article 370 has been placed in the hands of the Kashmir leadership. They have been complaining that, instead of being made "free sons of free India". They are often heard saying, "If India is going to keep us under the Kashmiri domination, then it is as bad as being under the Chinese." As early as 1949, in an impassioned plea to Prime Minister Nehru for taking Ladakh directly under the care of the Union Government, the Ladakhi Buddhist Association said, "Tibet is the cultural daughter of India, and we of the 'lesser Tibet' seek the bosom of the gracious mother to receive more nourishment for growth to full stature. Will the great mother (India) refuse to take to her arms one of her weakest, forlorn and distressed children?"

On account of the provisions of Article 370, the valley leadership acquired almost unlimited control over Ladakh, and even those institutional safeguards which were available elsewhere in the country were denied to the Ladakhis. The violent agitation of Ladakhi Buddhists in July-September 1989 was an expression of their strong resentment against what they called the Kashmiri domination and exploitation.

Some leaders and analysts continue to say that Article 370 is a matter of faith. But they do not proceed further. They do not ask themselves: what does this faith mean? What is its rational? Would not bringing the State within the full framework of the Indian constitution give brighter luster and sharper teeth to this faith and make it more just and meaningful?

In a similar strain, expressions like 'historical necessity' and 'autonomy' are talked about. What do these terms mean in practice? Does historical necessity mean that you include, on paper, Kashmir in the Indian Union on the one hand at a huge cost and give it back, in practice, on the other hand, on a golden platter? And what does autonomy or the so-called pre-1953 or pre-1947 position imply? Would it not amount to the Kashmiri leadership saying: "You will send and I will spend; you will have no say even if I build corrupt and callous oligarchy and cause a situation in which Damocles' sword of secession could be kept hanging over your head?"

Can Article 370 be abrogated? If so, how? It has sometimes been argued that it is not constitutionally permissible to abrogate this Article without the approval of the Constituent Assembly of the State. It is said that a plain reading of the Constitution makes the position clear in this regard. The relevant portion of Article 370 reads:

> Notwithstanding anything in the foregoing provisions of the article, the President may, by public notification, declare that this article shall cease to be operative....
>
> ...Provided that the recommendation of the Constituent Assembly of the State referred to in clause (2) shall be necessary before the President issues a notification.

An essential prerequisite of the Presidential declaration is the recommendation of the Constituent Assembly. In other words, even if the Union Government decides to abrogate this Article, it cannot constitutionally do so by itself as this would involve positioning of the State's Constituent Assembly and getting its recommendations. The amending powers under Article 368 of the Constitution would also not help.

On the face of it, the aforesaid argument is impressive. But no provision of the Constitution can be read in isolation. Article 1 is of far more fundamental importance. It reads:

"1. *Name and Territory of the Union.* India, that is Bharat, shall be a Union of States.'

The States and territories thereof shall be as specified in the First Schedule; and (c) such other territories as may be acquired."

Jammu and Kashmir is the 15th State in Schedule 1 of the Constitution, and Article 1 applies to it in its entirety. On the other hand, Article 370 is transitional. The very heading of part XXI of the Constitution reads: "Temporary, transitional and special provisions." Thus, at the time when Article 370 was framed, the understanding was that it would stay for a short time and cover the transitional period. Since the State's Constituent Assembly no longer exists, the question of its consent under Article 370 does not arise. Consent of a dead body or a non-existent body has no meaning. The Constitution can, therefore, be amended under Article 368 by the Union Parliament which represents the people of the State also. Thereafter, the aforesaid proviso requiring the recommendation of the Constituent Assembly could be deleted. After this deletion has been carried out, the President can make the necessary declaration and Article 370 would stand abrogated.

The current situation in the Kashmir shows that Article 370 has created a separate psyche and thus threatened the territorial integrity of the Union (*Frozen Turbulence*: Jagmohan, pp. 107, 130-31, 204, 226-27, 245-47).

While speaking on Article 370 in Lok Sabha on 26 June 1952, Dr. Shyama Prasad Mookerjee asked: "How is Kashmir going to be integrated with India? Is Kashmir going to be republic within a republic? Are we thinking of another sovereign Parliament within four corners of India—barring the sovereign Parliament?" He warned: "If you just want to play with the words and say we are helpless and let Sheikh Abdullah do what he likes, then Kashmir would be lost. I say this with great deliberations that Kashmir will be lost."

Dr. Mookerjee further asked: "Are not the people of Jammu and Kashmir entitled to the Fundamental Rights that we have given to the people of India? Who made Sheikh Abdullah king of kings in Kashmir. Did we do it for creating a sovereign republic within a sovereign republic? There is no scope for varied constitutional patterns and disparities between one federating unit and another."

Dr Mookerjee brought the following statement of Sheikh Abdullah to the notice of the Prime Minister in Parliament:

> We are a hundred percent sovereign body. No country can put spokes in the wheel of our progress. Neither the Indian Parliament nor any other Parliament outside the State has any jurisdiction over our State.

On the above statement, Dr. Mookerjee said: "Let Sheikh Abdullah declare that he accepts the sovereignty of this Parliament. There cannot be two sovereign Parliaments in India. You (Nehru) talk of Kashmir being a part of India and Sheikh Abdullah talks of a sovereign Parliament for Kashmir. It is inconsistent. It is contradictory. And why should he be afraid of accepting the sovereignty of this Parliament of Free India?

"Secondly, it is not a matter of changing the provisions of the constitution by the president's order? .... At present, Sheikh Abdullah's Government is responsible to the Maharaja according to the constitution, responsible to one who is being described as wrethched fellow, who has to be turned out lock, stock and barrel. In every speech of his, he says: "The Maharaja, the Dogra Raj is being finished. What is the use of flogging a dead horse. What is the use of saying it?"

Sheikh Abdullah says: "I want an elected head now." Why can you not tell him and others what you have done in the constitution that originally we provided for an elected Governor, but after a good deal of thought we did away with that.

"And then the Flag. The Flag has a significance. It will not do for the Prime Minister to say that it is a matter of sentiment. It was announced in the papers that Indian Flag will fly only on two ceremonial occasions and otherwise the State Flag alone will fly there. If you feel that the unity and integrity of India are not affected and it will not lead to fissiparous tendencies being generated, accept it and do it for all. But why do it as a matter of surrender to Sheikh Abdullah?

"Sheikh Abdullah wanted to call himself the Prime Minister.... We know one Prime Minister of India including Kashmir, that is the Prime Minister, who is sitting here. How can you have two Prime Ministers, one Prime Minister in Delhi and another Prime Minister in Srinagar?

"You are changing without giving much thought to the provisions of the constitution regarding citizenship.... Four classes of citizenship in Jammu and Kashmir—What for? They should be abolished. There should be only one class of citizenship.

"We have Kashmiri Prime Minister of India. We welcome him. What is the fear? Is it feared that Indians will go there and invade Kashmir and one of them will become the Chief Minister of Jammu and Kashmir?

"Why this anxiety on the part of Sheikh Abdullah to make a special provision for getting back those who ran away to Pakistan and who are not prepared to come?

"As regards the emergency provisions, it is amazing stand. If there is an emergency on account of internal disturbances, the President of India will not have the last say. Can you contemplate a more gratuitous insult to the President of India? I would expect the Prime Minister to tell whether the other emergency provisions apply or not. There are two other very important provisions in the constitution. Article 354 relates to application of provisions relating to the distribution of revenues while proclamation of emergency is in operation and the other Article is Article 356 relating to the provisions in case of failure of constitutional machinery in States. Has Sheikh Abdullah accepted the application of Article 356? The Prime Minister does not make reference to it. The Supreme Court's jurisdiction also has not yet been accepted.

On August 21, 1962, in reply to Pandit Prem Nath Bazaz's letter concerning Article 370, Jawaharlal Nehru wrote:

"As a matter of fact, much has been done in spite of the Article in the Constitution which is supposed to give a special status to Kashmir and gradually what little remains will also go. The question is more a sentimental one than anything else. Sentiment is sometimes important but we have to weigh both the sides and I think no change should be made in the matter for the present."

Towards the end of his life, and perhaps chastened by the bitter experience of India's defeat in the 1962 Chinese war of aggression, Nehru himself became somewhat more realistic about Article 370. Thus, on 27 November 1963, he said in the Lok Sabha: "Our view is that Article 370, as is written in the Constitution, is a *transitional*, in other words a *temporary* provision. And it is so...as a matter of fact, as the Home Minister has pointed out, it has been eroded, if I may use the word, and many things have been done in the last few years which have made the relationship of Kashmir with the Union of India very close. There is no doubt that Kashmir is fully integrated.... So we feel that this process of gradual erosion of Article 370 is going on...."

This shows that Nehru himself did not rule out future change with regard to Article 370. And so far as sentiments are concerned, it is quite clear by now that they have operated in the opposite direction and strengthened the separatist and subversive psyche which in turn here threatened the very unity and integrity of the country,. it is time that the seed that has given birth to an unhealthy plant is pulled out from its roots.

Retention of Article 370 has sometimes been justified by saying that it is not a wall but a tunnel. On December 4, 1964, Gulzari Lal Nanda, Union Home Minister, said, "Through this tunnel, a good deal of traffic has already passed; more will pass now." A few days later, M.C. Chagla, Education Minister, observed, "Through Article 370, the whole of the Indian Constitution could be applied to Jammu and Kashmir. M.C. Chagla wanted the separate Constitution of Jammu and Kashmir to be scrapped.

It should be evident that Article 370 and its by-product, the separate Constitution of Jammu and Kashmir, must go, not only because it is legally and constitutionally feasible to do so, but also because larger and more basic considerations of our past history and contemporary life require it. This Article and its accompanying paraphernalia need to be abrogated. It serves as an instrument of perpetrating injustices and inequities. It facilitates the growth and communication of corrupt oligarchies. It fans and feeds the forces of parochialism and obscurantism. It implicitly recognizes the two-nation theory. It acts as a breeding ground for separate emotions. It puts false notions in the minds of the youths, and it creates narrow grooves and narrow loyalties. It gives rise to regional tensions and conflicts, and even the autonomy assumed to be available is not attainable in practice. The distinct personality and cultural identity of Kashmir can be safeguarded without this Article. It is socially regressive and causes situations in which women lose their rights if they marry non-State subjects and persons staying for over forty years in the State are denied elementary human and democratic rights. And, above all, it does not fit into the reality and requirements of India and its vast and varied span. What India needs today is not petty sovereignties that would sap its spirit and aspirations and turn it into small 'banana-republics' in the hands of 'tin-pot dictators', but a new social, political and cultural crucible in which the age-old traditions of pluralism and tolerance, of truth and rectitude, of fairness and justice, and of compassion and catholicity, are melted, purified and moulded into a vigorous and vibrant set-up which provides real freedom, real democracy, and real resurgence to all (*My Frozen Turbulence in Kashmir*: Jagmohan, Allied Publishers Limited, pp. 230-34; 245-48; 251-52).

## Abrogate Article 370

Bhartiya Jana Sangh and later as the Bharatiya Janata Party (BJP) has been all along opposed to Article 370. Perhaps no other issue has figured as regularly in its party resolutions, and as many times, as Jammu & Kashmir's full integration into the Indian Union. For example, in a resolution titled 'Abrogate Article 370', passed in Kanpur in January 1966, the Jana Sangh said:

> Jammu & Kashmir is an integral part of India. Pakistan has aggressively occupied one-third part of the state since 1947. To get that aggression vacated and secure the liberation of Pak-occupied part of the state is the duty of the government of India.... The question of the constitutional integration of that part of Jammu & Kashmir (which is in our hands) with the rest of India is a purely internal affair of India. The temporary and transitional Article 370 of the Indian Constitution on

> the basis of which Jammu & Kashmir has a separate constitution of its own is a big hindrance in the way of such integration. It has created a psychological barrier between the people of the state and their counterparts in the rest of India, which has been exploited all these years by anti-national elements and Pak agents to the detriment of India's vital interests. Its abrogation, and application of the Indian Constitution in full to Jammu & Kashmir, is an essential prerequisite for the normalization of the situation within the state.

The nation was shocked on 26 June 2000, during the Vajpayee Government's rule in New Delhi, when the Jammu & Kashmir assembly adopted a report of the State Autonomy Committee (SAC) and asked the centre to immediately implement it. The SAC recommended return of the constitutional situation in J&K to its pre-1953 status, by restoring to the state all subjects for governance except defence, foreign affairs, currency and communication. MLAs belonging to BJP, Janata Dal (United), Congress and a few other regional parties voted against the motion.

The Union Cabinet, at its meeting on 4 July, rejected the J&K legislative assembly's autonomy resolution. L.K. Advani told the media on that day, "its acceptance will set the clock back and reverse the natural process of harmonizing the aspirations of the people of the state with the integrity of the nation." Advani added: "If the government were to accept it, it would encourage trends that will not be conducive to natural unity.' He emphasised that, although "there is a clear case for devolution of more financial and administrative powers from the Centre to the states", the NDA Government favoured this for all the states, and not for Jammu & Kashmir alone. In any case, devolution of greater powers to states was very different from granting autonomy to states. Advani also reminded that the issue of restoring the constitutional situation in J&K to its pre-1953 status had been discussed and settled a quarter century ago, in the 1975 accord between Indira Gandhi and Sheikh Abdullah. This agreement had clearly affirmed that "provisions of the Constitution of India already applied to the state of

Jammu and Kashmir without adaptation or modification are unalterable".

Advani further says: This was one occasion when both Atalji and I had to be very firm with the state's Chief Minister, Dr Farooq Abdullah, whose National Conference was in fact a part of the ruling NDA at the Centre. We advised him not to press for the implementation of the SAC report. Indeed, Atalji told Dr Abdullah to decide whether to continue in the NDA at the Centre following the Union Cabinet's rejection of the state assembly's autonomy resolution. To his credit, Dr Abdullah allowed the issue to lapse (*My Country—My Life*: L.K. Advani, Rupa & Co., pp. 678-79)

I am reminded of what late J.P. Mathur, a founder member of the Bharatiya Jan Sangh said and I quote: "Even if the BJP ever got the majority, it might not be able to repeal Article 370 so easily."

The BJP manifesto in the last Jammu and Kashmir election included abrogation of Article 370 but as the election drew near, it had to sleep over it and while forming the coalition government with PDP in Jammu and Kashmir, BJP had to agree to maintain status quo on Article 370.

Article 370 has become breeding ground for separatist emotions and in consequence a perennial headache for India.

# 9

# Sardar Patel and Article 370

In the course of a statement on Kashmir made in the Lok Sabha on 24 July 1952, Nehru defended the Article 370 on the ground that, as the issue had been referred to the United Nations, 'the whole matter was in a fluid state'. He went on to add that the matter relating to J&K's position in the Constitution was clinched in November 1949, and that it was Sardar Patel who was 'all this time dealing with it'.

Pandit Nehru was quite correct inasmuch as, when the Constituent Assembly adopted this particular provision, the Prime Minister had gone abroad, and all affairs of government were being looked after by Sardar Patel, the Deputy Prime Minister. But thereby hangs an interesting tale, recounted in some detail by V. Shankar, Private Secretary to Sardar Patel at that time. In his two-volume book, *My Reminiscences of Sardar Patel*, Shankar says that Sheikh Abdullah, "did not trust the Indian government and while he accepted a constitutional relationship with the Indian Union, he wanted to reserve to the government of Jammu & Kashmir of his choice the final word as to the detailed content of the accession—three subjects of defence, external affairs and communication—and any further accretion to such accession". Abdullah also wanted full freedom for the state's Constituent Assembly to form its own constitution.

Before going abroad, Nehru finalized the draft provisions relating to Jammu & Kashmir with Sheikh Abdullah and entrusted it to Gopalaswamy Ayyangar with the task of piloting these provisions through the Constituent Assembly. Obviously, Ayyangar had no idea as to how daunting this task was going to prove. Before formally moving the Article in the Constituent Assembly, Ayyangar spelt out his proposals in the Congress Parliamentary Party. His presentation, Shankar notes, provoked "a storm of angry protests from all sides, and Ayyangar found himself a lone defender with Maulana Azad an ineffective supporter". According to Shankar, "in the party, there was a strong body of opinion which looked askance at any suggestion of discrimination between Jammu & Kashmir state and other states as members of the future Indian Union and was not prepared to go beyond certain limits in providing for the special position of Jammu & Kashmir. Sardar was himself fully in accord with this opinion, but due to his usual policy of not standing in the way of Pandit Nehru and Gopalaswamy Ayyangar, who sorted out problems in their own lights, he had kept his own views in the background. In fact, he had not taken any part in framing the draft proposals with the result that he heard the proposals only when Gopalaswamy Ayyangar announced them to the Congress party."

Dismayed by the rough reception he had had to face at the meeting of Congress parliamentary party meeting, Ayyangar rushed to Sardar Patel and 'appealed to him to come to his rescue'. What transpired subsequently has been recounted by Shankar thus: "Sardar heard him (Ayyangar) and lapsed into silence. To my query as to what reply he would like to give, he said he would think it over. Later in the evening, he rang me up and told me that he had sent for Satyanarayan Sinha, the Congress chief whip, and had asked him to convene a meeting of the party executive, together with some of the prominent stormy petrels and they would discuss the matter; he wanted me to be present at the meeting. The meeting was held at the appointed hour and Maulana Azad was also present. The meeting was one of the stormiest I have ever witnessed. The opinion in opposition to Gopalsawamy's formula was forcefully and even militantly expressed...even Maulana Azad was shouted down. It was left to Sardar to bring the discussion down to the practical plane and to plead that because of the international complications, a provisional approach alone could be made...."

Reluctantly, it seems, the Congress Party fell in line with the Sardar's wishes. Indeed, it is this that explains why in the Constituent Assembly the discussion on this provision was so vapid and sketchy. Apart from Ayyangar's own speech, there was not a single worthwhile intervention, either for, or against. The steam, obviously, had been let off at the party meeting.

Curiously, Sardar's success at persuading Congressmen to reconcile with this 'temporary' provision of Article 370 brought about an estrangement of sorts between Patel and his lieutenant. Shankar writes: "I was somewhat taken aback at Sardar's acquiescence in the draft formula of Gopalaswamy and strongly felt that Sardar had compromised the position of the Indian Union and other states in accepting that formula as the basis. Frankly speaking, "I was resentful of Sardar's attitude and when we returned to his residence during the lunch break, I was silent and sullen and repaired straight to my office room. Maniben (Patel's daughter) came to call me for lunch; I declined to go and told her about the pain and anguish inwardly felt, adding that for the first time I nursed a grievance of betrayal on the part of Sardar. She conveyed my feeling of resentment to Sardar, who sent her back to tell me that I should join the lunch table at least for a talk. I did so, accordingly, as soon as I was seated, Sardar spoke, 'So you are annoyed with me for having accepted Gopalaswamy's formula.' I queried that if he felt that way, why did he not indicate his mind earlier. He said, 'I was deeply concerned at the situation. Gopalaswamy had acted under Panditji's advice. If Jawaharalal were here I could have had it out with him, but how could I do so with Gopalaswamy, who was only acting under orders? If I did, people would have said that I was taking revenge on his confidante when he was away. Gopalaswamy had appealed to me for help. How could I have let him down in the absence of his chief?'"

Shankar continues: "I then asked why he had let down the country and the other states whose constituent assemblies had been scrapped in accordance with his advice and policy. He conceded the validity of the criticism but pointed out the delicate international position of the state and the issue of its relationship with India. We felt that the present situation had to be tided over without giving up the eventuality and this had been done under the formula. He said that after all, neither Sheikh Abdullah nor Gopalaswamy was permanent. The future would depend on the strength and guts of the Indian government, and if "we cannot have confidence in our own strength we do not deserve to exist as a nation."

It is hard for me to yield to the justification given by Sardar Patel. There is no secret that Nehru and Patel were in conflict on matters of principles. Sardar had courage to call a spade a spade, at times shovel. He had gone to the extent of saying that if there is any secularist Muslim in India, he is Jawaharlal Nehru. I feel, Sardar Patel instead of caring for the feelings of Nehru and what people would think, should have thought of far reaching consequences of Article 370 and should have allowed Congress Parliamentary Committee to go its way, which may have resulted in not seeing through the Draft Article 370 in the Constituent Assembly.

All those mattered have gone, but Article 370 remained. No government had strength and guts to do away with it. Every move and effort to abrogate Article 370 so far has proved an exercise in futility.

# 10

# Regional Autonomy

Jammu's regional discontent also branched off into a demand for regional autonomy.

The proponents of regional autonomy, drew their inspiration from and had participated in the freedom movement in the State which was directed against the authoritarian rule of the Maharaja and supported by the Indian National Congress. They opposed the concept of an independent Hindu State and demanded accession of the State to the Indian Union under the leadership of Sheikh Abdullah in 1947, thereafter they demanded equitable share in political power of the people of all the three regions. For achieving this objective, they believed, abolition of monarchy and a secular democratic organization were indispensable.

They opposed suppression of Kashmiri urges by the ruler before 1947 and the Government of India after 1953.

## Nehru-Abdullah Commitment

The demand of regional autonomy received positive response from Nehru and the Sheikh. Releasing the Delhi Agreement, Nehru told a press conference in New Delhi on 24 July 1952, in the presence of the Sheikh, that the State Government was considering regional autonomies within the larger State. Separately, the Sheikh gave an assurance to the effect that the constitution of the State, when complete would give limited regional autonomy, particularly in the cultural spheres, to Jammu and Ladakh.

In essence, the underlying principle of the Delhi Agreement was autonomy of the State within India and autonomy of the regions within the State.

However, the agreement was strongly opposed by Shyamprasad Mookerjee and N.C. Chatterjee and Jammu Praja Parishad which started an agitation against its implementation and for full accession in November 1952.

Perturbed over the possible consequences of the Praja Parishad agitation Balraj Puri sought the intervention of Nehru on 6 January 1953. In that meeting he submitted his assessment of the situation as follows:

"The unhappy situation in Jammu is mostly due to the local nationalism of the various regions of the State taking an aggressive form. We regret that even Sheikh Abdullah remained essentially a hero of Kashmir nationalism and could not reconcile himself to the role of the leadership of the State....

"We are not very clear about the real motives of the Kashmiri leadership regarding their Jammu policy. But we feel circumstances were often created which deliberately encouraged Praja Parishad at our cost. We suggest political and constitutional changes to remove the present unrest.... Conditions must be created so that the people of Jammu may feel that they are free from the so-called Kashmiri domination. An announcement for granting some sort of autonomy to each region would considerably ease the situation. It is the logical end of what is being called "limited accession. We emphasize that the integrity of the State be maintained and feel that autonomy to each region would act as a unfying force between the peoples of all the regions."

## Jana Sangh Support

Jana Sangh President Dr Shyamaprasad Mookerjee also veered round to this view. In a letter to Prime Minister Nehru on 17 February 1953, he offered to withdraw the Parishad agitation and accept the Delhi Agreement, unity of the State and the principle of autonomy which would "apply to the province of Jammu as a whole and of course also to Ladakh and Kashmir Valley."

Sheikh Abdullah, reiterated the decision of his government to "give autonomy to the different cultural units of the State as will be provided in the Constitution that is being drawn up." Broadcasting from Radio Kashmir, Srinagar, on 17 April 1953, he said: "This will remove all the fears of domination of one unit over the other and will make for the voluntary unity and consolidation of the people of the State."

Nehru made a similar announcement on 2 July 1953 in which he said "The State Government was considering grant of autonomy to its regions, particularly Jammu, while framing the Constitution of the State." On the following day, the then Deputy Prime Minister of the State Bakshi Ghulam Mohammad, said, in a press statement, that Nehru's announcement reflected the policy of the State Government. He added, "Sheikh Abdullah has consented to the proposed scheme of autonomy for the constituent units of the State so as to ensure its unity."

Referring to inter-regional relations, Bakshi, who succeeded the Sheikh, observed in a radio broadcast from Srinagar on 9 August 1953, that "the rights and privileges that we secure for the State as a whole have to be shared in equal measure by the people of its different parts." He further added, "a genuinely democratic set up has to satisfy the demands of each one of the constituent units of the State with due regard to its basic unity and integrity."

A sub-committee of the State Constituent Assembly, consisting of Messrs D.P. Dhar, Syed Mir Qasim and G.L. Dogra, recommended a substantial measure of autonomy for each region with power of taxation and legislation.

As G.M. Sadiq became Prime Minister (later called Chief Minister) of the State in March 1964, hopes were revived for implementation of the idea of regional autonomy. For before coming to power, he had often made sympathetic references to the aspirations of Jammu.

## Karan Singh Formula

However, G.M. Sadiq was soon involved in a bitter controversy with the then Governor of the State, Dr. Karan Singh, who, in a statement to *Times*, London in November 1965, had proposed linguistic re-organization of the State and merger of Jammu with the adjoining Himachal Pradesh. Sadiq called it "an imported idea which was fraught with dangerous consequences and should be resisted with "all our might".

Taking cognizance of the problem, J&K Pradesh Congress Committee appointed a five member committee, with Sadiq as Chairman and Messrs Syed Mir Qasim, Shamsuddin, Bhagat Chhaju Ram and Trilochan Dutt as members to look into the grievances of Jammu.

After the assembly election of 1967, when Sadiq returned to power with a legislative party of his choice, his attitude hardened. He, his party and government launched a massive attack on the movement of regional autonomy. Other parties also joined the attack. These included PSP, CPI, local National Conference, political wing of Anand Marg and a number of ad hoc organizations. An EKTA Front was set up to coordinate the concerted anti-autonomy campaign.

In an article in *Indian Express* of 19 August 1967, Balraj Puri described the heat generated by the controversy as follows:

> The Pradesh Congress Executive condemned it (regional autonomy) as a disruptionist slogan. The All India Jana Sangh Working Committee at its meeting at Simla on 2 July strongly denounced any move to grant regional autonomy to Jammu. For "it would benefit only the supporters of Sheikh Abdullah and pro-Pakistan elements."

## Autonomy Campaign

On 18 April 1967, Puri addressed a crowded meeting at the Gulab Bhawan Jammu which was exclusively devoted to elaboration of the demand for regional autonomy. He said:

> The idea of regional autonomy rested on principles accepted all over the country. It was one of the basic

> principles of a federal and democratic country like India that each distinct cultural entity should be recognized and provided with opportunities of full growth. Even in unbillingual states, safeguards had been provided for each region within it. The basic principle had been implemented either through linguistic re-organisation of states or regional committees or sub-legislatures. The latest experiment was in Assam where hill areas were granted autonomy within the State.

The stand taken by Puri was endorsed by 180 prominent citizens belonging to all walks of life and communities including public men, social workers, writers, intellectuals, retired civil servants, doctors and advocates. In a one sentence statement they said "we support the demand of regional autonomy for Jammu within the framework of the State to promote friendly relations between its principal regions and restore its politics on healthy and secular basis."

## Erosion of Sangh

By collaborating with the Kashmiri leadership of the ruling Congress Party on this issue, the Sangh lost some of its credibility as a champion of regional interests of Jammu. The alternative solution, suggested by Jana Sangh, and supported by the Anand Marg, of the merger of Jammu and Kashmir State with Himachal virtually amounted to dividing the former State on Hindu Muslim basis and exposed its pretensions in favour of unity of the State. It had also undermined its position by proposing, before the Delimitation Commission, division of Jammu to carve out one Hindu majority constituency of Jammu, Udhampur and Kathua districts after merger of Poonch with the Shopian constituency of Anantnag (Kashmir) and Doda with Ladakh.

In a report on the situation in Jammu, *Nav Bharat Times* of 8 August, 1967 referred to the anomalous position of Jana Sangh. For "people failed to understand why it was opposing a demand in which interest of the people of Jammu seemed to lie." *Pratap*, the Urdu daily of Delhi lamented that Jana Sangh leader Prem Nath Dogra was allergic to the word "Autonomy".

The Congress Party also suffered some loss of support on account of its opposition to the autonomy move. The president of its youth wing Jammu and Kashmir Pradesh Youth Congress, Amrit Malhotra resigned from the party along with a large number of his Jammu colleagues to join the Autonomy Forum.

Sheikh Abdullah also joined the critics of regional autonomy. In a post-prayer meeting at Jammu, he condemned it as "a game of Indian imperialism."

"Jammu Autonomy Forum accused Sheikh Abdullah and Jana Sangh of appealing to communal sentiments of Muslims and Hindus respectively to oppose its move for regional autonomy.

"A statement issued by the Forum said that the communalizing of politics endangered the integrity of the State.

The forum regretted that the Sheikh had forgotten his own socio-economic plan for Kashmir promising decentralization" (*Hindustan Times*, 4 May 1968).

Recalling Sheikh's earlier commitments in favour of regional autonomy, Balraj Puri said: "It is surprising that Abdullah, who accuses the Government of India of eroding the autonomy of the State, is now dismissing similar urges of Jammu" (*Patriot,* 30 May, 1968).

In a message to the convention of Jammu Autonomy Forum on 19 November, 1967, Shamin Ahmed Shamim, MLA and Editor of the weekly *Aina Srinagar*, said:

> As I attach great importance to the protection of autonomy, individuality and personality of Kashmir, I have deep interest in the programme and objective of the Autonomy Forum.... Whatever else might be said against those who are demanding autonomy for Jammu, it would be height of injustice to accuse them of communalism or anti-Kashmirism. Far from wanting to divide the State, they want to restore the mutual relations between Jammu and Kashmir on healthy and stable basis.

Shamim also gave notice of moving a constitutional amendment bill in the State Assembly incorporating the principle of regional autonomy.

Bakshi Ghulam Mohammad, the former Prime Minister of the State, also supported the principle.

Outside the State, it had received sympathetic consideration at a seminar on Kashmir convened by Jayaprakash Narayan and attended by Persons like C.D. Deshmukh, Col. B.H. Zaidi, P.N. Sapru, Khushwant Singh and S. Mulgaokar. It stated: "all talks of emotional integration of Kashmir, normalization of its politics and settlement about any particular constitutional status are completely meaningless unless urges of both Jammu and Kashmir can be harmonized" (*Kashmir Times*, Jammu, December 1966).

Jayaprakash Narayan himself advocated "radical solutions including greater autonomy for Jammu and Kashmir State within the Union and within the State itself, autonomy for Jammu". (*Hindustan Times*, 31 March 1968).

## Gajendragadkar Commission

In order to "defuse" the situation, the State Government appointed, in consultation with the Union Government, the Jammu and Kashmir Commission of Enquiry on 6 November 1967.

P.B. Gajendragadkar, retired Chief Justice of India headed the Commission while Shankar Prasada and Badr-ud-din Tyabji, ICS retired Secretaries of the Government of India were its other members. Its terms of reference included examination of policies regarding development, recruitment and admissions (to institutions of higher education) and "consider generally the causes that lead to irritations and tensions and to recommend remedial measures". The Commission was required to suggest measures not only for equitable share of resources among the regions of the State but also for conveying "a feeling of equal participation in the integrated development of the State."

Concretising its demand, Jammu Autonomy Forum, in its memorandum to the Commission, suggested:

> While number of subjects proposed to be delegated to the hill areas of Assam should broadly form the basis of a similar division in case of Jammu and Kashmir State, the regional administration may broadly follow the pattern of Delhi Metropolitan Council with which Parliament shares some of its legislature and executive power over the Union territory.
>
> The memorandum stated that regional autonomy will not only solve Jammu's specific problems but help evolve rational and mutually satisfactory relations between Kashmir, Jammu and Ladakh.

The other party that came close to the Stand of Autonomy Forum was Jammu and Kashmir National Conference led by Bakshi Ghulam Mohammad. In its memorandum to the Commission, it said: "Situation can be remedied if power is decentralized and given to locally elected organs at Tehsil, district and provincial levels (with a Cabinet at the top) with provisions for consideration of special provincial problems through democratically evolved instruments of power for administration.... Powers of the government should be so decentralized that proper control and supervision can be assured. Means will have to be devised so that this feeling of neglet and isolation in one province when the seat of government is in the other can be eliminated."

Meanwhile Prime Minister Indira Gandhi in a public statement at Srinagar ruled out granting of regional autonomy to Jammu. Protesting against her remarks a resolution of the Autonomy Forum said: "Her statement implies a lack of respect for the august Commission and sympathy for aspirations of the people of Jammu" (*Hindustan Times*, 28 June, 1968).

The report of the Gajendragadkar Commission, submitted to the Government, in December 1968, made a positive contribution to the debate on inter-regional relations in two major respects. First it stressed the need for recognition of regional identities in various fields of government activity. It said:

> Although the Jammu and Kashmir State has been a single political entity for over a hundred years, it cannot be denied that geographically, ethnically, culturally and historically, it is composed of three separate homogeneous regions, namely Jammu, Kashmir, and Ladakh. In fact, the Pir Panjal range forms a natural dividing line between the Jammu and Kashmir regions.

Secondly, recognizing paramountcy of political aspiration, it conceded, real or imagined, from which certain even if all the matters were equitably settled, we feel that there would still be a measure of discontent unless the political aspirations of the different regions of the State were satisfied. In fact, we consider that the main cause of irritation and tension is the feeling of political neglect and discrimination, real or imagined, from which certain regions of the state suffer.

Summary of Recommendations of Gajendragadkar Commission is given below:

**Development Programmes:**

1. There should be a statutory State Development Board and statutory Regional Development Boards for the three regions—Jammu, Kashmir and Ladakh. The Regional Boards should be headed by Chief Minister or the Planning Minister and legislatures from the regions should be adequately represented on the State Development Board should be headed by the Chief Minister.

The functions of the Regional Development Boards will be:

(i) to draw up the regional Plans;

(ii) to assign priority to schemes and projects included in the regional Plans;

(iii) to supervise the implementation of the regional Plans.

In discharging these function it should be the special responsibility of the Regional Development Boards to pay due regard to the special needs of the backward areas of their respective regions.

The State Development Board will scrutinize the regional plans prepared as residuary Plan of schemes and projects which transcend regional boundaries or happen to be of an all-State interest and allocate Plan funds equitably (after taking into account the population, area and the specific needs of each region) to the regional Plans and the residuary Plan of all State interest.

The State Development Board and each of the Regional Development Boards will prepare at the end of each year a report of their respective activities giving details of the progress of the Plan programmes and Plan expenditure. At the end of each plan, similar detailed reports should be prepared by the Boards indicating the physical and financial targets and the physical and financial achievements. All these reports should be laid before the Legislature as soon as may be after they are prepared.

2. The State Government continued its policy of drift and inaction on the report of the Gajendragad Commission for about eight months till it convened an all party meeting on 30 July 1969 which, too, shelved a final decision on the crucial recommendations of the report regarding statutory Regional Development Boards.

The Boards that the government appointed, over a year after the Commission's recommendation, were neither statutory nor representative. Majority of their members were civil servants and experts. But as even such boards never functioned, the entire exercise of the Commission on the subject remained merely academic.

## Sikri Commission

In pursuance of its agreement with the All Party Jammu Committee, which spear-headed four-month long agitation in Jammu from December 1978 to March 1979, for constitutional and institutional changes to ensure an equitable distribution of political power among the three main regions of the State, the Government of Jammu and Kashmir set up a Commission of Inquiry on 2 June 1979 headed by Justice S.M. Sikri, Retired Chief Justice of India, it included Dr. Malcolm S, Adisehia (Member) and Dr. Z.M. Zaheer (Member-Secretary).

The Commission submitted its report to the Government on 25 August 1980, which was released in November 1980.

The Commission declined to consider the question of constitutional changes to satisfy political aspirations of the regions as it was, in its view, beyond its brief. Its major recommendations are as under:

1. A State Development Board be set up with the Chief Minister as Chairman with some members of the legislature as members.
2. A formula for financial allocation to the regions be devised taking into account their population, area, backwardness and natural resources.
3. Working of the Public Service Commission and Recruitment Boards be improved and recruitment should be on merit, without any reservation on the basis of community, region or district.
4. Viva Voce system in admissions to professional institutions be scrapped and merit at written examination should alone be considered.

The following is the official summary of the recommendations released by the Commission:

## Grievances and Relevant Issues

1. A State Development Board may be set up composed of the Chief Minister as Chairman and some members of the State Legislature as members and may be entrusted with supervision over the working of District Development Boards, formulation of allocation of funds for developmental expenditure, ensuring selection of meritorious boys and girls for special educational facilities and to report annually to the legislature on the working of the District Development Boards.

# 11

# Jayaprakash Narayan on Jammu and Kashmir

From 1953 up to 1975 JP continued his campaign for a settlement of the Kashmir issue through negotiations between the Government of India and Sheikh Abdullah as also with Pakistan. During this period he was condemned by Indian chauvinists as a traitor and many of his public meetings were sought to be disturbed with slogans like "Hang JP the traitor."

JP felt that the Kashmir issue was a black spot on the fair name of India. He was against forcible occupation of Kashmir. He wanted India to honour her commitment regarding deciding the fate of Kashmir according to the wishes of the people.

## Right to Secede

In 1968, Sheikh Abdullah invited JP to inaugurate the Jammu and Kashmir State People's Convention.

JP bluntly told a big audience in Hazoori Bagh, Srinagar, that even if he were the Prime Minister of India he would not be able to get Kashmir seceded from India. The only solution possible for the State was to seek appropriate status for it within the framework of the Indian Union.

JP continued his efforts for a dialogue between Sheikh Abdullah and the Government of India. In 1964, he had blessed the idea of a confederation between India, Pakistan and Kashmir. It was this proposal that Sheikh Abdullah and his colleagues took along with them when they went to Pakistan in 1964 to discuss it with Pakistan's leaders. General Ayub Khan, the then President of Pakistan, dismissed these proposals straightaway. JP, however, continued his efforts for a solution of Kashmir problem within the framework of Indian Constitution on bilateral basis, that is, between Sheikh Abdullah and Government of India, eliminating Pakistan from the negotiations.

## Support to Regional Autonomy

In a seminar on the Kashmir Problem which JP convened at Delhi in 1966 he lent his unequivocal support to the idea of regional autonomy so that the apprehensions of the people of the Jammu were allayed. The J&K state People's Convention convened by Sheikh Abdullah two years later he and his colleagues accepted the idea of regional autonomy.

## Search for Settlement

In his article in the *Hindustan Times* of 15 May 1964 with regard to Jammu Kashmir, J.P. wrote:

"I wish to take a look at our secularism in relation to Kashmir. Apart from other considerations Kashmir is deemed of great value to us because we wish to hold it up as an example of our secularism. I wonder if the spokesmen of secularism are aware of the irony of the present situation. The same Kashmir that is supposed to be an example of Indian secularism has occasioned a nasty upsurge of Hindu communalism. It is not easy to discern this process, because it is happening under the cover of nationalism. India being a Hindu majority community, it is not difficult, for Hindu communalism to trot out in the garb of Indian nationalism. Therefore it is all the more urgent for those who believe in a truly secular and composite nationalism to be on their guard.

"What is meant by Kashmir being an example of Indian secularism? It means that the people of India have given such proof of their non-communal outlook that the Muslims freely decided to live with India, which is a Hindu-Majority but secular country, rather than with Pakistan, which has a Muslim majority but is an Islamic state. But suppose we had to keep the Muslims of Kashmir within India by force, would that also be an example of our secularism? The very question exposes its absurdity. And yet how wide-spread is the mentality today that in order to defend the secular basis of our nation we must keep Kashmir, if necessary by force, within the Indian Union.

"I therefore wish most seriously to plead with the Prime Minister, the Congress president and other Congress leaders to look carefully at the cancerous process that is taking place within their party. As things are moving there will soon be little to choose at least in this matter between the Congress and the Jana Sangh. Shallow and timid Congressmen feel that the Jana Sangh is stealing their thunder. But by and large people's minds are sound, and they would rally round Pandit Jawaharlal Nehru-as they have always known him—if he were to give a clear and bold lead. And so would all the faint-hearted Congressmen who are eager to ride to victory on the communal wave. If some such event does not happen, I am afraid the secular base of our nation will be vitally damaged (*JP on Jammu and Kashmir*: Balraj Puri, pp. 56-57).

**Constitutional Integration without Emotional Integration Meaningless:**

In his Press statement released in Calcutta on 18 December 1964 J.P. said:

> The question we must squarely face is whether constitutional integration of Kashmir with India is more important in the national interest than friendship with Pakistan and justice to the people of the Valley of Srinagar. Legal technicalities will not provide the answer. What is needed is a mature and realistic reckoning. As far as I can see, the disadvantages of the present policy far outweigh the advantages.

Constitutional integration has little meaning in the absence of emotional integration. In this age and time, it is impossible to hold down by force any sizeable population permanently. If we continue to do it, we cannot look the world straight in the face and talk of democracy and justice and peace. Nor, on account of the historical circumstances, can we take shelter behind the internationally recognized limitations of the right to self-determination. Perhaps the most harmful consequence of the policy of forcible integration would be the death-knell of Indian secularism and enthronement of aggressive Hindu communalism. That communalism is bound in the end to turn upon the Hindu community itself and destroy it.

As for friendship with Pakistan, let us calculatedly determine how dearly we need that friendship. No country can afford to buy friendship at any cost. So let there be a reckoning of gains and losses. First of all, let us be mature enough to understand that if we persist in our present Kashmir policy, there can be no friendship with Pakistan.

Here is the pricing of Indo-Pak friendship as it appears to me. First, if Pakistan turns hostile, as I fear it would if we persist in the policy of full constitutional integration, the defence of the country would become a hundred-fold more difficult. Certain parts of it, such Assam, NEFA and Nagaland would be next to impossible to defend. Indo-Pak amity on the other hand would automatically result in large scale dis-engagement, thus strengthening considerably our defence capability. Our communications too would be automatically strengthened ten-fold. As far the defence of Ladakh, I am sure any amicable settlement of the Kashmir issue would make a provision for it.

Second, both history and geography destined the subcontinent of India to play a key role in South and South-East Asia. But as long as India and Pakistan remain at loggerheads, India's as also Pakistan's capacity to maneuver in this area-remains drastically restricted. No initiative taken by India can have the same value and attraction for the countries of this region unless India and Pakistan moved jointly. At present, they cancel out each other, creating a power vacuum that no one but China can fill effectively.

Third, what is true of the South-East Asia region is very largely true of the world. India's posture on the world stage is very considerably determined by her obsession with Kashmir and her consequent relations with Pakistan. In the Afro-Asia world, this quarrel between the two big Asian countries has cost both heavily in prestige and influence and diplomatic effectiveness.

Fourth, there is the vast economic harm the quarrel is causing both countries. It is beyond doubt that the development of each would have been much faster had there been cooperation between them in the economic field.

The last and in some way the most disastrous consequence of the quarrel is its human and moral cost and the alienation of peoples that it threatens to bring about. If the quarrel continues, Muslims in India and Hindus in Pakistan would continue to live under the shadow of suspicion and suffer severe spiritual unrest. The danger of communal rioting would be ever present. These conditions would be sure to cause mass human degradation on both sides the political division of the sub-continent cannot hide the fact that the people of India and Pakistan are really one people.

I am aware that settlement of the Kashmir issue would not in itself mean establishment of firm Indo-Pak friendship, but it would certainly remove the greatest obstacle on the way and create the necessary psychological conditions. I am also aware that friendship is not one-sided. But I am convinced that friendship is as precious for Pakistan as for India and they will be found to be as keen for it as we persuade ourselves to be.

A last word to the leaders of the government. At this critical moment in the country's life, it is their duty to lead and not to be led. The crippling fear of public opinion and party rank and file is only a reflection of the leadership's own weakness and division. It is for the leaders to shape public opinion and educate the back-benchers. If they fail in this they will do disservice to the country in this hour of decision.

## No Power can Transfer Kashmir to Pakistan

JP in his convocation address at Mysore University on 29 November 1965 said:

> He could not conceive of "any power on earth being able to transfer Kashmir from India to Pakistan, nor can I see how Pakistan can ever take the valley by force from India."

He further said: "In the face of Pakistan's aggression, surreptitious at first through armed infiltration, and then open and massive across the international border in Chhamb, the government had no alternative but to take action for the defence of the country.

"No other stand could have been right where Pakistan was demonstrably determined to take by force what it could not have by diplomacy—particularly when it has no legal or moral right to what it wants to grab."

"Pakistan by its repeated acts of aggression, had forfeited the right to have any say in regard to Kashmir's future."

He further said: "Kashmir could not exist as an independent state, because Pakistan would not allow it to survive. It would be foolish for any Kashmiri leader to nurse any hope on those lines. No solution had any chance of succeeding which involved deaccession of the state from India.

"Kashmiri and Indian leaders could find a just solution to the problem, if both sides are conscious of the limits set for them by circumstances".

JP continued India's case had been misunderstood. Many nations were under the misapprehension that India had deprived Pakistan "by force or something" what in justice belonged to her. Pakistan, he said, had never laid claim to Kashmir. Her plea was that the future of Kashmir should be decided according to the wishes of the people, hoping that they would opt for Pakistan "which is mere wishful thinking than anything else" (*Hindustan Times,* 30 November 1965).

The experience of history has repeatedly shown that in an atmosphere of mutual suspicion and hostility even minor disputes become insoluble. On the other hand, it has been found that once mutual understanding had been brought about, even the most complicated disputes become miraculously transformed and simple to settle this is as true of disputes between brothers as between nations.

## Sheikh Against Merger with Pakistan

It has been known these many years that Sheikh Saheb has been resolutely against Kashmir being merged with Pakistan. He did, no doubt, entertain ideas of some kind of an independent

Kashmir, but I believe he is realist enough to realize that (a) no solution of the Kashmir question could ever be accepted by India, after the last war with Pakistan, that involved deaccession of the state, or any part of it, from the Union; and (b) an independent state in that part of the world could have little chance of survival in face of Pakistan's consuming hunger for the valley of Kashmir and the emergence of the Chinese power in the region—a power that cannot be expected to exercise self denial in relation to its weak neighbours. Finally, it should be borne in mind that in every major step in war or peace, there is always an element of risk. No one who is unprepared to take risks can hope to be either a great soldier or a great statesman (*J.P. on Jammu and Kashmir*: Balraj Puri, pp. 149-54).

### Era of Indira Gandhi

After Shastri's premature and sad death, Indira Gandhi Era began. JP wrote a strictly confidential letter to Indira Gandhi on 23 June 1966, in which with regard to Kashmir he wrote: "The Kashmir question has plagued this country for 19 years. It has cost us a great deal materially and spiritually. We profess democracy, but rule by force in Kashmir unless we have auto-suggested ourselves into believing that the two general elections under Bakshi Saheb had expressed the will of the people, or that the Sadiq government is based on popular support, except for a small minority of pro-Pakistan traitors. We profess secularism, but let Hindu nationalism stampede us into trying to establish it by repression."

Kashmir had distorted India's image for the world as nothing else has done. There is no nation in the world, not even Russia, which appreciates our Kashmir policy, though some of them might, for their own reasons, give us their support.

No matter how much and how loud and how long we shout that Kashmir is an inalienable part of India and that, therefore, there was no Kashmir problem, the fact remains that a serious and urgent problem faces, and will continue to face, us in that part of the country.

That problem exists not because Pakistan wants to grab Kashmir, but because there is deep and widespread political

> the state, the government of Pakistan and the United Nations. Yet, while there are these four parties. I do think that basically this dispute is between the government of India and the people of Kashmir, then it seems to me very clear that both the government of Pakistan and the United Nations will have to fall in line. They will have no option but to reconcile themselves to whatever the people of Kashmir and the Government of India mutually agree upon.

As I read the situation, the real desire of the Government of Pakistan is to seize the valley. Twice they tried to capture it by force, but they failed. But they have been saying openly, except in the very early days, that it is for the people of Kashmir to decide. Now if the people of the state like Sheikh Abdullah, Mirza Afzal Beg, etc. are party to it then I think Pakistan will have to agree that the people of the state have given their verdict. I think some way could be found to demonstrate to the world that this agreement between the Government of India and the leaders of Kashmir has the backing of the people of the state. I personally do not think that a plebiscite is at all possible, or, would be agreed to by India. I also do not think that plebiscite would be a good way of deciding this question. I think it would be very wrong. But I think plebiscite is not the only way in which the wishes of the people can be ascertained. Even the world community is coming to recognize other ways of doing so, such as in Saba when Malaysia and Indonesia together agreed that the Secretary General of the United Nations should find out whether the people wanted to be a part of Indonesia or a part of Malayasia. May be, other ways could be found. I think even a general election, provided it is an honest general election, where the issues on which the people are supposed to express themselves are clearly placed before them and in which all the leaders of the people are allowed to take part, could convince the world. It may not convince the Government of Pakistan to begin with, though in their own hearts they would see that this solution was based on the verdict of the people. But it would certainly convince the world.

## Dispute Basically between Government of India and Kashmir

I would, therefore, repeat that the dispute basically is between the Government of India and the people of Kashmir. Of course, as I said earlier, the Government of India thinks that the issue is settled. I have read lots of press comments, particularly in the editorials of the language papers, to the effect that man like me is unnecessarily and foolishly stirring up trouble, that there is quiet on the Kashmir front, that the people have reconciled themselves to whatever arrangements have been made for them and so on. I do not know whether the Government of India really believe all this, but I shall not be surprised to learn that they really do so. They have their intelligence working there, but they may think that the present leaders of the Congress in Kashmir would work some miracle in the next few years and win the majority of the people of the valley of the state, to the side of India. I do not think that the situation is like that at all. I have not been to Kashmir since January 1947. That was the one and the only time that I visited Kashmir or any part of Kashmir, when Maharaja Hari Singh was still ruling and Mr. Kak was the Prime Minister and there was every danger of my being arrested. But was not. I have not been there. But I have tried to remain in touch with the situation through friends and others. Whatever information I have leads me to the conclusion that perhaps there is more discontent today amongst the Muslims of the state than at any earlier time. There is more anti-India feeling among them than before. This may not be all the time on the surface, but it is certainly below the surface and not very far below the surface. I do not think it would be possible for the Government of Kashmir, to win over the people, no matter what plans of development or what other plans of emotional integration they might have. I do not also think it is possible for them to solve the question by force. I hear a lot about a Kashmiri never having been known to have died for a cause throughout history. It may be so, but history changes and we would be shutting our eyes to the situation as it is growing or developing throughout the world. I think nationalism may be very stupid, but now it is there, it is the most important force today in the world against which no ideology, no religion, nothing else, seems to be an effective barrier. Nationalism is the most important force today in human society and there cannot be such a thing as the Kashmir Government being able to suppress that nationalism. I do not even know if Indians could ever behave like that, for it would be like India's soul committing suicide. Yes, it will be a suicide of the soul of India, if India tried to suppress the Kashmiri people by force. But suppose we undertake to do it, can we ever succeed? My clear answer is that we will never succeed and deep discontent will remain in the state. And this with two hostile nations, one of them a very powerful nation, a world power, on the borders. Possibly, if Kashmir were within the heart of India, somewhere in the middle of India and if we were ready to deny our whole history, and all our traditions, our culture and civilization, may be some Indian government could have settled the question by force, disperse the population and colonise the area by Hindus and others. But I do not think any of these things is possible in Kashmir.

I am absolutely certain, therefore, that any policy based on force cannot succeed. This view was shared by no less a person than Pandit Jawaharlal Nehru. For eleven years a policy based on force was pursued.

It is in the interest of the Indian people, it is in the interest of the people of Kashmir, the people of the whole state of Jammu and Kashmir, in the interest of this sub-continent and in the interest of the world that this question is settled between the two primary parties to the dispute.

If the Government of India is realistic it should try to reach an agreement with him. Sheikh Abdullah if it fails, it will not then be blamed by the world. The world will then be convinced that we have made a serious attempt, gone to the farthest limit to which we could under the circumstances. We would then have more friends in the world. The world public opinion cannot be treated with contempt as some people here in New Delhi pretend to assert. On the contrary, it is of the greatest importance that we pay some heed to that opinion.

## Reasonable Solution of Kashmir

The fact is that even after we settle with the people of Kashmir, we will have to, with the help of the Kashmir Government, may be, settle this question of the Cease Fire Line and Azad Kashmir, some kind of political settlement with the Pakistan Government will have to be reached.

After the last war with Pakistan, in which many Southern officers and men laid down their lives, emotionally South India has also got involved. However, I have said on an earlier occasion that after this war Pakistan has no locus standi in this dispute. While on the face of it, it seems to be nonsense because after all the dispute in the Security Council is there. The Cease Fire Line is there, Azad Kashmir is there—occupied Kashmir we call it and they call our portion of Kashmir as occupied Kashmir. Even then what I meant was, and I still stand by it, that when there are two parties to a dispute and they agree to talk it over, each party has a place in the talks. But then if one party draws its sword out and says, "all right you accept my version of it or otherwise I will chop your head Off", the only answer from the other party will be, "all right chop my head off, but then you can have no place in negotiations. "It is in that sense that I had said that after the war, Pakistan had no locus standi in the Kashmir dispute. There was the Kutch Agreement and hopes were held out by both sides that this agreement would lead to the easing of tension and behold the infiltration started. May be, at the parchment this was being done by Pakistan. I really could not understand this at all. The constitutional amendment in respect of Article 370 had been made before Kutch. Since Kutch there had been no provocation from the side of India, so far as I remember.

From all the information that foreign sources have given us, it seems to us that President Ayub Khan had been persuaded he was not in favour of it in the beginning—to go along with the hawks there on the assumption that India would not attack through the Punjab border and if India decided to fight it out in Jammu and Kashmir area then it would not be difficult to cut Jammu and Kashmir off from India; and in that way the whole of Kashmir state could be occupied and then the question would be settled for all times, as they think the Azad Kashmir issue had been settled. But our government decided that this could not be allowed to take place, and what was not expected to happen by Pakistan did happen. Whatever that might be, the Pakistan govt did embark on a military gamble. They had done this for the second time and it was particularly reprehensible since it had happened so soon after the Kutch Agreement. It was in that context that I had said that they had no locus standi in Kashmir. But I am not shutting my eyes to the fact that the Cease Fire Line is there, Azad Kashmir is there and the dispute is before the international community. In that sense Pakistan is certainly a party to it. However, as I said earlier if there is a real settlement with the people of the state to which all sections including those represented by Sheikh Abdullah are a party, then I think the grounds from under Pakistan's feet would be knocked out and their leaders will have to accept it sooner or later. They may raise a sort of hoo ha there about it and even start denouncing Sheikh Abdullah as a traitor, but ultimately they will have to accept it.

## Deaccession not Possible

That perhaps is the fairest solution of this problem could be that India agreed to Pakistan's keeping 'Azad Kashmir', the Cease Fire Line was rationalized, Jammu and Ladakh remained in India and the valley was made into an autonomous state, demilitarized and neutralized, neither a part of India nor a part of Pakistan. Now I do not think that after the last war such a solution is any longer practicable.

Besides, any autonomous or independent state of the valley, even if neutralized and demilitarized, is not likely to be allowed to remain autonomous or independent very long and there would always be present the danger of war between India and Pakistan, or between India and China, and also the danger of internal subversion, and the people of Kashmir would be most unhappy. Before the emergence of China as a great and aggressive power, perhaps such a settlement might have been arrived at with Pakistan being a party to it. But I do not know whether even this can be said now, after the last military adventure by

Pakistan. Frankly, I have to admit that I did not expect this from President Ayub Khan. I know him. I have had several talks with him. Some other friends also went with me last time (1964) when I went there on my second visit. I have been very much impressed by President Ayub's personality, by his sincerity about friendship with India and so on. Therefore, it was a shock to me that so soon after the Kutch Agreement he should have allowed a large scale secret invasion, which infiltration really meant. I am now not prepared to accept the bona fides of the Pakistan Government, any Pakistan Government, regarding an independent or autonomous state of the valley. Therefore, I think that whatever solution is possible between the government of India and the people of Kashmir it has to be within the framework of the accession. The utmost that the Government of India can do is to go back to the 1947-53 days, that is, go back to the time when the state had acceded to India only in three subjects. This will mean providing for the fullest possible autonomy. The centre may look after Defence, External Affairs and Communications, may be also Currency, but the rest should be the concern of the people of the state, the undivided state as today, a part of India. I am not saying that this should be done on the basis of partition. The state must remain as it is in the context of a settlement with leaders, genuine leaders or more popular leaders.

There are all kinds of difficulties about this formula based on full internal autonomy. One difficulty may be in regard to the partition of the state, The other difficulty might be relating to security. The state was autonomous to begin with but its autonomy gradually eroded and some sort of constitutional and other arrangements will have to be made to see that this sort of thing is not repeated again.

For, in the changed context, the slogan, 'Let the people decide', would sound hollow and would be laughed at. If Pakistan continued to sing that song, Pakistan would be placed in more or less the same position as perhaps India is in the world today on this issue. I do not think any body in the world will be with Pakistan in the new situation, and some kind of treaty, some arrangement about Cease Fire Line, etc. could be reached. In brief, this is my thinking at present on this subject.

I feel that a settlement must be acceptable both politically and morally.

Muslims of the valley have democratic and secular ideas and also believe in some sort of progressive economic ideas, which may perhaps be described as socialism. They are poor people, most of them, they are wedded to radical socio-economic programmes and ideas and I do not think they would get any of those things in Pakistan. They know that East Pakistan has lost its identity and its personality. The pathans have lost it, as West Pakistan is dominated more or less by Punjabi Muslims. I think Kashmiris will find such dominating even less palatable than perhaps East Pakistanis are finding it. So I would say an autonomous status for Kashmir within the Indian union would be in the best interest of the people of the valley also.

We should not try to force it down their throats. That would be morally wrong. It may be considered to be politically expedient, this kind of expediency in that geographical situation would not succeed. It would be a disaster.

## Morally not Politically Obnoxious to Rule by Force

In that case if we continue to rule by force and suppress these people and crush them or change the racial or religious character of their state by colonization, or by any other means, then I think that means politically a most obnoxious thing and morally also a most obnoxious thing to do. Kashmir has cost us a great deal and it is time that every one who is a patriot in this country thought seriously about a really good solution.

## Plebiscite No More Practical Solution

Coming to the substance of the matter, I do not think any responsible person, either in Pakistan or in India, has thought for many years now that plebiscite in Jammu & Kashmir was a practical solution of the problem any more. Even President Ayub Khan in 1964 had told me that, though plebiscite was the first priority solution as far as Pakistan was concerned, if India thought it was impractical, he was prepared to discuss any other solution which could be negotiated mutually between the parties concerned. For many years there have been only two alternatives open: a negotiated settlement or a forcible settlement. No doubt, India continues to demand that Pakistan should 'vacate' her aggression, but India knows very well that short of a war which she never seriously contemplates, it is impossible to win back the Pakistan occupied territories. Pakistan also knows equally well that, short of a successful war, she cannot win any of the territories which are part of India today. I am not quite sure if Pakistani leaders have now foresworn war with India, but, if they have, the only alternative left is a negotiated settlement. Therefore, the very word plebiscite is irrelevant to the present situation, and no amount of harping back on the original commitments made by the Government of India can avail.

In my inaugural address I had tried to point the way to a negotiated settlement in two stages: first, a settlement between the Government of India and the leaders of Kashmir, endorsement of which by the people of the State could be obtained at a general election or in some other agreed manner; second, a negotiated settlement subsequently with Pakistan. The second stage may not immediately follow upon the first, but once the people of the state had, in a credible manner, endorsed a settlement made by their leaders with the Government of India, a settlement with Pakistan must follow sooner or later. These, however, are my views, and it is open to the Convention to accept, reject or modify them.

Jayaprakash Narayan in his article published in *Hindustan Times* on 1st February 1972 wrote:

## Question of Quantum of Autonomy

The plebiscite issue is dead for ever. Even the Sheikh cannot put back the clock of history. No question can be raised now about the accession of Jammu & Kashmir to India. Anyone who thinks otherwise is living in a fool's paradise and has failed to grow with the time and grasp the historic significance of the tremendous changes that have taken place in the Indian subcontinent.

The only question that may still be considered to be relevant is that of the quantum of autonomy that Jammu & Kashmir should enjoy within the Union of India, and Jammu and Ladakh regions, in their turn, should enjoy within the constitutional framework of that state.

I myself have been a consistent advocate of a much larger measure of autonomy to the states in view of the vastness of our population and the diversity of our problems I have also felt that smaller states would make for better government and bring democracy nearer to the people and give them a better sense of participation and, further, that smaller States would also help in removing regional disparities with far less tension and at a faster pace. At the same time I have also been consistently emphasizing that the strength and authority of the Union Government should not be impaired in any way, nor should the territorial integrity of the country be allowed to be weakened. I believe that within these limits there is enough scope for mutual adjustment, accommodation and give and take.

## Hindu and Muslim Communalism Nailed

For these reasons I have never doubted there was any danger whatever to the integrity of our nation. I am sure India would continue to remain united and keep growing from strength to strength. We have colossal problems but I am confident that we shall conquer them.

## Cease-Fire Line be Made International Border

After so many years and at least three Pakistani overt and covert aggressions across the line; and particularly after the recent Indo-Pak war, the old cease-fire line has no reality or relevance left at all. This is a point on which I find there is general agreement in the country, including its official circles. No body, I think, barring some on the lunatic fringes, is wanting to take back by force the whole Pakistan-occupied part of the original state of Jammu & Kashmir. But there is general agreement that the old cease-fire line and the presence of the UN observers, whose contribution to assuring peace along that line has been nil, have become anachronisms now. It follows, therefore—and on this point too a national consensus has emerged—that the so-called cease-fire line should be rationalized and re-drawn and converted into a well-defined permanent international border so as to guarantee India's security in that region and make it difficult, if not impossible, for Pakistani adventurers to create any further mischief. If that were done, any UN presence in that area would become unnecessary and contrary to international law.

It is now recognized that the original cease-fire line was irrational and hastily drawn up without any regard to geography and the requirements of stability and security and the whishes of the people of the area, particularly those of the Maharaja and the then Prime Minister of the state, Sheikh Mohammad Abdullah.

This is a matter on which some amount of give and take may be necessary. One hopes that President Bhutto is sincerely concerned about establishing firm and friendly relations with India, which is so obviously essential in the interests of both the nations, besides eliminating at the same time the possibility of international intrigues which have wrought so much mischief in the past. I am sure that if Mr. Bhuto rises to the occasion, refuses to be anybody's tool, accepts the facts of history and desires lasting peace with India and mutual cooperation between the two countries, he will not find the Government of India to be unresponsive.

## 12

# The Solution Once and for All Man to Man Diplomacy

I may recapitulate the solutions suggested by Sardar Patel, Dr. Babasaheb Ambedkar, Balraj Madhok, R. Venkataraman, and Sharad Pawar to solve the Kashmir dispute.

Sardar Patel had told Minoo Masani: "He could settle the Kashmir issue in no time by arranging that the Kashmir Valley go to Pakistan and East Pakistan to India. Both countries would benefit from such an arrangement."

Sardar Patel had also told Dr. Rajendra Prasad: "When we had given away Punjab, Sindh and the NWFP, of what value could be the small valley of Kashmir for us. Will the people there ever live happily with us."

Dr. B.R. Ambedkar in his letter of resignation as Law Minister of India dated 10 October 1951 said: "...right solution is to partition Kashmir. Give the Hindu and Buddhist part to India and the Muslim part to Pakistan. Or if you like, divide it into three parts; the Cease-fire zone, the Valley and the Jammu-Ladhak Region and have plebiscite only in the Valley...."

R. Venkataraman as Defence Minister suggested in 1983 to Indira Gandhi that Ladakh may be made a Union Territory as demanded by the local people, Jammu given the status of a State, and that the Valley dealt with a separate entity, but it did not find any response.

Sharad Pawar believes the problem of Kashmir can be solved with a lot of understanding and the skillful negotiations. He says: "Despite the fact that the State has no economic viability, the clamour for independence has gained ground in recent years. If the group supporting such an untenable demand can be won over, with patient discussions, arguments and political debate, a solution is not out of reach."

"The most heartening aspect of the situation is that those who want the State to go over to Pakistan consist of a negligible fringe. A vast majority in the State do not desire absorption into Pakistan, considering the miserable state of affairs in the Pakistan occupied territory, across the border.

"The immediate issue in Kashmir is to locate the right type of leaders with grassroots hold on the people, and to encourage them to take an active leadership role in sorting out the problem. The State has been starved of local leadership in the last two decades, with too much blatant interference from New Delhi.

"All this has been compounded by the instigation of violence by Pakistan, often blatantly.

Since the new government has taken over at the Centre, vigilance in Kashmir has been intensified, with the defence forces playing a crucial role. The law and order situation in the State is not more manageable. The fact however remains that the minds of a vat section of people have to be won over. This will take some time."

Pawar is confident that a process of normalization can be initiated in Kashmir with a programme of tackling the terrorists. This has to be undertaken boldly and ruthlessly. It must be ensured that terrorists no longer receive the training they do across the border in Pakistan. At the same time, an effective dialogue should be opened with the sensible and moderate elements in the Jammu and Kashmir Liberation Front (JKLF). Simultaneously, the interference from Delhi that has been a marked feature of the past should also cease, leaving room for greater participation of local leadership in rebuilding the economy of the State. Visible, effective and equitable economic development of the State is one area where the Union Government can easily establish its credentials with the people of Kashmir.

Pawar realizes that terrorism as experienced in Punjab and Kashmir is politically motivated, unpredictable and therefore difficult to control. Terrorists are known to chose symbolic targets and they thrive on publicity.

"Terrorism, inspired, abetted and motivated by nations against countries amounts to surrogate warfare, where they are unable to mount a conventional military challenge. Terrorism is used to weaken the resistance of the "enemy" with aim of destroying him."

Pawar further says:

> Wrong policies in the past have marred the chances of settlement of issues in Kashmir. For example, the Muslim United Front in Kashmir was forced out of political existence in 1986 for its extremist views by "leaders" who today cannot even step into the State. The authorities are today prepared to discuss the Kashmir problems the groups that are far more extremist and militant than the MUF.

The main problem facing Kashmir is the militants, trained and inspired by Pakistan. Large sections of the misguided population continue to be held ransom and alienated. Unemployment and economic hardships have made the people desperate. The government is keen to ensure a better deal to the people and to see that major attempts are initiated in that direction. Long spells of Governor's rule have not helped bring a solution nearer. It is therefore time to look for alternatives, and restore popular rule in the State, as has been done in Punjab. This should be followed by a package of reforms to remove the economic backwardness of the people. This will be the only way to ease the feeling of neglect among the people. The State needs industries to supplement tourism which has been Kashmir's lone source of income.

According to Balraj Madhok, it is in the interest of India as a whole to delink Ladakh from the Kashmir Valley and give it Union Territory status directly under the Central Government.

Dr. Karan Singh, while he was Governor of Jammu and Kashmir in a statement to *Times*, London in November 1965, had proposed linguistic re-organization of the State and merger of Jammu with the adjoining Himachal Pradesh.

Shri N.V. Gadgil, in his book, *Government of India from Inside* writes: "...the mistake in not taking over the whole of Kashmir has enabled Pakistan to meet China through the Gilgit corridor and conspire against our interests. I have to record with regret that whenever I made proposals concerning Kahmir, Nehru reacted as if I were an enemy of Muslims. I always pressed him to take a firm stand in regard to Kashmir at some point and said we were all behind him. Nehru used to say that politics should always be flexible. I used to tell him that if he did not take a firm stand somewhere, he would get no time even to admit his mistake."

Jawaharlal Nehru was also infavour of partition of Jammu and Kashmir until 1953. He had agreed with Dulles that partition might be a better way to solve the problem than a plebiscite. He had suggested that the cease-fire line, with minor modification, would provide a reasonable basis for dividing the State of Jammu and Kashmir.

In 1957, Surahwardy met privately with Nehru and Harold Macmillan in London. Macmillan suggested to them that the only feasible answer lay in some form of partition. Nehru and Surhawardy both agreed but said that they could not state this publicly for domestic political reasons.

Nehru changed his mind in 1963.

In 1963, the American and British diplomats advised the Indian and Pakistani Prime Ministers that dividing the valley seemed to be the best way to resolve the dispute. Reacting Nehru said: "It would surely be bad to divide such a small and economically and culturally homogenous area." Nehru took a hardline against partitioning the Valley with Galbraith on 20 April 1963.

## Dispute Basically between Government of India and Kashmir

Jayaprakash Narayan said: "Perhaps there is more discontent today amongst the Muslims of the State than at any earlier time.

There is more anti-India feeling among them than before. This may not be all the time on the surface, but it is certainly below the surface and not very far below the surface. I do not think it would be possible for the Government of Kashmir, the Congress Government to win over the people, no matter what plans of development or what other plans of emotional integration they might have. I do not also think it is possible for them to solve the question by force."

How JP was prophetic can be said from the anti-India feelings of Kashmiri Muslims today.

JP further said:

> It is in the interest of the Indian people, it is in the interest of the people of Kashmir, the people of the whole State of Jammu and Kashmir, in the interest of this sub-continent and in the interest of the world that this question is settled between the two primary parties to the dispute.

JP felt that a settlement must be acceptable both politically and morally for this he suggested an autonomous status for Kashmir within the Indian union.

To sum up, the trends and undercurrents reveal that the polity and the administration of the State of Jammu and Kashmir are not in good health. The Congress (I) was in disarray. The National Conference showed no spark, no vigour. The drumbeaters of parochialism and fundamentalism are working overtime, and the secularists have surrendered initiative. Subversion is on the increase. The shadows of events from across the border are lengthening. Lethal weapons have come in. More may be on the way.

From religious platforms, the Moulvis invariably give political sermons. They concern themselves less with religion than with politics. Some of the 'religious czars' in their respective areas have built their entire political following by addressing Friday congregations. Even political stalwarts have been making important speeches from the Hazratbal and other shrines.

## A Fresh Approach—Man to Man Diplomacy

In the situation obtaining today, a fresh approach needs to be adopted and that approach, in my opinion could be Man to Man Diplomacy.

Much water has flown over the bridge. The efforts made by Prime Ministers right from Pandit Jawaharlal Nehru, Lal Bahadur Shastri, Indira Gandhi, Atal Bihari Vajpayee and Manmohan Singh have failed in spite of Tashkent Declaration, Simla Agreement, Agra Summit, Lahore Declaration, besides Delhi and Kashmir Agreement.

A very impartial observer has summed up the situation in Jammu and Kashmir as follows:

> The people of Kashmir did not support Pakistan either in the first war of 1947 or in the Second War of 1965. Pakistan was never in a position to generate on its own the dissatisfaction amongst the people of Kashmir against the Indian accession. Pakistan could take advantage of the dissatisfaction which had arisen by 1989 as a result of India's continued distrust of the people of Kashmir and its failure to fulfil the conditions of the terms of the accession.

The position has been greatly worsened as a result of the policy of wholesale suppression of the people which has been followed in actual practice by the para-military security forces in Kashmir since January 1990. The excesses committed by the security forces of India as a response to the misdeeds of the militants were not only disproportionate but were also directed against people who were non-militant. A very large number of innocent people have been killed or tortured, some of their women raped and many of their houses burnt to ashes. That is the main reason why the alienation of Kashmiri people against India.

Bashir Manzar editor of *Kashmir Images* published from Srinagar in his write up in *Indian Express* says:

> In the fight between the government and the separatist leadership, the common people are losing everything—

their dear ones; the education of their children; the economy; their pace of mind.

Bashir Manzar further writes:

"We must also ask questions of a section of society that seems to take pleasure in the sufferings of the common people. Having access to the internet, denied to the vast majority, they glamorize the stone pelting. They encourage the children of the poor to die while they themselves sit in safe office chambers and cosy drawing rooms. They urge other people's children out on to the streets, while shielding themselves behind curfew passes. They must be asked: As they instigate kids to pelt stones on government forces through their columns, write-ups, Facebook and Twitter posts, where are their own children, and why are they not on the streets?

"Are resistance and resilience meant only for the children of lesser mortals?

"The separatist leadership too has to face questions. It is this leadership that has been telling people what to do and what not to do. It is because of their protest programmes, coupled with the government's curfew and restrictions, that life in Kashmir has come to a standstill. They are not allowing the schools to open. They are not allowing people to open their shops and business establishment. They are not allowing government employees to attend to their duties. They did the same in 2008 and then in 2010 without achieving anything.

"It is important to question the government as to why its forces have not been able to learn how to control agitated mobs without killing and maiming people. The government has been bringing more forces, even the Border Security Force, without understanding that the situation can't be controlled by the armed forces alone."

India's army chief, General Bipin Rawat, chose to hold out dire public warnings of "tough action" against the stone-pelting young people to Kashmir. He declared that the government is prepared to give those who support terror activities an opportunity to join the "national mainstream", but warned that if they continue their action, the security forces would respond with "harsher measures". He also gave notice that those pelting stones at security forces during anti-militancy operations would be considered anti-national over-ground workers of militants. He added that the army would go "helter skelter" against local boys who pick up arms or aid besieged militants.

It is very rare to hear India's army chief use the belligerent language of threats to target not enemy soldiers or armed militants, but the civilian population.

Last winter, Harsh Mander visited the Valley with a solidarity team comprising Pamela Philipose, Tapan Bose, Navsharan Kaur and Dinesh Mohan.

The question that people asked them over and over again was this: "You say we are equal citizens of India. Yes, some of our boys pelted stones. But we know of far more violent mobs in other parts of India last year-the Jat and Patidar agitations, the Cauvery dispute and many others. To disperse those mobs, have security forces ever used pellet guns? In all those unrests, lathis, tear-gas and water-cannons were found to be sufficient by India's security establishment. But why is it that only for Kashmiri youth throwing stones, you use pellet guns?" No rational mind can blame the questioner.

Despite the fact that pellet guns fail to meet any standards of national and international law for crowd control, the government's proclamation that it will continue to deploy pellet guns, and the army chief's muscular warnings of "tough-action" against even those who do not use the gun are deeply worrying.

## Award for Gogoi

The army's commendation of Major Nitin Leetul Gogai, the officer who tied Farooq Ahmed Dar, a shawl weaver Irom Chil-Bars village in Budgam, Kashmir, to the bonnet of a Rashtriya Rifles jeep and paraded around several villages, with a placard tied to his chest, apparently using him as a human shield for his troops against stone-pelters, is a shocking move. For one, it has pre-empted due process-the army's own ongoing internal inquiry into the circumstances of the officer's action. The army chief, General Bipin Rawat, has said whatever the court of inquiry finding, there is no reason for disciplinary action against Gogai.

There is no evidence that Dar was a stone-pelter. In fact, by all accounts, he was among the pitifully small number of Kashmiris who defied the mood on the ground to vote in the Srinagar Parliamentary by-election held on that day. Gogai's action was also a violation of the ICCPR that lays down that no one shall be subjected to torture or to cruel, in human or degrading treatment or punishment.

Gogai's action was a violation of the right to life and liberty enshrined in Article 21 of the Indian Constitution. The Army is bound to uphold the Constitution. At all times, its actions must be aimed to protecting the citizens of the country. Dar is Indian citizen. Justifying torture or the degrading use of one civilian as something that helped to save hundreds of lives, including those of the troops under Gogoi's command, raises more questions than answers.

General Bipin Rawat has said Gogai was given the award "to ensure the confidence level of the officer and others operating in a similar environment". This should rightly raise concern about the message it has sent out to troops deployed in Kashmir and in other theatres in the country about the limits of acceptable conduct for the world's seventh largest professional army. Just as importantly, it should raise concerns about the message it sends out to an already alienated people in the Valley.

No matter how you look at it or try to defend it, tying Farooq Ahmed Dar to the front of a jeep and parading him through the villages of Kashmir was not illegal, but immoral. It humiliated an Indian citizen and deprived him of his dignity and essential human rights. This is why it was wrong for a soldier to do it. As Lt General H.S. Panag, a former Northern Army Commander, put it, "Whatever the provocation, the Indian army cannot take recourse to illegal acts."

The decision to award a commendation to the major was either an act of deliberate defiance of the widespread view that the young officer had erred, or a mistaken, muscular message to Kashmiris that the army will not tolerate their dissent. It was unfortunate. And that it should have happened whilst a court of enquiry is still to report is more than inexplicable—it's baffling.

As General Panag tweeted, "IA (Indian Army) traditions, ethos, rules and regs (regulations) swept away by the 'mood of the nation!"

Major Gogai's surprise appearance on television only added fuel to the fire. To quote Lt General Panag again: "The image of a 'stone pelter', tied in front of jeep as a 'human shield, will forever haunt the Indian Army and the nation!"

If we are to follow a humanist-democratic policy in Kashmir and to succeed in winning back the confidence and trust of the Kashmiri people, we have to reverse the entire policy which has been hitherto followed.

In the first place, we must change our attitude towards the people of Kashmir. We must realize that if we want Kashmir to be a part of India, it can only be on the basis that the people of Kashmir are regarded by us as our own people, as our brothers and sisters. It is only with this changed attitude that we can possibly win back their trust and friendship. The Indian security forces, while it is their duty to do all things necessary to end the militancy in the valley, must always keep themselves within the bounds of law while doing so. Moreover, a distinction must be made between militants and non-militants. The latter must not be tourtured, fired upon or otherwise harassed, out of mere suspicion or out of a sense of revenge. Offences against the non-militants must be stopped and the offending personnel of the Security forces must be tried, adequately punished and the punishments publicized. More power should gradually be given to the local police force of Jammu & Kashmir so that the military and para-military forces eventually be confined to their barracks within the State itself. They should be available only when their assistance is found necessary by the civil authorities.

## Confederation

Ever since its inception, the relations between India and Pakistan have not been friendly and this is not only because of Kashmir. The fact stands that there is 'deep-seated hatred between the Hindu and Muslim communities in India. If a solution has to be found in terms that the 'sore of partition should not fester again', it has to be found in the concept of united India. In spite of India being a secular State, the Muslims in India, feel as hostages and not as free Indian citizens. This is so in spite of the fact that Indian administration since independence has taken special steps to see that there should be no such feeling among the Muslims in India. In whatever way the Kashmir problem is solved, the facts remain, that India will have almost as many Muslims as there are in Pakistan and Bangladesh, and they have to feel as free citizens of India, if peace is to prevail in this sub-continent. The problem therefore is not essentially only of Kashmir, but of the whole post partition history of India. In this sub-continent, the Hindus and Muslims are bound to live together, whatever configuration is adopted. And whatever may be solution to the Kashmir question, unless the three Independent States of Pakistan, India and Bangladesh can remain on friendly terms, within this sub-continent, the future will always be uncertain. Therefore, solution has to be found which will enable all the three States to function together on friendly terms. This is the real problem in India and Kashmir is only a symptom. Some arrangement has to be worked out by which all the three independent States can function on friendly terms.

Chagla too in his plea before the Security Council said: "Kashmir is merely a symptom. It is not the disease. The disease is that Pakistan believes in a religious State; it believes in religion and the nexus between citizens."

Pakistan and India have been into an Arms rivalary, which strains the meager finances of two of the proverbially poorest countries in the world. The defence expenditure of India and Pakistan is three-fourth of the world. This is when both the countries have yet to fulfill the needs of the poverty-stricken people who are beyond proportion. They have yet to provide for the basic needs of their population like education, health, water and roads. If both the countries who are in the grip of rivalary reduce their expenditure on defence, they can see the welfare of their people.

In a seminar held in Delhi on Kashmir problem in 1966, JP said: "It is beyond doubt that the development of each (India and Pakistan) would have been much faster had there been cooperation between them in the economic field."

JP further said:

> The most disastrous consequence of the quarrel is its human and moral cost and the alienation of people that it threatens to bring about. If the quarrel continues, Muslims in India and Hindus in Pakistan would continue to live under the shadow of suspicion and suffer severe spiritual unrest. The danger of communal rioting would be ever present.

But should there be a rethinking on this matter by the people of Pakistan, which has lost politically and economically more than India by the partition, India should be glad to consider joining Pakistan and Bangladesh in a confederation which will be for the joint benefit of the people of these three countries. All interested in Hindu-Muslim unity should consider, if that can be secured without Indo-Pakistan unity. Today Hindu Muslim unity in India exists superficially. According to Justice Chandrashekhar Dharmadhikari, Hindu-Muslim unity in India is a fiction and not a reality. It is constantly in danger of disruption with Indo-Pakistan relations at low level. Let us not forget that to the Father of the Nation Hindu-Muslim unity was axiomatic, and the partition was literally on his dead-body.

We agreed to the partition out of the compulsion of circumstances. We do not want to undo history. But if we now look upon Kashmir as a Muslim-majority area and hence entitled to secede thinking that it is not proper for it to remain in India, we would be repeating the mistake after over six decades.

There is more at stake in Kashmir than merely a piece of territory. Kashmir is the symbol and touchstone of our secular structure. The dismemberment of Kashmir would start the dismemberment of India as a whole and produce migrations and conflicts of a character and magnitude—much worse and larger than the aftermath of Partition. Let the leaders of both India and Pakistan as well as leaders of other countries especially the Great Powers beware of this danger and not encourage the

Pakistani leaders to start or continue something that will spell disaster for the whole region.

Would the leadership atleast in countries, namely India, Pakistan and Bangladesh wake up to the relations of the great benefits that await them should they choose to come together?

Today, there are as many Muslims in India, as there are in Pakistan and Bangladesh, and the Muslim Community is divided into three parts, namely Pakistan, India and Bangladesh. The community has also lost any legal or moral claim over India. It is of course true that India is treating them absolutely on a par with other Indian citizens, but it is a fact that even today they are looked at with suspicion, and are held responsible for the partition. And as a result of the 1971 war, and separation of Bangladesh from Pakistan, the whole concept of Muslims of India being a separate Nation has been falsified. The two parts could never work together. And the Indian Army only separated what was already a severed link. Further the fact that the majority Muslim Area of the State of J&K, voluntarily joined India, and was absolutely peaceful after the accession brought to the world's notice the falsity of the claim that the Muslims in India are or were a separate Nation. In fact, till 1986, the State of J&K was absolutely quiet and it appeared that Pakistan had reconciled itself to the State's accession. All countries including the U.S.A. have recognized the Simla Agreement and even after Raphel's statement, the U.S.A. made it clear that they have no intention of disturbing India's integrity. If now there are going to be talks between India and Pakistan on the Kashmir question, India can never give up its territorial claim of Kashmir, and as Lal Bahadur Shastri said, "Kashmir will be the last issue between India and Pakistan." Pakistan wants it to be the first issue, a position which India has never accepted.

Kashmir is directly concerned with seven countries—India, Pakistan, Bangladesh, China, Russia and America. It is, therefore, necessary for the people of Kashmir to raise their mind to the supramental level and evolve a world approach to their problems. They must liberate their minds from the events of the past and develop an objective and scientific outlook.

Some have gone to the extent of saying that Afghanistan, Mayanmar, Cylone, India, Tibet, Nepal, Bhutan and Pakistan should form a confederation, then there will be peace in the world, thereby problem of Kashmir will be solved.

George Fernandes, while he was Defence Minister of India suggested that all necessary initiatives should be taken to form a confederation with Pakistan and Bangladesh and, if possible, Nepal, Afghanistan and Sri Lanka, with a united Kashmir as one distinct entity in that confederation. Such a confederation alone will enable the countries of the sub-continent to overcome their prejudices and mutual distrust, and result in saving between 30 and 40 thousand crores of rupees a year which are now squandered away on maintaining huge armies and equipping them with killer weapons manufactured by the world's armament manufacturers located in Europe and in America.

Fernandes further suggested: "A tremendous redistribution of resources towards development would strengthen the entire sub-continent and the economic benefits would bind the confederation in the same manner as is being done in Europe today. Kashmir would no longer be used by Western powers as the breeding ground for weapon-users or drug peddlers engaged in keeping the third world from standing on its own feet" (*Kashmir Through the Ages*: Suresh K. Sharma and Usha Sharma, pp. 85-93).

Acharya Vinoba Bhave in his book, *Message of Love* wrote: "The Kashmir problem will be solved only when the conditions in the world will change and countries like India, Pakistan, China, Russia, Afghanistan and all other countries who are concerned with Kashmir will think in their heart of heart to solve Kashmir problem. The day these countries think on these lines, all the problems of the world will be solved.

"But as far as the Kashmir problem is concerned, it will be solved when Kashmiris themselves gather inner strength and for this purpose the people of every village should join hands and resolve to die for each other."

Vinoba further said: "Party politics will not help. Political parties divide people instead of uniting them. This is my appeal to all India in general, but more particular to Kashmir. Here the approach should be spiritual rather than political. Political approach will break the villages which will draw Government's interference; it will not help for the development of village. Spirituality will create the feeling that we are all one and are prepared to die for each other."

The following persons have made their suggestions to solve Kashmir dispute.

**Kuldip Nair, High Commissioner of India to U.K.** says

> One possible solution is on the basis of the Trieste-type agreement (October 20, 1954), which provided for the partitioning of the Free Territory of Trieste between Italy and Yugoslavia along the then existing demarcation line between the two, with minor changes. The agreement granted travel facilities between the two sides.
>
> A solution on the lines of the Trieste agreement may help settle the Kashmir problem. This may also satisfy the Kashmiri youths because they will enjoy local autonomy. Both India and Pakistan will be able to integrate permanently the Kashmir territory on their side. If the problem remains unsettled, the two countries will continue to be distant neighbours. (*Kashmir Through the Ages*: Suresh K. Sharma and Usha Sharma, pp. 137-42)

Arun Sahani, General Officer Commanding-in-Chief, South Western Command writes in *Indian Express*:

> As a first step, there must be a consensus amongst political parties on the national narrative; national and state political leaders need to speak in unison. This will lend clarity of thought and direction to the people in the Valley while strengthening the hands of the elected leaders and governmental agencies. In addition, the local leadership needs to interact at the grassroots with village and urban elders and teachers, so as to ensure that young boys and girls are not influenced by malicious propaganda.

Sadique Ali Committee in its report stated:

"Mishandling and foreign interference of more than one variety have conspired to make the situation in Kashmir insoluble. Yet a fair and wise solution is imperative not only in the interest of the two countries, but of peace and goodwill among nations.

"A lasting solution of any human conflict must be based on just principles and the long view. India and Pakistan, whatever their present differences, have to live together; and they cannot but live in friendship. Persistent conflict is sure to destroy them both.

"It would be very much worthwhile for both the governments to sit together determined to find a satisfactory solution. Representatives of the two governments, no doubt, have met in the past, but they did so under the shadow of third parties on relying on finding a solution with their help. It is necessary to lift this shadow and seek a solution without the interposition of any outside agencies."

Waheed-Ur-Rehman, Youth President of PDP writes in *Indian Express*:

"The challenge in Kashmir today is to connect the youngsters who are below 18 and, tragically enough, many of those who have recently died are in that age group. In three earlier cycles of protest, in 2008, 2009 and 2010, the major casualties were largely among those who were below 18.

"We need to understand that these youngsters need good parenting rather than policing. We need to listen to them patiently. Similarly, social problems need societal interventions, rather than security. Security forces can't replace society in conflict areas. In villages, we have lost the idea of eldership. We used to have a culture of respecting our elders. Today, elders are irrelevant in villages. The reason for this societal breakdown is the despair set in by a never-ending conflict that rules every sphere of the life of the people. We need to understand the reason behind the rage.

"Kashmiri youth are politically very conscious and understand the nuances of each discourse. Over the years, there is a feeling of defeat which they carry with them."

Kashmiri youth is angry, it is not India's enemy. Today, the young think that if they inflict injury on themselves, New Delhi may feel their pain. It's more of an emotional problem than a geographical or economical one. But Delhi lacks emotion or empathy for Kashmir and its responses have often been in terms of economic packages rather than serious and honest political outreach.

When India says Kashmir is its integral part, the term "integral" is geographical in nature and doesn't take the people into account. On the other hand, Pakistan calls it its "jugular vein" and addresses its constituency in Kashmir more emotionally than geographically. Many people in Kashmir carry the grudge that a country which unites in seeking justice for victims of rape and molestation like Jessica Lal or Ruchika Girhotra conveniently ignores similar victims in Kashmir. The mysterious deaths of 2009 "rape and murder" victims, Aasiya and Nilofar, in Shopian are repeatedly cited as a case in point.

Every year, thousands of our young boys and girls get scholarships under the Prime Minister's Special Scholarship Scheme (PMSSS). Our students, who go out to study or work, get harassed and beaten up across cities and towns in mainland India. This defeats the very purpose of such programmes and instead, sows the seeds of hatred in the hearts of Kashmiri youth.

It is the common people of India who look at Kashmiris with suspicion and contempt. This is much more dangerous. It's another feeling of defeat for our youth, which further taints the idea of the political mainstream on the ground in Kashmir.

Mufti Mohammad Sayeed had firmly positioned his politics on annoying none and still creating relevance for all. His was an accommodative, inclusive and participatory politics. Unfortunately, the process of reconciliation started by him ended tragically.

Today, while there is an urgent need to resuscitate that process, there seems no serious movement in that direction.

One can only regret the absence of spaces in our country for social and political engagement on the "Kashmir issue" and "issues of Kashmir". We need people-to-people relations that sustain and outlive us.

A healing touch and not a military crackdown should form the core of the Kashmir policy. The policy of consistent inconsistency practiced by earlier Central Governments hasn't helped. Delhi has to be different this time. It's high time Modi invokes and emulates Mufti's legacy (*Kashmir through Ages*: Suresh K. Sharma and Usha Sharma, p. 78).

Sajad Padder from Centre for International Relations, Islamic University of Science and Technology, Awantipora, Jammu & Kashmir

Describing the cause of youth unrest in Kashmir, Sajad Padder Says:

"Since the late 1990s, a few trends are quite common here. One is the behaviour of the Valley's youth on the eve of elections. They become active political agents and vote overwhelmingly. What peoples them to do so?

"They crave for a dignified life and revocation of draconian laws like AFSPA. But once elections are over, it's *déjà vu* all over again. Nothing changes except power between political elites. Corrosive institutions and inept politicians is a deadly combination for any society.

"The next phase is when separatist politics take centrestage. The killing of innocents often trigger panic. Then our youth demands 'azadi'. The word 'azadi' lacks a clear-cut definition. For some, it amounts to the 'right to self-determination', while, for others, it stands for demilitarisation and control over natural resources, particularly water.

"The deep sense of anger and deprivation drive our youth into streets, ready to face bullets with stones. Instant overthrow of political system becomes their primary motto. What follows is curfew for weeks together. Internet services are suspended. Life returns to normalcy only after a long lull.

"Now, look at the health of our institutions. Every institution, from academic to religious is highly politicized.

The two mainstream political parties. Peoples Democratic Party (PDP) and National Conference (NC) are equally responsible for it, although the All Parties Hurriyat Conference (APHC) must acknowledge its share of blame as well.

"Where is the heaven our poets and politicians often speaks about? It's absolute hell and there is little hope."

If the Kashmir problem is solved peacefully, amicably and equitably before conditions deteriorate beyond control, Kashmir might become the much-needed bridge over the gulf of differences that has opened wide between the two sister States, viz., India and Pakistan. Kashmir can become both the source of friendship as also the cause of eternal enmity and war between the two countries. It is for Indian leaders to decide what they want to make of it, a beautiful common pleasure garden where Hindu and Muslim culture could fructify in a composite cosmopolitan culture or a battleground for the two communities and the two countries. Whether the Kashmir Valley goes to India or to Pakistan, of one thing there should be no doubt—that the future progress and prosperity of this beautiful land depends on good neighbourly relations between the two countries (*Kashmir Through the Ages*: Suresh K. Sharma and Usha Sharma, pp. 277-78).

# Annexure

## V.K. Krishna Menon's Marathon Speech on Kashmir at the Security Council

V.K. Krishna Menon's marathon speech lasting for eight hours, spread over two days has been extracted from the proceedings of the U.N. Security Council's

1. Seven hundred and sixty-second meeting, 23 January 1957.
2. Seven hundred and sixty-third meeting, 24 January 1957.
3. Seven hundred and sixty-fourth meeting, 24 January 1957.
4. Seven hundred and sixty-fifth meeting, 24 January 1957.

### (1)

**Krishna Menon:** The Government of India has given consideration to the statement made by the Foreign Minister of Pakistan before the Security Council on 16 January. That is a statement coming from the neighbouring country, with which it is our desire to establish, maintain and continue the most intimate friendship. It has been made by a person who has been associated with the service of India for well over a generation and who, today, occupies a place of prominence in his Government.

Before I deal with the subject that is before us, I would like to make this preliminary observation. Yesterday in India, India and Pakistan signed a trade agreement. If this was merely a trade agreement for the exchange of commodities, as might happen between any two peoples, it would not be of any importance. This, like so many other agreements reached between our two countries, marks a further step forward in the effort, in justice, to get over the difficulties, which have arisen from time to time. It touches not the feelings so much as the standards of living of our people on both sides.

With that background, I will endeavour, therefore, not to introduce invective or anything irrelevant to the subject before us, or which would in any way swim against the current of co-operation and fraternity between our two countries.

The present consideration of this matter arises from a letter dated 2 January 1957 (S/3767) from the Minister for Foreign Affairs of Pakistan to the President of the Security Council. It is important for me to mention this, because, as I develop the position on behalf of the Government of India, it will be obvious to the Security Council, that, in this matter, it is necessary to place developments, phases, incidents and events in their right perspective. It is not possible to understand a problem, especially a complex problem which has engaged, in the first instance, the attention of the two countries, and the attention of other parties, including the Security Council, over the years—to which I shall refer later so that the significance of documents, arrangements and declarations can become realistic and true to fact.

The statement made in this Council on 16 January began, it is true, with a brief mention of the partition of India. It then went on to the position that India accepted "a spurious offer of accession" of the State of Kashmir, and it would appear that what was sought to be conveyed was that we are here in regard to dispute about territory.

Mr. President, I believe that you and all but one or two members of the Security Council are newcomers to this subject. It is quite true that it is not individuals but States that represent Governments here. And even with regard to States, apart from the five Permanent Members of the Security Council, the bulk of them if not all of them, are newcomers to this subject. I have duty to the Security Council and to my Government, as well as to the cause of international peace and security, to present this problem, even at the risk of trying the Council's patience with detail, in such a way as to enable the picture to be true to fact.

It will be recalled that the last time the Security Council considered this matter was on 23 December 1952, which is more than four years ago, a fact which is more than four years ago, a fact which is not without significance, because, at a later stage in his remarks, the representative of Pakistan attempted to convey to the Council the feeling that there was a crisis developing in this matter. I shall refer to that factor in a moment.

It was the Government of India that came here in the first instance on 1 January 1948. It is not usual for a Government of average ability and intelligence, as mine is, to come before the Security Council and to invite its attention to the wrongs it has done. In this particular case it has done nothing wrong, and in any case the matter is clear in itself.

Therefore, I shall now refer to annex 28 of Security Council document S/1100, which is on page 139 of the Security Council Official Records, Supplement of November 1948. The original text is in English, and it is dated 1 January 1948. I hope the Secretary-General will bear with me, when I say that it is essential for us to quote these documents, with all the details, because, at variance with the practice of the General Assembly, the Security Council's documents require considerable research if you wish to find some particular point in them. There is no volume of resolutions on this subject: you have to search for the resolutions and put them together. That may be a good thing, because one learns more about them. I should like to read the beginning and the end of this:

> Under article 35 of the Charter of the United Nations (Krishna Menon: Which means that we did not come here with a request for drastic action as we were entitled to do) any Member may bring any situation (Krishna Menon: And I emphasize this word situation, for we

> did not bring here a dispute but a situation), whose continuance is likely to endanger the maintenance of international peace and security to the attention of the Security Council (Krishna Menon: Then we went on to say): Such situation now exists between India and Pakistan.....

*We felt, as indeed my predecessor in this chair pointed out to the Council at that time, that there is no dispute about territory,* If it were a dispute about territory, I say with great respect that the Security Council under the Charter would be incompetent to deal with it because that would be either a political or a juridical question, and under Chapter VI or Chapter VII the Security Council would deal with questions of international peace and Security. *So we brought here a situation and not a dispute.*

But that is not the most important part. We went on the say:

> The Government of India requests the Security Council to call upon Pakistan to put an end immediately to the giving of such assistance. (Krishna Menon: Immediately, on 1 January 1948, and today we are nine years away from it), which is an act of aggression against India.

I shall quote these words more than once before I have concluded, in order to discharge my responsibility as the representative of my Government:

> ...Which is an act of Aggression against India.

*That is the crux of the question.* What we are considering here is not merely various resolutions or the method by which a problem may be resolved otherwise. What is before us, as I shall point out later, is this question of aggression, because the whole United Nations is founded upon the basic principles of international law and behaviour. That is based upon equity. And he who asks for equity must come with clean hands. Therefore, our starting point is that we came here in order to file a complaint, to ask for redress on a charge of aggression. If Pakistan does not mention this starting point, then we have to point out why we were so concerned about it. Even today we have frontier raids one way or another. But why did we then ask the Security Council to deal with this matter? "If

Pakistan does not do so,"—that is to say, halt the aggression,—"the Government of India may be compelled in self-defence", and I interpolate that self-defence is not only a right of the Member States of the United Nations but, I submit, it is an obligation that Member States have under the Charter, because they have an obligation to maintain the sovereignties of their own countries—"the Government of India may be compelled in self-defence to enter Pakistan territory"—which we did not do,—"in order to take military action against the invaders. The matter was, therefore, one of extreme urgency and called for immediate action by the Security Council for avoiding a breach of international peace."

As the delineation of this picture becomes more complete, it will be clear that the efforts of India and of the Security Council and the approaches made to Pakistan by mediators have, at earlier stages, been primarily addressed to the halting of hostilities.

Therefore, our country was faced with the position that part of its territory was invaded, and that invasion had to be resisted. It had to be rolled back. The normal practice of war would have been to defend by attacking the invader. But this was in 1947. And it is a fact, which remains true to us even today, that these were the same people who were party of our country but ten years ago. What is more, between January 1947 and October, when these thing started, our two countries had only just passed through the holocaust of fratricide, that is, of Indian people killing Pakistanis, and Pakistanis killing Indians. We witnessed an orgy of violence. And it was the desire of our Government that nothing should be done to rekindle these embers, which were still burning.

That is the original position, and I shall keep coming back to it. We are here on a complaint of aggression. That aggression has not been resolved: it has not been got rid of. So long as there are forces of other countries in a place where they have no right to be, irrespective of our rights, I think the Security Council is called upon, under the provisions of the Charter, to act.

In this context, so many trees have grown, and a very considerable amount of undergrowth, that it is impossible to see the wood properly, and it will be my attempt to present it as best as we can. We shall try to assist the Security Council to see this picture as it was. As I said, five years ago we debated this, and in five years—even apart from the nine years—a great many things have happened. It is part of the inevitable practice of nations that the changes in conditions that time brings about and which may go to the root of a question have also to be taken into account.

From there, with great respect to my colleague, the Foreign Minister, I shall follow his example of looking at this problem since the partition of India.

India became an independent country on 15 August 1947. We are not concerned here with the political issues but with the constitutional and other issues relevant to this problem. The independence of India was attained by an act of the United Kingdom Parliament. The Independence Act of 1947 is that Act, and at later stages we shall draw attention to the clauses relevant to these matters. On 17 June 1947, the United Kingdom Parliament passed the Independence of India Act whereby India was created a self-governing dominion and a successor State to British India. Popularly, we speak of the British Parliament having partitioned the country into two; constitutionally that is not correct.

What happened was that British India obtained independence. India, under the British Crown, obtained independence and in that process Parliament constituted certain territories—which we had agreed on before politically—into another dominion. Therefore, as regards our State, for example, in the United Nations, we did not have to be admitted anew. We came there as a successor State to the India that signed the Covenant of the League of Nations, that signed the Treaty of Versailles, and which also went to San Francisco to help in establishing this Organization, at which time my distinguished colleague from Pakistan was one of the representatives. So India became the successor State by this Act of 1947: The 1935 Act, that is to say, the Act of the British Parliament passed in 1935 and which came into force around 1936, became the Constitution Act.

It was amended in order to deal with certain anomalies, such as the reference to the Crown, the Viceroy, and so on. Various such amendments were made during that period. That is the Constitution Act. Now this Act—and it is important to remember it—deals with the Federation of India. British dominion in India or British suzerainty in India consisted of the overlordship of what is now called by that very ugly word, the sub-continent, that is, the Indian peninsula.

That territory consisted of two groups of political species: *one was the British provinces directly ruled under the ultimate direction of the Secretary of State from London: and the other were the Indian states. There were 565 of them when we obtained independence.* Therefore, the problem arose as to what was to be done with the States, because the States were not directly ruled: they were indirectly ruled.

The British Government, with the wisdom, which is often not credited to it but which in fact exists, had foreseen that India was likely to become independent. Therefore, as early as the third decade of this century they had tried to define the relations between the British Crown and these states by what is called a doctrine of paramountcy. It is necessary, for purposes of record and for any future misunderstandings that may arise—not in this particular issue to state that we do not necessarily accept everything that everybody says about the doctrine of paramountcy. It does not appear anywhere else in international law.

Roughly speaking, for this purpose the doctrine of paramountcy is this: that when we speak of the relations between the Indian States—and here again let me emphasize that when the British speak about the relations between the Indian States or we speak about constitutional law—it is the relations between the Crown and the head of the State, because all treaties were between the Crown and the Princes. There were no treaties ratified by any parliament or legislatures. The relationships were established on account of the treaties, which were really charter, given, by the British Crown and the Princes. And the British Government of the day, the Viceroy of the day, argued that this established a privity between them, a privity of contract, a privity of relationship between them and expounded for the first time, in 1926, this doctrine of paramountcy.

Under the doctrine of paramountcy, when India gained independence, the British Government proposed that the Crown was withdrawing. The Crown was withdrawing from the peninsula. The Crown was withdrawing from effective control of British India. And that is a point which I particularly would like the representative of the United Kingdom to take special note of.

When were these changes necessary in the relations between the Princes and the Crown? Because the Crown was going on legal theory, fixed in a two-fold way, through the Viceroy, on the one hand, and the Governor-General, on the other. It was a fact that he had the Indian Army, it was a fact that he had Indian revenue, it was a fact that he had the Indian police, it was a fact that he had the Indian customs organization which enabled him to arrange the relations with the States.

Some gentlemen around this table are well aware, in constitutional practice, of the difference between status and function. Functionally, therefore, it was the British Government of British India that maintained these relations. It is quite true that there was a constitutional aspect. Therefore, for the purpose of the record we want to read into it that whatever remained, in the British Government, by virtue of this function, remains in the Government of India by virtue of its succession. Therefore, the doctrine of paramountcy was limited by this phraseology.

In order that there may be further support for this argument, I wish to draw the attention of the Council, and particularly the representative of the United Kingdom, to the fact that a distinguished jurist who was Viceroy of India in this period when these changes were dreamed of in 1926, told the Princes that they had no sovereignty and that they had no independence at any time. There is a classic phrase which says: Over and above all treaty obligations are certain rights that rest in the Government. And therefore at no time was the independence of the Indian States the kind of sovereign independence that would have enabled them to become Members of the United Nations. It is quite true, as it is said in the Cabinet Mission's Memorandum, that they were competent to discuss some political relationship other than accession. That is possible. But they would not have been independent, like Columbia, or Cuba, or France or any of the countries around here, because they had no international status. I want to submit that the British Government, or any Government in the world, cannot just make a country like that.

Independence rests upon function, upon territory, upon the capacity to exercise sovereign rights and, what is more, upon the recognition by the world. Therefore, when we speak about the three alternatives, this has to be born is mind. My government in view of the complications that arise in these matters, is anxious that this should be on the record somewhere, even though it might not have an immediate bearing on what you are going to consider.

The mission of the British Cabinet was in India in 1946 and on May 1946 it issued statement in the form of memorandum. For the convenience of the Council, my delegation has prepared these documents for the purpose of ready reference. The memorandum to which I have just referred appears in our document No. 4. I shall, at some stage, ask for these documents to be circulated as United Nations documents. I believe we are entitled to ask that. But for the purpose of reference the President has a copy, and copies have also been given to the other Members of the Council.

It will be seen that in our document No. 4—which, for convenience, we have handed to the President and this colleagues in the Council—the position is briefly set out at the end of page 3 and the beginning of page 4. I do not want to take up the time of the Council by reading out the whole of this document, but it says in part:

> This means that the rights of the States (Krishna Menon: And the important word is 'rights') which flow from their relationship to the Crown will no longer exist and that all the rights surrendered by the States to the paramount power will return to be States.

That is one statement. The reference is to rights; there is no reference to the other relationships that have been created, and it will be seen that this is referred to in the British Prime Minister's statement in Parliament, because, over and above rights, there are functional relationships set up. The document goes on to say, on page 4:

> Political arrangements between the States on the one side and the British Crown and British India on the other will thus be brought to an end. The void will have to be filled either by the States entering into a federal relationship with the successor Government or Governments in British India, or failing this, entering into particular political arrangement with it or them.

Now this is the basis to which my colleague has referred as being the relationship between the States and India in the future. And, therefore, when the British withdrew from India the *Pax, Britannica,* of which we had heard a great deal, became limited by this fact. This new State that had been set up had to weave these threads of unity afterwards. The greater part of the States where in geographical and other contiguity to India, and, therefore, both in the British House of Commons and in the Chamber of Princes—which then was the organization for consultation between the Mission and the Princes, and of which my colleague sitting behind me was at that time Chancellor the representative of the Crown, the Viceroy of India, made his announcement as to what all this meant.

There is a statement of what Lord Mountbatten actually did say which appears in Mr. Feroze Khan Noon's statement, and we want to deal with that. It says:

> The Viceroy and Governor-General, Lord Mountbatten, who represented the suzerain—the King of the United Kingdom and Emperor of India—however, advised the Princes of India on 25 July 1947 that, in deciding the question of accession, they must pay due regard to the communal composition, the wishes of their peoples and the geographical location of their States.

I am not willing to really on my memory in regard to this carefully considered document. We have done all the research we can; we are familiar with the subject. There is no such statement of that character. What is more, the statement does not refer to communal representation. What it says is this—and this is the statement of 25 July 1947 by Lord Mountbatten in the Chamber of Princes:

> You people are now free to join either Dominion, or you can be even, in a sense, independent, but of course you cannot evade geography; you cannot evade all that has happened in the past. So you people have to make up your mind.

He said to them:

> It was necessary to set up two States Departments.... But when I say that they are at liberty to link up with either of the Dominions, may I point out that there are certain geographical compulsions which cannot be evaded. Out of something like 565 States, the vast majority are irretrievably linked geographically with the Dominion of India. The problem, therefore is of far greater magnitude with the Dominion of India than it is with Pakistan. In the case of Pakistan the States, although important, are not so numerous, and Mr. Jinnah, the future Governor-General of Pakistan, is prepared to negotiate the case of each State separately and individually.

The rest of it refers to our internal arrangements. The Viceroy went on to say that, in order that there might be a smooth passage over, he was arranging to have a clause inserted in the Independence Act in regard to internal arrangements.

On page 5 of the document it is stated:

> Let us turn for one moment to the Cabinet Mission Plan of 16 May 1946. In this plan the proposal was that the States should surrender to the Central Government three subjects—Defence, External Affairs and Communications. That was a plan which, to the

> best of my belief, every Ruler and every State accepted as reasonable, fair and just.

But the key phrase in his statement is this:

> You cannot run away from the Dominion Government which is your neighbour any more than you can run away from the subjects for whose welfare you are responsible. Whatever may be your decision, I hope you feel that I have at least done my duty by the States.

I have spent sometime on this statement because there is reference here to a distinguished national of the United Kingdom who performed such great services to both our countries and to the Commonwealth and to whom we referred as the Representative of the Suzerain of India at that time, and it is essential that there should be no mistake in this matter. Lord Mountbatten did not at that time—nor did the British Parliament at any time in regard to the States—ever refer to communal representation, by which, in India, is meant the grouping of Hindus and Muslims. There was no reference and it was not the idea at that time that the States should be represented in that way in any of these documents.

But then the other document on which my distinguished colleague relies is the document of 3 June 1947, which is a statement by Mr. Attlee, then Prime Minister of the United Kingdom in the British Parliament on the transfer of power. I will not labour the Council by reading this document, but it will be found that this document definitely says that this was concerned exclusively with British India. This is what the Pakistan Foreign Minister says:

The basis of the partition of the British Empire in India (Krishna Menon. If by that is meant British India plus the States) as set forth in the statement of the then Prime Minister of the United Kingdom of 3 June 1947, was that Pakistan would be constituted by the contiguous Muslim majority areas in the north-west and north-east of the sub-continent, and India would comprise contiguous non-Muslim majority areas. It was thus universally assumed that, following the basis adopted for

Partition, Princely States with the Muslim majority in population contiguous of Pakistan would accede to Pakistan.

There is nothing like this in the 3 June document. What is more, it makes a special reservation to say that this does not concern the Indian States, but is exclusively concerned with British India. And it is not splitting hairs on this matter, because he was trying to explain the basis on which the grouping of territories in the partition had taken place. This is merely an explanation of that character. It is explained in paragraph 18 of Mr. Attlee's statement:

> His Majesty's Government wish to make it clear that the decisions announced above relate only to British India and that their policy towards Indian States contained in the Cabinet Mission Memorandum of 12th May 1946 remains unchanged.

Therefore, I submit that this 3 June document has nothing to do with this matter, and I have said that, because there is some irrelevancy as to such claims as Pakistan puts forward for Kashmir.

Now it will be seen from that that, while these territories, were enabled to be independent as I have said, before, there were a large number of practical arrangements between these various areas. There were 565 States scattered all over India from north to south and east to west. A great many of them were territories which were separated by bits of British Indian territory. There were questions of communications, questions of customs, questions of postal arrangements and various other matters; and over and above those, there was the question of defence. I shall not read out that part, but it will be noted that the Viceroy referred to this question as follows:

> You Princes cannot defend yourselves; you have to be, in a larger grouping. That is the only way to do it.

In the statement made later in the British Parliament by the Prime Minister he referred to the fact that arrangements should be made to carry on in the intervening period. That was at the time when the British were still ruling India and when we had not been partitioned *de jure*. The Viceroy and Governor-General was still the head of the Government and, at that time, prior to the partition, these arrangements were being carried on, and it was suggested that a standstill arrangement should be made by the two States with whoever they wanted to function.

Therefore, the first part is contained in Section 7 of the Indian Independence Act of 1947, which says:

> His Majesty's Government in the United Kingdom have no responsibility as respects the Government of any of the territories which, immediately before that day, were included in British India.

The suzerainty of His Majesty over the Indian States lapses, and with it, all treaties and governments in force at the date of the passing of this Act between His Majesty and the rulers of Indian States, all obligations of His Majesty existing at that date towards Indian States or the rulers thereof, and all power, rights, authority of jurisdiction exercisable by His Majesty at that date in or in relation to Indian States by treaty, grant, usage, sufferance or otherwise....

Therefore, there was a void which had to be filled and that is done by a proviso:

> Provided that, notwithstanding anything in paragraph (b) or paragraph (c)—(Krishna Menon: which I have just read)—of this sub-section, effect shall, as nearly as may be, continue to be given to the provisions of any such agreement as is therein referred to which relate to customs, transit and communications, posts and telegraphs, or other like matters, until the provisions in question are denounced by the Ruler of the Indian State or person having authority in the tribal areas on the one hand, or by the Dominion or Province or other part thereof concerned on the other hand, or are superseded by subsequent agreements.

This is the period between 17 June, when this Act was passed, and 15 August, when we became independent, and 14 August, when they became independent. We are the younger State by Six hours.

Arising from this, standstill agreements, as they were called, were formulated. And the purpose of the standstill agreements was to carry on business in the way indicated here, and, so far as we were concerned, that included the matter of the Security of the country, because, as I have said, there were areas interspersed all over. They were on our coasts, and they were very vulnerable in the post-war era. Therefore, the two Dominions had to make their own arrangements in this connexion, as the Viceroy had pointed out. Mr. Jinnah, who afterwards became Governor-General of Pakistan, was to negotiate with these States separately. Mr. Zafrullah Khan, who represented Pakistan in the Security Council meeting on 16 January 1948, referred to these agreements, so far as they were concerned and pointed out what they actually meant. He said:

> In any case, the (Krishna Menon: The Maharajah) had entered into a standstill agreement with Pakistan. It is necessary to explain what a standstill agreement is. India, being one political entity before the division on 15 August 1947, had a common system of defence, of railways, post offices, telegraphs, telephones, and a host of other matters. If on 15 August, when at least a nominal division took place between these two Dominions—in some places, the actual division also took place on that date—all these matters **had had** to be adjusted, the situation would have been impossible. A new currency could not be started merely by a stroke of the pen.

Mr. Zafrullah Khan went on to say:

> Each State would come to a standstill agreement with the Dominion of India or the Dominion of Pakistan, according to its own situation and requirements, providing that these matters—mainly communications, and so on should continue to run on the old basis.

There was a further statement by Mr. Zafrullah Khan. At the Security Council meeting on the next day, he said:

> I explained yesterday to the Security Council what the standstill agreements mean. Kashmir had arrived

> at a standstill agreement with Pakistan with regard to her communications, supplies, and post office and telegraphic arrangements.

I want the Security Council to take note of this last part, it was with regard to communications, supplies, and post office and telegraphic arrangements, and nothing else. Mr. Zafrullah Khan went on to say, "This agreement became operative on 15 August".

The history of the standstill agreement is contained in the telegrams exchanged between the Prime Minister of Jammu and Kashmir, on the one hand, and the Prime Minister of Pakistan, on the other, and there was a similar exchange of telegrams between the responsible Minister in New Delhi and the Prime Minister of Jammu and Kashmir.

As a result of the telegrams that passed between the Prime Minister of Pakistan and the Prime Minister of Kashmir, a standstill agreement was arrived at. The contents of that agreement have been submitted to this Council by no less an authority than Mr. Zafrullah Khan, who was Foreign Minister of Pakistan at that time. It must be stated there were no signatures on these, because they were agreed between the governments by means of telegrams.

So far as the Government of India is concerned, on the same date an identical telegram was sent to the Government of India, and India was in the process—and this is important—of negotiating these standstill agreements, and they are contained in the second set of telegrams. In a telegram from the Prime Minister of Jammu and Kashmir to the Government of India it was stated:

> Jammu and Kashmir Government would welcome standstill agreements with Union of India on all matters on which these exist at the present moment with outgoing British Indian Government. It is suggested that existing arrangements should continue pending settlement of details and formal execution of fresh agreements.

It may be said here that the "existing arrangements" comprised the use of Indian forces if there was internal rebellion in one of the States. That had been practiced for a long time, but it is not necessary for me to bring that out. The Government of India telegraphed back:

> Government of India would be glad if you or some other Minister duly authorized in this behalf could fly Delhi for negotiating standstill agreement between Kashmir Government and Indian Dominion. Early action desirable to maintain intact existing agreements and administrative arrangements.

Before the Prime Minister could come to discuss these matters, Kashmir was invaded. Therefore the standstill agreements which they were trying simultaneously to conclude with the two countries were interrupted, not by the action of the Government of Kashmir or by the Government of India, but by the active aggression complained of. Therefore, it was not possible for the standstill agreement contemplated to go on, and other developments followed.

There is only one matter to which I wish to refer. We propose to put in, for the reference of the Security Council, the standstill agreement used by the Government of India with regard to all the Dominions and States. This document is important, because we did not cook it up for Kashmir. It is a standard document There are no other agreements and, therefore, if Kashmir had concluded an agreement with us, the purpose of it would have been as contained in this document. I will not read the text, since it would take too long, but the schedule of this document is important and the standard form was different from the substance given of it by Sir Zafrullah Khan. I am pointing out the difference between the standstill agreement of India and the standstill agreement of Pakistan. The schedule included air communications, arms and equipment, control of commodities, currency and coinage, customs, Indian State's forces, external affairs, extradition, import and export control, irrigation and electric power, motor vehicles, national highway, opium, posts and telegraphs and telephones, railways, salt, central excises, relief from double income tax and other arrangements relating to taxation, etc.

All these subjects are contained in the schedule of the standstill agreement. Therefore, if there had been no interruption by invasion, it is normal to conclude that a standstill agreement would have included external affairs, control of State forces and of other matters which spring from the sovereignty of a country.

I should like to say that there is nothing inconsistent in a State concluding a standstill agreement with two different countries, especially a State of this kind, where there were railways communications and postal communications with India and Pakistan. That is why Sir Zafrullah Khan, with great accuracy, pointed out what they had, and this is what we would have had, because this is a pattern which is not altered, but at that time the invasion of Kashmir began.

There is telegram No. 1, the chronology of which is important. I have already referred to the telegrams sent in connection with this matter by the Prime Minister of Kashmir to the Government of India. The representatives will note that the date of this telegram is 12 August 1947. On 16 August, four days later, the Government of Pakistan telegraphed that it had agreed to standstill agreement and a few days later the Chief of Staff of the Jammu and Kashmir forces, Major-General Scott, a British Officer, submitted his first report to his Government, the Kashmir Government which still had not acceded to anybody, before the border raids from Pakistan. That does not mean there had been no raids before.

All of us know, especially now with all our discussions, about United Nations forces, that it takes some time for this sort of thing to travel. Anyone, on 31 August 1947, the Chief of Staff of the Jammu and Kashmir army submitted a report to his Government on border raids from Pakistan. So the invasion had begun. That was what prevented the officials of the Kashmir Government coming over to India at that time.

On 4 September, on the basis of a telegraphic report submitted by its Chief of Staff, Major-General Scott, the Kashmir Government protested by telegram to the West Punjab Government against armed Muslims from Rawalpindi district infiltrating into the State. Protest were also made to the Deputy Commissioner.

Two days later there was a marked increase in this activity.

> A patrol visited Alibeg, twelve miles west of Bhimbar and Major-General Lovett, commanding the Seventh infantry Division—that is to say, presumably of the Pakistan forces—was informed. On 13 September, a Pakistan Army patrol visited Alibeg and Jatlai, fourteen miles west of Bhimbar, both in the State territory. They are all contained in the diary kept by General Scott.

On 17 September—we are now only one month after independence—a band of 400 armed raiders, twelve miles south-east of Ranbirsinghpura drove away herds of cattle belonging to State nationals.

On 18 September, railway service between Sialkot and Jammu was suspended by Pakistan authorities without any reason and in contravention of the Standstill Agreement. So if there was an agreement it was broken by the conduct of the Pakistan Government on 18 September—and this action was not isolated. Armed gangs entered Kashmir in Palandri, Poonch, across the State border. By 18 September the invasion had gained momentum.

On 28 September, hundreds of armed men with service rifles, automatics and spears attacked a Kashmir State patrol near Chak Harka. On 30 September hundreds of armed Pathans entered Dhirkot Than, inside the State territory.

On 3 October, the Jammu and Kashmir Government protested telegraphically to Pakistan against hundreds of armed people from Murree Hills in Pakistan operating in Poonch—part of which is now occupied by Pakistan, part of which is in the other side; it also protested against the essential supplies, including petrol, rice, salt and cloth being withheld. That is the second violation of the Standstill Agreement.

On 4 October, armed men renewed their activities in the Chirala area and near the Jhelum river and fighting between the raiders and the State forces began. Now we had reached a state of war.

On 10 October, two sections of the Pakistan army followed by an armed gang attacked Pansar village in Jammu. I submit with great respect and a sense of responsibility that what I have now read out is one of the key points in the consideration of the whole of this question—that is to say, Pakistan informed us that they were not involved in this matter. They said they were trying to stop them. The Security Council asked them not to get involved and not to do anything. Even as early as 10 October, long before the Indian forces had been there, Pakistan had invaded the State of Kashmir. How does it become important? Because irrespective of whatever claims, whatever relations, whatever titles the Indian Government may have on Kashmir, Pakistan certainly had no rights because it had no accession, no relationships of any kind. At best it was foreign territory. It was an act of aggression. So, on 10 October 1947 the invasion began. And here the diary says that two sections of the Pakistan army followed by an armed gang attacked the village. And this item appeared in the Pakistan papers:

> The North West Frontier Province Premier is reported to have announced that firearms would be distributed among the people liberally so that all except the 'enemies of Pakistan' can have them.

## A very Familiar Sound

On 13 October, 1947 the following was stated in a newspaper:

> Pakistan has cut off from Kashmir supplies of petrol, sugar, salt and kerosene oil, although a standstill agreement between them has been signed.

Norman Cliff, who was the correspondent of the *News Chronicle* (London) not an Indian paper from Kashmir, published this news, in that newspaper.

On 15 October the Maharaja appealed to the British Prime Minister, probably by force of habit, because that was the practice in the past days. The Kashmir Government cabled to the British Prime Minister about the economic blockade of the State by Pakistan and the beginning of the invasion from Pakistan in Poonch. He went on to say:

> People all along the border have been licensed and armed with modern weapons under the pretext of general policy,

> which does not appear to have been followed in the case of internal districts of West Punjab—whereas military escorts are made available for several other purposes, none is provided for safe transit of petrol and other essential of life. Protests merely elicit promises which are never implemented. As a results of obvious connivance of the Pakistan Government, the whole of the border from Gurdaspur side up to Gilgit is threatened with invasion which has actually begun in Poonch.

That is to say, away from the western border, the western district towards the south of the State right up to the mountain area on the frontiers of Sinkiang, the Soviet Union and other countries. In all those areas supplies are made. Some days later, the Jammu and Kashmir Prime Minister telegraphed the Prime Minister of the North West Frontier Province—that is, a province of Pakistan and the Deputy Commissioner of Rawalpindi, both in west Pakistan, about people armed with modern weapons infiltrating from Hazara and Rawalpindi districts in West Pakistan into the State and asked them to stop the infiltration. The invaders continued their progress along the Jhelum Valley road towards Srinagar. Srinagar is the summer capital of Kashmir, founded about 2,300 years ago by the great Emperor Asoka. Their triumphant march was temporarily stemmed at Uri, a town fifty miles from Srinagar, by the demolition of the bridge and the gallant resistance of about 150 men under the command of a Brigadier of the Kashmir army who was killed fighting a memorable last-ditch battle. The raiders managed to construct a diversion which was about a mile long, requiring considerable engineering skill, as, according to *The Dawn* of Karachi of 7 December 1947, it was completed in two days—that is to say, in this invasion the Pakistan sappers or engineer regiments—their REME's—must have participated. It was not possible for them to do otherwise. A fact will be noticed here to which I will refer later. These men were resisted only by the national militia, by the local population. They were not welcomed as liberators. They fought a last-ditch battle; they resisted these people. That was on 22 October.

On 24 October the Maharaja, who was the head of the State and according to the Constitution, the only person competent to sign an accession; nobody else could do it—appealed to India for military help.

May, I halt here for a moment. Until no one from India, either Army or ministers or anyone, had gone into Kashmir to persuade the Maharaja. No police had been sent. We did not put any pressure on him; in fact, if I may interpolate, in a previous period Lord Mountbatten, on behalf of the Government of India, told the Maharaja of Kashmir, "You will accede to Pakistan if you wish and we will not take it as an unfriendly act" because the Government of India at that time was concerned about not having these States suspended in a vacuum, being the centres of trouble and difficulty, especially a frontier area.

If they had acceded in the normal way, we would have accepted it, as indeed we accepted the sorry partition to which we subscribe and which we have no desire to undo. The Maharaja appealed to India.

On 25 October Lord Mountbatten attended the Defence Committee at which General Lackhart, the Commander-in-Chief in India, read out a telegram from the headquarters of the Pakistan Army—and this is of importance to my colleagues of Australia and the United Kingdom—stating that some 5,000 tribesmen had attacked and captured Muzaffarabad and Domela and that considerable tribal reinforcements could be expected. Reports showed that they were already little more than thirty-five miles from Srinagar. It was quite normal for those two British officers to exchange telegrams, especially at that time; Pakistan had not acknowledged its invasion. Obviously, the Commander-in-Chief and British officers were working outside the policy region.

On 26 October 1947, the Maharaja asked for protection—I shall deal with the letter when we come to the question of accession—and he offered accession to India. This is the position up to 26 October and I will deal with the document regarding accession to India of Kashmir and the surrounding States later, but it is necessary for me to dwell at some length on the history of this period, between that time and the cease-fire. If the members of the Security Council will look at the pages of Document No. 1 from page 5 onwards they will see what happened in Kashmir. It is stated on page 5:

> ...it is a fact that several top-ranking British officers serving in Pakistan did have an inkling of these preparations and plans, though I do not suggest that they took any hand in their execution.

We came to know later (Krishna Menon: that is, the Government of India came to know later) that, as soon as the June 3rd plan was announced, Kashmir became the subject of attention and study in certain military circles. Why was there a demand on the Survey of India for so large a number of maps of Kashmir. (Krishna Menon: that is, from our Ordinance Department in Delhi?) What was the mysterious 'Operation Gulmarg', copies of orders in respect of which fell into the hands of those who were not meant to receive them?

This was because the Government of India also had an intelligence service. The document goes on to say:

> ...the appearance at the psychological time of Jinnah's private secretary to Srinagar, the presence of Jinnah himself at Lahore, cannot be ascribed entirely to coincidence....

On 28 October 1947, it is recorded in a diary written at the time:

> In the middle of today's Defence Committee, Auchinleck rang up Mountbatten (Krishna Menon: Auchinleck was a British Field Marshal and Supreme Commander of Armed Forces for the partition of personnel and physical assets of these forces) from Lahore to say that he had succeeded in persuading Mr. Jinnah to cancel orders given the previous night for Pakistan troops to be moved into Kashmir.

I have read this in order to convince the Council that as early as 28 October 1947 the invasion by Pakistan, by a State and not by irregulars, not by a lot of hooligans, but under the command of the Governor-General, had already taken place.

The Pakistan Commander-in-Chief was a British officer at that time who, in the absence of General Masservy, telephoned the Military Secretary of the Governor of the West Punjab, with whom Jinnah was staying. General Gracey replied that he was not prepared to issue any such instructions without the approval of the Supreme Commander; that is to say, in those transitory stages it was not quite clear—in fact Pakistan voiced and published a complaint that Gracey had no business to disobey these commands. He was under the command of Auchinleck.

At Gracey's urgent request Auchinleck flew to Lahore that morning and explained to Jinnah that an act of invasion would involve automatically and immediately the withdrawal of every British officer serving with the newly formed Pakistan army.

I would like to say that in all these matters, the British officers who served with our army and, so far as we know, the bulk if not all the British officers serving with the Pakistan army, remained aloof from the lethal operations.

An order given by Mohammed Ali Jinnah in 1947 for Pakistan troops to launch an attack on the province of Jammu was ignored by General Douglas Gracey, who was then acting as Commander-in-Chief of the Pakistan army. This was revealed on 20 March 1956 at a meeting of the Kashmir Liberation Conference held in Dacca under the auspices of the Ali-Pakistan Millat-e-Islam Convention by ex Major-General Akbar Khan of the Pakistan army. This was the ex Major-General Akbar Khan who afterwards appeared on the Kashmir scene under the name of General Tariq; who later was charged by the Pakistan Government with the offence of treason, and went to prison. Major-General Akbar Khan said that General Gracey thus jeoparadized the chance then available of liberating Kashmir. This was the view of the senior Pakistan officer at that time: that the British Commander-in-Chief, by refusing to carry out these orders had thrown away the chance of liberating Kashmir.

Mr. Jinnah gave his order after a conference held on 27 October 1947 at Lahore with Pakistan army chiefs. General Gracey said that before launching the attack he would confer with Field Marshal Auchinleck, who was then responsible for superintending the partition of the old Indian Army and the transfer of troops from it to the new Indian and Pakistani armies. Akbar Khan said that Mr. Jinnah's directive was correct and wise; that General Gracey's insistence on conferring with Field Marshal Auchinleck was unjustified because Auchinleck was not in any way concerned with the operations of the Pakistan army—and there is something to be said for Akbar Khan's arguments. He then described the acceptance of the United Nations cease-fire order in Kashmir and Jammu as inopportune. Instead, Pakistan should have accepted the United Nations mediation in 1948 when the District of Poonch was under the control of the "Azad Kashmir Government."

During this period, various acts of brigandage, of rapine and plunder took place and if I had the time I would go into this at great length. But what is the political importance of this? The political importance is that if the Kashmir territory was aligned with Pakistan by kinship, by lines of blood, race or religion, that is a strange way of showing that friendship, by invading its country, and the raping and plunder of the raiding forces continued up to Baramula which is only a few miles from Srinagar. The town was sacked and burned. In spite of the risk that I may take of prolonging this statement, it is necessary at least to look into some parts of this situation.

In his budget speech to the Legislative Assembly of the Frontier Province on 7 March 1949, Premier Abdul Qayyum Khan advocated a special grant for the tribesmen and justified an allotment in these words:

> The House will recall with pride the fact that in our greatest hour of danger the masud responded to our call by rushing to the rescue of the oppressed Muslims of Jammu and Kashmir State.

I know of no rule of international law which confers upon a State the right to go and protect someone else in another State, even if he is oppressed. If that were the case, no State would be stable.

On 31 October 1947, the Prime Minister of India telegraphed to the Prime Minister of Pakistan:

> Raiders from the Frontier Province or along the Muree road come from Pakistan territory and it is the easiest thing in the world to stop them at the two bridges which connect Pakistan territory to Kashmir.

We did not blow up those bridges because at that time we were very careful not to go anywhere near Pakistan territory.

They were not so prevented (said Mr. Nehru) and their equipment and arms including artillery and automatic weapons bear witness to the help being given to them. We are credibly informed that regular officers of the Pakistan army are advising the raiders.

The Minister of Health in Sind, another province of Pakistan, at that time appealed to all trained and demobilized soldiers to proceed as volunteers to the Kashmir front.

Prime Minister Nehru stated that there could be no doubt whatsoever that all these invaders had come across from Pakistan territory.

He said:

> We have a right to ask the Pakistan Government how and why these people could come across the frontier Province or West Punjab, and how they have been armed so effectively. If this is not a violation of international law and an unfriendly act towards a neighbour country?

The United Nations Representative found that it was a violation of international law. The Prime Minister continued:

> Is the Pakistan Government too weak to prevent armies marching across its territory to invade another country, or is it willing that this should happen? There is no third alternative.

Now comes perhaps the most important evidence of the direct implication of Pakistan in this raid. While this was going on, the Government of India was still trying to settle matters and attempting not to have a repetition of what happened in the previous months in the north-west of India and the north-east of Pakistan. It is in that connection to which the telegrams mentioned by the Foreign Minister of Pakistan refer and to which I shall come in a moment.

Mr. Jinnah invited the Prime Minister to go to Lahore, but he was unable to go owing to ill health. However, the Governor-General went, and what happened? At that time discussions took place and it was said that both sides should call off their troops; that is to say, the Indian army should be withdrawn and the raider, as they were then called should also leave. But the Pakistan side, represented by Mr. Jinnah, had all along been saying: "We really cannot do anything about these people. They are co-religionists. How can we stop them?" Therefore, either the Pakistan Government had not control over them, or they were abetting them, or there was a combination of both. Mr. Jinnah, therefore, proposed that both sides should be withdrawn. Lord Mountbatten asked the common-sense question of how Mr. Jinnah could be responsible for withdrawing the tribesmen if he had no control over them, to which Mr. Jinnah replied, "If you do this I will call the whole thing off".

Independent evidence has been offered by London newspapers which in no way could be regarded as being disposed too favourably towards India in these matters at that time. Alan Moorehead, correspondent of the *London Observer* in Pakistan, wrote as follows: "The Pakistanis look on this as a holy Muslim War". I read that deliberately, because that is the position even today. This afternoon when we go into these questions we shall be able to cite evidence that that is the position, that is to say that India is threatened by a campaign of hatred and preparation for an aggression against its territory. We shall not fire a shot and we shall not allow a soldier to leave our borders, but just the same as anyone else we shall discharge our duty of self-defence. This correspondent wrote:

> They look on this as a holy Muslim War. Some of them I have seen talk wildly of going to Delhi.

Alan Moorhead motored to Peshwar and the Khyber Pass from where this crusade began. He wrote: "Everywhere recruiting is going.... This is happening not only in the tribal territory.... But inside Pakistan itself." That was at the end of October and the beginning of November 1947.

There is also photographic evidence. An Associated Press photographer, presumably an American, flew over a section of

Kashmir and said that he saw more than twenty villages in flames. The villages, in an area ten miles long and ten miles wide, apparently had been set fire to by the Muslim invaders, who were scouring the Valley and moving in the direction of Srinagar.

In a report in the *New York Times* by Robert Trumbull, dated 10 November 1947, we read the following:

> Baramula, India, 10th November—The city had been stripped of its wealth and young women before the tribesmen fled in terror at midnight, Friday, before the advancing Indian Army. Surviving residents estimate that 3,000 of their fellow townsmen, including four Europeans and a retired British Army Officer, known only as Colonel Dykes, and his pregnant wife, were slain. When the raiders rushed into town on 26th October, witness said: "One party of Masud tribesmen immediately scaled the walls of Saint Joeph's Francascan Convent compound, and stormed the Convent Hospital and the little church. Four nuns and Colonel Dykes and his wife were shot immediately. The raiders' greed triumphed over their blood lust". A former town official said: "The raiders forced 350 local Hindus into a house, with the intention of burning it down. The group of 100 raiders is said to be holding another five, a hostages, on a high mountain, barely visible from the town. Today, twenty-four hours after the Indian Army entered Baramula, only 1,000 were left of a normal population of about 14,000".

Here again is another account concerning *Father Shanks,* who was one of the Christian missionaries working in the area. It is a story that Father Shanks would never tell. He described the attack on the Convent without mentioning his own name, as follows:

The tribesmen—great,, wild, black beasts they were—came shooting their way down from the hills on both sides of the town.

They climbed over the hospital walls from all sides. The first group burst into a ward firing at the patients.

A 20-year old Indian nurse, Philomena, tried to protect a Moslem patient whose baby had just been born. She was shot dead first. The patient was next.

Mother Superior Aldetrude rushed into the ward, knelt over Philomena and was at once attacked and robbed. The Assistant Mother, Teresalina, saw a tribesman point a rifle at Mother Aldetrude and jumped in front of her. A bullet went through Teresalina's heart.

At the moment Colonel Dykes, who had assured us we would not be attacked raced from his room a few yards along the terrace to get the Mother Superior out of danger, shouting at the tribesmen as he ran. But the Mother Superior fell shot, and Colonel Dykes collapsed beside her with a bullet in the stomach.

Mrs. Dykes ran from her husband's room to help him. She too was shot dead.

While this went on Mr. Gee Boretto, an Anglo-Indian, was killed in the garden before nine nuns. Then the nuns were lined up before a firing squad.

As the tribesmen raised their rifles a young Afridi Officer, who once studied in a convent school at Peshawar, rushed in and stopped them.

At least there are living features of human quality in these incidents.

He had been told his men were raiding a Convent, and had run all the way from the town. That saved all our lives by a few seconds.

He did not find Mrs. Dykes until the following day. She had been thrown down a well.

We have another report, as follow:

> A Pakistan Army convoy was sent to rescue us. On the way from Baramula we stopped at the village of Boniyar to seek the staff of the World Wide Evangelistic Crusade Mission.

Then we have the following report:

> In Baramula the townspeople told me of a young Muslim who had sacrificed his life rather than recant in his creed of religious tolerance. His martyrdom had taken place almost under the shadow of the convent walls, and in the memory of the devoted Kashmiri's he was fast assuming the stature of a saint.

He—Mir Maqbol Sherwani—must have been a sort of Rabinhood character, from the stories the townspeople told me, championing peasants who could not pay their exorbitant taxes, pitching into the police when he found them beating up some luckless victim, bolstering up the resistance of the people against their many oppressions.

When the tribesmen invaded Kashmir and terrorized the countryside, Sherwani, who knew every footpath in the Valley, began working behind the lines, keeping up the morale of the besieged villagers, urging them to resist and to stick together regardless of whether they were Hindus, Sikhs, or Muslims, assuring them that help from the Indian Army and People's Militia was on the way. Three times by skillfully planted rumours he decoyed bands of tribesmen and got them surrounded and captured by the Indian infantry. But the fourth time he was captured himself.

On 22 December 1947, the Prime Minister of India handed over to the Prime Minister of Pakistan a letter in Delhi requesting the Government of Pakistan to deny to raiders (1) all access and use of Pakistan territory for operation against Kashmir, (2) all military and other supplies and (3) all other kinds of aid that might tend to prolong the present struggle.

I should like to draw the attention of the Council to that date, namely 22 December. We waited one week before coming here. The request was the same, that is that the country had been invaded. What was our requests? This is what should be taken into account when there is an adjustment of values in the minds of members. Our territory had been invaded and the army was in a hopeless position, having been sent to Kashmir on less than twenty-four hours notice. I shall later disprove, if it is necessary, that there was any preparation on the Indian side. We have documents signed of their own will by the British Commander-in-Chief, the British Air-Marshal of the Indian Air Force and other personnel of the Indian army at that time, that the matter was never even broached by anyone before the question of defence arose.

In this context, if any other country, any other people—and it is not surprising that we did because we were the same people—had made a request of this kind, would it not have been answered by an ultimatum of war on their territory? And what did we ask? We accepted at face value the statements made that these were marauders.

The Security Council, even though it has sat on this for over nine years, cannot forget the facts of history and its obligations to the Charter. We made this moderate request for not giving this aid. I am sure that everyone around the Security Council table would say that a country so invaded has the right under normal practice to say, "We shall retaliate and we shall not withdraw until such and such a time." This was merely a request from one friendly Government to another, providing that we were not in a state of war even then.

Nothing happened after eight days: We would not have come here if any improvement had taken place. On 1 January 1948, India complained to the Security Council under Article 35 of the Charter. Even then we did not come here with the idea of using international forces to restrain, or imposing economic sanctions, or removing Pakistan from its seat in the Assembly, or anything of that kind. We came here to complain to the Security Council under Article 35 of the Charter, requesting that the Government of Pakistan be asked to prevent tribal and Pakistan nationals from taking part in the fighting in the State of Jammu and Kashmir and to deny to the raider access to and use of its territory in operations against Kashmir, military and other supplies, and all other kinds of aid that might tend to prolong the fighting in Kashmir.

Are these the words either of a belligerent Government or of Government with expansionist ideas, with the desire to follow its neighbour—as often pointed out, a neighbour far stronger than we are militarily today? Is this the language they should use?

We came here asking the Security Council to do these things, and it was a modest request. That is still what is pending before the Security Council. The issue that is pending before the Council is one that its members dare to evade only if they are prepared to defy the Charter. Everything else that has gone afterwards makes no difference. I go so far as to say that it makes no difference even if for argument's sake it is said that we were guilty of evasions after this incident, because international law is based upon equity. Anyone who comes here must come with clean hands, and I submit that our hands were clean.

What is more; we did not use our strong arm even at that time. We came here with a limited purpose. It may well be that, if we had forced that position at that time and not relied upon the processes that followed afterwards, perhaps, this matter would have been resolved long ago. And, what is more, we would not have been giving the material for the kid of ill-informed adverse propaganda that goes on. We would not have sown the seeds of doubt in the minds of people sitting around this table.

Therefore, I repeat this point, to which we shall come back again and again, that it must be planted firmly in your minds that the issue is aggression. The issue is invasion: it is a violation of territory. It is not necessary for me to prove the unquestioned sovereignty of India in regard to Kashmir. It is sufficient for me to prove that we were in possession—even, if you like, in a state of temporary possession but I am not going to concede that. I want it to be shown on the record that I am not going to concede that, because we have suffered often here by accepting a hypothetical proposition and by saying, "Let us assume this for argument's sake", or saying, if A, B, C and D happened, then we will do D". Then we discuss D, everybody forgets A B and C and we are committed to course D. Therefore, I urge the Council to be extremely careful.

However, suppose, for example, that that was the position. I ask my South American friends to think of the doctrine on which their countries are based. We were in possession legally and in fact. They were invaders, and they had no standing in international law or international practice or according to the Charter, other than as wanton, naked aggressors into the territory of India.

While we made this complaint and it was being considered, what happened? I have not the records here, but I am sure the Secretariat will inform us that the Pakistan Government certainly must have had notice before 11 January, the Foreign Minister of Pakistan, Mr. Zafrullah Khan, who is now a judge of the International Court of Justice—a jurist of standing—informed the Reuters correspondent that it was impossible for Pakistan to guarantee that no Pakistan nationals or other people passing through Pakistan should not go to Kashmir and "participate in the struggle for freedom." That is to say, we were two sister States brought together under the struggle of partition and with feelings of understanding. We agreed to the partition of India as the price of our freedom and also in order to save much bloodshed. Having done that, we came under the same Act of British Parliament. Here in one part of the country is this rapine going on, and that is called a struggle for freedom. I say with great respect to them—and I do not want to be misunderstood—that we in India, I know something of the struggle for freedom. It was great struggle for freedom that made the independence of Pakistan possible.

Now we turn to the most respectable of the journals of the world, that is, the *London Times*. On 13 January, that is, twelve days after we came here, it stated:

> That Pakistan is unofficially involved in aiding the raiders is certain. Your correspondent has first-hand evidence that arms, ammunition and supplies are being made available to the Azad Kashmir forces.

Here may I interpolate that my Government uses, the words "Azad Kashmir" without accepting the connotation of the word "Azad". Although "Azad" means "free", we do not accept the term as meaning free Kashmir forces. They are enslaved Kashmir forces or whatever they are. But we have to use the language as it is given, and it should be understood that we do not regard it in its liberal sense.

The times went on to say that a few Pakistani officers were also helping to direct their operation and that, however much the Pakistan Government might disavow intervention, moral and material support was certainly forthcoming.

Both in the municipal laws of many countries and in international law, aiding and abetting either before or after the act is participation in the act itself. Let us assume for a moment that the units of the Pakistan Army were not operating, which we are not prepared to admit. The reason, of course, is that our army officers and their army officers were brother officers. They had met them in Kashmir. They knew them by their first names. They had all worked together in the same regiments before being divided by the partition. We do not want any documentation of this. Let us assume that there was not participation of the regular army, as it was suggested that there could not be. According to this *Times* correspondent, if there was not intervention, there was moral and material support. If the correspondent of the *Times* or any other newspaper suggested this in an article in this way, that would not be sufficient for the conduct of affairs to nations, but it is the start of a whole series of incidents. Certainly, it comes from a source that was not biased in our favour.

Now we come to the stage before the Security Council. We came here with a request that the aggression must be halted. If the Security Council were to tell us that in that letter we did not ask for more drastic action, that we did not ask for condemnation, that we did not ask for Pakistan to be declared an aggressor, we pleaded guilty. We plead guilty in the sense that we were not prepared and we had no intention at that time, nor have we now, to aggravate the situation. What we wanted was the undoing of the wrong rather than finding fault with somebody.

That is why in that letter, which is phrased in language that is not the language of war, we were simply asking from people who were committing rapine and murder to remove the weapons and not to let them go on with it. That is all we wanted.

Therefore, if the Security Council takes the view that generosity and moderation in these matters, and not asking for the extreme remedy, is a misdemeanor, then I am afraid we must plead guilty, but I hope that the time will not come when the United Nations takes that view.

So we came here on 1 January in 1948.

On 15 January the Pakistan Government "emphatically deny that they are giving aid and assistance to the so-called invaders or have committed any act of aggression against India". This is letter from the Minister of Foreign Affairs of Pakistan to the Secretary General of the United Nations, Annex. 6 to UNCIP's First Interim Report, document S/100.

I do not know whether the Security Council wants me to read the whole of it, but this is an official letter submitted as truth to the Security Council. And what does it say? It says:

> Pakistan Government emphatically deny that they are giving aid and assistance to the so-called invaders or have committed any act of aggression against India.

There are three statements there to which I would request the Security Council to address itself. One is the denial of giving aid and assistance, and the other is that they do not regard the so-called invaders, the rapine in Kashmir, as invasion of territory which is beyond their border. The third statement is that they plead not guilty to aggression. Either they deny the fact or they deny that indirect assistance is not aggression.

In either case, I say that it is serious violation of all canons of international behaviour. The letter goes on to say:

> On the contrary and solely with the object of maintaining friendly relations between the two dominions, the Pakistan Government have continued to do all in their power to discourage the tribal movement by all means short of war.

That is to say, not only did they deny it, but they came and told the Security Council that they were taking deterrent action to prevent it. I ask any member of the Security Council to tell me whether, even assuming that they were exclusively border raiders, whether it was possible for their army to march across long distances over Pakistan territory, whether they could get fuel anywhere, especially at that time, and where these trucks and this machinery came from, and where the officers came from and where the weapons came from?

If it is true that Pakistan could not stop the raiders from going across their country, by what right does this Member State come and say here "We shall take Kashmir under our protection", if they cannot prevent libertines and marauders from walking across their country and making themselves free with the resources that are there? And if a Pakistan Government were to tell us that they cannot stop a belligerent force from marching across that territory, by what right then can a Member State say that they are competent to take anybody over? That means it is not a State, it is territory over which anarchy prevails, if that is true.

But I submit that it is not true. The Pakistan Government at that time had an army which was in no way inferior to the Indian army. It was part of the size, and so on, as decided by the British Government and the two States. They had all the material. What is more, what was required here was not militant action, but its denial.

Can anyone tell the Security Council that the march of people across long distances over Pakistan territory could not have been stopped by an organized Government? But if that is true alone, it would not be as strong as it is and as condemnatory as it is. But side by side with it stands all the statements I read out to you, where these Ministers call upon person after person, and they call them heroes; they call it liberation; they ask people to give assistance; they ask for volunteers; they ask for funds.

The Chief Minister, the Prime Minister of the Punjab, afterwards accused in certain financial matters, says that he spent this money on Kashmir. And not without evidence—there it is. Then in a subsequent part of the letter, the following is said:

Governor-General of Pakistan (Krishna Menon: that is Mohammad Ali Jinnah, the founder of Pakistan) explained that he had not control over the forces of the Azad Kashmir Government or the independent tribesmen engaged in the fighting.

This is the same Mr. Jinnah who was asked by Lord Mountbatten: "How can you be responsible for these people?" Then he said. "I will call the whole thing off". I will tell the Council in what context later.

The document which I read is attacked to the letter from the Minister of foreign Affairs for Pakistan to the Secretary-General of the United Nations, and is to be found in paragraph 23 (1) of Annex. 6 of UNCIP's First Interim Report, to which I referred a while ago. The UNCIP in its First Interim Report says:

> Another element, the significance of which had not been fully appreciated before the Commissioner's departure from the sub-continent, was the Azad Movement which constitutes and organized political and military body, is assisted by the Pakistan High Command and is engaged in active revolt against the existing Government. This Movement has co-operated since October 1947 with invading tribesmen and individual Pakistan nationals.

I submit that if I did not say anything else, and if read out this paragraph where the United Nations Commission reports that the Azad Movement was an organized political and military body, assisted by the Pakistan High Command and engaged in active revolt against the existing Government, with which the Pakistan Government has co-operated since October 1947, before the complaint came here and which they have denied and with invading tribesmen and individual Pakistan nationals, that one statement alone coming from United Nations sources as a finding on fact—not an opinion but as a finding on fact—would, in my submission be adequate to prove the charge of aggression.

In view of the composition of the Security Council, I will ask the members to look at some evidence that comes from American sources. Russel K. Haight Jr., a former American soldier who served for two months in the Azad Kashmir Army, gave a secret interview to *The New York Times* correspondent, Robert Trumbull, in Lahore stated that Pakistan had provided petrol. The following is the report:

> Mr. Haight also found Pakistan army personnel running the Azad Kashmir radio station, relaying messages through their own Pakistan army receivers (Krishna Menon: I repeat relaying messages through their own Pakistan army receivers) organizing and managing Azad encampments in Pakistan, and supplying uniforms, foods, arms and ammunition which, he understood, came from Pakistan army stores through such subterfuges as the 'loss' of ammunition shipments. Mr. Haight characterized the Azad Kashmir Provisional Government, headed by Sardar Mohammad Ibrahim Khan as 'Pakistan Puppets'. He also deeply implicated high Pakistan Government officials, notably the Premier of the North West Frontier Province.

This is from *The New York Times* of 29 January 1948, and is also quoted by Lord Birdwood who has written a book on Kashmir, again not a friendly book to India. But those are the facts.

The next authority probably will be regarded as sympathetic to India, although many things have been written. Therefore, I will not read it. However, the representative of Australia would be interested to know what was said in the Australian Continent about this. I do not have an Australian extract here. But there is "Kashmir and the United Nations" by "Criticus" in the New Zealand Labour Party's weekly. *The Standard* at Wellington, and it was published in India. It was carried on 28 November 1951 in *The Standard.* It reads:

> ...thousands of Muslim tribesmen equipped with arms by the Pakistan Government invaded Kashmir. This was obviously an act of open aggression....

I think it will be admitted that Lord Birdwood, with his background as Field Marshal acquainted with India, had contact with the British officials and Pakistan, and this is what he says:

> At GHQ in Rawalpindi (Krishna Menon: that is the main army headquarters of Pakistan), as in so far as they were prepared to discuss the matter, I was assured that no regular unit was moved before May:

That is May of 1948.

Yet a battery of mountain guns with an infantry escort were in action in an unsuccessful attack on Poonch on 17th March, while on the Indian side General Russell believed that regular (Pakistan) troops were involved in January.

General Ressell was a British officer serving in the Indian Army. The document continues:

> He accordingly asked to be relieved of his command....

We readily agreed because we did not want British officers to fight British officers on other side, and we did not want to involve the United Kingdom in any trouble between Pakistan and ourselves. Although General Rusell was a very loyal and an extremely able officer, he asked to be relieved the moment he knew the Pakistan Army was in action. And what did the Government of India do? We would have been entitled—and I ask the representative of the United Kingdom to bear with me—to tell this man, "You have signed an agreement with the Indian Army, and this is ordinary military duty. We did not do anything of the kind. We relieved him, and we asked General Cariappa, as Commander-in-Chief, to take over. And General Cariappa, when the British Government left, was a brigadier. It was not as though we had ready-made officers to deal with these matters.

The statement adds that General Cariappa was convinced that at this stage Pakistan was using regular forces. General Cariappa, by the way, was an army officer who recently retired, and who must be very familiar to my Australian colleague, since he was High Commissioner for two or three years afterwards.

General Cariappa, the statement says, based his opinion on the fact that a number of prisoners of regular units had been taken. Now it cannot be said that the Pakistan Army sent a few persons to be taken prisoner for no reasons. General Cariappa faced his Pakistan friends with the charge—and anyone who knows General Cariappa would understand how he does this. The statement adds:

> This he was able to do since an invitation to the Pakistan Armoured Corps 'Week' in Lahore came through to him from his old friend, Major General Iftikar, who was then commanding the 10th Pakistan Division in Lahore.

All these men had been brother officers in the same army only a few days before.

This is the position. I should like to stop there so far as the invasion in concerned, and to come back to the political aspect.

On 1 January we made our complaint I read out to the Council a while ago what Sir Zafrullah Khan said on the eleventh. I read out all the denials between that date and Pakistan's reply. Nine years ago, on 1 January, we made this complaint, and I read out what the complaint was. On 17 January the Council passed a resolution. That resolution was based upon our letter and took into account Pakistan's reply.

Broadly speaking, what is that reply? It is denial of the charges; it is a denial that they had given any assistance, it is a denial that there had been any aggression; and then it is a counterclaim on various other matters. But there is no principle of international law or international behaviour which says that if, in respect of a situation or particular problem, a complaint is brought, other misdemeanours in something else can be pleaded in bar. Therefore, I do not propose at this stage to go into the irrelevant intrusion of other complaints made by Pakistan. If the Security Council so desires, in its judgement, it's up to it, but so far as I am concerned I propose to keep to the subject of Kashmir.

Therefore, the position is that we made certain complaints. We asked for certain remedies. Pakistan denied the facts that we alleged. A little later that denial was disproved, not only by what I have read out to the Council from outside sources but by the United Nations Commission itself. Then—I ask as a simple matter of analysis—what remains? We make a complaint; we assert certain facts; those facts would amount to aggression—and I presume the Security Council would not argue that they do not amount to aggression. If those facts amount to aggression and the answer is a denial that the facts took place, and if, afterwards, the Security Council finds that that denial was not correct, then what remains? All that remains is the aggression.

The defence is taken away, and therefore, in the letter that was put before the Security Council, the answer they gave was:

> The situation in their view is due to the aid which the invaders, consisting of nationals of Pakistan and of tribesmen from the territory immediately adjoining Pakistan from the north-west, are drawing from Pakistan for operations against Jammu and Kashmir, as State which has acceded to the dominion of India and is part of India.

That is quoted in the reply, which goes on to say:

> They have requested the Security Council "to call upon Pakistan to put and end immediately to the giving of such assistance which is an act of aggression against India". They have also threatened that if Pakistan does not do so, the Government of India may "enter Pakistan territory, in order to take military action against the invader".

At this moment I want to refer to that last paragraph. I have read out what we said. Does that amount to a threat? What we said to the Security Council was, "We want to refrain from doing this. We may be driven to a position where we have nothing else to do, because invasion must lead to war and must spread." Therefore, what we said to the Security Council was not, "If you do not do this we are going to invade". That is not what we said. In fact, right through the Kashmir operations, at a great cost of human lives, we kept this war restricted. That is story by itself.

Then comes the denial. The letter from the Minister for Foreign Affairs of Pakistan to the Secretary-General of the United Nations dated 15 January, 1948 says:

Pakistan Government emphatically deny that they are giving aid and assistance to the so-called invaders or have committed any act of aggression against India.

That is a total, straight denial. They deny they are giving aid and assistance to the "so-called invader", or that they have committed any act of aggression. The document continues:

> On the contrary and solely with the object of maintaining friendly relations between the two dominions the Pakistan Government have continued to do all in their power to discourage the tribal movement by all means short of war.

This is elaborated in Paragraph E (5) of document II, which is annexed to the letter in Annex 6 of document S/100. Paragraph E (5) is a reference to Kashmir, and states:

> That India obtained the accession of the State of Jammu and Kashmir by fraud and violence and that large-scale massacre, looting and atrocities on the Muslims of Jammu and Kashmir State have been perpetrated by the armed forces of the Maharajah of Jammu and Kashmir and the Indian Union and by the non-Muslim subjects of the Maharajah and of the Indian Union.

Now let us assume that all these facts have substances. I do not for one moment say that they have. In fact, they are entirely untrue. But supposing they were true; what rights under the Charter does Pakistan have to go and punish somebody else for that reason? That is not the function of a neighbouring State. So that the aggression is justified by the fact that, first, India obtained an accession by fraud and by violence—something which we shall go into this afternoon—and that, therefore, they are entitled to invade. In other words, it is taking the law if—it was the law—into their own hands.

That is war. That is aggression. If one returns to that, then it will be case of each side claiming right on its own side, and I say that, irrespective of the truth or otherwise of this matter, this entry would amount to aggression.

Numerous attacks on Pakistan territory have been made by the Royal Indian Air Force, armed bands of the Indian Union in the State of Jammu and Kashmir.

This has been denied by Indian army officials, who were at that time British officers. No preparations were made for going to Kashmir; in fact, we lost all our men who went there on the first day.

The Security Council met for the first time on 6 January 1948; that is, we complained on 1 January, the Council met on the 6th and did some preliminary business, and Pakistan filed a reply on the 15th from which I have read. On 17 January 1948 the Council adopted the following Resolutions:

> Having heard statements on the situation in Kashmir from representatives of the Governments of India and Pakistan;
>
> Recognizing the urgency of the situation;
>
> Taking note of the telegram addressed on 6 January by its President to each of the parties and of their replies thereto in which they affirmed their intention to conform to the Charter.

Calls upon both the Governments of India and Pakistan to take immediately all measures within their power (including public appeals to their people) calculated to improve the situation and to refrain from making any statements and from doing or causing to be done or permitting any acts which might aggravate the situation.

And further request each of those Governments to inform the Council immediately of any material change.

I request you, Mr. President, to take not of this phrase "to inform the Council immediately of any material change" because it appears afterwards:

> In the situation which occurs or appears to either of them to be about to occur while the matter is under consideration by the Council, and consult with the Council thereon.

My Government submits that from that day onwards, the basic ideas, the basic principles of the Security Council's resolutions have been violated by our sister State of Pakistan because the appeals to the people were in the opposite direction, as a I pointed out. Nothing was done to improve the situation. More help followed and, what is more, as the years went on, this became, as was said by the Commission, a large-scale undeclared war. If it is true that there was the regrettable behaviour of committing aggression and then trying to defend it, it was even worse when the Security Council called upon the party concerned to take no further action. And that is part of the answer which the Government of India has to give at this stage: to point out how, during these nine years, every one of these have been violated, and violations are continuing. That is why I said in the beginning that it is not sufficient to catch an argument somewhere at a cross-section and say that that is the picture. You have to look at what is behind, at what is going on, and what is likely to go on in the future if the words of the Foreign Minister are to be construed in their proper meaning.

Now, the "material change" to which I referred. On 20 January, three days later, the Security Council further considered the matter and this is its resolution:

> Considering that it may investigate any dispute or any situation which might, by its continuance, endanger the maintenance of international peace and Security; that, in the existing state of affairs between India and Pakistan, such an investigation is a matter of urgency.

Adopts the following resolution:...

I want to point out that this resolution of 20 January 1948 is one which binds the Security Council. It was a decision of the Council in regard to its own conduct.

A. Commission of the Security Council is hereby established, composed of representatives of three members of the United Nations, one to be selected by India, one to be selected by Pakistan, and the third to be designed by the two so selected.

Each representative on the Commission shall be entitled to select his alternates and assistants.

B. The Commission shall proceed to the spot as quickly as possible. It shall act under the authority of the Security Council and in accordance with the directions it may receive from it.

That sentence gives all the weight that is necessary to the findings to which I previously referred. It is not as though the

Commission's report were an unofficial document. It was in obedience to this mandate.

.... It shall keep the Security Council currently informed of its activities and of the development of the situation.

I regret to say that, as a material matter, the Commission did not do so.

It shall report to the Security Council regularly, submitting its conclusions and proposals.

C. The Commission is invested with a dual function:

(1) To investigate the facts pursuant to Article 34 of the Charter;

(2) To exercise, without interrupting the work of the Security Council, any mediatory influence likely to smooth away difficulties; to carry out the directions given to it by the Security Council; and to report how far the advice and directions, if any, of the Security Council have been carried out.

D. The Commission shall perform the functions described in Clause C:

> In regard to the situation in the Jammu and Kashmir State set out in the letter of the representative of India addressed to the President of the Security Council, dated 1 January 1948, and in the letter from the Minister of Foreign Affairs in Pakistan addressed to the Secretary-General, dated 15 January 1948; and
>
> In regard to other situations set out in the letter from the Minister of Foreign Affairs of Pakistan addressed to the Secretary-General, dated 16 January 1948; when the Security Council so direct....

So I submit that, even according to that resolution, any reference to all these irrelevant matter is outside the competence of this resolution. This was what we both accepted.

E. The Commission shall talk its decision by majority vote. It shall determine its own procedure....

G. The Secretary-General of the United Nations shall furnish the Commission with such personnel and assistance as it may consider necessary.

These two resolutions may be taken together for consideration. The Government of India accepted the resolution of 20 January. It accepted that resolution, despite its undisputed and irrevocable claim to sovereignty over this territory, in view of the fact that the situation was likely to lead to difficulties in its faith in the United Nations—then perhaps more fresh than it is today, but still a faith that is founded in the Charter and the recognition that, whatever may happen in the intervening period, by and large truth catches up. Governments that have a responsibility for their own territories will not sit back and brook aggression from a neighbour. Therefore, we accepted these two resolutions and agreed to the setting up of the Commission in order that it might perform its dual functions, and I submit that, in the performance of the first of these functions, the Security Council has before it the facts. It would take me many a long day to sift all the paragraphs, all the statements, all the questionnaires, the assurances given in great detail, but the fact does remain—and this is to be corroborated after—that the Commission did report that there was aggression, that there was material change in the situation—of which the Security Council was kept in the dark, and thereby, the Council, while it was passing resolutions and, in my humble submission, often out of its generosity presumably, was taking the view that there are two sides to some kinds of *truth*. At that time changes were occurring in the situation, and it is not as though those changes stopped there, those changes still continue, so as to make it impossible to pursue the root of the matter on the lines that were thought of five years ago.

The Security Council, therefore, adopted this resolution and, having done so, went on to inquire about various things. Meanwhile, the Security Council changed the title to the "India-Pakistan Question". We stated at that time that we had no objection to the use of any words which might be desired, but we maintained that the Kashmir question was the subject of the complaint.

On 21 April the Council adopted another resolution. That resolution was a modification, and it gave new instructions to the Commission providing for the withdrawal of the troops and the holding of plebiscite, and the membership of the Commission was increased to five. On 5 May of that year, the Government of India formally informed the Security Council of its rejection of certain parts of this resolution, and that correspondence is contained in document S/734/Corr.I. India, however, expressed its willingness to confer with the Commission. The letter stated:

The Government of India has given the most careful consideration to the resolution of the Security Council concerning their complaint against Pakistan over the dispute between the two countries regarding the State of Jammu and Kashmir. The Government of India regret that it is not possible for them to implement those parts of the resolution against which their objections were clearly stated by their delegation, objections which, after consultation with the delegation, the Government of India fully endorse.

If the Council should still decide to send out the Commission referred to in the preamble of the resolution, the Government of India would be glad to confer with it.

That letter was signed by Mr. Nehru, the Prime Minister of India and Minister for External Affairs. Irrespective of the fact that we did not agree to the expansion, of the terms of reference the Government of India felt that it would be inhospitable and discourteous to the United Nations not to see the members of the Commission. There are cynics who say that that was where our troubles began, but would be wrong to take that view, because if nations, out of risks and fears in this direction, would not enter into negotiations, then they would not be able to assist in the implementation of the functions of the Charter. But, and I say this in all sincerity, that carries with it, the fact that one should not penalize those who necessarily do to stick to the letter of their communication, that is to say, they do not confine themselves to that, but are prepared to go a little further in exploration. Therefore, while we rejected this resolution and refused to accept it, we agreed to receive the Commission. At that time Mr. Gopalaswami Ayyangar, who was the Minister in the Indian Cabinet responsible for these affairs, spoke before the Security Council and he registered objections. I will not read the whole of his speech which was very long, but it is apparent from the preliminary discussion in January 1948 that it all turns upon what we agreed to. I have made no comment on this, but if I were to do so, I could say that it went to the very substance. Mr. Gopalaswami Ayyangar said:

> I would now proceed to review briefly some of the detailed provisions of the draft resolution presently under consideration. By way of anticipating possible claim from the other side, I desire to say a few words on the question of accession…'whether the State of Jammu and Kashmir is to accede to India or Pakistan'. The contention has been advanced (Krishna Menon: And this is our position) that the accession is for a temporary period (Krishna Menon: To do that it will be necessary to repeal an Act of Parliament) and a limited purpose, and when that period elapses as that purpose has been served, it ceases to be operative.

That was the contention. Mr. Gopalswami Ayyangar went on to say:

> We, on our side, repudiate this claim (Krishna Menon: This was as early as 1948, so it was not an afterthought) The accession which took place on 26th October 1947 was both legal and lawful. It has been followed up by India in the discharge of all the obligations that her acceptance of the accession has imposed upon her. She has saved the Jammu and Kashmir State from disintegration. She is now resisting those who are attacking that integrity even today. She is protecting the State's large population from the unfriendly attentions of raiders from outside.

The accession therefore subsists today and will subsist even after the fighting ceases and peace and order have been resorted.

That has been the basis of our position from 1948 onwards, it has never moved. Mr. Gopalaswami Ayyangar went on to say, "Until then, *Pakistan has no constitutional position*". He went on to make a statement which is very important from our point of view:

> After the fighting ceases, the whole of the State will have to come under one Government. By the whole of the State, I include also the area which is now under the control of the rebels and raiders. When the whole of the state thus comes under one administration—and that, the administration of the State of Jammu and Kashmir—India's garrisons will need to be planted at her frontiers on the west of the Jammu and Kashmir State. The planting is necessary for enabling India to discharge her obligations for the defence of the State which she has taken over under the Instrument of Accession.

That is an undertaking which is not only sanctified by our Constitution, it is enjoined by an Act of Parliament of the United Kingdom, which is the basis of our Constitution. These obligations that we are carrying out were also agreed to by the Security Council. The Security Council at no time challenged either sovereignty of Jammu and Kashmir or the validity of the accession, and that is the only thing that stays. Therefore, wherever this resolution goes into the question of treating these two countries as though they were two parties to a complaint we have resisted that position and we have not subscribed to that part.

If it were necessary, I would go into the details of the 21 April resolution. But I do not think it is necessary because we are now covered by the resolution that followed. The Commission was appointed by the 21 April resolution. We did not accept that resolution, but what did Pakistan do? Pakistan protested against the resolution without accepting it. It, however, chose Argentina as a member of the Commission on the same day. We objected to certain parts of it, but we agreed to receive the Commission. Pakistan protested and said they would not accept the resolution.

So if the resolution of 21 April has any value, then it depends upon the juridical argument: What is the status of a Security Council resolution under Chapter VI which makes recommendations. And they can have value as part of the process of conciliation only if the two parties agree. In the first instance, we did not agree entirely but we did agree to its function. Pakistan rejected it. Then they came in as a matter of conduct. By conduct they ratified parts of it, and therefore it has been necessary for the Security Council to examine the conduct and how far and into what regions this conduct travels. And so when, as was hinted—not said but hinted—in the observations of the representatives of Colombia and Cuba the other day; they were quite rightly concerned about the position of the Security Council—it is necessary to look into the substance of it and see what we agreed to and what we did not agree to.

As a result of this resolution, and in spite of the fact that both sides were unhappy about it, the Commission did go and it was well received in India. We did our best to make it acceptable in Kashmir and they spent a great deal of time.

### (2)

**Krishna Menon:** Before I continue the observations I was making this morning, I should like to submit that the length of these observations does not arise from any particular desire on the part of my delegation to prolong these proceedings. It arises from the fact that this matter has not been before the Council for many years and, as I said this morning, there are very many new members—and the basic positions have to be understood if the Indian case is to be presented adequately. Therefore, if the Security Council desires to hear all the aspects of this matter as far as they are relevant, it will be necessary for my delegation to take the necessary amount of time. But I do not want to prejudice the Security Council by creating any feeling that the length of these observations arises from any other reason.

I was dealing this morning with the resolution of the Security Council adopted on 21 April 1948, and I pointed out that we objected to several paragraphs of it. But we were quite willing to confer and, as a result of that, the United Commission started functioning.

It is not really relevant to my purpose to go into the activities of the Commission. But they met at Geneva on 16 June, and a study of the documents will reveal that at that time the Commission was concerned, and very much concerned, with the on matter—and was that the matter of stopping the fighting. If the relevant paragraphs of the Commission's report were read, it would be quite clear that the concern of the Commission was somehow or other to bring about a cease-fire.

I read the following from the Commission's report:

> At the fourteenth meeting, it was agreed that the question of an immediate cease-fire should be explored and that the Government of India should be asked for its observations regarding the ways and means by which such a cease-fire might be brought about.

The Commission went on to state:

> That its immediate objective to bring about a cessation of hostilities rather than to deal with specific provisions contained in resolutions of the Security Council.

Thus, the Security Council resolutions adopted earlier in the year had been disregarded by Pakistan in the sense that it had introduced other forces and heavy fighting had been taking place in the northern areas. What I said this morning referred very largely to the offensive in Western Kashmir. While that offensive was going on, however, and despite the injunctions of and the undertakings given to the Security Council that any material change in the situation should be reported, a considerable offensive was taking place in the Northern areas; I shall refer to the details of this latter offensive when I deal with the Northern areas.

As a result of this heavy fighting, the Commission was naturally concerned about the immediate objective of achieving a cease-fire. The Commission met in Geneva, and finally got to Karachi on 7 July. It was at that time that there occurred the new development which has been described as a "bombshell" in a book written by Mr. Korbel, who was then the Chairman of the Commission. I read from the Commission's report as follow:

> The Commission stopped in Karachi from 7 to 9 July. The principal representatives were received informally by the Minister for Foreign Affairs and Commonwealth Relations, Sir Mohammed Zafrullah Khan. He reviewed at length, and along the lines of the expositions made before the Security Council, the general background of the problem and the broader issues involved in the dispute between India and Pakistan. In the course of this interview—

And this is the relevant passage:

> The Foreign Minister informed the members of the Commission that the Pakistan Army had at the time three brigades of regular troops in Kashmir, and that troops had been sent into the State during the first half of May. Sir Mohammed Zafrullah Khan stated that this action had been taken as a result of the spring offensive by the Indian Army.

The Security Council resolution had asked for information with regard to any material change in the situation. The above-mentioned information given by Sir Mohammed Zafrullah Khan was regarded as a material change in the situation and was communicated to the Security Council. I read again from the Commission's report:

> At the nineteenth meeting, on 20 July, a confidential cable was drafted and dispatched informing the Security Council of the presence of Pakistani troops in Kashmir. The Commission adopted a resolution requesting the Security-General of the United Nations to appoint a military adviser.

It was the presence of these troops which had been denied all along, but was admitted by the Foreign Minister of Pakistan when the Commission arrived in Karachi—that created a new state of affairs.

As later stage, the Pakistan Government gave the reasons for this invasion. The report continues:

> Sir Mohammed Zafrullah Khan stated that three main reasons had motivated the entry of Pakistan troops into Kashmir: protection of the territory of Pakistan from possible aggression by Indian forces; prevention of a fait accompli in Kashmir by the Government of India; and prevention of the influx of refugees into Pakistan.

I submit that none of these reasons have anything to do with the people of Kashmir. We have heard a great deal about their future and their destiny, but if the protection of the territory of Pakistan from Indian forces does not sound like a preventive war I do not know what it is—that is the situation where a Member State gets the right to go into a neighbouring territory for fear that it might be attacked from that State. So protection of its territory, the first reason, is not a reason that is sanctioned by the principles of the Charter.

With regard to the prevention of a fait accompli in Kashmir by the Government of India, so far as the legal position is concerned, whether the Pakistan Government accepted it or not, it had been put before the Security Council; and if the view was that a fait accompli must not be brought about, then the Pakistan Government intended, in spite of the resolution of the Security Council, to decide this by force of arms, that is to say, to use its troops in order to prevent a fait accompli.

The third reason was to prevent the influx of refugees into Pakistan, and I would say that of all the reasons given this is the one that least holds water. After the partition there were seven or eight million people leaving in each direction. Refugees came from Pakistan into India and from India into Pakistan—one of those horrid scenes in our common history which I hope we shall be able to forget some day. But the idea of troops moving in to prevent the influx of refugees into Pakistan is difficult to understand. The only refugees who went into Pakistan presumably were those who preferred Pakistan as a home. Are we to understand that the Pakistan Government was going to prevent the influx those refugees by the use of an army?

So there are three reasons given; none of which in my submission have any substance.

This other matter to which I referred just now was a matter of serious concern to the Government of India and the Commission notes that. The Commission says—these are their findings—that Pakistan had not informed the Security Council of the presence of its troops in Kashmir because at the time they had been sent into the state the question had been entrusted to the Commission, whose daily departure was expected. This is Sir Zafrullah Khan's explanation. The matter put before the Commission immediately after its arrival in Karachi, in the view of the Foreign Minister of Pakistan—that is, the presence of foreign troops in Kashmir—did not raise the question of international obligations since Pakistan had never accepted any in regard to non-interference in Kashmir.

This view was repeated in Mr. Khan Noon's statement before the Security Council, that is to say that Pakistan had no international obligations in regard to non-interference in Kashmir. I submit this is a violation of the provisions of the Charter. Therefore, the explanation that is given, that is, that the Commission "is coming here so we will not let it know", when the Security Council had asked six months there had been no denial. Then, to buttress this argument, the Foreign Minister went on, says that Commission, to dwell at length on economic and strategic considerations. Now if it is right to lead an army into a country for economic and strategic reasons, then I think that the causes of his negation are even more justified.

The Commission goes on to say:

> The Minister for Foreign Affairs...argued that India, if it had control over Jammu and Kashmir, would be in a position to divert all five rivers of the Punjab, that is, Chenab, Jhelum, Beas, Sutlej and Ravi, the last three being already under Indian control, and thus could reduce to a desert one—third of the irrigated areas of West Punjab.

I think the most amazing paragraph is paragraph 68 of this report which says that the Foreign Minister pointed out:

> ...that, if the Radcliffe Award had followed the terms of reference under which the Boundary Commission had

> operated and had included all Muslim majority areas in West Punjab, the Pakistan boundary would have been much further to the east.

Now what is the implication of that paragraph? The Commission pointed out that Lord Radcliffe had given an award and that award, in this particular respect, was not satisfactory to Pakistan and in many respects it was not satisfactory to us. And here the Foreign Minister is saying that if the Radcliffe Award had been given the other way then of course the question of Kashmir would have been further east and the question of direct access would not have arisen. Therefore, by implication, this invasion is a method of modifying the Radcliffe Award by force. At the time it became public knowledge—we knew all the time that it was going on—that Pakistan had invaded Kashmir, this created a great deal of feeling in India, and the Prime Minister made reference to it in some speeches he delivered, against which Pakistan protested. And the response of the Commission is significant in this matter to show how it felt about it. At the thirtieth meeting on 6 August the Commission considered a telegram received from the Government of Pakistan protesting against a speech delivered by Prime Minister Nehru on 25 July in Madras and asking what measures were contemplated by the Commission. The Commission felt that in view of the presence of Pakistani troops in Kashmir any representation to the Government of India about this speech of the Prime Minister would be ill-advised and therefore the receipt of the telegram was acknowledged without comment. The Commission exchanged views concerning alternatives—this is another significant part—to a plebiscite, keeping in mind that the study of the alternatives could not be seriously undertaken without the consent of the Governments of India and Pakistan.

During these same meetings, the Government of India and the Government of Pakistani produced before the Commission the various conditions which they regarded as necessary for establishing a cease-fire. The Pakistani position, so far as I understand it, subject to correction, as set out in paragraph 50, was that a cease-fire should come after arrangements for a political settlement—a very familiar argument in the United

Nations. The principles which the Government of India regarded as necessary for agreeing to a cease-fire, as set out in paragraphs 46, 47 and later, were the following. When the Commission, under its Chairman, Mr. Graffe, interviewed the Prime Minister, the following points were submitted on behalf of the Indian Government: (1) The regular Pakistani forces should be withdrawn from the State of Jammu and Kashmir, (2) Indian forces should remain along fixed lines and occupy certain advanced strategic positions, and (3) the evacuated territories situated outside of the fixed line should be provisionally administered by existing local authorities, or, if necessary, by local authorities to be designated by the Commission, and should be supervised by observers of the Commission, but remain under the sovereignty of the State of Jammu and Kashmir until the final settlement of the dispute between India and Pakistan.

Therefore, these principles, which were put forward ultimately and which to a very great extent found favour in the Commission, were based upon the idea of the sovereignty of the State, that is to say that it is indivisible, that its parts cannot be taken by invasion, that the Indian forces have the right and the duty of protecting this area and that the invaders must evacuate. That is the crux of the case: the invaders must evacuate territory and, if it is necessary, there should be local authorities there—not Governments but merely local authorities—for the maintenance of law and order under the supervision of the Commission. That was the position, as may be seen from the resolutions that were adopted later.

As a result of these discussions, the Commission, having put to both the Government of Pakistan and the Government of India the various points of view, and in view of Pakistan's objections as set out in the report, at its meeting on 13 August finally formulated the resolution which forms the basis of the Kashmir question so far as the Security Council is concerned. This is the well-known resolution of 13 August 1948 which brought about a cease-fire. As I stated a short while ago, the concern of the Commission at that times was to a large extent the establishment of a cease-fire so that the fighting might be stopped. I shall not read out the resolution, as it is a very long one, but there are certain points of it to which I must draw attention. This resolution was referred to in a statement by the Foreign Minister the other day, and I believe that in the interests of clarity and accuracy one ought to draw attention to it.

The representative of Pakistan stated:

The main provisions of this international agreement for a plebiscite are:

Cease-fire and demarcation of cease-fire line. (Krishna Menon: We have no quarrel with that)

Truce agreement providing, *inter alia,* for (a) withdrawal of tribesmen and Pakistan nationals... (b) withdrawal of Pakistan troops and the bulk of the Indian Army... (c) a plebiscite to be conducted....

This might appear to be of very little importance if one did not know the history of this matter, because this resolution is really conceived in three consecutive parts. The part referring to the plebiscite is not part II but part III, which has very considerable relevance to the whole approach to this problem. Part I is concerned only with a cease-fire. It places responsibility on the High Commands of the Indian and Pakistani forces "to refrain from taking any measures...". I shall not read out the whole resolution. It establishes the cease-fire as between the two High Commands. Part I, paragraph E, is relevant in this connexion:

> E. The Government of India and the Government of Pakistan agree to appeal to their respective peoples to assist in creating and maintaining an atmosphere favourable to the promotion of further negotiations.

Neither before 13 August nor after 13 August until the present time, as the Council will come to see when we deal with present conditions, has there been any appearance that this has been done by the Government of Pakistan as reflected in the public opinion of Pakistan. This is not to say that the peoples of Pakistan are against the peoples of India, but there has been a campaign of hatred and a campaign of a holy war against India.

Now that the cease-fire has been established, so far as the Government of India is concerned that is an agreement into which it has entered and which should be supervised by an international body of observers.

Part II relates to the truce agreement. The plan of this programme is that first there should be a cease-fire, then there should be third part. Part II is divided into three sections: A, B, and C. Paragraph 1 of Section A states:

1. As the presence of troops of Pakistan in the territory of the State of Jammu and Kashmir constitutes a material change in the situation since it was represented by the Government of Pakistan before the Security Council, the Government of Pakistan agrees to withdraw its troops from that State.

That is to say, one of the principles laid down in this resolution was that a material change in the situation had been brought about, and as a result of that it was necessary as one of the first conditions of the truce that there should be a withdrawal of the troops of Pakistan from the territory of Jammu and Kashmir.

The second paragraph states:

> The Government of Pakistan will use its by endeavour to secure the withdrawal from the state of Jammu and Kashmir of tribesmen and Pakistan nationals not normally resident there who have entered the State for the purpose of fighting.

Our submission is that there has been no withdrawal of these nationals to the extent that is required in this matter. What are called other armies in Kashmir are under the control of the Pakistan command. They are officered by Pakistan officers, and the administration is under Pakistan control. Therefore, to say that paragraph 2 of the truce agreement has been carried out is not accurate.

The third paragraph states:

> Pending a final solution, the territory evacuated by the Pakistan troops will be administered by the local authorities under the surveillance of the Commission.

This is an integral part of the conditions of the principle for which India asked and which is incorporated by the Commission in its resolution. What is the position today. I shall deal later with the political conditions, but there are no local authorities. The administration in that area is directly under Pakistan administration through its own officials, and the authorities in Kashmir are controlled from Karachi. So there is no such thing as local administration much less supervision by the Commission. So this part also has not been carried out.

Now we come to some of the other more important matters. Section B begins with "When". It states:

> When the Commission shall have notified that Government of India that the tribesmen and Pakistan nationals referred to in Part II A hereof have withdrawn, thereby terminating the situation which was represented by the Government of India to the Security Council as having occasioned the presence of Indian forces in the State of Jammu and Kashmir, and further that the Pakistan forces ware being withdrawn from the State of Jammu and Kashmir, the Government of India agrees to begin to withdraw the bulk of their forces from that State in stages to be agreed upon with the Commissions.

That is to say, it is only when the Commission has notified that the tribesmen and Pakistani nationals have withdrawn and, secondly, when the conditions on which we came here namely, an invasion, have disappeared, it is at that time that the Government of India must withdraw the bulk of its forces. That was the position taken in August. It was something undertaken on the basis of conditions.

Pending the acceptance of the conditions for a final settlement of the situation in the State of Jammu and Kashmir, the Indian Government will maintain, within the lines existing at the moment of the cease-fire the minimum strength of its forces which, in agreement with the Commission, are considered necessary of law and order.

Therefore, this Part II B is recognition of the fact that the Security of the State is the concern of the Government of India. That is again amplified in the phrase that follows in paragraph 3:

The Government of India will undertake to ensure that the Government of the State of Jammu and Kashmir will take all measures within their power to make it publicly known that peace, law and order will be safeguarded....

They were given the responsibility for law and order and the responsibility for Security. What is more, it was a condition that the Indian forces should withdraw only when all others had withdrawn, and the reason for bringing the case had disappeared. That is set out in Section B.

In the discussions that have gone on in this Council after this period—1952 and subsequently—these matters have been put on one side. The reason is not hard to seek, because we were confined to one problem, a problem that could be implemented only after this came into effect.

However, so far as the Government of India is concerned, in spite of this condition in Section B, we have withdrawn a considerable part of our forces. There is an army in Kashmir, and, so far as Kashmir which is not under foreign occupation—and as far as India is concerned, that is the Indian Army. It is the Kashmir Army. It could not more be called a foreign army than the British Army would be called a foreign army in Lancashire. It is a part of the army and the local militia that the Kashmiris are entitled to have. In spite of the fact that these foreign nationals are there in spite of the fact that the aggression has not been liquidated, we have withdrawn a considerable part of our troops.

The Foreign Minister made some arithmetical calculations and told us that India had 80,000 troops in this area and, what is more, that that constituted one-twelfth of the population. I think that if we applied these mathematic in one place it might be useful to apply them in some other place. There are today forty-five battalions in those outposts around "Azad Kashmir" and there are only a half a million people there. Therefore the Security Council can work out the mathematics in that. I am not referring to other areas at the moment; I am referring to the half million people in what is called the Azad area, where there were, at the time when the Commission was investigating, thirty-two battalions, which have now become forty-five battalions. Therefore, if we face the question of having troops, that is the position.

On this matter, I also wish to submit that Kashmir is the northern extremity of India. The Indian Army is deployed in the various sectors of the country, and this is one area where it has to function, not only for the protection of Kashmir and all that is involved therein but because it is the place where it normally would be located.

If we are to take this into account, then, as I shall point out later, we shall have to take into account the divisions of the Pakistan Army that are located about five, ten and twenty miles from our border. That is, if it is right to have the Pakistan Army in Abbottabad or in Murree or in any of these areas, then it is necessary for the Indian Army to be held somewhere. Therefore, the idea that this is an occupation, as it has been represented to the Council, is a total misnomer.

Then we come to Part III, which is the crucial part. Part III states, and I would request you, Mr. President, to give your very careful attention to this:

> The Government of India and the Government of Pakistan reaffirm their wish that the future status of the State of Jammu and Kashmir shall be determined in accordance with the will of the people and to that end, upon acceptance of the Truce Agreement both Governments agree to enter into consultations with the Commission to determine fair and equitable conditions whereby such free expression will be assured.

The commitment about a plebiscite is usually spoken of as though it were the law of the Medas and Persians, but what does it amount to? It amounts to an expression of a wish on the part of the two Governments. The expression of a wish is far less than what may be called an international obligation. However, I do not wish to argue that point. But take the other one, that it should be carried out upon the acceptance of the truce agreement. No truce agreement has been signed, because Pakistan armies have not vacated and, what is more, there are continued violations.

As I shall point out later, large number of conditions have changed under which it is no longer possible to consider the matter in these terms. So any suggestion that the Government of India—and there is no further charge—has a commitment that it is not honouring, I deny totally. So far as we are concerned, the commitment is for the acceptance of a truce agreement. It is not to hold a plebiscite but to enter into consultations.

First of all, there is no truce agreement. Therefore, if number two does not happen number three is out of court. Number two is the truce agreement. I have given the reasons why the truce agreement is not being carried out. Therefore, number three means that it is only when number two has been accomplished that number three comes into the picture at all. The character of number three is not just a matter of taking a plebiscite, but that the Government enters into consultations.

This means that the two parties shall enter into consultations in the same way, shall we say, as was arranged in connexion with elections in Indo-China. That is all there is to it. Those consultations have taken place, even without a truce agreement, and nothing has come of them.

Now this resolution was not accepted by Pakistan. We accepted this resolution, and as I told the Security Council a while ago, we had previously set out the principles that should be embodied. While the resolution was not one that totally met our point of view, with a view to resolving the position the Government of India accepted this resolution which was adopted by the Commission on 13 August.

But still there was no cease-fire. The fighting was going on in the northern areas. It was becoming more intense. The Commission reported to the Security Council and made further efforts.

It is essential in reading the document of 13 August, which is a resolution of the Commission, to appreciate that this document should be read along with the assurances given in writing by the Commission to the Government of India because they form one document. If you like, that is a contract; these are the warranties. This document cannot be regarded as isolated from the context of the assurances given.

Those assurances were set out in a letter that was sent by the Prime Minister of India to the Commission on 20 August 1948. May I say here that the facts of this letter were not private, as is sometimes hinted in some newspapers, between the Commission and the Prime Minister. They were published and in the next stage of negotiations, Pakistan and India came to an agreement on the resolution of 5 January Pakistan, if agreed to that, had cognizance of these conditions. That letter says the following:

> On the 17th of August, my colleagues, the Minister without Portfolio, and I discussed with you and your colleagues of the Commission now in Delhi the resolution which you had presented to us on the 14th instant. (Krishna Menon: That is, the resolution that had been previously adopted by the Commission and presented to us.)

Then, a little further on, it goes on to say:

> During the several conferences that we had with the Commission when it first came to Delhi, we placed before it what we considered the basic was fact of the situation which had led to the conflict in Kashmir. This fact was the unwarranted aggression, at first indirect and subsequently direct, of the Pakistan Government on Indian Dominion territory in Kashmir. The Pakistan Government denied this, although it was common knowledge. In recent months, very large forces of the Pakistan regular army have further entered Indian union territory in Kashmir and opposed the Indian army which was sent there for the defence of the State. (Krishna Menon: Which is envisaged by this resolution.)

This we understand now, is admitted by the Pakistan Government, and yet there has been at no time any intimation to the Government of India by the Pakistan Government of this invasion. Indeed, there has been a continual denial and the Pakistan Government have evaded answering repeated inquiries from the Government of India. In accordance with the resolution of the Security Council of the United Nations adopted on the 17th January 1948, the Pakistan Government should have informed the Council immediately of any material change in the situation while the matter continued to be under the consideration of the Council. The invasion of the State by large forces of the regular Pakistan army was a very material change (Krishna Menon: I am sure the Council will agree.) in the situation and yet no information of this was given, so far as we know, to the Security Council.

The Commission will appreciate that this conduct of the Pakistan Government is not only opposed to all moral codes as well as international law and usage, but has also created a very grave situation. It is only the earnest desire of my Government to avoid any extension of the field of conflict and to restore peace, that has led us to refrain from taking any action to meet the new situation that was created by this further intrusion of Pakistan armies into Jammu and Kashmir state. The presence of the Commission in India has naturally led us to hope that any arrangement sponsored by it would deal effectively with the present situation and prevent any recurrence of aggression.

I would like the Council to take note of that sentence, that is to say, the fact that the Commission was intervening in this matter and brought this resolution to us. They had reason at that time to think that the aggression would be terminated, but nothing of that kind happened. The letter continues:

> Since our meeting of the 18th August, we have given the Commission's resolution our most earnest thought. There are many parts of it, which we should have preferred to be otherwise and more in keeping with the fundamental facts of the situation, especially the flagrant aggression of the Pakistan Government on Indian Union territory. We recognize, however, that, if a successful effort is to be made to create satisfactory conditions for a solution of the Kashmir problem without further bloodshed, we should concentrate on certain essentials only at present and seek safeguards in regards to them.

There then follow the safeguards which are very material:

(1) That paragraph A.3 of Part II of the resolution should not be interpreted, or applied in practice, so as (Krishna Menon: that is the paragraph with regard to local authorities.)

(a) to bring into question the sovereignty of the Jammu and Kashmir Government over the portion of their territory evacuated by Pakistan troops (Krishna Menon: that is to say, that neither the invasion by Pakistan nor the fact that they evacuated it under orders from the Commission would in any way affect the sovereignty of the Jammu and Kashmir Government. That was the condition we made.)

(b) to afford any recognition of the so-called 'Azad Kashmir Government', or

(c) to enable this territory to be consolidated in any way during the period of the truce to the disadvantage of the State.

That is what has happened since: the portion being administered from another place. It then goes on:

(2) That from our point of view the effective insurance of the Security of the State against external aggression, from which Kashmir has suffered so much during the last ten months, was of the most vital significance and no less important than the observances of internal law and order, and that, therefore, the withdrawal of Indian troops and the strength of Indian forces maintained in Kashmir should be conditioned by this overriding factor. (Krishna Menon: That is to say, we emphasized the point that we have the responsibility for Security.) Thus at any time the strength of the Indian forces maintained in Kashmir should be sufficient to ensure security against any form of external aggression as well-internal disorder.

(3) That as regards Part III (Krishna Menon: That is, ascertaining the will of the people) should it be decided to seek a solution of the future of the State by means of a plebiscite, Pakistan should have no part in the organization and conduct of the plebiscite or in any other matter of internal administration in the State.

Therefore, it was not as though there were two peas in a pod and two people with some equal jurisdiction over this. The plebiscite was merely a concession, merely a method, whereby some peaceful settlement could be brought about. Therefore, we made the reservation. Then the Prime Minister went on to say:

> If I understood you correctly, A.3 of Part II of the resolution does not envisage (Krishna Menon: This is the Commission's position being taken) the creation of any of the conditions to which we have objected in paragraph 3(1) of this letter. In fact, you made it clear that the Commission was not competent to recognize the sovereignty of any authority over the evacuated areas other than that of the Jammu and Kashmir Government.

I ask the Council to take notice of this; that is, the Commission says that they have no authority to recognize any sovereignty other than that of the Jammu and Kashmir Government. In the face of that, how can the Security Council contemplate with equanimity the position that part of the territory has been invaded, usurped, annexed and assimilated? The next paragraph says the following:

> As regards paragraph 3 (2), the paramount need for Security is recognized by the Commission (Krishna Menon: That is say, the sovereign function of defence is placed upon India) and the time when the withdrawal of Indian forces from the State is to begin, the stages in which it is to be carried out and the strength of Indian forces to be retained in the State, are matters for settlement between the Commission and the Government of India.

That is to say, there is no mention of the words "the Government of Pakistan" so far as that is concerned.

The next paragraph reads as follows:

> Finally, you agreed that Part III as formulated, does not in any way recognize the right of Pakistan to have any part in a plebiscite.

Then the Prime Minister concludes:

> In view of this clarification (Krishna Menon: These are all clarifications given by the Commission, and I shall read out the confirmation in a moment) my Government, animated by a sincere desire to promote the cause of peace and thus to uphold the principles and prestige of the United Nations, have decided to accept the resolution.

To complete this chapter, may I now be permitted to read the acceptance of the Commission:

> I have the honour to acknowledge the receipt of your communication dated August 20, 1948, regarding the terms of the Resolution of the United Nations Commissions for India and Pakistan which the Commission presented to you on the 14th August 1948.

The Commission requests me to convey to Your Excellency its view that the interpretation of the resolution as expressed in paragraph 4 of your letter coincides with its own interpretation, it being understood that as regards point (1) (c) the local people of the evacuated territory will have freedom of legitimate political activity.

In this connection, the term 'evacuated territory' refers to those territories in the State of Jammu and Kashmir which are at present under the effective control of the Pakistan High Command.

The Commission wishes me to express to Your Excellency its sincere satisfaction that the Government of India has accepted the resolution and appreciates the spirit in which this decision has been taken.

Therefore, here are assurances given and discussed for a very long time; clarifications sought and given; and, in categorical terms, the letter signed by the Chairman of the Commission on 25 August, which completes the resolution of 13 August. Therefore, I submit that the Security Council in considering this resolution—I will come to the next one in a moment—has to read it along with these clarification and assurances. Otherwise, the Security Council has said to us that we are to accept one part of what the Commission says, and not the other. Our acceptance of this document was along with those clarifications. Pakistan did not accept this.

I should also add that whatever is said here also refers to the Northern Territories—that is to say, the territories where, as I shall point out later, owing to the instrumentality of the local commanders, who are not local people at all affiliations have been received and a considerable amount of fighting has taken place. In regard to these Northern Territories, the Prime Minister said:

> The authority of the Government of Jammu and Kashmir over this region as a whole has not been challenged or disturbed, except by revolting bands of hostiles, or in some places like Sardu which have been occupied by irregulars or Pakistan troops. The Commission's resolution, as you agreed in the course of our interview on the 18th, does not deal with the problem of administration or defence in this large area. We desire that, after Pakistan troops and irregulars have withdrawn from the territory, the responsibility for the administration of the evacuated areas should revert to the Government of Jammu and Kashmir and that for defence to us.

That is to say, in regard to these problem, territories of Baltistan and Gilgit, and all those areas, there is a difference—a difference between the local authority issue in West Kashmir, Where it was suggested there were some local movements, and this one. And the Government also said:

> The only exception that we should be prepared to accept (Krishna Menon: They did not accept it, but they were prepared to do so) would be Gilgit. We must be free to maintain garrisons at selected points in this area for the dual purpose of preventing the incursion of tribesmen, who obey no authority, and to guard the main trade routes, from the State into Central Asia.

India has considerable trade through these areas into the Central Asian region and the lower provinces of Asia, of Russia, of China and of Tibet.

In answer to this northern areas question, similarly, the Commission agreed. I shall read out the paragraph which relates to this agreement:

> The Commission wishes me to confirm that, due to the peculiar conditions of this area, it did not specifically deal with the military aspect of the problem in its resolution of 13 August 1948. It believes however, that the question raised in your letter could be considered in the implementation of the resolution.

The Commission, therefore, tried to make a further effort, because the cease-fire could come about only if there were agreement of the two sides. It met in Geneva in September, prepared its procedure, and then reported to the Security Council in Paris. Then it proceeded to the peninsula and produced a series of proposals on 11 December, which were passed by the Commission in its private sitting, were communicated to the Governments of India and Pakistan. India accepted them on 23 December, and I believe that Pakistan accepted them on 25 December.

So, by 25 December, we had a situation where the resolution of the Commission, as passed in its private sitting on the 11th, was accepted by both Governments, and that became the resolution of 5 January, the resolution was first set up by the Commission and put to the two Governments; their agreement was obtained, and it was formalized.

This is a convenient moment to point out how we stand with regard to this, because these are the two resolutions to which we have given any agreement at all—that is the resolutions of 13 August and of 5 January. My submission is that so far as those resolutions are concerned they stand by their texts and by this intention. That is the first point. The second point is that they should be read together and their sequence taken into account. The third point is that these resolutions are also to be read along with and to be conditioned by the assurances I have read out to the Council and the other assurances that are given by the Commission with regard to the resolution of 5 January, which are printed in *aide memories* which were submitted to the Commission and which are in the records of the Security Council. It was stated therein:

> The Prime Minister emphasized, (1) that if the Government of India, were to accept the Commission's plebiscite proposals, no action could be taken in regard to them until Parts II and III of the Commission's resolution of 13 August had been fully implemented.

That is one of the things that is said in regard to the resolution of 5 January:

(2) that in the event of Pakistan not accepting these proposals, or having accepted them, not implementing parts I and II and the resolution of 13 August, the Government of India's acceptance of them should not be regarded as in any way binding upon them (Krishna Menon: I shall come back to this in a moment).

(3) Part III of the Commission's resolution of 13 August provided "that the future status of the State of Jammu and Kashmir shall be determined in accordance with the will of the people and to that end, upon acceptance of the truce agreement, both Governments agree to enter into consultation with the Commission to determine fair and equitable conditions whereby such free expression will be assured."... While the Government of India adhered to their position in regard to a plebiscite, they had pointed out that, in view of the difficulties of holding a plebiscite the present conditions in Kashmir, other methods also be explored. The Commission had itself recognized the difficulties of carrying out a plebiscite in Kashmir. The Government of India feel that the exploration of other methods should not be ruled out.

For the present purposes I am satisfied to put in these *aide memories* for the information of the Security Council. If, in further debate, there should be any challenge upon them then I would have to argue what is in these *aide memories*. But the main thing is this:

(2) that in the event of Pakistan not accepting these proposals, or having accepted them; not implementing Parts I and II of the resolutions of 13 August—

and our submission is that Parts I and II of the resolution are not implemented, and that therefore the Government of India cannot be regarded as being bound by those resolutions, because that is the consecutive character. It is a concertina resolution Unless (A) is accomplished, (B) cannot be undertaken; unless (b) is accomplished, (C) cannot be undertaken. Apart from what (C) means—something to which I have referred—(B) has not been implemented, and so unless there is a truce, unless there is evacuation, how does the Security Council even contemplate the idea of anything in the nature of an assessment of the will of the people in the occupied areas of Pakistan, with forty-five battalions of these forces, the entire army of Pakistan, right up on our frontier? And when I deal with the military preparations in that area, the Council, I hope, will begin to sit up and take notice. That has nothing to do with the welfare of these people. The people in the "Azad" areas, the people in Gilgit, the people in Chitral and the people in Baltistan—they do not go around in aeroplanes, and the Council will be bound to enquire what is the purpose of the airfields and airstrips in these areas.

I think it would be regarded as unfair to the Council if I did not refer to the fact that this resolution of 5 January deals, in the main, with implementation of Part III—that is, the resolution of 13 August, which deals with the cease-fire and the truce and leaves the plebiscite in one paragraph. What the resolution of 5 January does is to elaborate the ways in which a plebiscite should be taken. Practically, the whole of this resolution deals with the methodology of this plebiscite; but it is not as though it is laid down categorically. There are so many "ifs" and "whens" in this which are integral to the commitments made by India. The Council will bear with me if, on behalf of the Government of India, I try to clarify this matter, because it is a serious thing to tell a Government that is not honouring its commitments; and it can only honour the commitments which it has undertaken. A commitment does not become a commitment by an assumption of what has gone before.

Now, what is this resolution of 5 January 1949? It reads as follows:

The Untied Nations Commissions for India and Pakistan, having received from the Governments of India and Pakistan, in communications dated 23 December and 25 December 1948, respectively, their acceptance of the following principles which are supplementary to the Commission's resolution of 13 August 1948:

1. The question of the accession of the State of Jammu and Kashmir to India or Pakistan will be decided through the democratic method of a free and impartial plebiscite.

As everybody will notice, it says *"will be decided*—a simple futurity. *It does not say "shall be decided".*

The next paragraph governs this one; paragraph 2 of this resolution of 5 January governs the first one:

2. A plebiscite will be held when it shall be found by the Commission that the cease-fire and truce arrangements set forth in Parts I and II of the Commission's resolution of 13 August 1948 have been carried out, and that "when" still remains "when". And I shall submit later on that the "when" not only remains so, but it is no longer possible.

Paragraph 3 of the resolution deals with the functions of the Plebiscite Administrator.

*I must say a word about the Plebiscite Administrator.* Our position in this matter was that we did not like it, but that there was really no objection to a man working out the details if he wanted to so that he could put them into operation when the time came. We had no feeling about people coming into the country or seeing things for themselves and so, when it was pressed upon us, we agreed to a Plebiscite Administrator being appointed subject to all this expert advice.

Now we come to paragraph 4:

(a) After implementation (Krishna Menon: And I ask the Council to take note of these words) of Parts I and II (Krishna Menon: The previous paragraph said when) of the Commission's resolution of 13 August 1948, and when the Commission is satisfied that peaceful conditions have been restored in the State, the Commission and the Plebiscite Administrator will determine in consultation with the Government of India (Krishna Menon:

Not with the Government of Pakistan) the final disposal of the Indian and State armed forces, such disposal to be with due regard to the Security of the State and the freedom of the plebiscite.

There is one verbal implementation which I should like to make. It has always been understood that the expression "disposal", used in this resolution, means, to the Government of India, "disposition". The Council will see that is its meaning if it looks at the word "disposition" used in other places.

So paragraph 4, again, reiterates this fact, that nothing can happen until Parts I and II have been carried out. Part I has been signed, although there have been serious breaches of the cease-fire—one of them of a serious character which developed into a miniature battle.

Hence, the whole of the resolution of 5 January is concerned with the minutiae of the plebiscite, but even in that, it makes it quite clear at what time it will be taken. This is a plan of action. It is a blueprint. But you cannot operate it, you cannot pull the trigger on it until Parts I and II are in operation. Part I is in operation; therefore, there is no fighting—and, so far as we are concerned, it will remain in operation. But Part II is not in operation; and, what is more, the conditions that could have made Part II in operation have been breached before this without the knowledge of the Security Council and without conveying the information, and afterwards, and is being breached continually. In fact, a division of Kashmir which is wrong both de jure and de facto, has taken place. This is sheer violation of all the commitments made by the Government of Pakistan to the United Nations. That is the limit of our commitments in this matter.

That finishes the first part of my submission to the Security Council; that is, it takes us to what our commitments are. So far as I can remember, three or four resolutions were adopted by the Security Council before 13 August 1948 and 5 January 1949. I think that we should consider those two resolutions as one plan. The Security Council will appreciate, when it has gone through the papers and pondered, that all the previous resolutions are absorbed by these; the resolutions of 13 August and 5 January really take into account all the previous resolutions. It is the submission of my Government that all the resolutions which may follow can only flow from these. Therefore, the binding conditions, whether they bind us or whether they are conditional bindings, or provide for denunciation and escape, all have to be taken into account. The only things that bind us in regard to Kashmir, so far as the Security Council and the world are concerned, are these resolutions with all the conditions I have mentioned. And I would say that, while we are not a member of the Security Council, as a Member State which has earnestly tried to discharge its solemn obligations to the international community, the Council will think many times before it is led even to think, let alone express a view, that the Government of India has in some way tried to get round international commitments.

I shall try, in the course of my next submission, to deal with the matter of what a commitment is, what a decision is, and what a recommendation is.

One gathers the impression that there is some desire to know about the Constituent Assembly since, in our view erroneously, the Council seems to persist in the idea that this is some world-shaking matter. I must confess that the atmosphere of crisis has been created, or some sort of D—Day or zero hour, for 26 January. But whatever may be the background which we are able to understand, we have the duty to point out what the facts are, and I have therefore, decided to change the arrangement of my presentation. Logically, this should come much later, but in order to suit the convenience of the Council, and because, I want to tell you, I am not in a fit condition to sit through a third session continuously, I have changed the order to my presentation. Therefore, I propose now to take up first of all the claim—and by claim I mean the title or the argument, or the case, or whatever it may be, that Pakistan may have for Kashmir. Secondly, I shall deal with the accession, and then with the Constituent Assembly, because if I do not deal with accession, the Constituent—Assembly becomes unintelligible. I shall be able to do all that this afternoon. I think it is very necessary that this political, social—if you like, logical—aspect of this question should be understood.

From what we have heard in the Security Council, from all the discussions, the debates, the writings and everything else that goes on in Pakistan and which have been communicated in the views expressed by the foreign Press, there is some idea that over and above the Security Council decisions there is a basis for the affiliation of Kashmir to Pakistan, that there is some natural affinity.

*What are these considerations?* We accept some of these considerations, but we argue that they are either equally or more applicable to us. For the moment, I am putting on one side whatever title we may have derived. I am talking of the extra-legal considerations and the extra-security considerations. The first of these is geographical contiguity, which is commonly accepted by all of us.

The answer to that is that Kashmir has a frontier with Pakistan on the west and slightly to the north-west. It has a frontier with India and communications with India. It has a frontier with Russia and China and Tibet. Therefore, Kashmir has a large number of frontiers.

Geographical contiguity is very often governed to a considerable extent by the historical past, and Kashmir's economic relations and commercial relations have been very much more with India than with Pakistan. This did not arise in the old days, because it was one country. Therefore, it is a question of a common frontier and of contiguity, it is not as though the accession of Kashmir to India is the accession of some far-off island which is separated from the rest of our territory. To put it at its worst, contiguity is a common factor.

The other matter is one on which my Government will not in any circumstances alter its position. We refuse to recognize what is called the "two-nation theory". India is a secular State, where any person, Hindu, Muslim, Christian, Buddhist or whatever he is, is an equal son or daughter of India, with right of citizenship guaranteed by our Constitution. India claims Islam as one of the Indian religions, just as it does Christianity or any other. Therefore, we refuse to accept the thesis that because the population of a particular area is of one religion, some political issue is involved.

We are not a theocracy, we are a modern secular State governed on democratic principles, where the right of citizenship is based on residence, upon domicile, and upon loyalty to the Constitution. Therefore, we totally disregard this argument with regard to Muslim majorities and Hindu minorities. Some of you may say that that is a very nice view, but it is not how the world is run. Then how do we look at it? Pakistan has a population—I am subject to correction—of between seventy and eighty millions, because I believe that their census, like ours, was taken in 1951, and our populations increase by one and a half per cent a year. Roughly speaking, Pakistan has a population of somewhere about 75 millions; Pakistan is in two parts and is separated by the Indian mainland extending for about 1,000 miles.

The proximity of Kashmir, ethnically and otherwise, is to West Pakistan, and I have no accurate figures of the Muslim population of West Pakistan, at the very outside, cannot be more than about 30 millions and there are nearly 50 million Muslims in India. If our Government were to accept the view that because people are Muslims they should belong to another State, I ask the Security Council, in all conscience to consider what would happen to the considerable Muslim minorities in my country. They are distributed over the whole of our land. In some places they are sparse minorities, in some places they almost form the majority in the area. Are we to say that they are second-class citizens? We refuse to accept that position in India. We have almost as many Muslims in India—and I qualify and word "almost"—as in the whole of Pakistan. We do not regard it as either a foreign culture or a foreign religion. What is more, whether it be in Pakistan or in India, whether they be Hindus, Muslims, Christians, or whatever they are, their ancestries are pretty much the same. One religion does not mean one race, nor does it mean that there is a separation as between the two religious groups in that way.

We have this considerable Muslim population inside India, but it is not regarded as a minority. There is no question of the Muslims having any special sheltered treatment; they would not have it. They are equal citizens in our country, taking their place in our Government, in our public services, in our industry, in our agriculture, and in everything else, just like everybody else. The secular State is one of those ideas and one of those possessions which we regard with great jealousy, because in this world the rivalry of religion and the amount of violence that has been carried out in the name of religious loyalty has been to an extent that should shame humanity at any time. Therefore, we are not prepared at any time to accept any view, whatever resolutions anybody may pass, that there is any justice or anything that a modern community can entertain in this idea of what was spoken of in the address of the Foreign Minister, who attributed it to Lord Mountbatten, about what is called communal representation or communal affinity, or something of that kind.

The whole connexion of Kashmir is, with the mainland. Its capital was founded in the third century B.C. I am not an antiquarian, I have not studied it, but the history of Kashmir is a continuous one. It has been ruled by Hindu kings, by Muslim kings, by Sikh kings, by Afghans, and by all kind so of people, but it has always been part of the mainland of India. Therefore, these are extra-constitutional, extra-legal, extra-United Nations considerations, by which I mean they are considerations which are outside the principles of the Charter, on the and hand and which do not come into any of the resolutions or any of the decisions which we have made. However, it has necessary for me to put them forward because it was on them that the other argument was based, that the accession was wrong, that we got by force or by fraud.

What, then, is the interest? Mr. Zafrullah Khan said that there are strategic interests. Well, I would argue first of all that the strategic interests of a country should not always be placed in the picture when we are taking about the fortunes of the people in that country. But let us leave that alone. What is there are strategic interest?

The strategic interests of a country like India, with its big land mass in the Indian Ocean, are at least as vital in the world as the strategic interests of its neighbour, and we are not aware of any strategic interests in our mind which are inimical to the strategic interests of Pakistan. Therefore, this strategic interest, which was advanced by the former Foreign Minister, in our opinion, one that should not appeal to the Security Council.

What is the actual position with regard to this evaluation? I outlined briefly this morning the relation of Kashmir to India, that is, that when the British left India these States were to accede to one country or to the other, to one Dominion or to the other. That was the position. That way was prescribed in the Constitution, and it would be of interest to know that the way of accession was not thought out after the partition. It is contained in the Act of 1935 passed by the British Parliament. The way of accession is for the Head of the State to submit an instrument of accession and for the Government of India to accept it or the Government of Pakistan to accept it. So an offer of accession and an acceptance completes accession. That creates a union within a federation.

On 26 October the Maharaja of Kashmir who was the Head of the State—I am now dealing with the constitutional necessities—submitted to the Governor-General of India—in the constitution of that day the Governor-General of India was the Head of the Government, but not today; he was the representative of the British Crown because at that time we were an independent British dominion—an instrument of accession. The text of it is set out in Document 4. I will not read it because it is a legal document in conformity with what is said in the constitution. I will read it if it is challenged, but otherwise I will not do so. It is set out in the Constitution, in the Act of 1935, as amended. That instrument was sent over and on the 27th, Lord Mountbatten, Governor-General of India, accepted the accession. Lord Mountbatten said:

> I do hereby accept this Instrument of Accession.

Dated this twenty-seventh day of October, nineteen hundred and forty-seven.

The Accession is complete. We should look at these caveats more frequently than we have done. It has been suggested time and again that there is something like provisional accession, that you can go in and come out.

This is a very serious matter for us, a serious matter not only for India but for every country seated around this table. We fare a federation; we are not a confederation, and the units that accede to federation stay in once they have acceded. There is no provision in our Constitution, there is no contemplation in our Constitution for the secession, and that is not peculiar to us. Our institutions are largely derived from Anglo-Saxon parliamentary institutions which affected the constitutions of the countries of Western Europe and North America. In these countries there is no provision of secession at all. That is to say, under the Government of India Act, as in force on 15 August 1947, the relevant extract of which is in document 4, it has been set out how a State should accede. Once that accession has taken place there is no provision in this to go out. The only provision there is in regard to variation. A ruler may, by a supplementary instrument executed by him, and accepted by the Governor-General, vary the instrument of accession of his State by extending the functions which, by virtue of that instrument, are exercisable by any dominion, authority in relation to the State. But, of course, the Government of India also has to agree. If the two sides agree, it is possible to vary the conditions of the relationship between the constituent unit in the federation and the Central Government. That is all that is permitted by the law. Therefore, when anyone suggests to us that there should be a divorcement of this territory from our Federation, we are being asked to act against our constitutional procedures. Now I freely admit that when, constitutional procedures, as your learned colleague will advise you, are against well-known principles of international law, international law prevails.

But in this particular matter, the Constitution of India was presumed to be known to the United Nations when it was admitted as a Member. These provisions were there even before we were independent. Also, it is well-known in international law that in a Federation of our kind there is no right of secession. I want here to refer only to two instances. One is the well-known instance of the United States and it is possible to quote case after case to show where the constituent States of the United States have a greater degree of sovereignty than the units of our Federation—one can say this without going into domestic affairs—because they have residuary powers in those States. But it has gone to the Supreme Court of the United States time after time. I think the leading case in this matter is a case called *Texas* v. *White*, where the Supreme Court ruled once and for all that there was no such right vesting in a State. The issue was not whether they wanted to secede, but that was the point that had to be decided. For our purposes it is better, even more to go into the general principle of secession. If you want me to, I can quote it. But any textbook on this subject will tell you that in a Federation there is no right of secession. Our Constitution in this sense is different from the constitution of some other countries. In *Texas* v. *White*, the Supreme Court settled the constitutional question. The book Studies in Federalism, edited by Bowie and Friedrich states that "the Supreme Court settled the constitutional question of the right of secession, as it had in fact been settled by the Civil War" (p. 789).

I did not want to refer to that because the Civil War was not exactly judicial process. But, at any rate, it certainly showed the determination of a people to retain the unity of their country and which side really asserted itself. But in this case the Supreme Court said:

> When, therefore, Texas became one of the United States, she entered into an indissoluble relation.

That is a provision of a constituent unit in the federation. In other words, a federation does not recognize divorce. Once it is in, it is a sacrament; it cannot be separated; it is an indissoluble relation. The Supreme Court continued:

> All the obligations of perpetual union and all the guarantees of republican Government in the Union, attached at once to the State.

That is to say, Texas by the fact of its admission, became an American State. It is not only Texas, but it is America, the United States of America. The Supreme Court continues:

> The act which consummated her admission into Union was something more than a compact.

A State, in my submission, can no more banish itself from a federation than an individual can banish himself from a State. He has no right of divorcement from the Community to which he belongs. There may be rules of exile in a country, but there federation than an individual can banish himself from a State. He has no right of divorcement from the Community to which he belongs. There may be rules of exile in a country, but there is no way in which a man can disqualify himself except by committing a crime. The act which consummated the admission of Texas into the Union was something more than a compact; it was not a contract and therefore could not be dissolved. The Supreme Court continued:

> it was the incorporation of a new member into the political body. And it was complete and final.... There was no place for reconsideration of revocation, except through revolution or consent of the States.

It is possible for the Parliament of India, in the exercise of its sovereignty and according to its constitutional procedures which would require the consultation and the assent of the constituent State to separate it, but that is the kind of sovereignty that Professor Dicey spoke of when he said that a Parliament can do everything but make a man or woman. But that sovereign right is not what is at issue here. The issue is: What was the formal relationship which was contingent, which was conditional and which could be altered? Even if it was so, then a dispute about territory, to which the previous representative in this Chair, Mr. Gopalaswami Ayyangar, referred to and refuted, would have been very simple; but there is not such thing. I would refrain from quoting the general principles, on this subject, but I want to refer to another instance, particularly in order that the representatives of the United Kingdom and Australia can come nearer to this problem.

Australia has six states. It is a confederation. But power is much more dispersed, shall we say, than in Canada and Western Australia, at one time, had ideas of separation. A plebiscite was taken. Some 130,000 people—in round numbers voted for separation, and 30,000 people voted for remaining in. The plebiscite, then, was in favour of separation. That was before the Statute of Westminster, and therefore any alteration of the law would require the consent of the British Parliament. It went to Parliament, and the Parliament appointed a joint committee of the two Houses which sits in judicial session on these matters. The case was argued by counsel on both sides, and the Parliamentary view about this was recorded in the joint committee's decision—that Western Australia could not secede. At any rate, if it were to secede, the decision had to come from the Australian Parliament—and then it would not be secession, but it would be separation.

The right of secession, then, does not exist in our federation. This may be abstract law, but it is of very great importance to us. And I want to ask the members of the Council to address their minds to what would happen to what is now called India if this principle were not strictly enforced.

I have mentioned that there were 565 states before the British went away. A handful of them are part of Pakistan; the remainder are part of the Indian Union. If every local Maharaja had a different idea the next morning and started seceding, our unity would disappear in no time. What is applicable to Kashmir would be applicable to every state that has acceded if once we said that the accession is not permanent but provisional.

Therefore, the Government of India, out of considerations of Security, out of considerations of international law and the law of India, and the law that has been given to her by the British Parliament, cannot ever accept the idea that accession is anything but an indissoluble bond. When Kashmir acceded, that matter was finished. Therefore, there is no such thing as going out. In this country, as I said, they decided in other ways, and now it is being confirmed by the law courts of the country. Accordingly, any suggestion to us that the accession is provisional or temporary is very wrong.

We might then be asked: What is the meaning of the letter written by the Earl of Mountbatten, when he was Governor-

General of India, to the Maharaja, about consulting the wishes of the people? I do not want to evade this question.

As I pointed out, there is a document of accession. There is an offer and there is an acceptance. That concludes the arrangement. I will not call it a contract—but that concludes the arrangement. The letter of Governor-General is a separate document and has nothing to do with this. What does that document do? It makes no guarantees. It expresses the wish of the Government of India—not as part of the law, but as part of a political policy. We are entitled to ask that the Security Council should make a distinction between what is a policy of a government at any time and the constitutional law or the principles of international law that govern these matters.

Therefore, when the Governor-General of India wrote to the Maharaja and said, "In accordance with the general policy that we follow, we will consult", he did not say anything about a plebiscite; he said that the wishes of the people would be consulted. I shall deal with this more in detail when we consider the question of the plebiscite. Whatever we may have said in that way has, first of all, nothing to do with Pakistan and nothing to do with the international community; it is something between the people of Kashmir and ourselves. It is a pledge to them and to nobody else.

The Foreign Minister of Pakistan has quoted a telegram in which may Prime Minister says to the former Prime Minister of Pakistan, Mr. Liaquat Ali, that this is a pledge to all the world—a pledge to you and everybody else. I am going to deal with those telegrams of the Prime Minister, because they must be read in the context in a which they were sent. And we have always communicated this view to the Government of Pakistan.

In the telegram of 31 October 1947, from New Delhi to Karachi, the Government says:

> Kashmir's accession to India was accepted by us at the request of the Maharaja's Government and the most numerous representative popular organizations in the state, which is predominantly Muslim. Even then it was accepted on the condition that, as soon as the invader

had been driven from Kashmir soil and law and order restored, the people of Kashmir would be able to decide the question of accession.

That is why the Constituent Assembly question becomes important—because, while we have no international commitment in this matter, we have a moral commitment to the people over there that commitment in the context of things that appeared. Therefore, when we consider this question of consulting the wishes of the people, the plebiscite and so on, we should bear in mind that there are two aspects of it. One is the aspect of whether there is a commitment by the Government of India to other parties than the Security Council of the United Nations, and the other is the aspect of whether there is a commitment that has come in the context of the United Nations. And that is where the consultation of the people has arisen.

First of all, the reason for stating this wish was the previous history of Kashmir. Kashmir was ruled at that time by a Maharaja who was far from having given it a popular Government. The leaders of the national movement were in prison. The national movement in India was in close association with it, and the leaders of the Indian national movement have shared the prison life of these people. So this great national movement, which was kept under suppression by the Maharaja—was really Kashmir in a political and social sense. And a Government like the Indian Government, which had installed itself after a peaceful revolution, could not feel happy in merely accepting the accession—not for legal reasons, but political reasons—of the Maharaja. It therefore consulted what was at that time the only widespread movement in the place—the national Conference.

While we are on this subject, it is well to say that the national movement in Kashmir started as a communal movement. It was first called the Kashmir Muslim Conference—and then, as soon as it became mature, it dropped this sectarian outlook and made itself national. For twenty or twenty-five years, they struggled and endured all the rigours of opposing the law; and went in and resisted the Maharaja's rule.

Therefore, when we accepted this accession, we did thing we could. And after that, if conditions had not been what they were, that it is to say, if the country had not been invaded, if there had not been all that followed in the wake of the invasion, if the country had not been divided by the cease-fire line into the occupied part and the free part—the part occupied by Pakistan and the part that is free in India—then it would have been possible to do something else.

It is in that context that the telegram to which the Foreign Minister of Pakistan has referred was sent to the former Prime Minister of Pakistan. And I would request the Security Council to read the text of that telegram, because it was more a message from the heart than from any political deliberations. It was a time when India and Pakistan were emerging from the background of the great mass slaughter on the north western frontiers and it was hoped on both sides to prevent any further spread of this bloodshed.

If the telegram is to be quoted, the net paragraph should also be read. The Foreign Minister of Pakistan quoted a paragraph and it is accurate as for as it goes. But I submit that the Security Council, in looking at the document, has to look at the previous and the succeeding paragraph, if necessary. Now, this is what the succeeding paragraphs say:

> I have no doubt that you realize that the raiders from the frontier province or along the Murree Road came from Pakistan territory and that it is the easiest thing in the world to stop them at the two bridges which connect Pakistan territory with Kashmir.

In other words, it was an appeal to him to stop the bloodshed at these bridges. They were not so prevented, and the equipment of arms, including artillery and automatic weapons, bears witness to the help being given them.

The telegram goes on:

> We are credibly informed that regular officers of the Pakistan Army are advising these raiders. Even now, it would be easy for your Government to stop the passage of them and their supplies to the Kashmir territory.

Now, the statement made by Mr. Khan Noon should be read in the context of the telegram of 31 October 1947 from the

Prime Minister of India and of the reply by the Prime Minister of Pakistan.

At the Security Council's seven hundred and sixty-first meeting, I said that Mr. Khan Noon had referred—not only as regards the subject with which I am now dealing but also as regards other subjects—to private conversations between the Prime Ministers. I asked the Council's indulgence—and it was freely given—so that I might have an opportunity to consult my Prime Minister. At that time, I did not have before me the full text of the telegram in question. I have no obtained the necessary information from my Prime Minister. This is what he says:

> As far as we can find out, Sir Feroz Khan Noon's references to statements by me all relate to certain messages sent by me to Liaquat Ali Khan within the first ten days or so of the invasion of Kashmir in 1947.

I would ask the Security Council to place itself within the context of that background. I continue to read from my Prime Minister's communication to me:

> During those days, we had no knowledge of the part that the Pakistan Army was playing in this invasion, that is, obviously helping the raiders. It was later, in November, that we came to know the presence of the Pakistan Army itself in Kashmir, because our troops came into contact with them there. You will notice (Krishna Menon: And here the Prime Minister is referring to me) that, at the time that I had suggested to Pakistan to make a joint request to the United Nations to undertake a plebiscite in Kashmir, Pakistan did not accept this, and in fact continued its aggression for a year subsequently, that is, throughout 1948.

We went to the Security Council to avoid all-out war with Pakistan. Later, the fact of Pakistan's aggression came out clearly. The military situation in Kashmir state began to be unfavourable to them.

The resolution of the United Nations Commission of 13 August was agreed to by India, subject to clarifications.

Pakistan did not agree to this resolution and continued the aggression. Owing to a further deterioration of the military situation, they agreed to the United Nations resolution of 5 January, which supplemented the 13 August resolution.

Now, this goes back to very early period of the tumult. It was our hope that Pakistan would join us in setting the matter.

At this point, I should like to say something that I shall have to repeat later. If an offer is made and it is not accepted at the time it is made, it cannot be held for generations over the heads of those who made it. It is quite true that at one time we told Pakistan, "Let us go to the United Nations together and ask for a plebiscite". They did not agree. When they did not agree, that offer lapsed. They cannot come here nine years later and say, "You mentioned the word 'plebiscite'." That is the position. We have made many offers to Pakistan at various times. Some of these offers may be reconsidered, if necessary, when the time comes. But, if an offer made to an opposing party is not accepted within a reasonable time, it cannot be maintained that it is still an open offer. The offer terminates when it is not accepted. In very many cases, we have said that explicitly; where we have not done so, it must be taken as the normal state of affairs.

This is the position as regard accession. There can be no conditional accession. That would be against our constitutional procedure. It would amount to denying citizens of India the right to live in a free country, where they have the fundamental guarantees of freedom. It would amount to making those citizens run the risk of having to live a different kind of life elsewhere—a risk which we are not prepared to have them run.

It has been said that we obtained this accession on the one hand by force and on the other hand by fraud. In anything that I shall now say on the question of force, I do not wish to be understood as referring to the word "fraud". So far as force is concerned, I would say this: Force did play a part in this accession. Force affected the timing so that the Maharaja had no alternative but to ask for protection. Apart from any questions of accession, apart from any questions of the law relating to this matter, I would ask the Security Council this question in all conscience: If a State is being invaded, is it not the most natural thing in the world for that state to ask a neighbour to come to its protection? Is such a request to be regarded as the imposition of force from outside? We used no force in connexion with the accession. I believe that the Security Council is familiar with communications in this respect from General Lockhart, the British Commander-in-Chief of our Army, and from Air Marshal Elmhurst, the head of the Air Force at that time—in any case, I shall circulate these communications. These officers were commissioned by His Majesty, the King of England, and were on temporary service with us. They had nothing to expect from us by way of reward, but they categorically stated that any suggestion that there was any conspiracy in connexion with the accession was entirely wrong.

Thus, I repeat, we used no force. The only force we used was that necessary to repel the invader—and I believe that that is a force which we are entitled to use, and indeed are enjoined to use, under the Charter.

With regard to the other suggestion that some sharp practice was involved, I set out this morning the conditions of the Standstill agreement. Had the State concluded the standstill agreement with us, we should immediately have become responsible for its foreign affairs, defence and communications—but, as I said this morning, this matter was interrupted by the invasion. The Security Council will recall the chronology of the invasion which I read out this morning.

Therefore, it can be seen that it was not we who used force—or that other word which I do not want to use. The accession was legal. As I have already said, at one time, before the Maharaja had made up his mind, we asked the Governor-General to tell him to accede to Pakistan if he so wished. Lord Mountbatten told the Maharaja categorically that we would not regard such accession to Pakistan as an unfriendly act. But that was before all these events which I have described took place. Thus, there was no question of our trying to inveigle the Maharaja into any kind of accession.

Questions may be asked regarding the right of the sovereign —that is, the Prince—to make the accession for the State. In this respect, we have the very reputable and, in this particular case, very helpful authority of Mr. Jinnah. Mr. Jinnah was President of the Muslim League and a founder of Pakistan. He said the following on 17 June, 1947, before he became Governor-General of Pakistan.

Constitutionally and legally, the Indian States will be independent, sovereign States on the termination of paramountcy, and they will be free to decide for themselves to adopt any course they like. It is open to them to join the Hindustan Constituent Assembly (Krishna Menon: That was what they called us):

Or the Pakistan Constituent Assembly (Krishna Menon: That was their name).

Or decide to remain independent.... I am clearly of the opinion that the Cabinet Mission's memorandum of 12 May does not in any way limit them in this choice.

Just two weeks before the partition took place, Mr. Jinnah reiterated this attitude before the Muslim League. He said:

> They are free to join either of the two dominions, or to remain independent. The Muslim League recognizes the right of each State to its destiny.

There are other statements by Mr. Jinnah in which he says that the person to whom the accession should be offered is the Ruler. If that were not the case, there would be no legality. The Ruler is the repository of power. Whether, morally speaking, he is democratic or not is another matter. In an Indian State, however, all power flows from the Ruler—in some cases, this is true only in theory; in many cases, before independence, this was also true in form. There was, therefore, no one who could have offered the accession.

I come now to the question of Constituent Assembly. In acceding to India every State—not only Kashmir—had the right, if it so wished, to call its own Constituent Assembly.

They could have discussed various other matters, the allocation of various sources of revenue and all kinds of things like that. But the majority of State, in fact all of them after some time—some of them had toyed with the idea—decided that it was a waste of time and energy in procedure, so they elected members to the Indian Constituent Assembly. When the subject was under discussion and they did not see the reason, the Princes of India—patriotic men and women as they were—all realized the importance of allowing a united India to emerge, and—it was the Princes who came forward, without making any difficulties in regard to this matter, and decided to go into the Indian Constituent Assembly. But in Kashmir a different situation had arisen on account of this trouble, and therefore that matter was left alone. Besides, in Kashmir, there had been a powerful national movement which in 1944 had asked for a constituent assembly, and their demand for a constituent assembly is part of their national upbringing. I would ask the Security Council whether any democratic government could disregard a very well-established feeling of that kind.

What I am here concerned in pointing out is that this idea of a constituent Assembly was not something either strange in the relationships between India and the Indian states, or something that we conjured up just because the matter was before the Security Council. It was there long before there was an invasion of Kashmir; it was part of the demand of the people to the Maharaja. But the Maharaja had his own plans, like some countries have for their colonial territories and will not give them any power, and he would have none of it.

So the national movement in Kashmir wanted this constituent assembly. Then came the war, the invasion and all these troubles and the matter was kept in suspense. Kashmir acceded in three main subjects only. There were various other matters, because under the British rule there were varying relations between British India and the Indian States and in the case of Kashmir there were a large number of problems, of customs and so on, to be resolved. So they decided to have their own constituent assembly.

What does this constituent assembly amount to? So far as the Security Council is concerned it has to look at the documents.

These are constitutional documents and I would ask the Council to look at the document which is the source from which the constituent assembly in its present form derives its existence; then its scope will be seen; because it has been presented as if this constituent assembly were a device rather in disregard of all other processes. It is contained in the proclamation of the Yuvraj of Kashmir, the son of the old Maharaja, who is elected by the people every five years—this is a democratic process. He is the head of the state and he issued proclamation on 1 May 1951, and this is the proclamation:

> Whereas it is the general desire of the people of the State of Jammu and Kashmir that a Constituent Assembly should be brought into being for the purpose of framing a constitution for the State (Krishna Menon: That is its terms of reference).

Whereas it is commonly felt that the convening of the Assembly can no longer be delayed without detriment to the future well-being to the State (Krishna Menon: Again a purpose with which we do not disagree).

And whereas the terms of the proclamation of the Maharaja (Krishna Menon: His father) dated 5 March 1948 in regard to the convening of a national assembly as contained in clauses 4 to 6 of the operative part thereof do not meet the requirements of the present situation (Krishna Menon: it is out of date).

I, Yuvraj Karan Singh, do hereby direct as follow:

> A constituent Assembly consisting of representatives of the people, elected on the basis of adult franchise shall be constituted forthwith for the purpose of framing a constitution for the State of Jammu and Kashmir.

For the purpose of the said elections the State shall be divided into a number of territorial constituencies each containing a population of 40,000 or as near thereto as possible, and each electing one member. A delimitation committee shall be set up by the Government to make recommendations as to the number of constituencies and the limits of each constituency.

Elections to the Constituent Assembly shall be on the basis of adult franchise, that is to say, every person who is a state subject of any class, as defined in the notification No...is not less than twenty-one years of age on the first day of March, has been a resident in the constituency for such period as may be prescribed by the rules, shall be entitled to register in the electoral rolls of that constituency, provided that any person who is of unsound mind or has been so declared by a competent court, shall be disqualified for registration.

The vote at the election shall be by direct and secret ballot.

The Constituent Assembly shall have power to act notwithstanding any vacancy in the membership thereof (Krishna Menon: That is in order to provide for the places from which people could not be elected, in the occupied area. There again, they tried to work it out as smoothly as possible without talking about annexation or anything of that sort. They simply left that place vacant).

The Constituent Assembly shall frame its own agenda and make rules for the governing of its procedure and the conduct of its business.

The Government shall make such rules and issue such instructions and orders as may be necessary to give effect to the terms of this proclamation.

Then it goes on to say that all things done before the issuing of this proclamation with a view to facilitating the provision of electoral rules for the purpose of election to the Constituent Assembly shall, in so far as they are in conformity with the provisions of this proclamation—therefore anything that is not in conformity with this proclamation, or the decision of any conference, is not binding at all—will be deemed to have been done or taken under this proclamations as if it was in force at the time such things were done or such steps were taken.

This is the proclamation which states the terms of reference so to speak of the Constituent Assembly. It is quite clear from this proclamation that the function of this Constituent Assembly is to make a constitution for Kashmir. It could not make a constitution for defence, external affairs or communications, or do anything against the fundamental rights of the Indian Constitution, because it had accepted accession by that time.

Now we turn to the document which is the Constitution adopted by the Constituent Assembly and look at what it says. The burden of the argument here is that this Constituent Assembly is going to create a new relationship, and my answer is: in terms of international law; the actions of a Constituent Assembly are not creative, they are merely declamatory; they do not make anything new.

We, the people of the State of Jammu and Kashmir, having solemnly resolved, in pursuance of the accession of this State of India (Krishna Menon: If anything is wrong, it is the accession that is wrong not the Constituent Assembly; the relationship with India was not brought about by the Constituent Assembly, it was brought about by the accession) which took place on the twenty-sixth day of October, 1947, to further define the existing relationship of the State with the Union of India as an integral part thereof, and to secure to ourselves justice, social, economic and political; liberty of thought, expression, belief, faith and worship; equality of status and of opportunity, and to promote among us all fraternity assuring the dignity of the individual and the unity of the Nation.

In our Constituent Assembly this seventeenth day of November, 1956, do hereby adopt, enact and give to ourselves this Constitution.

So if there was a date, that was 17 November 1956. This Constitution creates nothing. It is in pursuance of the accession. If the relationship of Kashmir is not acceptable—as it is not—to Pakistan, then the thing, to quarrel with, so far as the Constitution is concerned, is the Instrument of Accession and the Government India. The Constituent Assembly could do nothing; it was done in pursuance of the accession. In other words, this is the act of a sub-sovereign body.

It is the by-laws; if you like—it is for the internal government of the country; where an enormous amount of social reform is taking place, where land reform has resulted in the abolition of the old form of landlordism and where no one can hold more than twenty-three acres of land, where education has spread. They went to arrange all their economic affairs. Furthermore, I want to draw the Council's attention to Part I of the Constitution, which states, in paragraph 1 (2):

> This section and sections 2, 3, 4, 5, 6, 7, 8 and 158 shall come into force at once (Krishna Menon: That is to say when this Constitution is put in draft) and the remaining provisions of this Constitution shall come into force on the twenty-sixth day of January, 1957....

Now what are the reserved clauses? I have mentioned sections 2, 3, 4 and 5. Section 3 reads:

3. The state of Jammu and Kashmir is and shall be an integral part of the Union of India.

That provision came into force in November.

4. The territory of the State shall comprise all the territories which on the fifteenth day of August, 1947, were under the sovereignty or suzerainty of the Ruler of the State.

5. The executive and legislative power of the State extends to all matters except those with respect to which Parliament has power to make laws for the State under the provisions of the Constitution of India.

All those provisions which relate to federation matters, to matters of the relationship between the State and the Federation, are matters of past history.

In this connection the Presidential Order of 1954 is important. That is part of our Constitution. It is not as though the 26th is a zero hour. As a matter of fact, the Security Council is in a somewhat difficult position. Actually nothing will happen on 26 January except, in all probability, before midnight of the 25th the Constituent Assembly will dissolve itself.

Can the Security Council tell them that they should not dissolve themselves? The Security Council has been asked to put itself in a position where its actions would have not meaning in this connexion. If there were any issue, that issue should be in regard to accession. Is Kashmir a part of India? There I think the Security Council is tied up by the findings of the Commission; it is tied up with constitutional law and practice; it is tied up with the law of federations and, what is more, it is tied up with the principles of the Charter.

The Security Council, of course, in its profound wisdom may do what it likes. I now speak from memory, which is not always very good, but the Foreign Minister of Pakistan either said or suggested that there should be some restraining action in the character of an injunction. Members know that an injunction is an equitable process, a process arising from equity. And what invader can ask for equity? Therefore, that question does not arise.

I want to submit, therefore, that the whole of this crisis atmosphere which has been created about 26 January is just unreal. The 26th of January with us, as with Dr. Walker in Australia, marks the foundation of our Constitution. It is India's national day. Therefore, this new State has finished its municipal constitution. Its conduct is municipal—it is dealing with its legislature, how many members of Parliament there should be, what to do with the land laws, what taxes they should raise and are competent to raise in connexion with the Federation of India, what the powers of the Speaker of the House or the Advocate General might be—these are the matters contained in this Constitution. A great many of them are already in operation. The Constituent Assembly in Kashmir as was the case in India sits both as a parliament and as a Constituent Assembly. When it sits as a constituent assembly it is to preside over by its chairman. When the chairman leaves the chair and the speaker presides, it becomes a parliament. The same body functions in two different ways. Whenever the Constituent Assembly completes consideration of a particular measure which is necessary for the welfare of the people, the Parliament enacts it. It is part of what has already been done and there is not crisis or zero hour, there is no action from which restraint can be exercised. The only thing that could be restrained would be to undo the act of accession. The right thing for the Security Council to do, in the submission of the Government of India, would be to ask for the observance of the Charter and for the vacating of the aggression. That is the problem before the Council.

I have taken this out of the General scheme of the argument in order to meet the wishes of the various members of Security Council who had intimated privately that they would like to hear about it. That is the position as regards the Constituent Assembly. I hope that the Security Council is not going to find itself in a position where it will subscribe to a decision which is so devoid of reality, which will expose it to ridicule, which is so unconnected with the events of the day and which is contrary to the constitutional procedures of a sovereign State, of a Member State whose constitution is presumed to be known to the United Nations in international law. What is more, there are large numbers of people who subscribe to the same kind of legal system to which we subscribe.

I should like, therefore, to erase from the minds of members this idea of a crisis or a zero hour of something happening on 26 January. It is a day which is observed in every part of India in general jubilation as the day when the Constitution of India was inaugurated. It traces its origin to midnight, 25-26 January 1930 when, on the banks of the Ravi, the present Prime Minister, the President of the Indian National Congress, stated that all men are entitled to their freedom. Therefore, should any country oppress us, where there is a rule of that kind we shall try peacefully to terminate it. That was the declaration of independence in 1930, and this is the anniversary of that day.

There is nothing in this, therefore, which should attract the attention of the Security Council with regard to the Constituent Assembly process. I have taken pains to inquire about what actually is going to happen on that day. I understand that all that will happen will be a formal meeting of the Assembly in order formally to wind up their affairs because they no longer have any function. Parliament may then sit the next day.

This was not arranged in view of the meeting of the Security Council. It is part of its normal proceedings. It has finished its functions long ago. There is no particular reason whey it should do this on the 26th, except that it may thus spare the expense of having two separate celebrations, one to wind up the Constituent Assembly and another for its national day. The appointed day in this respect follows the Constitution of India.

I have so far argued that the claims in regard to this are based, on the one hand, upon something which is extra-legal and extra-constitutional and outside the decisions of the Security Council, and I have submitted the view of the Government of India in refutation of that position. There are no considerations which are so generous in this matter, no considerations which, on their own merits, indicate that this must have been the course. To the extent that the Foreign Minister of Pakistan has quoted authority, I have proved, if my documents are correct—and they are open for scrutiny to anyone—that those conditions not only did not exist but that they referred to other matters. The legal and constitutional aspect of it relates to the accession.

I should like once again to repeat that this is a matter—and I quoted this position this morning—on which the Government of India has at no time made any recession. What is more, the Commission has at no time raised this point; that is to say, it is accepted on all sides. The members were concerned with the issues of international peace and Security, and that is the function of the Security Council.

I ask you, Mr. President, to look at Chapter VI or even Chapter VII, if you wish, and I ask where is the provision to challenge the merits of accession. The Security Council is called upon here to deal with pouring oil over troubled waters. So far as we are concerned, we have not only helped to fetch the oil, but we do not trouble the waters at all. We ask the Council to restrain others from making the water muddy.

If those two issues are out of the way, then what remains? What remains is aggression. That is what remains in any claim that can be made with regard to what is called a plebiscite.

As regards the commitments which we have made, I am prepared to face them quite squarely, because the Government of India has a responsibility to explain its position before a world body such as the United Nations.

We did not ask the Security Council at the end of five years to spend several days on this matter. Our sister State of Pakistan desired to do so, and we were quite prepared to come here either in June of last year, when there were rumours about it, or at the present time. You, Mr. President, notified us about this meeting, and we are here.

Now, what is this commitment? The commitment is that in various resolutions it has been said that it is the wish, that it is the desire, to refer that matter to the people of the country, and so on. I do not know whether you want me to quote this again, as I have quoted it so many times, but it is all there.

No one, least of all any responsible person from India, says that the question of plebiscite was not considered at one time under certain conditions. It is an error, if I may say so, to ask a Government to consider what it has offered and what it has considered outside the context of any circumstances.

Any lawyer here would know that even in a civil matter, even in a matter between individuals inside a country, all the surrounding circumstances have to be taken into consideration. The nature of these commitments is twofold. The plebiscite, I think, has, first of all two aspects, and one aspect has two sub-aspects.

One aspect is the commitment we may have made to the people of Kashmir, that is to say, what came out of us by our own volition in the context of the national life of India. That is represented by the communication made by Lord Mountbatten to the Maharajah on the 27th, which states that "it is wish of the Government in accordance with our policy"—he did not say anything about a plebiscite—"to have a reference to the people." That might be any kind of reference; it might be a referendum; it might be a plebiscite; it might be a general election; it might be Gallup Poll; it might be anything. That was the position at that time, but let us assume that it was a plebiscite. Even he attached conditions to it: when the soil was cleared of the invader and peace and order was restored. I cannot state the authority of my distinguished colleague from Pakistan on the question of peace and order, because in one part of his statement he says there is peace and order but in another he says there is not. I think he is right, because there is peace and order in the territory we administer.

That is one commitment. Now I should like you to look at this. This is very much like an equitable doctrine, and therefore, I think that one may make an analogy. Suppose that you, Mr. President, with all the wealth you possess, make a testamentary disposition to your children willing them your property and saying that you give so much money for this and so much for that, and that at the end of it you say to your eldest son, "It is my wish that out of this money you should build a library", or something of that character. That has no force in law; it is the expression of a wish. All that binds the young man is what you have said. The expression of a wish is not binding in any equitable relations. It may be respected. We try to respect it.

Therefore, our first commitment, if it is a commitment, is to the people of Kashmir. No other party comes into it. Secondly, it is in consonance with the policy of the Government of India. Policies of Governments are matters which the Governments alone can decide. Thirdly, it was effective when the soil was cleared of the invader; and, fourthly, when peaceful conditions had been restored.

That is why my friend and predecessor, Mr. Gopalaswami Ayyangar, when he came here, said that the garrisons of India must garrison the Northern area, that the troops must be kept to prevent tribesmen coming on the Western frontiers of Western Kashmir and on and north-western frontiers of north-western Kashmir. The whole of the territory comes under the sovereignty of Jammu and Kashmir, as is admitted by the Commission.

Therefore, that condition, even so far as we are concerned, does not exist. But we did our best. We hung this up for sometime, right from 1948 till about 1952, hoping that something would happen.

The members of the Security Council are all of sovereign independent States given to the democratic way of life. Can the Security Council ask us that the people of Kashmir should be without franchise without the guarantee of fundamental rights without being able to introduce the economic legislation that is necessary for their planning, their education and things of that character? How is that to be done? It is to be done by command from the Government of India? That is not how our country is governed. These provisions are made by the constituent assembly for that reason. Therefore, while it was not possible for us to do it in one way, we did it in another way.

So in Kashmir, there is a legislature, a constituent assembly that functions. In that parliament there is an opposition, small as it is. In 1952 there were fifteen newspapers and journals in Kashmir, in a very small area where the majority of people are not literate; today there are forty-eight. What is more, as I shall point out later, in the last two or three years more than 500 primary schools have come into this area. So, it can be seen that the Government of Kashmir is advancing in all state matters in this way. Therefore, to the extent that the wishes of the people could be consulted, we did so.

The Foreign Minister also made a reference, not very complimentary to us, to the election of this constituent assembly. I am prepared to face this issue also. The proclamation asked for a universal franchise, secret ballots, and so on. The constituent assembly elections were announced; the electoral rolls were prepared; the electoral constituencies were delimited. All the arrangements were made. The candidates came forward. A fact that has not been mentioned is that the opposition candidates who afterwards withdrew did not come from the people who are either Moslems or those who wanted to go to Pakistan or were suspected of wanting to go to Pakistan; they came from the orthodox Rajput Hindu sections of the community who were against India for its being a secular State. We did not stop them but they realized that in this large country, where there is a big nationalist movement, they did not have a chance. Having filed their nominations, and all arrangements having been made before the elections dates, they withdrew their candidacy.

According to our election laws, in common with the election laws of the United Kingdom, Australia, and, I believe, other countries, each candidate has to deposit a certain amount of money, and if he does not poll one-tenth of the votes he forfeits the deposit. What is more, he looks very ridiculous if he polls a microscopic number of votes. These people, having used the elections for propaganda purposes, withdrew their candidacies. They were not forced to withdraw or anything of that character. The result was that the others were returned unopposed. There are many unopposed elections of this type.

Whilst the case is not an exact parallel, I would ask my colleague from Pakistan to look at the election in India in 1937. Then a national movement of that character, in the context of the first election, swept everything before it.

The test of this is in the municipal elections. Sometimes we have candidates withdrawing from elections. Where there is no forfeiture of deposits there is not obligation of withdrawal. There are many elections of municipalities and local bodies in Kashmir, and in all these elections the same party has come out on top. Therefore, the idea that there was a one-party state or a kind of election to order is entirely inconsistent with what goes on in India.

With great respect to the Security Council, I would submit that when a country has the largest democratic electorate in the world, when it has a constitution guaranteeing the fundamental rights, when every man and woman in its may vote and, what is more, when 200,000,000 people will go to the polls in two month in that country, I think that to speak of such a country as sifting elections is a charge that cannot pass muster. I shall not say anything more than that.

You cannot compel people to be opposed. If there are unopposed returns, it does not mean that the system is not functioning. The constituent assembly does not sit in secret. The world press is there.

Kashmir is the centre of the world's visitors. Last summer we had 62,000 people in Kashmir as visitors, and 9,000 of them were foreigner, and the majority Americans. And they did not stick to the towns. They went around all over. Therefore, any suggestion that this Constituent Assembly was an arranged pocket affairs is very much of a mistake. What is more, in that Constituent Assembly, as regards the very men whose names were referred to by the Foreign Minister of Pakistan as now having fallen from favour and therefore, were in prison, when

I go into the facts the Foreign Minister will probably be pleased to withdraw some of these names.

But at any rate that is another matter. However, what I say is this: that the candidates who were elected are people who have been participants in the national movement for a very long time. For the convenience of the Council I have submitted as document 6 the statement made by Sheikh Abdullah to the Jammu and Kashmir Constituent Assembly is an extremely interesting document and we do not make any apologies for submitting it. Sheikh Abdullah is in detention. He is in detention under the law of Kashmir. I will come to that in a moment, before I finish the whole submission.

Sheikh Abdullah said:

> As a realist I am conscious that nothing is all black or all white, and there are many facets to each of the propositions before us. I shall first speak on the merits and demerits of the State's accession to India. In the final analysis, as I understand it, it is the kinship of ideals which determines the strength of ties between two States. The Indian National Congress has consistently supported the cause of the State's peoples' freedom. The autocratic rule of the Princes has been done away with and representative governments have been entrusted with the administration. Steps towards democratization have been taken and these have raised the people's standard of living, brought about much-needed social reconstruction, and above, all, built up their very independence of spirit. Naturally, if we accede to India there is no danger of a revival of feudalism and autocracy. Moreover, during the last four years, the Government of India has never tried to interfere in our internal autonomy. (Krishna Menon: we were not permitted to so by our Constitution.) This experience has strengthened our confidence in them as a democratic State. (Krishna Menon: This is Sheikh Abdullah speaking.)

The real character of State is revealed in its Constitution. The Indian Constitution has set before the country the goal of secular democracy based upon justice, freedom and equality for all without distinction. This is the bed-rock of modern democracy. This should meet the argument that the Muslims of Kashmir cannot have Security in India, where the large majority of the population are Hindus. Any unnatural cleavage between religious groups is the legacy of imperialism, and no modern State can afford to encourage artificial divisions if it is to achieve progress and prosperity. The Indian Constitution has amply and finally repudiated the concept of a religious State, which is a throwback to medievalism, by guaranteeing the equality of rights of all citizens irrespective of their religion, colour, caste and class.

The national movement in our State naturally gravitates towards these principles of secular democracy. The people here will never accept a principle which seeks to favour the interest of one religion or social group against another. This affinity in political principles as well as in past association, and our common path of suffering in the cause of freedom, must be weighted properly while deciding the future of the State.

We are also intimately concerned with the economic well-being of the people of this State. As I said before while referring to constitution—building, political ideals are often meaningless unless linked with economic plans.... As you know, and as I have detailed before we have been able to put through our 'land to the tiller' legislation (Krishna Menon: And he goes on to talk about legislation that has taken place. Then he continues as follows):

> In the second place, our economic welfare is bound up with our arts and crafts. The traditional markets for these precious goods, for which we are justly known all over the world, have been centered in India (Krishna Menon: That is, their economic life is tied up with us). The volume of our trade, in spite of the dislocation of the last few years, shown this. Industry is also highly important to us. Potentially we are rich in minerals,

> and in the raw materials of industry; we needed help to develop our resources. India, being more highly industrialized than Pakistan, can give us equipment, technical services and materials. She can help us too in marketing.... It is around the efficient supply of such basic necessities that the standard of living of the man in the street depends. (Krishna Menon: Then he goes on to talk about the disadvantage.)

To begin with, although the land frontiers of India and Kashmir are contiguous and an all-weather road link dependable as the one we have with Pakistan does not exist. (Krishna Menon: But now it does; at the time he spoke it did not). This must necessarily hamper trade and commerce to some extent, particularly during the snowy winter months. But we have studied this question and with improvements in modern engineering, if the State wishes of remain with India, the establishment of an all-weather stable system of communication is both feasible and easy. Similarly, the use of the State rivers as a means of timber transport is impossible if we turn to India, except in Jammu where the river Chenab still carries logs to the plains (Krishna Menon: their timber trade is with Pakistan).

In reply to this argument it may be pointed out that accession to India will open up possibilities of utilizing our forest wealth for industrial purposes and that, instead of timber, finished goods, which will provide work for our carpenters and labourers can be exported to India where there is a ready market for them. Indeed in the presence of our fleets of timber-carrying trucks, river transport is a crude system which inflicts a loss of some 20 to 35 cent in transit.

Still another factor has to be taken into consideration. Certain tendencies have been asserting themselves in India which may in the future convert it into a religious State wherein the interests of Muslims will be jeopardized (Krishna Menon: He has put in every argument). This would happen if a communal organization had a dominant hand in the government and Congress ideals of the equality of all communities were made to give way to religious intolerance. The continued accession of Kashmir to India should help in defeating this tendency. From my experience of the last four years, it is my considered judgement that the presence of Kashmir in the Union of India has been the major factor in stabilizing relations between the Hindus and Muslims of India. Gandhiji was not wrong when he uttered words before his death which paraphrase. I lift up mine eyes unto the hills, from whence cometh my help.

As I have said before, we must consider the question of accession with an open mind, and not let our personal prejudices stand in the way of a balanced judgment. I will now invite you to evaluate the alternative of accession to Pakistan.

The most powerful argument which can be advanced in her favour is that Pakistan is a Muslim State, and, a big majority of our people being Muslims, the State must accede to Pakistan. This claim of being a Muslim state is of course only a camouflage. It is a screen to dupe the common man, so that he may not see clearly that Pakistan is a feudal State in which a clique is trying by these methods of maintaining itself in power.

I am only quoting Sheikh Abdullah. He goes on:

> In addition to this, the appeal to religion constitutes a sentimental and a wrong approach to the question. Sentiment has its own place in life, but often it leads to irrational action. Some argue, as a supposedly natural corollary to this, that on our acceding to Pakistan our annihilation or survival depends. Facts have disproved this Right-thinking men would point out that Pakistan is not an organic unity of all the Muslims in this—sub-continent. It has, on the contrary, caused the dispersion of the Indian Muslims from whose benefit it was claimed to have been created. There are two Pakistan's at least a thousand miles apart from each other. The total population of Western Pakistan, which is contiguous to our State, is hardly 25 million (Krishna Menon: I was wrong; it is less than I said) while the total number of Muslims resident in India is as many as 40 million.

*As one Muslim is as good as another, the Kashmir Muslims, if they are worried by such considerations, should choose the 40 millions living in India.*

Looking at the matter too from a more modern political angle, religious affinities alone do not and should not normally determine the political alliance of States. We do not find a Christian bloc, a Buddhist bloc, or even a Muslim bloc, about which there is so much talk nowadays in Pakistan. These days economic interests and a community of political ideals more appropriately influence the policies of States.

We have another important factor to consider, if the State decides to make this the predominant consideration. What will be the fate of the one million non-Muslims now in our state? (Krishna Menon: Out of the four million population of Kashmir in 1941 more than one million were non-Muslims, and a great many of these were Buddhists of Tibetan race. The statement continues):

> As things stand at present, there is no place for them in Pakistan.
>
> Any solution which will result in the displacement or the total subjugation of such a large number of people will not be just or fair....

(Krishna Menon: I will leave this now and come back to the other course he has pointed out. The third course which is suggested is), Why do they not remain independent? (Krishna Menon: And I am reading this in order to show that it is not as though these people were jockeyed into some position. They had all this before them.)

The third course open to us still has to be discussed. We have to consider the alternative of making ourselves an Eastern Switzerland, of keeping aloof from both States but having friendly relations with them. This might seem alternative in that it would appear to pave the way out of the present deadlock. To us as a tourist country it would also have obvious advantages. But in considering independence we must not ignore practical considerations.

Firstly, it is not easy to protect our sovereignty and independence in a small country which has not the sufficient strength to defend itself on our long and difficult frontiers bordering on many countries.

Secondly, we must have the good-will of all our neighbours. Can we find powerful guarantors among them to pull together always in assuring us freedom from aggression? I would like to remind you that from August 15 to October 22 of 1947 our State was independent (Krishna Menon: This was before accession) and the result was that our weakness was exploited by our neighbours, with whom we had a valid standstill agreement. The State was invaded. What is the guarantee that, in future too, we may not be the victims of similar aggression?

He has developed this point, so I have read this out at length because this idea of accession is obtained.

Now, therefore, what is the nature of our commitments outside? I have dealt with the position with regard to the Kashmir people and ourselves. The outside commitments are what arise from the mention and I want to use this word "mention"—of the word "plebiscite", and from its use as a provisional mechanism, or the idea that it can be part of a plan which is a concerted plan implementing itself in consecutive stages. That is what is being argued. First of all, I do not know whether I need repeat the arguments. I said this morning and this afternoon, but all of these commitments can be tied up in these two resolutions of the Commission—that is, the resolutions of 13 August and 5 January.

The resolution of 5 January is an implementing resolution. It provides the mechanism, provided the decision is made. Our commitments for a plebiscite are, first of all, conditioned by the withdrawal of Pakistani forces and nationals by the large-scale disbandment and disarmament of the Azad Kashmir army, by the restoration of the unity of the country, by the return of refugees, by the restoration of law and order and by conditions of Security.

I have not the resolution before me; if I had, I would probably make this statement longer, but I do not want to do so. So if the Council will recall to mind the various "whens" and "afters" and "ifs" that were in that resolution, it will appreciate that there can be no shadow of doubt in any rational mind that what was conceived was a plan conditional upon a contingency.

But whether they are incapable of performance or not, we had no commitment in this matter because the Government of India takes serious exception to the suggestion that we dishonoured our commitments. It is incumbent upon those who make these charges to prove them beyond all doubt.

We have made no commitments. What is the nature of commitments, Mr. President? You have long experience of international affairs. Commitments are treaties between nations; they are international obligations in the way of final acts, declarations, protocols and things of that kind. In this particular case what happened was that the Commission produced a resolution and we two agreed to it. There is no bilateral agreement between Pakistan and ourselves, technically.

We have always said that the Government of India will never agree to the interference of Pakistan in the sovereign affairs of the State, and that the plebiscite is not Pakistan's business but has to be taken by a Plebiscite Administrator, who has to decide its terms. And in any case none of these things can take place so long as the territory—more than 42,000 square miles out of 84,000—is under occupation.

I have not referred as yet to the story of the occupation of the North. I would like to do during the next instalment of this statement, and I have to ask all those concerned to forgive references to individuals and nationalities which are of a character which is not intended to hurt them at all since they are the facts of history.

Thus we have not commitments in this way. Our commitment is contingent upon the performance of part II, and even then —even if part II is performed—what is the promise that we have made? The promise we have made is to confer with the other side.

For this purpose, if the President so desires, we could take a hypothetical position. First of all, I said that there was no agreements on the level of treaty. There is no international agreement of the type that is a protocol or a final declaration of conference. What there is, is an agreement on a plan of settlement, which is a very different things.

Now, for the purpose of argument, my Government will be prepared, not to admit that there is anything more than that, but to examine this problem as though it were a treaty. And I want to emphasize this because we have suffered in the past by making hypothetical propositions. Supposing we assume—which we cannot assume—that whatever we have said in the way of a treaty is a plebiscite; what are the obligations under international law with regard to treaties? I am not going to quote any law because this is not a juridical body. But there are principles of international behaviour. There are some conditions which are laid down from the interpretation of treaties. They are here in Oppenheim's "International Law". If anyone is apprehensive that I might be unfair in quoting only parts of it, I am prepared to read the whole, but it will take a long time. I shall quote the parts which I think are relevant, and if there is any doubt, I will read the remainder:

> It is taken for granted that the contracting parties intend something reasonable, something adequate to the purpose of the treaty, and something not inconsistent with the generally recognized principles of international law.

I say that what the Security Council is being asked to believe that we have committed ourselves to is not anything reasonable. That is to say, to plunge a country that has got law and order institutions into a whole mixture of foreign intervention that is already on its frontier, to make this gateway of invasion into another way of interference, another way of the violation of sovereignty, is not reasonable. It is not reasonable to assume that there could be freedom of the poll in Pakistan—occupied area when there are—as I will tell the Council later—how many divisions of the Pakistan army within five and thirty miles of its border, when there are forty-five battalions of Azad forces ready to line up; with modern troops and equipment. We have some idea of this equipment; we do not live far away. There are airstrips built in these places—again I am going to give the particulars. So far as we are concerned it is not a military secret, although it may be a secret to others. But there it is. When there is an armed fortress and, what is more, when there is all this appeal to hatred and invasion, and language such as that used by the Foreign Minister himself—which at an appropriate stage, I propose to quote—it is not reasonable to expect that a country will unsettle things that are settled.

It is not reasonable now. Then it must be adequate. Would this be adequate for this purpose? It was Sir Owen Dixon, who said that no plebiscite would ever be adequate because, supposing the plebiscite by majority decided for Pakistan, there would be even more trouble. And, what is more, how would the adequacy of this plebiscite be justified in the present conditions?

Oppenheim says further: "It must not be inconsistent with the generally recognized principle of international law" and that is the main sheet anchor of our position. For the Security Council to take a step in this matter today which does not take our primary position—that is our territory has been invaded—into account would be inconsistent. Kashmir was never a part of Pakistan. Kashmir never acceded of Pakistan. Kashmir was in no way historically connected with the present Pakistan, and therefore, its entry into that territory, irrespective of our claims, is an act of invasion.

Assume for the moment, for argument, what is not a fact—that our claims have flaws in them, either legal, political or moral, that would not justify an act which is a clear violation of international law, as I shall point out in the findings of the United Nations Commission. An act of taking troops across our frontiers, being responsible for the aiding of ravage and rapine—that is not in accordance with recognized principles of international law. I will go further and say that many invasions have taken place since the Council asked that were should not be such invasions; and what is more, there has been a withholding of information from Security Council. This is not in accordance with international law.

International law is based upon the principle of equity, of fair-play and of international morality, and no party can come before this body and ask for equity unless it is prepared to deal it. The rule of equity in civil law is: those who want equity must come with clean hands.

Oppenheim says further:

> If, therefore, the meaning of a stipulation is ambiguous, the reasonable meaning is to be preferred to the unreasonable; the more reasonable to the less reasonable.

The purpose of the treaty is to get a settlement in Kashmir—that is the consistent meaning, not the meaning that is inconsistent with the recognized principles of international law. That is the first set of conditions in the interpreting of a treaty must be taken into consideration if the meaning of any one of its stipulations is doubtful, not only the working of the treaty, but also the purposes, the motives, and the conditions prevailing at the time.

There are two things here to be taken into account. Firstly, "the motives that led to its conclusion." The representatives may recall that earlier this afternoon I referred to the anxiety of the Commission to get a cease-fire.' I did not do this merely to draw attention to the fact that it had some relationships with this. The motive in getting agreement is to stop the fighting. Therefore, to talk now of something, which would lead to greater violence is not in conformity with this. The second is, "the conditions prevailing at the time". I shall deal with that at length later. Then it stated:

> The principle *in dubio mitius* must be applied in interpreting treaties (Krishna Menon: That, again, is important). If therefore, the meaning of a stipulation is ambiguous, that meaning is to be preferred which is less onerous for the party assuming an obligation. (Krishna Menon: in this case, we are asked to be the parties who are to assume the obligation, and, therefore, if there is an ambiguity, the meaning that is less onerous to us must be taken) or which interferes less with the territorial and personal supremacy of party (Krishna Menon: what could be more on all fours with the present case?) or involves less general restrictions upon the parties.

It is also stated:

> If two meanings of stipulation are admissible according to the text of a treaty, such meaning is to prevail as the party proposing the stipulation knew at the time to be the meaning preferred by the party accepting it.

That is the case here, because when we accepted the two resolutions we accepted the stipulations and the meaning of their letters of assurance and the aide memoire. These were known to the other side. Therefore, that meaning is to be preferred. There are a large number of other conditions, but these are sufficient for my purposes. It is also stated that:

> It is well-established rule in the practice of international tribunals that so-called preparatory work (travaux preparatories), i.e. the record of the negotiations preceding the conclusion of a treaty, the minutes of the plenary meetings and of committees of the Conference which adopted a convention, the successive drafts of a treaty, and so on—may be resorted to for the purpose of interpreting controversial provisions of treaty, and so on—may be resorted to for the purpose of interpreting controversial provisions of treaty (Krishna Menon: That is what I have done, I have gone into the minutes of the Commission, into the letters, and so on). The Permanent Court of International Justice has frequently affirmed the usefulness of preparatory work.

Therefore, even if there were, and there is not, a high-level treaty as between our two countries, or an agreement of the nature of a treaty obligation, either registered with the United Nations or entered into with the Secretary-General, it would still be bound by these commitments. We say that one of our commitments in this matter is accession. There we have a commitment. We have accepted the obligations which are laid on us under our Constitution. We have no obligations which are laid on us under our Constitution. We have not only accepted a legal obligation, but also political and moral obligations, because to throw accession away would be to throw the whole of India into chaos and we would upon the door to dismemberment, and our unity and national sovereignty is something which we prize. Therefore, under the circumstances, we are not prepared to permit a challenge to the validity of this accession. That is our commitment, and on that commitment we stand.

We have another commitment to which I shall refer a length later. That is the cease-fire commitment, and we shall honour it. But we have no other commitments.

The Foreign Minister of Pakistan said that in regard to this Kashmir matter, he had no other international obligations than those that are to be found in these resolutions. I agree with that, but to a limited extent in the sense that we have to interpret this agreement in the terms of these two resolutions to which I have referred, but if it means that the international obligations of the Charter are not binding, then I join issue with him. I am prepared to confirm that I subscribe to the view that in the discussion of any procedure, of any particular decision, of any agreement reached, these resolutions are what are binding in the circumstances I have submitted to you. But it would be wrong, so far as are concerned, for a Member State to argue that there are no other international commitments. That Charter is a commitment for every State, and when the time comes to sum up these observations at the conclusion of thee meetings of the Security Council, we shall fall back upon our bounden duty to ask all of you to address yourselves to the provisions of the Charter. Therefore, no Member state, in our submission, may say there are not other international obligations. I feel sure that that is not the meaning of the statement made by my colleagues, but I wish to be clear on this point.

**Firoz Khan Noon** (Pakistan): I am sorry but that is a misinterpretation of my statement.

**President:** You have no right to interrupt.

**Krishna Menon:** I will read out the quotation. I thought that by not doing so before I could save time, but it will be seen that my slow procedure is the quickest in the long-run. The representative of Pakistan said:

Pakistan is equally convinced that the international agreement for the plebiscite is one indivisible whole (Krishan Menon: we agree). No party to the dispute has the right to accept it in part. If India, a party to the dispute (Krishna Menon: Which does not exist) makes an attempt to freeze the situation as it exists, Pakistan would consider it as a repudiation of the international agreement...I want to make it clear that Pakistan recognizes to international obligations with regard to the State of Jammu and Kashmir except those she has voluntarily accepted together with the Government of India in the resolutions of UNCIP dated 13 August 1948 and 5 January 1949 (S/PV. 761, p. 37).

I should not have referred to this without quoting it, but I submit that, in my own reading of this, it does not exclude our commitments under the Charter. It simply means that there are no other agreements of the type of these resolutions or plans of that charter outside these two resolutions. I was trying, in my statement, to elicit information on this point in the reply of my colleague. So far as the Government of India is concerned, for the moment we assume that this means that so far as commitments of this kind are concerned, these are the only two resolutions. That is also our position.

Could I now rest on this instalment at this time?

## (3)

Krishna Menon was dealing yesterday with the responsibility for the non-performance or the non-implementation of the plan that was put forward by the United Nations commission for India and Pakistan on 13 August 1948 and 5 January 1949, the resolutions of those dates together forming one document—a plan of settlement and not a resolution with the character of a decision. That plan, I pointed out, was a plan which contained contingencies, and, for the performance of Part III, which is the plebiscite, called for the achievement of what are generally called conditions precedent. This issue has been, for a long time, how these conditions precedent should be brought about.

In view of the urgency of the cease-fire because of the considerable slaughter that was going on, the very strongly expressed and repeated views of the Government of India on the necessity of avoiding further bloodshed, and the insistence of Pakistan, on the other hand, that the cease-fire could come only after political considerations—in view of all that, this plan was put forward and accepted by us with these contingencies in it.

The important point to remember is this when that plan was put forward, it was not contemplated by the authors—it was not the intention of the Commission or of the Government of India or of the Government of Pakistan—that this should be something lasting over a period of eight or nine years.

At any rate, before we approach this problem, we ought to look into the responsibility for non-performance.

I not only freely conceded, but I volunteered the point, that, if there is a plan which requires conditions precedent and if one party, willfully and *mala fide,* impedes the performance of those conditions, then there is a charge of inequitable behaviour against it.

Those are the charges which the Foreign Minister of Pakistan set out in his statement before the Council. On pages 19 to 21 of the verbatim record of his statement, contained in document S/ PV. 761, there are eleven points put forward to show how India obstructed the performance of Part II. If these were correct, they would not by themselves answer the whole case because, as I said yesterday, there are certain basic conditions which, overruling Pakistan's objections, the Commission laid down, and which are incorporated in these agreements.

Before I attempt to deal with points seriatim, there are two matters which I wish to dispose of. One is that I see before me a draft resolution under the names of Australia, Columbia, Cuba, the United Kingdom and the United States of America. I want to say here and now that I am making this statement today without any reference to the resolution, and the reason I want this to go on the record is that I want the people of my country to appreciate that this resolution has been put forward by its five sponsors before hearing the statement of the representative of India—especially after I said last evening that I still had to argue this case. I am not making my detailed comment on it at the moment. All I want the Security Council to be seized of is this: For the purpose of this morning's statement, I am not taking this resolution into account.

The next point on which I want clarification or a ruling by the President is that I would request reference to sub-paragraphs (5) and (6), on pages 19-20 and 21, respectively, of the speech of the Foreign Minister of Pakistan, in document S/PB. 761.

These refer to the good offices of Commonwealth Prime Ministers. Now if the reference implies that this matter came before the meeting of Commonwealth Prime Ministers, then on behalf of my Government I want to register categorical denial. I myself have been present at every meeting of the Commonwealth Prime Ministers since Pakistan and India became members of that group. There has been no meeting of Commonwealth Prime Ministers in the sense that these meetings which are usually convened at convenient intervals were devoted to this matter. This matter was sought to be raised by Pakistan and it was never agreed to be discussed.

If, on the other hand, the Foreign Minister of Pakistan is referring to private conversations that might have taken place between Prime Minister and Prime Minister, or with small groups of Prime Minister, then I would ask for a ruling from the President. Either these paragraphs stand withdrawn or we have freedom to refer to confidential documents, because my Government cannot take up the position of having the name of our Government and our Prime Minister and of his colleagues used in this way without referring to the documents. I have the confidential reports of these conversations. We have regarded them as top secret documents. But I will take the responsibility, so far as we are concerned, of going into their contents, provided that is the wish of the Security Council.

We cannot have allegations made from private document without opportunity to use those documents in rebuttal. Therefore I ask for your ruling, Mr. President. Either these paragraphs must stand withdrawn or I will quote from the documents.

**The President**: The President has heard the statement of the representative of India and he cannot make a ruling on any statements made in connexion with the question before this body. The representative of India has the right to make a reply as he chooses and to make such statements as he may make, as the representative of Pakistan also has the right to make his own statements and deny whatever the representative of India has stated here. But the President cannot make a ruling on a statement made by a representative before this Council.

**Krishna Menon**: With great respect, that is all I ask for, because the responsibility for the revelation of these conversations does not rest on the Government of India. When confidential conversations are referred to by responsible persons in a forum that is not concerned with that, then the Government of India has no alternative but to tell the whole story, and that is all I ask for. Therefore, I should like to refer to the first proposal of the statement of the Foreign Minister of Pakistan. It is necessary to refer to these allegations seriatum because we are not able to subscribe to these things and, what is more, they are contradicted or modified by the documents available to the Security Council in such a way as to make this picture very different from what is sought to presented. I will read the first allegation:

> (1) In March 1949, the United Nations Commission convened a joint committee of the India and Pakistan representatives, at which it was agreed that both India and Pakistan would submit their plans for the withdrawal of forces to that committee. Pakistan did so: India first asked for more time and later refused to honour this agreement. (*S/PV.* 761, pp. 19-20).

The charge is that the Commission asked for the withdrawal of forces, that Pakistan offered a plan and that we did not co-operate. If that were true in the way it was put, that is certainly a grave lapse on the part of the Government of India and may be counted as a point in part of non-performance. I now wish to refer to paragraph 229 of the third interim report of the Commission. The Commission has something very interesting to say about this:

> In early March the Commission received the first concrete indication of the manner in which one of the parties envisaged the implementation of the truce.... The Pakistan delegation held (a) that the objective of the

> truce agreement is to create a military balance between the forces on each side and (b) that the withdrawal of her regular forces depended upon plans acceptable to the Pakistan Government for the synchronization of this withdrawal with that of the bulk of the Indian forces.

What I read out now is the Commission's findings. But in another part of the report, paragraph 169, the Commission says:

> The Government of India did not agree with the premises on which the plans of the Pakistan delegation were based. The Indian delegation informed the meeting that it was unable to respond to the Pakistan delegation by presenting a similarly comprehensive plan, until a basis for agreement was reached. The meetings were adjourned. Subsequently, on 28 March the Commission received the Government of India's own views.

What is said in the statement of the Foreign Minister of Pakistan is that the Government of India did not submit its views: the Government of India refused to honour this agreement. But I will read out what the Commission said:

> ...the Commission received the first concrete indication of the manner in which one of the parties....

The Pakistan delegation held such and such a view. We pointed out before in our statement, the Commission had already rejected both the (a) and (b) proposals of Pakistan. Now the principle which the Commission had rejected, that was brought before the Commission. The Government of India reiterated its position. What is more, the Commission goes on to say that on 28 March the Commission received the Government of India's own views. So both parts of that statement are inaccurate.

The next allegation is as follows:

(2) After many months of efforts, the United Nations Commission came to the conclusion that India was not prepared to withdraw the bulk of its forces from Kashmir and was seeking to cover this refusal by misinterpreting the Commission's resolutions on the subject. The Commission, therefore, proposed that the differences arising from the interpretation of the two

resolutions—which constitute the international agreement on Kashmir—should be submitted to the arbitration of Admiral Nimitz, the designated Plebiscite Administrator. This proposal was endorsed by a personal appeal from President Truman of the United States and Mr. Attlee, the then Prime Minister of England, in August 1949. Pakistan accepted this proposal: India rejected it. (S/PV. 761, pp. 19-20).

Apart from the statement in regard to arbitration, there are two definite allegations here that the Government of India misinterpreted the resolutions of the Commission.

What are the facts? It is true that India rejected the proposal for arbitration that was made by the Commission at that time. May I say, this was not a question of general arbitration; it was arbitration on the topic which we are talking about, and these were the reasons which should have been set out. The arbitrator in this particular case was to have the authority not only to arbitrate in this particular case was to have the authority not only to arbitrate on this issue given to him, but also, if necessary, to determine the points on which he should arbitrate. I ask representative on the Council to show me one instance in the whole law of arbitration where the arbitrator is asked to say what he is going to arbitrate on. That strikes at the root of all arbitration. Arbitration is usually the appointment of a tribunal, to whom a case is referred with a request to give an award or find a reconciliation between two points of view. In this case this arbitrator was asked to arbitrate on whatever he was going to arbitrate on. That is to say, he would be the plaintiff and the judge. This was a novel procedure and without precedent, and could hardly be justified; and I ask anyone to show me an instance in the whole international arbitration procedure where this has been done.

The main difference between India and Pakistan in this particular matter of arbitration was on the disbanding and disbanding of the Azad forces—forces which Pakistan had all along denied were there. There was Pakistan participation; they did not communicate with the Security Council. The Security Council was happily passing these resolutions in total ignorance of what was going on. The information having been withheld. And later when this matter came up, the Commission gave assurances to us. Mr. Luzano, who was Chairman of the Commission at that time, wrote a letter on behalf of the Commission, which I read out yesterday. The main difference between India and Pakistan was on the disbanding of the Azad forces, because we did not think that a plebiscite could be held, nor could we agree to the idea of an insurgent government being recognized. And certainly it cannot be the idea of the Security Council—as it seems to be the plan going around—that the Security Council is going to stand behind some sort of insurgent authority.

The Commission had given us the assurance that there was to be large-scale disbanding and disbanding of these forces and it was on the basis of this assurance that India had accepted the resolution of 5 January 1949. This was, therefore, not a matter for arbitration but for affirmative or immediate decision.

The withdrawal of Indian forces has nothing to do with the Government of Pakistan. In fact, Mr. Zafrullah Khan asked that he should be informed as to the plan of this withdrawal. That is to say, our military operations should be disclosed to him. The Commission rejected the idea wholesale. Therefore, it was said that this was a matter for the Government of India and the Commission or its successor.

If arbitration was to be according to the UNCIP resolution, which is all we accepted, Pakistan could not be a party to those arrangements—I laid stress on this yesterday; the Commission agreed that Pakistan had nothing to do with them and had not right to be consulted at all. It was not a matter for us to decide with Pakistan.

In December 1949 the President of the Security Council, General McNaughton, acting as the Council's mediator in this dispute, formulated certain proposals for the demilitarization of the State of Jammu and Kashmir. Pakistan accepted these proposals; India rejected them.

What are the facts here? General McNaughton tried to place India and Pakistan on an equal level in this matter. Our position from the very beginning, irrespective of what the Security

Council may say, has been that this is not a dispute over territory. This is a complaint about aggression. And, irrespective of the assumption that there may be flaws in India's claim that the invader has no rights. General McNaughton's proposals tried to treat us as though we were two co-defendants in that matter. What is more, he equated Azad Kashmir with the Jammu and Kashmir Government and gave the former also a status in the matter, despite the Commission's definite findings against it.

He gave a formal recognition, therefore, to this Government which not even Pakistan recognized at that time. Pakistan did not recognize the Azad Government—perhaps for other reasons, but there it is.

These proposals of General McNaughton failed to take account of our respective positions in this dispute and did not preserve the agreements of 13 August and of 5 January. This only puts before the Security Council the position that I stated yesterday and shows that it was not something that we made up for this meeting. This has been our consistent position all along.

Now we go to paragraph 4:

The Security Council then appointed Sir Owen Dixon and authorized him in March 1950 to bring about the demilitarization of the State within five months. He formulated the demilitarization proposals in July 1950 and discussed them with the Prime Ministers of India and Pakistan. Pakistan accepted those proposals, India rejected them.

First let me say, by way of introduction to this particular point that the whole of the proceedings after 5 January are not concerned with the whole issue. They are only concerned with part 2, to bring about demilitarization—nothing else. It is a very small compass.

Sir Owen Dixon, now Chief Justice of Australia, went to India and to Kashmir and to Pakistan and he tried to establish, in the same way as General McNaughton did, a parity between India and Pakistan. What is more, he also brought in Azad Kashmir as though it were a de jure Government, and he also tried to establish parity between the State forces and militia on the one hand and Azad forces on the other.

It is not correct to say in this connection that we rejected Sir Owen Dixon's proposals. Sir Owen Dixon's proposals are interesting in this connexion. He came to two or three important conclusions, not that we accept them, but the Security Council should known about them. One conclusion he came to was that a wholesale plebiscite was neither desirable nor possible. So he suggested alternative plans for what has been called a compartmental plebiscite. At that time—and I want to say now that the Government of India is making no fresh commitment in this matter—we said we were prepared to look at it. We said at that time that we were prepared to examine this proposal, that is to say, to take a plebiscite over the different areas or perhaps agree that some parts had to go to India and other parts had to go to Pakistan. At that time we were certainly prepared to examine those proposals. It was not India that rejected them. Pakistan rejected from wholesale. That is the record.

There is something else that Sir Owen Dixon said. I referred to it yesterday and I shall refer to it again. That is that when they crossed the boundary they violated international law—a polite way of saying that they invaded another country.

Now I go to paragraphs 5, 6 and 7. I shall take all these together for your convenience, Mr. President, and the convenience of the Council, because they all deal with the same proposition. I should like to restate that there was no question of this Kashmir question being on the agenda of the Commonwealth Conference of Prime Ministers. The Government of India has objected and will continue to object to the discussion of this problem in any international forum other than the Security Council, which is seized of it.

It would be very wrong for me simply to say that there was no Prime Minister's meeting dealing with this or that no formal objection was made. There were conversations in 1951—I believe it was the second Conference after India decided to become a republic. There were talks with Mr. Menzies, the Prime Minister of Australia. I believe that there were talks before with the late Mr. Mackenzie King. There were always talks on large numbers of subjects; some of them had nothing to do with this matter at all. There was also an occasion when

Mr. Menzies and Mr. Attlee sat together with my Prime Minister for a private conversation, and Mr. Liaquat Ali Khan, the Prime Minister of Pakistan was also present.

In view of the delicate nature of Commonwealth relations and the bringing in of the names of these Prime Ministers, and for various other reasons, which will become more apparent when I read this resolution—and if I can claim the attention of the representative of the United Kingdom—I should like to read this note recorded at that time by my Prime Minister:

> This evening I attended an informal conference about the Kashmir question. This was originally fixed to be held at 10, Downing Street, but, owing to Mr. Menzies' illness, it was decided to hold it in Mr. Menzies' room at the Savoy. We met at 8.30 p.m. The Prime Ministers of the United Kingdom, Canada, Australia, New Zealand, Ceylon and Pakistan were present. We discussed the matter for about an hour.

I might recall here that the reason for having this informal meeting was that we had refused to have the matter discussed formally in the Prime Ministers Conference.

Mr. Menzies and Mr. Attlee made some preliminary remarks about the extreme desirability of the Kashmir issue being settled, more especially because of the world situation. They referred to a plebiscite having been agreed to and only the conditions relating thereto being subject to dispute. Mr. Menzies expressed his opinion that probably a limited plebiscite would be more desirable. He added that, as there were legitimate apprehensions in the mind of India in regard to the security of the State, it should be easily possible for a brigade or so of Commonwealth troops to be placed there for security reasons till the plebiscite ended. Australia would be glad to provide such troops as it was thought it would be a service rendered to the cause of world peace. Some reference was also made to the heavy expenditure on the defence of India and Pakistan (Krishna Menon: Then my Prime Minister gave his reply).

Mr. Attlee then turned to me. I said I was at least equally desirous of a settlement of the Kashmir question. This was to the advantage of both India and Pakistan, and we had made many attempts but thus far without success. They show obviously that it was not quite so simple as it appeared on the surface, or otherwise it would have been settled long ago. No doubt it will be settled sooner or later. I gave a very brief account of some of the difficulties and points that had arisen and added that two aspects were prominently before me. One was that no steps should be taken which might lead to an upsetting of the somewhat unstable equilibrium that had been gradually established between India and Pakistan during these past few years.

There was a grave danger that if a wrong step was taken it would rouse passions all over India and Pakistan and raise new issues of vital importance. That would be a tragedy.

The second point was that I could not deal with any proposal without reference to my colleagues in Delhi and Kashmir. So far as the Government of India was concerned we had gone there on the invitation of not only the legally constituted Government but also the largest popular party. Our responsibility was confined to defence, foreign affairs and communications. For the rest, the State Government was responsible, and we could not interfere with its discretion though we could advise them. It was neither possible nor advisable for us to come to a decision without the concurrence of the State Government.

This was in the early stages of our accession. The relations had not yet been built up.

Then the Prime Minister of Pakistan stated that the said Government was just a puppet appointed by me, and I could remove them or change them at any time. I took exception to this and told them something about the background of Kashmir and the National Conference and Sheikh Abdullah.

I had given a very brief resume of the events in Kashmir in the last few years, finishing up with Dixon and the proposals. I pointed out that Dixon had concluded that an overall plebiscite was not feasible and had therefore explored the possibility of a partial plebiscite. To the general principle of this I had agreed, subject, of course, to the other matters connected with it being considered and decided upon.

I made it clear that there was no point in discussing these matters until the principle was accepted by Pakistan, because at that time, in the discussions with Menzies, this agreement was to be by Pakistan and not by us, because we had agreed, subject to details, to the principle that Sir Owen Dixon had put forward.

Mr. Liaquat Ali Khan indignantly repudiated this. The Prime Minister of Pakistan thereupon said there was no question of an overall plebiscite not being feasible. There might be some difficulties, but obviously it could be done. I agreed that it could be done, though it might take time.

The question of feasibility did not refer to the practical difficulty of having an electoral roll, but, according to Dixon, to various other factors (Krishna Menon: Which are set out in the Dixon reports and some of which are referred to briefly in these conversations. I continue to quote):

> Mr. Menzies stated that he had not been able to understand why the Government of the State (Krishna Menon: This is important because it comes from Mr. Menzies) should be pushed aside or suspended because of the plebiscite (Krishna Menon: and here I would point out that was exactly what Pakistan was pressing for. Mr. Menzies went on):
>
> It could very well continue, although matters connected with the plebiscite might be handed over to the Plebiscite Administrator. Attlee agreed with this.

Now, the Government of India, I would recall, has raised no objections in this connexion—provided other conditions are satisfied. The conversations among the Prime Ministers then touched on the ethnic and linguistic divisions of the State. I quote from the conversations:

> I told them, also, that there was a basic difference between our approach and Pakistan's to the two-nation theory, and the insistence on religious differences coming into politics. While we had reluctantly accepted certain facts we never accepted their theory, and we

were not prepared to apply it to Kashmir in any event. (Krishna Menon: and here the reference is to the theory of a Muslim State and a Hindu State). That would be bad for Kashmir, but would be worse still for India and for Pakistan. It would go counter to the principles that governed us and might produce upheavals both in India and Pakistan. We had only recently witnessed an upheaval of this kind in Bengal, which had with difficulty been controlled by the Agreement between the two Prime Ministers.

Mr. Attlee pointed out rather warmly that past history did not quite fit in with what I had said. The division of India had largely been based on a religious basis. He did not like this religious basis at all, and he had tried to avoid it, but facts were too strong. Further, he said that ethnic and linguistic divisions were equally dangerous, and we in India were having to face this difficulty in various parts of the country. I said that we were not enamoured of ethnic and linguistic divisions, but in the circumstances, we certainly thought that any religious approach to a political problem was dangerous and explosive. We had never accepted that principle, and we did not propose to do so in the future. Right from the beginning of the Kashmir trouble, we had laid stress on this fact and had informed the United Nations Commission repeatedly that this appeal to religion must be avoided. In spite of this, the Pakistan Press was full of religious appeals and calls for 'jehad' (Krishna Menon: that is, holy war).

If this kind of thing was going to take place before and during the plebiscite period, then there would be no plebiscite but civil upheaval, not only in Kashmir but all over India and Pakistan.

Mr. Menzies then said that he quite agreed that religion should be kept out of the picture, and he had been much disturbed when he saw the Pakistan Press in Karachi.

(Krishna Menon: And this is Mr. Menzies speaking, not the Government of India):

Which was writing most irresponsibly on this subject....

The Prime Minister of Ceylon was silent throughout. Mr. Attlee then referred to river waters in connection with Kashmir and mentioned the international committee set up by Canada and United States. I mentioned that Mr. St. Laurent had drawn our attention to this last year, and I had stated subsequently that I would be perfectly agreeable to having subsequent consideration of the water problem as between India and Pakistan.

The delegation of Pakistan has not raised this objection during this series of meetings of the Security Council, but, had they done so, we should have had the answers. I continue to quote from the conversations of the Prime Ministers:

> The Prime Minister of Pakistan at one stage referred to ethnic divisions of Kashmir and said that, if necessary, a plebiscite could be held separately in these areas. At no time, however, did he accept the idea of a partial plebiscite. He insisted on an over—all plebiscite for the State, though this might be taken separately in different areas—presumably to allow these areas to decide for themselves.

As Mr. Menzies was not feeling too well and had a temperature, the conversations ended rather suddenly at about 10 p.m. Mr. Menzies concluded it by saying that we might perhaps think over the various suggestions made in the course of the conversations. These were, according to him, that, firstly the State Government should not be touched (Krishan Menon: Now, this is Mr. Menzies' opinion) and should continue except in regard to functions relating to the plebiscite: secondly, the Commonwealth might provide a security force and thirdly, the plebiscite might be held in different areas.

In the course of the conversations, no reference was made either by Mr. Liaquat Ali Khan or by me to the proposal about a Commonwealth force being sent. There was no mention of these talks being resumed.

I am sorry to have had to read out this long document. However, we have other matters to consider in relation to the countries involved—particularly in relation to Australia, which, though separated from India by miles of sea, is a very close neighbour of ours; in fact, we hope, as time goes on, to establish even closer relations with Australia then we now have. That is why I have read out this document.

**The President:** I call on the United Kingdom representative on a point of order.

**Sir Pierson Dixon** (United Kingdom): I am sorry to interrupt the representative of India, but I should like to make this brief observation.

Of course, I fully recognize that, since the representative of Pakistan has made an allusion to the discussions among the Commonwealth Prime Ministers, the representative of India naturally wishes to say something in that respect. I should, however, like to put this consideration to him, through the President: Of course, Mr. Menon is perfectly free to do what he likes in this respect, but, in view of the particularly intimate nature of these discussions among the Commonwealth Prime Ministers, I wonder it is desirable to give this textual account which he has been giving. I say this simply with this object in mind of preserving what is a rather special and particular institution—an institution which the three representatives of Commonwealth countries seated round this table value greatly, I know.

The representative of Pakistan made an allusion to these discussions. It seems to me that a summary is quite different from a textual account.

I have raised this point of order merely as a domestic concern of the three representatives of Commonwealth countries seated at the Security Council table.

**Walker** (Australia): I should like briefly to associate myself with the remarks made by the representative of the United Kingdom and to endorse his suggestion that it might be preferable if we did not follow the practice here of going into private conversations. I would just emphasize the fact that Mr. Menon read from his own Prime Minister's account of the private meetings. It has not been the practice in the past to publicize such private conversations. Of course, I recognize the right of the representative of India to bring before the Security Council any material which is at his disposal.

**The President**: The position of the Chair on the point of order raised is clear. On matters mentioned by representatives before this Council, if they are not insulting or libelous, the Chair cannot make any ruling. However, the representatives of the United Kingdom and of Australia have made an appeal to the representative of India, and I refer that appeal to him.

**Sir Pierson Dixon** (United Kingdom): I think that I may have spoken of three members of the Commonwealth, of course, I meant four.

**Krishna Menon:** I do not intend to take seriously Sir Pierson Dixon's forgetting one member, the sub-conscious mind projecting itself. I am prepared to leave it at that.

I must say that this intervention by the representatives of Australia and the United Kingdom is most extraordinary at this stage of the discussion. I can only conclude that, because of the general fatigue caused by listening to me, they could not have heard the point I raised with you, Mr. President. That would have been the time for the representatives of the United Kingdom and Australia to have said that they agreed with the representative of India that these matters should not be aired here, so let the representative of Pakistan, who has circulated these allegations all over the world, formally withdraw them. I am surprised beyond measure to see a diplomat of the experience of Sir Pierson Dixon telling me that when charges of dishonesty, charges of a serious character of breaking an agreement and of not trying to honour the second part of this agreement, are categorically made in the statement of the representative of Pakistan. I should not reply to them.

I presumed that the representatives of Australia and of the United Kingdom would have read the statement of the representative of Pakistan. What does it say? At the end of paragraph (5) it is stated "India rejected it" (S/PV.761, pp. 19-20). At the end of paragraph (6) it is stated: "Pakistan accepted this proposal; India rejected it" (*Ibid.,* p. 21). At the end of paragraph (7) it is stated "Pakistan accepted this; India once more rejected it" (*Ibid.*). The same thing is repeated all the time. These are definite allegations which reflect upon my Government and upon the Prime Minister of India, who participated in these conversations. I was entitled to read them, and my responsibility lies only with my Government.

Secondly, I should like to say here that I yield to no one in my desire to maintain Commonwealth relations, and I suppose that in my time I have contributed as much to this as anyone else at this table. I deeply regret that Sir Pierson Dixon did not raise his objection before, and I resent the observation of the representative of Australia that the account I was reading was my Prime Minister's account, thereby implying that it is not to be trusted. That may well be, but there is a different way of putting it. In that case, since the matter is now in court, let the Prime Minister of Australia come here and say what happened.

The time for this point of order was earlier than now, but even at this time I am prepared to have it taken out of the record, provided that the representative of Pakistan takes paragraphs (5), (6) and (7) out of the record. Why does this extreme sensitivity arise in regard to us? Why did not the representative of the United Kingdom, as the senior member of the Commonwealth, jump up and say, "It is not right for you, who are so close to us, tied to us with military alliances, and who we have always supported. Why don't you withdraw this, since it is not decent to refer to private conservations".

Am I to sit here and hear my Government challenged, and not use the material at my disposal? I went out of my way when I came here this morning to try your patience, Mr. President, by asking you to deal with this matter, and I think it is entirely wrong that an attempt should be made to convey the impression that we are behaving in a way that is inconsistent with all the nice things that the representative of the United Kingdom said. One way to preserve Commonwealth relations is to appreciate that it is a two-way relationship.

**Sir Pierson Dixon** (United Kingdom): In view of what my colleague from India has said, I must make it clear that all I appealed to him to do was not to read out the textual account of these private conversations. I did not suggest that he should make no allusion to them, because my colleague from Pakistan has already made that allusion. As I said when I raised this point, clearly my colleague from India will wish to make a reply. The only point I was making, and I had hoped it was clear to the Council and to my colleague from India, was to suggest to him the undesirability of reading out a textual account which, as we have heard. Contains a lot of quite intimate remarks about people's health and that kind of thing. It does not seem to me that it is conducive to the development of this discussion to do it in that way, and I should have thought that was a perfectly reasonable point.

With regard to the time when I should have raised that point, that surely is entirely within my discretion. I must say that it never occurred to me that Mr. Menon would in fact read out actual textual accounts. Had I thought that, I might have raised the point when Mr. Menon asked for a ruling.

**Walker** (Australia): I said that I thought that the representative of India was at liberty to use any material and information at his disposal. In my concluding remarks, I only intervened in support of my colleague, Sir Pierson to reinforce his appeal that detailed records of these private conversations should not be read out here is that could be avoided. I think that Mr. Menon misunderstood my remark that the record from which he read was his own Prime Minister's record. At private conversations the various participants normally keep their own records, and it is certainly not my introduce any such competing material or to make any suggestions at all regarding the accuracy of the record kept by the Prime Minister of India. I just did not that the document being read from was not an official report of the Conference but just private record.

**The President**: While it is interesting to listen to this British Commonwealth family discussion, an appeal has been made to the representative of India, and the representative of India may proceed.

**Krishna Menon:** With great respect, I submit that this is not a "family discussion". It is a point of order raised in connexion with the proceedings of the Security Council. If, in the exercise of your office as President, you at any time call me to order I will obey you. But I am not going to be pushed into the position of not stating the position of my Government. I look around this table and I know that I have got to fight my battles. We will see more about it in the subsequent meetings. The record is there.

I stated categorically and very plainly that I was going to read the notes of these discussions and that is in the record. Therefore, there can be no reason for Sir Pierson Dixon to tell the Council that if he had known or if he had thought that this was as intimate as this, that and the other and something else was going to happen—I do not think that is correct.

In what position is the representative of the Government of India? Certain allegations are made about a private conversation by one party, a conversation at which I was not present. Would the Council have been satisfied, if I simply had said that paragraph (5), (6) and (7) (S/PV, 761, pp. 19-21) are inaccurate or if I had given an incorrect narration of it? When the representative of Australia tells me "That is you Prime Minister's record", he should have told me that "That is your version of what your Prime Minister's record is". That would be another step removed. Therefore, I had no option. But at the same time, if I am allowed to, I will make an appeal to Sir Pierson Dixon to exercise some degree of fair play in dealing with different members of the Commonwealth—at least in public. As an earnest of my intentions, I am prepared, if the President agrees, that in the written record a summary which does not relate to the matters which are relevant to these items (5), (6) and (7) may be included. The only reason I read everything out was that I did not want it to be said afterwards that I was selecting extracts. Therefore, as I said, I do hope that the representative of the United Kingdom will be able to follow the practice that has obtained in the past of at least in public exercising some degree of fair play as between two members of what the President calls "the family". The objection should have come several days ago when these items (5), (6) and (7) were read out. I should have objected then, but I did not want to interrupt because the President would have called me to order as I am not a member of the Security Council. I therefore say as an earnest thereof that I am prepared to have inserted in the official records only, if the President agrees with us that is a correct summary of what I said here, a summary of the contradictions or the untrue allegations that are made in these paragraphs (5), (6) and (7). I think that in the position we find ourselves here it is necessary for me to substantiate every statement I make from the record. It may be boring, but then we have suffered in the past in this discussion by trusting too much to the good sense of everybody all around. We therefore propose to state our case in such a way that at least posterity will know where the truth is. Therefore, this is my response to the appeal of Sir Pierson Dixon. I do not expect any response in return. Not that it would not come, but I do not expect it. Is that agreeable to the President?

**The President**: Yes.

**Krishna Menon:** Now we come to paragraph (8) (*S/P V.* 761, p. 21) which refers to some mediation or some endeavour by the then President of the Security Council, Mr. Muniz. This is the same point about arbitration, so I do not want to repeat the argument which I have given. Paragraph (9) also relates to the same thing.

Paragraph (10) relates to the intervention of *Dr. Graham,* the United Nations representative, stating that he "put forward a number of proposals on the subject of the demilitarization." It sates that "each one of these was accepted by Pakistan, but rejected by India". Now, there can be no objection to going into the facts of this case because Dr. Graham is not a member of the Commonwealth. The full position in regard to paragraph (10) is that India also accepted and not, as was said here, that India rejected it. India accepted the proposal that demilitarization should be a single and continuous process. That is the first denial. The second is Pakistan's assertion that it accepted without exception all demilitarization proposals which were rejected by India, that is not correct.

Dr. Graham suggested in his proposals of 4 September 1952 the following criteria for fixing the quantum of military forces on each side of the cease-fire line, the actual figures to be decided at a conference of civil and military representatives of the two Governments. On the Pakistan side of the cease-fire line a minimum number of forces are required "for the maintenance of law and order and of the cease-fire agreement, with due regard to the freedom of the plebiscite". That is Dr. Graham's proposal.

On the Indian side, a minimum number of forces are required "for the maintenance of law and order and of the cease-fire agreement, with due regard to the security of the State and the freedom of the plebiscite". India considered that these principles—and this is where the contradiction comes in, the contradiction to the Pakistan allegation—were conceived in the right spirit and as a basis for the evolution of a suitable definition of functions of the forces on both sides of the cease-fire.

India considered that the principles contained the germ of a settlement but despite several efforts to evolve a suitable draft in terms of the language used in the Commission's resolution, no understanding could be reached with the Pakistan Government. Paragraph 10 says it was accepted by Pakistan and rejected by India; the facts are exactly the reverse.

From the informal discussions in the Indian and Pakistan Committees in December 1953, the Indian Committee suggested that after the withdrawal of the Pakistan Army the disarmament of the Azad forces which, as will be remembered, was part should remain 21,000 Indian troops in addition to the State Militia on the Indian side and a Civil Armed Force of 6,000 men on the Azad side, half 'Azad', half 'non-Azad', all of them armed, if necessary. The Indian side therefore made some concessions in this matter: first, a substantial increase in the civil armed forces on the Pakistan side, which was totally against the assurances that had been given to us, from the 4,000 originally proposed to 6,000; secondly the readiness to come to a satisfactory solution about the ration between the armed and unarmed forces, as well as the type of equipment to be supplied and even to the extent of all the civil force being armed, if necessary—previously India had insisted that half of the force should be armed and the other half unarmed; thirdly acceptance of the Pakistan point of view about the security of the northern areas and the consequent need for the retention of their scouts, that is to say, as a matter of compromise although it no longer binds us—and I want that to go into the record—we even agreed that in the places which these people have militarily occupied we were prepared to recognize the existence of the scouts which were established, as I shall point out later under the British administration and who surrendered this territory without anybody's authority. In spite of these concessions, the Pakistan Committee did not accept proposals. I ask whether that corresponds to the allegations made in the paragraph referred to.

Paragraph 11 deals with the resolutions adopted by the Security Council at its 61th meeting urging:

> ...the Governments of India and Pakistan to enter into immediate negotiations under the auspices of the United Nations representative for India and Pakistan in order to reach agreement on the specific number of forces to remain on each side of the cease-fire line at the end of the period of demilitarization, this number to be between 3,000 and 6,000 armed forces remaining on the Pakistan side of the cease-fire line and between 12,000 and 18,000 armed forces remaining on the Indian side of the cease-fire.

Our answer to this is that while the Government of India could not accept a resolution which suggested a number of forces which in India's view was insufficient for security, the Government of India did enter into further negotiations with Dr. Graham—and it is only normal to suggest that the Government of India must be the judge of what forces are required for the security of the forces themselves in his very large area. There was no question of total rejection at that time; we did enter into negotiations with Dr. Graham afterwards.

That concludes the comments with regard to the allegations made. It will therefore, be seen that out of these eleven statements made, every one of them is incorrect. In the majority of them, the position is exactly the reverse. And if arguing a case before this body has any value on the decisions it makes or any impact on the Governments represented here, I beg to submit that this refutation, with chapter and verse from the documents, must be regarded as an important item.

Therefore, the charges of non-performance, in my submission, are wrongly laid at our door. On the other hand, while we are not responsible for the conditions of non-performance, as I have already pointed out, we went a long way, even departing from the assurances we had received, even allowing these rebel and Pakistani forces on the other side to be armed and virtually taking into account the position that time had passed and some crystallization had taken place. All that went by the board. Therefore, it is not as though we did not try very hard, it is not as though we did not meet Dr. Graham or Sir Owen Dixon, or any of these people, or even that the Commonwealth Prime Ministers agreed with the view of the Pakistanis.

At this stage, especially in view of the intervention of the representative of Australia, I will take the liberty of reading paragraph 21 of Sir Owen Dixon's report to the Security Council which is an important paragraph. And if the Security Council decides, and I hope it will, that the primary concern is obedience to the Charter and the sanctity of the provisions of the Charter with regard to territories, then it will pay heed to this. This paragraph states:

> Upon a number of occasions in the course of the period beginning with the reference on 1 January 1948 of the Kashmir dispute to the Security Council, India had advanced not only the contention to which I have already referred that Pakistan an aggressor, but the further contention that this should be declared. The Prime Minister of India, at an early stage of the meeting (Krishna Menon: that is, the meeting with Sir Owen Dixon) made the same contention and he referred to it repeatedly during the conference. I took up the positions, first that the Security Council had not made such a declaration; secondly, that I had neither been commissioned to make nor had it made any judicial investigation of the issue; but thirdly that, without

> going into the causes or reasons why it happened, which presumably formed part of the history of the sub-continent, I was prepared to adopt the view that when the frontier of the State of Jammu and Kashmir was crossed, on I believe 20 October 1947, by hostile elements, it was contrary to international law, and that when, in May 1948. As I believe, units of the regular Pakistan forces moved into the territory of the State, that too was inconsistent with international law (S/1791, p. 29).

We have not held back anything that is used against us. But this was finding of one of the investigators who, on balance, was not favourable to the Indian position and had a considerable number of reservations. But on this issue, with his judicial training and with the facts before him—every lawyer knows that whatever may be the right of the occupant, no trespasser has a right to priority—he said that. So here is a categorical statement in a report of the U.N. Representative that there was an aggression.

Therefore, we say that, even assuming for argument's sake—which I do not assume and I do not ask the Security Council to accept—that India has not been forthcoming in all these matters. The primary question remains that Pakistan came here as an invader; it tried to change the situation by force of arms—we did not obtain accession by force of arms—it tried to unite Kashmir with its country by force of arms and, what is more, the worst part of it was that it did not keep the Security Council informed about it and kept the information away from the Security Council not only once but continually and this has been repeatedly referred to in the report of the Commission.

Another condition that the Commission laid down—and as I said before they were obsessed by this conception of the cease-fire when this agreement was concluded that they realized that it was necessary to create an atmosphere of settlement. Our submission and the statements of Pakistan Ministers are included in document 2. I want to say that this document is not up to date or even complete. A great amount of vitriolic abuse has been showered on our country and our statesmen by name, some of which is unprintable and some of which I would like to read out later. There is so much that I can give you only samples.

That is, in our opinion, a serious condition that has seriously affected the non-implementation. That is to say, it is not possible to agree to open out one's country to the entry of other people during a plebiscite period or to throw the whole of the established conditions into an unsettled state when, on the other side, there is always this campaign of war. Some of these statements, which I do not propose to read out are by members of the Legislative Assembly. The Pakistan Government statements. There is the press of Karachi, and papers founded by Mr. Jinnah himself, and statements of their own Ministers.

For example, there is a statement by Sardar Abdul Rab Nishtar, who was at one time in charge of Kashmir affairs and was the Governor of West Punjab—not an irresponsible person. This is what he said:

> Mr. Nehru understands only the language of force. We will have to exhibit our strength if we want to take Kashmir.

Another statement:

> We would not mind being cut into pieces but will certainly conquer Kashmir.

These are the people who accepted the agreement.

Then there is this statement by the Chief Minister of the Northwest Frontier Province, from whose territory these raiders came in the beginning:

> You can take it from us that the day we became desperate and lose all hopes of a just solution of the problem, not only the entire Pathan population of Pakistan and the tribal areas will rise up for the holy 'Jehad' in Kashmir, but our brothers from across the Afghan frontier will also throw in their lot with us for the cause.

That is an invitation to another country for a military attack upon our own people. The Governor of West Punjab, Sardar Abdur Rab Nishtar, also made this statement:

> So long as a single Pakistani is alive, nobody dare snatch Kashmir from Pakistan by force...if the problem is not settled immediately, the whole of Asia would be engulfed in the flame of war which might lead to a world conflagration.

*The Times* of Karachi of 16 August 1956 contains the following report of a statement made by Choudhry Mohamed Ali, who was then Prime Minister of Pakistan and who is, I believe, coming to Washington shortly as Ambassador:

> I am ready for the liberation of 'Kashmir', he said, and added, 'but I want the people to get ready'. The freedom of Pakistan would not be complete without Kashmir, he asserted, and exhorted the people to acquire the spirit of unity, faith and discipline.... He said the Kashmir dispute was now going before the Security Council (Krishna Menon: that refers to this meeting); but asserted that the nation would not rest there.

That statement was by the Prime Minister, by a man who is reputed to be a man of extreme moderation in language. We are told in his statement that this reference to the Security Council is only preliminary to other action. That is what the Foreign Minister of Pakistan told us the other day—and I shall refer to that later. That is to say, the Security Council is to be given a chance—but, if necessary, "we will do something else".

I would be taxing to the Council if I were to read a great deal of this material. Some of it, a I have said, is from the newspapers, and any Government can say "We have a free press and they can print what they like", though it may not correspond with the facts that obtain in a particular place.

The Chief Minister of West Punjab had this compliment to pay to the Security Council.

If the United Nations proves to be a band of thieves (Krishna Menon: that is all of us) we will have nothing to do with it. We will prove that we can liberate Kashmir with the strength of our arms.

In this particular matter, it is also to be noted that even foreign observers who are not friendly to India in their comments on these matters, such as magazines published in the United States, have pointed out that the whole conception of the State of Pakistan in regard to its alliances is to attack India.

Here is Mr. Falk, of Chicago, in *Newsweek*:

> Pakistan is taking the United Nations for ride. This is evident from your report and from my observations in that country, where I worked until recently. Pakistan thinks it did us a favour by joining SEATO and the Baghdad Pact. They do not worry about the danger of Russian aggression. Pakistan leaders merely humour our concern about Communist expansion in order to get economic and military 'Bakshish' and to strengthen their hand against India.

And here is Mr. A.T. Steele, writing in the *New York Herald Tribune*:

> The average Pakistani thinks very little about the Communist threat if he thinks of it at all. His hostility is toward India rather than the Soviet Union. And he assumes that in the event of a showdown with India, the American military supplies will be drawn upon.

In regard to these last two statements, I want to say that our quoting from them has no reference whatsoever—and I want to say this categorically—to the intensions of the United States in regard to this matter. We are talking only about Pakistan opinion.

I will put these statements aside now. One could read all of them—and I hope the members of the Council will. They do not make very pleasant reading, but it is reading that is pertinent to the argument that we have put forth.

Then we have the situation involving the whole constitution of Pakistan itself. That is entirely an internal matter and we have no wish to interfere in it. In so far as it affects this situation of a State which is heterogeneous in character, where the people who do not belong to the Islamic religion do not have equal rights with the others in certain respects If that is challenged I will quote from the constitution, if it comes to that—it is not possible for us to take the view that the campaigns that go on are not of this character.

The next point I wish to refer to relates to the various violations that have taken place. And I want to say here and now that my Government does not wish to make a point of the normal kind of skirmishes and crossings of the frontier that can take place on a military cease-fire line which represents no natural division but is a line which is reached for convenience, so that the local villagers may not know about it, may go and snatch cattle, and so on. We are not referring to that kind of thing.

There have, however, been major incidents. I do not want to burden the Council with a description of a whole set of them. I shall therefore refer to only one—and that is what has been called the Nekowal incident.

Nikowal is a small village on the Indian side of the Jammu-Sialkot border. I refer to this incident because it developed into the proportions of a minor battle. On 7 May 1955, the Pakistan border police—and these police are not just body scouts in uniform, but armed police—opened fire without warning at an Indian party consisting of Major Badhwar, an officer on loan to the Central Mechanized Farm—he was there not on military duty—nine civilian employees and a small military escort of eight persons who were supervising the ploughing of land at a distance of about 500 yards from the village, on our side.

As a result of the firing by the Pakistanis, Major Badhwar and five other ranks and six civilians were killed, and one of the other ranks was wounded. We lost an officer and five men there.

On 8 and 9 May, the United Nations observers conducted a joint investigation at the site of the incident, on a complaint lodged with the United Nations observers' team of Jammu. Observers declared this incident to be a border violation by the Pakistan border police.

Immediately on receipt of the information about this incident, the Government of India lodged an emphatic protest with the Government of Pakistan and, in accordance with the internationally accepted principle for claiming compensation, demanded compensation of the Government of Pakistan, in the amount of 1,200 thousand rupees, for the moral and material wrong done to the Government and nationals of India as a result of this incident.

After a long correspondence in regard to the liability to pay compensation—not with regard to the incident, but with regard to the liability to pay compensation—the Prime Minister of Pakistan wrote as follows on 19 May 1956, and I should like to say that this is not a private letter but one that has been quoted in Parliament:

> While, for reasons given above, I do not consider that my Government is at all liable to pay any compensation in respect of the Nekowal incident, I am personally conscious of the human suffering involved in an incident where a number of lives have been lost. Having regard to this aspect of this matter, we would be prepared to make an ex gratia contribution of one lakh rupees to the rehabilitation of the relatives of those who lost their lives on the Jammu side of the frontier.

The point about this is that we agreed to this ex gratia arrangement in order not to exacerbate the situation.

This is only one of the incidents that have taken place and, by the time the United Nations observers get around to it, the trouble has already occurred.

There have been a considerable number of attempts at probing our frontiers. If I so desired, I could have given you a number of instances. They have taken place not only on the cease-fire line—and I am confining myself to Kashmir—but there have been offensive actions against us on the Indo-Pakistan border. And may I say here that we have few troops on this border. When statements of that kind are made, they are inaccurate. We have armed police outposts. And there have been skirmishes which have resulted in considerable loss of life in one or two instances, in which the army had to be called in.

Therefore, the responsibility for non-performance in regard to the conditions of Part II, in regard to the violations of international law, in regard to the campaigns of hatred that go on, and in regard to the non-maintenance of the peaceful atmosphere, is not on our side.

There is one other aspect of this item that I want to mention before I leave it, and that has to do with the northern areas. The northern areas are those areas Chitral, Gilgit and Baltistan—there is a map attached to one of these documents of which are very sparsely populated areas and which, to a very considerable extent, even under British occupation, have been left to the people who were there. In this areas, fist of all, Pakistan—against the resolutions of the United nations—has annexed territories and incorporated them. What is more, such incorporation had taken place before the resolutions of the United Nations, and the United Nations Commission was not informed about these matters; they came to know about it later. Now, what happened in regard to this area known as Gilgit, which is strategically very important to India and for its defence, where in the British Command? The territory was handed over to the Maharajah by the British when they left. Therefore, there is no question of this not being part of Kashmir. And the Maharajah sent there a Governor, and what was done was that these scouts arrested the Governor under the Command of Major Brown. On 31 October the Gilgit Scouts led by Major Brown and other officers—presumably of the Pakistan Army—surrounded his house and he never suspected that these people were going to attack him. But there were rifle shots exchanged and one round was fired in the air to frighten them away. But what happened was that this man arrested him, put him in prison and handed over the territory. Major Brown made a declaration, or something of that kind, and it was through him that this particular territory went over to Pakistan.

The point here is this, that there has been not even a popular rising in this place. The custodians of this area were the Scouts under British Command. The British Government had no responsibility in this matter because after they handed over the territory the Scouts remained as in independent force. But the British personnel handed over this territory and the accession was received from them. Now in view of the time, I propose to make that story very short. It is now occupied; it has been incorporated, and there is a considerable army in that area.

The other area to which I want to refer it Chitral. Chitral is mentioned as one of the territories of Pakistan in the Pakistan Constitution. Therefore, it is an outstanding instance of annexation de facto and de jure. And the Commission has said time after time that there can be no change in the sovereignty.

It is sometimes argued that Chitral was not part of Kashmir. But there are the records of the British Government, most of which are in our possession, which show that this area was under the suzerainty of the Maharajah of Kashmir, and all those territories that were under suzerainty were part of the State. Irrespective of the value of Chitral to one side or the other. Whatever may be done in the far future if ever there was an agreement between the two sides; the annexation of this territory, the receiving of accession from a former feudatory to the Maharajah who had no right to do so, is a direct piece of annexation.

Then there is the other argument, the final argument, in regard to non-performance, that the whole of the position of Pakistan in regard to the conclusion of the truce, if one were to summarize it briefly and state it in one point, which probably would not be as accurate as it should be. They insist on what they call a military balance. That military balance has been rejected by the Commission. I wish to refer the Council to paragraph 2 of annex 12 of the third interim report which says:

> The Commission, however, cannot accept interpretation that 'the declared objective of the truce arrangements is to create a military balance between the forces on each side'. There can be no other objective of the truce arrangements than to establish peaceful and normal conditions throughout the State such as will be conducive to the organization and holding a plebiscite. Similarly the process of synchronizing the withdrawal of the Pakistan and Indian forces to be arranged between the respective high commands and the Commission, in effect tends to create a corresponding situation on either

> side as withdrawal of one and reduction of the other. But in no way does this affect the ultimate aims of the resolution of 13 August....

I will not read the other paragraph in view of the time, but I would like to refer to paragraphs 203, 204 and 225 in the same report which deals with the same problem. The Commission has at no time agreed to the idea of military parity or a military balance. If it agreed to a military balance, then it would mean placing these two sides in a position of equality. The position which the Commission held was that it was inconsistent with the sovereignty of Jammu and Kashmir, inconsistent with the reference of the Security Council and, what is more, a condition in which the security of the State could not be maintained.

I shall now deal with the position to which I made some references today in quoting to the Council the international practice in regard to the interpretation of treaties and what are the conditions that should govern. I am not going to repeat that, nor am I gong to quote legal doctrine. But there is a well-established legal doctrine. But there are the main supporters of the United States of America and the United Kingdom, which say that the passage of time and the change of circumstances must affect the nature of agreements reached. That is very commonsense proposition. It is not necessary to quote Latin phrases in support of it.

With regard to time factor, the Commission, and India, and I presume, Pakistan expected the operation of part 3 of the agreements, that is the plebiscite, to be taken in reasonable time.

In that background, that the plan was accepted with all its reservations. Is it reasonable to expect that it would stand still in regard to the territory of Kashmir, over which India has active control, in the social, economic or political respects, taking into account the conditions that obtain in India itself? Therefore, considerable changes have taken place—economic, social and communication developments, for example and all these have brought about big changes in the state of affairs. What is more, the disturbance of the existing conditions is calculated to impoverish the people of Kashmir. When I refer to the conditions that prevailed there, under a later heading, it will be clear to the Security Council, if it is disposed to receive the facts and the arguments, that that is the position.

The other change factor I have already referred to, namely the consolidation of the occupied territory. Time after time it has been said in this report that there should be only local authorities—meaning *de facto* local authorities. There should be no consolidation of territory. Western Kashmir is practically a Province of Pakistan, administered by its Central Government. It has no local government and, therefore, has become integrated in that way.

The same applies to other areas, directed by the Pakistan Army or the Pakistan Government. This consolidation, the factual division of Kashmir that has been made by Pakistan occupation on the other side of the cease-fire line, is a change—condition which makes the operation of Part II very difficult.

We want to refer to other changed conditions of vital importance to our country. The Commission noted that there were forty-five battalions of Azad forces on the Azad Kashmir side. That does not apply to the northern areas, but only to Western Kashmir, where there is a population of 500,000 and it is there that there are these forty-five battalions today, according to our estimate. And these forces are officered by Pakistan officer and Pakistani-trained officers who go to Pakistan military schools, where there are a large number of commandoes organized for guerrilla warfare. These commandoes were organized and thrown back into the population. Their number may be only a few hundred—the last time I heard, there were only 800 of them, but that is not an absolute figure. They are being trained for guerilla warfare. This is something affecting the whole conception of the opening of the territory for a plebiscite. It would be imprudent for any country not to take note of these conditions. The Commission says in paragraph 203:

> The resolution of 13 August 1948 recorded one major change in the situation as contemplated by the Security Council during its deliberations in the early part of that year, namely, the presence of Pakistan troops in the State

> of Jammu and Kashmir. It did not, however, record a second element which has developed subsequently into a serious problem.

This, again, after the Security Council was seized of the situation and after the resolutions asking them not to make changes:

> in the implementation of that resolution: The Azad (Free) Kashmir movement, whose fighting forces today (Krishna Menon: that was in 1949) number some thirty-two well-equipped battalions. This movement, Muslim in character, has become the centre of strong and violent resistance to the accession of the State to India. It controls a considerable part of the western area of the State, claims to be fully organized as a government and its political activities appear to be directed toward the accession of the State of Pakistan. The Government of India, of course grants no recognition to the Azad organization and holds, officially at any rate, its existence to be a problem of internal public order. On the other hand the Government of Pakistan has rendered important assistance to the Azad movement; it has officered the Azad forces with officers of the Pakistan Army. Units of the Pakistan Army itself are present in Azad Kashmir and have operated in the closest cooperation with the local forces. However, Pakistan has not given formal recognition to the "Azad Kashmir Government". In a letter dated 6 September 1948 Pakistan informed the Commission that it could not make commitments on behalf of the Azad organization. The Commission has never negotiated with its representatives; having no international standing the organization can have no international responsibility.

The Commission states in paragraph 204:

> At the time that the Commission adopted the resolution of 13 August 1948 it had reason to believe that the Azad forces did not constitute a properly organized and equipped military forces and that consequently their

> disposal, once the Pakistan Army had withdrawn from the State, would not constitute a major difficulty....

The Security Council must draw its own inferences as to why the Commission came to the conclusion at that time that it was not a serious factor because the Pakistan did not inform it.

Paragraph 204 continues:

> In accepting the 13 August resolution, India apparently agreed that these forces could be dealt with after the truce became effective....

Does that sound unreasonable on our part?

Four months later, during the conversations which immediately preceded the Commission's resolution of 5 January 1949, the Government of India stressed the importance it attached to the disbanding and disarming of those forces as a condition vital to the holding of a plebiscite. The Commission agreed that a large-scale reduction and disarming of the Azad forces should take place.

Provision for this was made in the resolution of 5 January.

Then, the Government of India said, in a communication, that it was prepared to regard this as a matter of chronology. It did not ask that it should be done first, but that it should be done before the plebiscite was taken.

I am going to read another paragraph but I should like to omit all the others in view of the time. The Commission states in paragraph 225:

> There is, indeed no doubt that the Azad forces now have a strength which changes the military situation and to that extent makes the withdrawal of forces, particularly those of India, a far more difficult matters to arrange within a structure which considers only the regular forces of two armies. Although it might be a matter of discussion whether the numerical strength of the Azad Kashmir forces has actually increased since August 1948, there is no question that those forces, who have since then been working in close co-operation with the Pakistan regular Army and who have been

> trained and officered by that Army, have increased their fighting strength. It is reasonable to suppose that, if the Commission had been able to foresee that the cease-fire period would be prolonged throughout the greater part of 1949 and that Pakistan would use that period to consolidate its position in the *Azad* territory, the Commission would have dealt with this question in part II of the resolution of 13 August.

Could there be anything more conclusive in favour of what I have been saying? Therefore, those are changed conditions in regard to the army of that area.

I have already referred to the war of propaganda; therefore I do not propose to repeat it. Now comes the international position of the State of Pakistan. Here I want to preface my observation by saying that whatever I say does not constitute in any way a reflection upon the motives of the six other States represented around this table that are in military with one party in this situation.

My government has stated its position in regard to these matters. Wherever there has been opportunity of direct communication with Governments or of personal contacts, we have explained that we do not doubt their motives. We do not for a moment say that their purpose is to arm Pakistan against India. The question is, what will happen to this considerable amount of equipment that now goes into this territory, whereby the entire military balance has been altered?

If the representative of the United Kingdom, whose country had the responsibility at the time of the partition, would go into the history of that period, he would find that one of the main problems discussed at the time of partition was the balance of military forces and equipment on either side in order to maintain stability. Now that equipment has been upset; and therefore, the neighbouring country of ours, in dispute with us always threatening war and crusades and keeping up a campaign of hatred, has now at its disposal very considerable quantities of equipment for use on the ground and in the air. When we come to the question of the military preparations, I shall read out such information as we have. Therefore the equilibrium that obtained, at the time of the conclusion of the signing of this plan, which is called the Commission's resolution, no longer exists.

Whenever there is talk about the withdrawal of troops, which the Foreign Minister of Pakistan mentioned in his observations, all these factors have to be taken into consideration.

When India was partitioned, some seven or eight million people from either side went to the other country. It was an exodus which inflicted a great deal of hardship on the populations concerned. Fortunately for us, we have practically settled all of them. With an idea of the problem of the refugees, the Council will be able to see that there is a steady stream coming from the other side, with which we have to deal, but any change in this situation, any stirring up of trouble here, any attempt to unsettle conditions today, would start a scare and an influx of refugees. The first thing that happens when there is an influx of refugees is the slaughter of populations of the community in the country concerned. It may happen in India, and I fear it will happen in Pakistan.

To sharpen the statement I have to make this morning, I might take the problem of refugees itself. The Pakistan Foreign Minister, in speaking to the Security Council, referred to the 500,000 refugees that have gone into Pakistan. I do not know whether those refugees referred to were people from Kashmir alone or whether this is a reference to the 1947 period, when they were trekking both ways. I have no doubt that 500,000 people went through Kashmir into Pakistan. More or less may have gone; it is immaterial.

However, what is of relevance to us is the position now and the treatment of the minorities. Our present figures—and we have a very considerable organization for dealing with this—show that the migration of Hindus from East Pakistan to India was four million. The migration of Hindus from West Pakistan to India was 4.7 million. The migration of Muslims from India to East Pakistan was 1.5 million. The migration of Muslims from India to East Pakistan was 1.5 million. The migration of Muslims from India to West Pakistan was 6.1 million.

However, the important part today is the return of these people to India. The return, not of Hindus, but the return to India of Muslims have migrated to East Pakistan is at the present moment one million. What I said yesterday about our being a secular State stands vindicated. One million of the Muslim faith have come over from East Pakistan to us. About 100,000 have come over from the West to us.

In Kashmir itself, the Jammu and Kashmir Government have a very well-organized refugee organization. Whilst the Foreign Minister says that 500,000 people went through Kashmir at that time, the present figures show that 450,000 Muslim refugees from Pakistan-occupied Kashmir have returned to Kashmir and they have been rehabilitated. We have figures of them because this rehabilitation costs money, and the figures show that 450,000 of them have been rehabilitated. Similarly, 122,429 non-Muslim refugees have come into Kashmir from Pakistan-occupied Kashmir. That is to say, taking the two between them, ultimately nearly 600,000 people have come in as against 500,000 who went out. What is more, they are all rehabilitated.

Today our problem is the problem of people of either faith coming into India because of better economic conditions, because of the secular conditions, and so on. In case the Foreign Minister challenges me on that, I shall read a very short extract from a statement by his own Prime Minister of today. Mr. Suhrawardy questioned a member's statement during a discussion in the Pakistan National Assembly in October 1956 with regard to the treatment of peoples in their own country and why people of a non-Muslim faith should be loyal. This is what he said:

> You tell me today what signs have they (Krishna Menon: that is, the non-Muslims) shown of loyalty to Pakistan. My answer is clear. What have you done for them to get their loyalty? In what way have you shown them that you treat them in the same manner in which you have treated the Muslims? How many posts, offices, jobs, positions of honour and position of responsibility have you given them.

That is the statement of the present Prime Mistier of Pakistan. In East Pakistan there have been Government regulations in the way of official circulars asking firms not to employ people who are not of the Muslim faith and for the exclusion of non-Muslims from the cloth trade, which is held 80 per cent by them, and official instructions to all foreign oil companies for the exclusion of non-Muslims. There is an increase in the number of crimes against this particular section of the community, and the whole system of education is being placed on a religious and non-secular basis. What is worse, there is the wholesale cancellation of licences for fire-arms for the non-Muslim population, while there is a free distribution of them to the other side.

Those are the changed conditions that exist. In view of those changed conditions, how can the Security Council consider that the position that existed in 1949 exists today? If there were a possibility of the total withdrawal of all these forces and the restoration of law and order and peaceful conditions, that would be different. This is what has happened.

The repercussion of all these matters in India is very considerable. The instability that will be created in our part of the world is such that any attempt to inflict any hardship on the minorities in Pakistan is bound to have equal repercussions in spite of a very stern policy of our Government in regard to racial or religious offences. In spite of that, it will create trouble. When violence breaks out, it will break out in a very large way.

In dealing with changed conditions in the State, I must also refer to the economic and social position in the Indian-administered area.

In the first five-year plan, the State laid out $9 million; in the second five-year plan, $32 million. It has abolished what used to obtain in the old, feudal days, the compulsory levy of grain on the peasants. Debt conciliation boards have scaled down rural debts by 80 per cent. An area of over 50,000 acres has been brought into cultivation. About 3½ million pounds of fertilizer are distributed each year. One hundred half million pounds of fertilizer are distributed each year. One hundred thousand acres of land have been reclaimed during the last two years. Electric power has begun to go into the villages. Local installations of power plants and the purchase of bulk electricity from neghbouring India contribute a very considerable part of the light and power in the area. Four hundred and twenty-five miles of new roads have been built, and a large number of the old roads have been improved. New bridges have been built. The customs duties between India and Kashmir have been abolished. Factories have been opened for the manufacture of minerals the tanning of leather, and so forth. An industrial revolution is taking place in the area.

The most important change, however in so far as it affects the other factors which have been mentioned; relates to the visits of foreigners to Kashmir. During the days of the trouble, when actual hostilities were going on, we restricted, for security reasons, the entry of foreigners into Kashmir. In 1944, which was before the days of the trouble and a peak year for tourists, 27,000 people went to Kashmir in the tourist season: last year, 62,000 people went there, out of which 9,000 were non-Indians, that is, European and American tourists.

I turn now to the field of education. Over 500 new primary schools have been established, 126 middle schools, and seven colleges. Thanks to the operation of UNICEF, there has been an extensive campaign to improve health conditions, particularly as regards tuberculosis, which is one of the troubles in Kashmir.

In this connexion, I should like to read a few brief comments made by foreign observers. This is what a special correspondent of the *Manchester Guardian*—a United Kingdom newspaper—had to say:

> In Srinagar, rations have gone up from 18 to 24 ounces (Krishna Menon: of course, this may sound very small to representatives of Western countries) and the price has gone down by 10 per cent. The import duty on salt has gone, water rates have been lowered, Government servants' wages raised; and, to silence anti-bureaucratic feelings, peoples tribunals to examine corruption and nepotism are being set up; ...co-education is to go and education is to be free for all.

A special representative of the *Sunday Times,* one of the organs of British conservative opinion, said the following—which I quote because the Foreign Minister of Pakistan made references to suppression in the Indian-administered area of the State:

> The Prime Minister (of Kashmir) moved unescorted among crowds who garlanded him, and peasants showered lumps of sugar, signifying a sweet welcome, on his car; while everywhere there were shouts of 'long live' and women sang 'our breadwinner has come.'

This is what the special correspondent of *The Times of London* had to say:

> More than ` 20 million of debts have already been reduced to ` 3,500,000.... Irrigation is being extended, and improved seed and artificial fertilizer supplies at cost price.... Electric power is being increased, and industries...improved and expanded.

Similar accounts were contained in *The Economist* of London, *The New York Times,* Swedish newspapers, Egyptian newspapers, and so forth. Statements to the same effect have been made by ordinary visitors to Kashmir.

I have now described the changed conditions on our side of the State, that is, the Indian-administrated side. These changed conditions have a bearing on the Council's consideration of the present problem. The Council must view the resolution adopted in 1949 in the light of all the changed conditions and circumstances to which I have referred.

I turn now to conditions in the Pakistan-occupied part of Kashmir. In this connexion, I shall quote from our document No. 3, which, like the other documents to which I have refereed and shall refer, I ask to be received as an official document of the United Nations.

First, I shall read excerpts from a memorandum to the members of the Pakistan Constituent Assembly from the All-Jammu and Kashmir Muslim Conference, that is, the large national organization of Azad Kashmir to which the Commission referred as wishing to accede to Pakistan:

> For the last few years the people of Azad Kashmir in general, and those of Poonch (the sword arm of Pakistan and Azad Kashmir) in particular, have been subjected to great torture and terrorization. Account of this terrorism is very heart-rending. The Azad Kashmir Government, acting on the advise of the Ministry of Kashmir Affairs, is primarily and mainly responsible for the conditions that prevail in Poonch today. (Krishna Menon: The memorandum then goes on to describe these conditions as follows):
>
> Martial law imposed in Poonch last time was without any justification.... At least a dozen houses were blasted with dynamite, a number of poor families rendered homeless. Ruthless and random firing by mortar guns took place, resulting in many deaths....

Arrests of men, women, and in some cases of children were effected. About 400 persons are still under detention in the concentration camp at Pullandri.

These statements are interesting in the light of the reference which has been made to person detained by the Kashmir Government in the Indian-administered area of Kashmir. I continue to read from our document No. 3:

> ...the people have been arrested without any warrants of arrest, on mere suspicion or personal vendetta.... They are rotting in the concentration camps at Bagh, Bari, Pullandri and Sarswahy. They are forced to live under sub-human conditions...in Pullandri Jail 340 persons are detained in two rooms which have been built to accommodate only thirty-six person. Eighteen hundred gallons of water are required daily in this prison, but only 800 gallons are supplied.
>
> ...there is a concentration camp at Muzaffarbad also. The face of Ghazi Feroze Ali, Secretary of the Pullandri Muslim Conference, was blackened. He was dragged through the bazaar, garlanded with shoes (Krishna Menon: that is a form of insult in our part of the world) and the police spit upon him and hissed and hooted

> him for hours.... The same treatment was meted out to Abdul Aziz Maloti.

Women are arrested and subjected to unbecoming and insulting treatment:

> and there follows a description of ceases of molestation which I do not wish to read out.

The memorandum then refers to the collection of arms, and states that persons practicing legal professions in that part of the world have been terrorized. I continue to quote from the document:

> Arrests and detentions without trial are a common feature of public life now....

For the last six years people of Azad Kashmir have not been allowed to elect a government of their own. The refugees of Jammu and Kashmir half a million of whom are on this side of the cease-fire line, are living in sub-human conditions. Their rehabilitation has been entrusted to unpopular, callous and unsympathetic so-called leaders who serve the personal purposes of the officers of the Kashmir Affairs Ministry....

To say that Azad Kashmir has been developed economically is to deceive the world and yourselves....

The submission is not meant for propaganda purposes. It was sent to the Pakistan Constituent Assembly by a political party seeking some redress. The following quotation from the memorandum is very important to the Council's consideration of this case:

> The Kashmir Affairs Ministry (Pakistan) are the actual rulers of Azad Kashmir.... People of Azad Kashmir are stunned to see what Pakistan means to them and those in Indian-held Kashmir have become hesitant in their blind love for the Crescent....

The memorandum then demands the recall of all Punjab constabulary from Azad Kashmir immediately and the recall of most of the non-Kashmiri officers, the appointment of courts of inquiry, and the establishment of a legislative assembly.

I repeat that this memorandum is not meant for purposes of agitation or propaganda. It was sent to members of the Pakistan Constituent Assembly by the All-Jammu and Kashmir Muslim Conference.

I should now like to read out some excerpts from an appeal made to the members of the Pakistan Constituent Assembly by important representative of the people of Azad Kashmir. This appeal is also worthy of the Security Council's attention.

For the last seven years the people of Azad Kashmir and the Jammu and Kashmir refugees have not been given a chance to elect their own government. Governments have been imposed upon them.... The Ministry for Kashmir Affairs wields totalitarian control over the administration of Azad Kashmir.

The people who signed this appeal are all responsible persons in terms of Pakistan political life, according to their designations. They made this submission on the Azad Kashmir side. I have said nothing about the local conditions in the northern area, because it is very largely inaccessible, but the people live under very primitive conditions and the developments that have taken place in these areas are of a military character, to which I shall refer later.

In his statement, the Foreign Minister of Pakistan referred to conditions of repression and imprisonment in the heart of the Kashmir State which is not occupied by foreign forces. He read out a large number of names, and said that these people were in prison at the present time. I should like to say, because this will go out to India, that some of the persons he mentioned are not in prison now; they have been out of prison for a long time. He said that Prem Nath Bazaz, a Hindu, was in prison. He is not in prison. He was imprisoned for year, and was released a long time ago. The people were detained on the orders of the Kashmir Government. It was stated that Mr. Ghulam Ahmad Ashai is now in prison, but he was released in 1954. Another person mentioned, Mr. Pir Maqbool Shah Gilani was released about a year ago. Mr. Abdula Ghani Goni was released on parole in the middle of last year, and finally some months ago. Mr. Ghulam Mohammad Dar was released towards the end of last year, and Mr. Sardaruyddin Mujahid was released on 10 September last year.

I am putting all these facts before the Security Council because an attempt has been made to show that there is a reign of terror in our part of this country. Last summer 62,000 people entered Kashmir as visitors, and 9,000 of them were non-Indians, they were foreigners. A great many of them were newspaper correspondents, cinemamen—because it is a great place for taking photographs—tourists and writers. They traveled all over the country, and that fact is sufficient indication that there is not an iron curtain.

Reference has been made to Sheikh Abdullah. I have already read from his statement to the Constituent Assembly to show what his political position is. Sheikh Abdullah was placed under detention by the Government of Kashmir. There is a detention law in Kashmir, just as there is a detention law in India. This is piece of legislation which, in spite of our desires to maintain an abstract liberty, we found to be necessary in view of subversive movements in the country. Today, under this law, there are forty-nine people under detention in the whole, of Kashmir, a good many of them for acts which have nothing to do with political crimes.

What is the procedure under this law? First of all, their offences must be stated to the detenus. A man cannot just be detained, he must be told why. They have access to a tribunal of high level judicial persons who have to investigate the cases. Objection might be taken to this legislation, and there are some people in India who seriously object to it. The cases are examined by the judicial tribunal, which can order the release of a detenu, and the Government cannot refuse that release. They are not brought to public trial because there are reasons which may affect relations between States, not only with the State of Pakistan, but with other States. You have already heard, when I read from a document this morning, that my colleague from the United Kingdom quite rightly felt very concerned. I was more concerned, but I did not get any remedy for my concern though he got his. That is how the world is, Mr. President. If some of these men were brought to trial, the Government could not withhold any evidence under our system, whoever that evidence might affect. It would create an enormous number of difficulties, but I do not want to ask the Council to go into all the details. I simply wish to say that, even taking quantum of it, there are forty-nine persons under detention, some for short periods, some for longer.

It is quite true that the former Prime Minister of Kashmir is under detention, but may I say, without any offence whatever, that the present Prime Minister of Pakistan was arrested in 1948. It is one of those things that happen in times of social changes. My Prime Minister was under detention for a long time, and he has said that he learned a great deal during that period. The present Prime Minister of Pakistan was a prisoner of the former Pakistan Government, but I must say that he has not retaliated in the same way.

With regard to Sheikh Abdullah, in a document which I am now going to put in there are at least five or six extracts from testimonials to Sheikh Abdullah given in previous times by Pakistan publicists and ministers, and there is no name that was too bad for Abdullah at that time. The question is, at which time did he turn quisling.

The letter of the former Prime Minister, Sheikh Abdullah, has been put in as a document by Mr. Khan Noon, and I am sure that he will agree with me that the only way to understand correspondence is to put in both the letter and the reply. Therefore, I have assisted him by providing technical assistance in putting in the reply of Mr. Sadiq, the President of the Kashmir Constituent Assembly. The letter of Sheikh Abdullah, which was put in as a criticism of the Government and against accession and so on, was sent to the President of the Constituent Assembly in order to make certain protest. The President of the Constituent Assembly was elected. He sent a reply, so if the Security Council looks into the one letter it must look into the other. Therefore, in document 7 we have put the two together.

I have a great many more notes here about which I wished to talk, but I think you have heard me long enough. I shall only deal with the essential point that remains. I have no time to contradict every paragraph that appears in the statement of the Foreign Minister of Pakistan. There is, however, a misquotation from a Commission document which gives a totally erroneous impression of its meaning. I think that in saying that I am being moderate enough.

The present series of meetings are being held because of the letter dated 2 January from the Minister for Foreign Affairs of Pakistan to the President of the Security Council. In presenting his case, the Foreign Minister of Pakistan has done two things. First, he delivered what are threats. He indicated that trouble would brew. We have had an opportunity of comparing some of these statements with the statements made in 1947. They have, shall I say, a very close family resemblance, that is to say, if this is a beginning, especially if you read it parallel to the other statements I read out a while ago, that this does not end with the Security Council and they proposes to do something themselves, and so on. Mr. Khan Noon said:

> Here I would like to say that it is sometimes argued by India that everything is peaceful (Krishna Menon: we have only said they are peaceful now on the Indian-administered side on the contrary, we have said it is not on the other side) so why bother about Kashmir? But I warn you, (Krishna Menon: he warns the Security Council) that is a calm before the storm.

Now I ask you gentlemen whether this is the language of the Charter: "But I warn you, that is a calm before the storm. Everything is not peaceful." Mr. Khan Noon contained:

> We have just seen a telegram which states that on 11 January our Minister for Information Mr. Amir Azam Khan made a statement in Karachi that the Indians have massed their troops on our border. The excuse that Mr. Nehru gives is that he fears an attack from Pakistan, whereas we have not sent one soldier to our border. The fact that he is afraid of a war breaking out because of the Kashmir problem should assure the Security Council closes the door on a peaceful settlement we cannot say what will happen. If the Indian troops are there because

> India fears war between India and Pakistan, that should be a sufficient answer to those people who say that all is quite in the kingdom of Kashmir (Krishna Menon: It is not a kingdom any more) and India and Pakistan and the Security Council need not take any action.

Then he gives some advice to the Security Council:

> Please do not be misled by the fact that we are peaceful, that we want a peaceful solution.

The Security Council has had sufficient evidence adduced before it by me to show the nature of these intentions. Then he goes on to say:

> We are looking to the Security Council to do justice to these poor and poverty-stricken people (Krishna Menon: I have also read to you the conditions on either side) of Kashmir to whom it has promised a free and fair plebiscite under the auspices of the Security Council, which plebiscite has been denied to them for the last eight years.

That is a denial of fact because what has been promised is what is under Part III of the agreement.

I shall first deal with this statement. There is an allegation here which is of a serious character and I say with the highest respect to the Foreign Minister of Pakistan this should have been a subject of protest to my Government. That is the normal practice between two neghbouring Governments if either masses troops on its border. Now what is the position? In actual fact we have reduced the military strength in Kashmir recently. I referred this to my own Prime Minister and this is the truth. There is no truth whatsoever in the statement made by the Pakistan Minister for Information on 11 January. Of course, the Minister for Information, as you know, in peacetime is the reincarnation of the Ministers of Propaganda in wartime.

The United Nations observer teams are located all along the cease-fire line in Jammu and Kashmir. If there had been any massing of troops in that area, as alleged by Pakistan, the matter would have been immediately dealt with by the chief military observer of the United Nations group. That is with regard to the cease-fire.

If the complaint is that we are massing troops on the Indo-Pakistan border, along the Indo-Pakistan border in the Punjab—that is in the western area—there has been no increase in the strength of our troops. The Prime Minister at the moment is Minister of Defence as well as Prime Minister, so he ought to know. If at all, the strength of troops deployed on the border has decreased as the majority of border posts have been handed over by the army to the Punjab armed police as the local police, not of the State Government. I do not know why and where the information came from; it may be that some observation from the air miscarried. They probably mistook Pakistan troops for Indian troops; they look alike. That is quite possible, but I think the interesting part of it is that on this day, when we were supposed to be making all these great troop movements in preparation for war, the great majority of our generals were taking part in a polo tournament in Calcutta. That is not the way to wage war. Therefore, there is no substance whatsoever to it. This part of the propaganda of the Minister of Information. The Foreign Minister has only relayed what his minister of propaganda put out.

As against that, we have to take the position that not merely are their troops in Kashmir—and all of you sitting around this table representing independent State realize that the security of a country is a vital concern. All the Pakistan military concentrations of any importance are on our border. Abbottabad is sixteen miles from the Kashmir border. It is one of the main military concentrations. Rawalpindi, which is the General Headquarters, is thirty-one miles from the Kashmir border. Murree, where another concentration of the 12th Infantry Division of the Pakistan army is located, is fifteen miles from our border. Jhelum is four miles from our border. Kharian is thirteen miles from our border. Sialkot is six miles away, so that we are ringed around by Pakistan concentrations the whole time. In document 2, which has been distributed, there is a map which shows how this encirclement is carried out, so that when we talk about security we are just not producing an argument.

If you want any further details since the Foreign Minister has taken the liberty of making a public statement about the disposition of our troops which turns out to be inaccurate, I take the liberty of telling you how their troops are deployed in the Kashmir area. I did not ask the Pakistan Government where they got their information. I only pointed out that it was inaccurate. This happens to be accurate. Scouts in the northern area of Pakistan-occupied Kashmir—that is the Gilgit area—number 3,000. They are officered by Pakistan regular army officers. Formerly, there was a distinction between the A and B categories of the Azad battalions, but now it has almost disappeared. The militia has now become a regular army. All "Azad" Kashmir battalions and their training and equipment are on a part with Pakistan regular troops. Regular Pakistan army officers with Pakistan forces and scouts in Pakistan-occupied Kashmir are more than sixty. The Commanding Officer and Adjutants in most of "Azad" Kashmir battalions are from the Pakistan Regular Army. There is sprinkling of regular Pakistan officers also in all "Azad" Kashmir battalions and in the Scouts Organization.

As far as the deployment of troops is concerned—because it affects our security, as I have the distances—there is one corps in the Rawalpindi area, one armoured division in the Rawalpindi area, the 12th Infantry Division under the operational control of the 15th Infantry Division, three infantry brigades in the Sialkot area, and this division is under its operational control. In other words it is these nerve centres that control the entire territory of Kashmir under Pakistan occupation. Kharian and Jhelum are being developed as big based, only four miles from us and a new component for the armoured division to be used as a base for supplies of the new military equipment coming in under American aid.

Lashkars are being trained for military operations in the "Azad" Kashmir territory. Personal are drawn from the "Azad" Kashmir battalions and are trained by Pakistan personnel.

This is another important part of it. Most of the airstrips and landing—grounds are being widened and improved to take the latest type of jet aircraft. We have the length of these airstrips and the increased that have been made recently and we are quite satisfied that the increase in the length of these runways is for the purpose of taking the jet planes which they could not have taken before.

The 12th and 15th Infantry Divisions have been under the operational control of that part of Kashmir. Formerly this was the responsibility of the 12th Infantry division. The ex-armed forces personnel are being organized by ex-Major-General Akbar Khan and others, to raise a volunteer corps to liberate Kashmir. This is the same Akbar Khan who was not supposed to be in Kashmir but appeared under the name of General Tariq and who was prosecuted by the Pakistan Government for conspiracy against the Pakistan Government and now; I suppose, a new patriotic phase has emerged and he is going to liberate Kashmir. So the former insurrection leader has also been put into this thing. I would like the Security Council to take note of this position.

In regard to air bases in Northern Kashmir, Gilgit and Chitral are the two important airfields; they are on the Soviet-Chinese-Indian border and, according to the reports that we have, are being expanded and developed. Out course, that equipment can not be manufactured in Pakistan. Heavy Machinery and radar are reported to have arrived there. The Azad Kashmir forces have not air arm of their own. Before November 1948 there were only two cross runways in the Gilgit airfields; one was 915 yards and the other 650 yards. They were for the small observation planes of the British days to come down on. But now the runways have been increased to 2,000 and 2,500 yards. I do not think I will read out the remainder because it is highly confidential information.

I have said, and I would like the delegations of the countries which are in military alliance with Pakistan—and particularly the United States—to accept my assurance, that in any observations I make, no reflection that such assistance as they give is intended to be used against us. But unfortunately weapons of war have no magazine for intentions; their only magazines are for projectile power. You cannot decide before hand which way they will fire.

I will not quote statements from the newspapers or from legislators or agitators, it is too serious a matter for that. But I will quote the present Prime Minister, speaking at Lahore on 2 December 1956, not long ago, defended Pakistan's policy of military alliances. He said that when the Government of Pakistan decided to remain neutral and weak there was no immediate danger to its own independence—it is quite obvious it was not its own security:

"I see no country that is prepared to attack, engulf or destroy us". That includes us, because Mr. Suhrawardy was formerly a member of our National Party. "I see not country that is prepared to attack, engulf or destroy us". I hope he still lives with that statement. The immediate disadvantage to Pakistan, however, is that it will no be able to assert its rights. The Prime Minister continues: "We may have to keep our rights on Kashmir, on canal water or to bow our heads to a superior and more powerful neighbour".

Then he went on to refer to India's attitude towards Pakistan. It is not a defensive affairs, and these alliances therefore are intended to negotiate from strength, as it is called, whatever that means.

The Foreign Minister said in Rawalpindi on 21 October: "There is only one country in the world inimical to Pakistan and that is Bharat"—that means us. They do not like us, but this word occurs in our Constitution and we have no objection to it, we are not ashamed—"on account of its intransigent policy in Kashmir." There is only one country inimical to Pakistan, but they have signed a trade agreement and we are always common sufferers under certain conditions.

Sir Firoz Khan Noon said at Lahore the previous day, speaking in justification of Pakistan's adherence to military alliances and specially the Baghdad and SEATO Pacts, defended it on the grounds that "a powerful neighbour country which was inimical to Pakistan had in fact forced it to seek friendship elsewhere. That country had grave differences with this country and the two pacts have enabled Pakistan to ensure its defence against aggression. The country's freedom could only be preserved with the help of those friends".

These are the two most restrained statements on this subject. I could quote a great many more, but it is not my purpose to aggravate this matter because so many other countries are involved; in spite of all the reservations I have made, it would be bound to leave a feeling that we were extending this debate to other matters such as the general world policies of certain countries.

At this moment it is necessary for me in a few minutes to say what our position is.

There are certain proposals made by the Pakistan Government. I had intended to deal with them this morning but it is not necessary for me to deal with them now because of the resolution which is before us; no doubt they will be discussed at that time. But if I deal with these proposals briefly it should not be considered that we have exhausted our observations in this subject. The proposals are as follows:

In view of this grave situation the Government of Pakistan request the Security Council to take action on the following lines:

(1) Call upon India to refrain from accepting the change envisaged by the new constitution adopted by the so-called Constituent Assembly of Srinagar.

I explained yesterday that the Constituent Assembly does not proceed from the resolutions of the Jammu Conference or anything like that; it has its origin in the proclamation of the Head of the State, the text of which I read out to you, and its purpose is the creation of a constitution for Kashmir itself. The relation of Kashmir to India, so far as we are concerned, is decided by the accession. Therefore, it is not the Constituent Assembly that should be attacked and I do not see what restraint can be imposed upon the exercise of the sovereign rights of an independent country. How can the Security Council turn round to us and say that a constituent party to a federation cannot have its own constitution, to order its own life in its own way? If anything is to be attacked it must be the accession, as I pointed out yesterday and I submitted that the Security Council is in no position under the Charter to go into the legality of the accession; and so far as we are concerned it is complete.

The second paragraph of the proposal reads:

(2) Under Article 37 (2) of the United Nations Charter, spell out the obligations of the parties, under the terms of the international agreement for a plebiscite as embodied in the United Nations Resolutions.

I think it would be repetition several times over for me to point out the fallacy in the last three lines. There is no international agreement for a plebiscite; there is international agreement on a plan for which there are certain pre-conditions. In these matters we must not jump from one thing to another; it does not mean the same thing. We are always willing to have the obligations of this body under the Charter spelled out.

Then there are remedies proposed. I do not think I shall deal with these in detail, but so far as the remedies in paragraph 77 are concerned, before those who are applying their minds to it make their final decision I would request them, particularly those who regard themselves as in close relations with us, to refer to the Commission's report on this subject made nine years ago.

It is a bad policy to subscribe oneself to a course of action for reasons that are not related to this subject. So far as paragraph 77 is concerned, we reserve our comments, except to refer to the paragraph in the Commission's report in regard to the introduction of other troops and forces in the area, and the answers that have been given. This was a Pakistan request, made by Sir Mohammad Zafrullah Khan nine years ago; it was reviewed and the Commission turned it down. I want to submit also, for those who are very constitutionally minded, that this is a contravention of the Charter.

I would like to say that the substance of my submission before the Council is that the Government of India asked the Council to carry out the provisions of the Charter, which is what it will do. We, on the other hand—and I make a solemn declaration on the part of the Government of India—shall not force. We shall not do a single thing that will upset stability. We have no desire—and we have never done it in the past—to change the status quo in regard to any of our difficulties on our frontiers by the use of force. The most outstanding instance is the Portuguese colony of Goa on our western side. It is Indian territory under imperial occupation. We had a moral duty as a national movement to bring about their affiliation. There are our friends from the Fourth Republic of France who had possessions of this kind in India. We patiently negotiated with them, as they did with us for over seven years; while if it were a question of force, it could have been decided one way or another before. Therefore, we do not change the state of affairs by the use of force.

I have been asked by the Government of India to state, therefore, that not a gun, not a soldier, not a shot, will be fired by us. There will be no aggressive action taken so far as we are concerned. It is little late in the day for Mr. Khan Noon to come and tell us about a no war declaration—which sounds very well except when you read the conditions. It was a request that was made to his predecessor when he was prime Minister and Foreign Minister eight or nine years ago, and repeated time after time to this successors, including the Ambassador to Washington at the present time. Therefore, while it may have the same label, it has not got the same substance.

I am to assure you that so far as we are concerned, even in order to redress our wrong, even in order to restore our territories, to asset the sovereignty which this Council has at no time challenged and, what is more, repeated time after time, and in order to pursue the purposes embodied in our Constitution, and to establish the integrity of our land, we are not prepared to use force. But at the same time, in view of the threats that have been made, if our territory is violated, then we shall use he provisions of the Charter to defend what is ours under the law and in terms of our possession. And this merely a very humble statement of the position of the Government of India.

It has no relation whatsoever with our armed dispositions. I have with the utmost frankness told the Council what our armed disposition is. Our is perhaps the only country in the world which has reduced its military budgets. We spent somewhere about 18 per cent of our total revenues on military expenditures, as against 37 per cent of Pakistan's. Our army has gone down in numbers and in its offensive power, while the other army has gone up. But believing as we do that it is not possible to equate this position, especially in the context of these military alliances, by entering into an arms race, and that probably the risks of peace are not greater than the risks of war, we are taking this line.

The Security Council composed as it is, in the circumstances in which we find ourselves of not having considered this question for five years, and, I hope in view of the submissions I have made has a serious responsibility to pronounce on this question. I say that the fundamental question is whether the Security Council is prepared to say to itself, whether each Member State which the Members represent is prepared to say to itself, that from an aggression, whatever may be the rights of the other side, other consequences beneficial to the aggressor can follow?

That is the issue we are considering in another context and in other places. Therefore, to disregard all that has been said by the Commission—and not in the one paragraph, but in many—and, what is more, as I said this morning, to draft resolutions on this subject before another side has submitted its case, is not to proclaim the sense of justice and equity of this august Organization.

Therefore, my Government, in full faith, in the allegiance of the Security Council to the principles of the Charter, believing in our rights in law, in morality and in ethics, and what is more, knowing what are the interests of the peoples of India and Pakistan, knowing the consequences of unsettlement, remembering the grim tragedy of 1957, knowing the passions that are aroused when there is quarrel between neighbours, asks you to be careful. We ask for your prudence; we ask for your sound judgement in not jumping into a situation without taking all these facts into consideration.

The Government of India here is not in the dock. We came here as complainants. A distinguished colleague of ours appears to have mentioned this today: why should we be so much on the defence? If it sounds to people that we are on the defence, it may be because we indulged in some understatements both in the past and in the present. We are here not in order to ask for condemnation of anybody. We are here in order to state what are our rights under the Charter. Have we the right to be free from threat? Have we the right to feel assured that the machinery of the Security Council, and its resolutions are not going to be sued as a smokescreen for the preparation of aggression against us? have we the right so far as the Council is concerned—and I say that it cannot impose it—to live side by side with our neighbour, free from the threats of a holy war? Have we the right to enable our peoples, the great majority of whom are under subsistence levels, to devote our energies, our attention, our resources our friendships, or the economic and political development of our peoples?

These are the questions that face us and while I have no desire to conclude in this way, I cannot but help referring—and I would not have done this if it had come from any other representative of the Government of Pakistan except our old friend Mr. Khan Noon—to what he told this council. He said that between the friendship of the Indian and Pakistan people stands Mr. Nehru. I ask the Council to consider that statement, coming from a leading Indian personality only ten years ago, who is a family friend of most of what may be called the ruling families, if you like, the persons in Government positions in India, who knows our intentions and who represented the Government of India as a whole in many circumstances, and telling our people that between the two of us lies the personality of our Prime Minister.

If that is not incitement to revolt against the Government, I ask what is? It is the only part of that statement that has caused our delegation intense pain. That comes on top of the kind of thing that is written in Pakistan. What I have here is from the *Dawn*. I am ashamed to read it, but it is my duty to do so. The *Dawn* is a paper founded by the founder of Pakistan. It is still regarded as a kind of most important organ, I believe. It says:

> The Security Council will have barely ten days to decide upon some concrete, tangible, unequivocal and compelling step whereby that rapacious brigand of Asia,